STUDIES IN
AMERICAN SOCIOLOGY
UNDER
THE GENERAL EDITORSHIP OF
STANFORD M. LYMAN

VOLUME III

Robert E. Park, Berlin, 1900, from a drawing by Clara Cahill Park.

MILITARISM, IMPERIALISM, AND RACIAL ACCOMMODATION

An Analysis and Interpretation
of the Early Writings of Robert E. Park

Stanford M. Lyman

The University of Arkansas Press

Fayetteville 1992

96 95 94 93 92   5 4 3 2 1

This book was designed by Chang-hee H. Russell using the Bembo typeface.

The paper used in this publication meets the minimum requirements of the American National Standard for Permanence of Paper for Printed Library Materials Z39.48-1984. ∞

Library of Congress Cataloging-in-Publication Data

Lyman, Stanford M.
    Militarism, imperialism, and racial accommodation: an analysis and interpretation of the early writings of Robert E. Park / Stanford M. Lyman.
        P.   cm. -- (Studies in American sociology: v.3)
    Includes bibliographical references and index.
    ISBN 1-55728-219-6 (alk. paper)
    1. Park, Robert Ezra, 1864-1944.   2. Sociology--United States--History.
    3. Militarism. 4. Imperialism. 5. Race relations.
    6. United States--Race relations.
    I. Title.   II. Series.
HM22.U6P3448   1992   91-19209
301'.0973--dc20   CIP

Dedicated to
The Faculty in Sociology
and Social Institutions
at the University of
California, Berkeley, 1951–1961

My Teachers

Democracy is not something that some people in a country can have and others not have, something to be shared and divided like a pie—some getting a small and some getting a large piece. Democracy is an integral thing. If any part of the country doesn't have it, the rest of the country doesn't have it. The Negro, therefore, in fighting for democracy for himself is simply fighting the battle for our democracy. . . .

Robert E. Park*

We can no longer impassionate ourselves for the principles in the name of which Christianity recommended to masters that they treat their slaves humanely, and, on the other hand, the idea which it has formed of human equality and fraternity seems to us today to leave too large a place for unjust equalities. Its pity for the outcast seems to us too Platonic; we desire another which would be more practicable; but as yet we cannot see what it should be nor how it could be realized in facts.

Emile Durkheim**

*Robert E. Park to Horace Cayton. Quoted in Winifred Raushenbush, *Robert E. Park: Biography of a Sociologist* (Durham, N.C.: Duke University Press, 1979), p. 177.

**Emile Durkheim, *The Elementary Forms of the Religious Life,* trans. by Joseph Ward Swain (New York: The Free Press, 1965), p. 475

CONTENTS

Selected Works of Robert E. Park

Militarism and Nationalism

The German Army: The Most Perfect Military Organization
in the World

ILLUSTRATIONS

(following page 176)

from "The German Army: The Most Perfect Military Organization in
    the World"

The Kaiser and King Albert of Saxony at a review.
Field Marshal Count Von Moltke.
William I, King of Prussia from 1861 to 1888.
At the German Army maneuvers—a field battery opening fire.
A military steeplechase.
"Auf Dem Fechtboden"—a course in fencing is part of the regular
    training of the German officer.
Grenadier guards drawn up in front of the Schloss in Berlin, with the
    Kaiser, General Von Bock, and three of the imperial princes.
At the German Army maneuvers—an infantry skirmish line.
At the German Army maneuvers—infantry awaiting attack.
A German cavalry band on the march.
Officers of the Grenadier Guards.
Troops drawn up in Unter den Linden on the occasion of the Austrian
    emperor's visit to Berlin, on May 4, 1900.

from "Recent Atrocities in the Congo State"

A lad with both hands destroyed.
A Belgian official of the Congo Free State with a native corporal.
A boy maimed by Congo soldiers.
Congo Soldiers.

PREFACE

Robert E. Park (1864–1944) is recognized as one of the giants of early American sociology. Yet, despite his prominent place in the history of the discipline, a conventional approach to his theoretical outlook and empirical studies has decreed the banishment of his early writings—i.e., virtually all of his works published before 1913—to a limbo land that not even his biographers have penetrated very deeply. Hence, Park's description and analysis of imperial Germany's military organization (1900),[1] his exposé and critique of Belgium's King Leopold II's atrocities in the Congo (1904, 1906, 1907),[2] and his studies of the black community in Winston-Salem, North Carolina (1905, 1913),[3] and of Booker T. Washington's agricultural education program at Tuskegee, Alabama (1908),[4] are not considered part of the annals of American sociology nor even a portion of his sociological *oeuvre*.[5] The present book intends to remedy this situation. It provides an interpretation of these and a few other of Park's early writings and offers a new and different outlook on his sociology.

Because autobiographical notes and biographical studies of Park are readily available,[6] it is only necessary here to present a brief sketch of those aspects of his life that are relevant to his early writings. Robert Ezra Park was born at his maternal grandfather's farm, six miles from Shicksinny, Luzerne County, Pennsylvania, on February 14, 1864, to a twenty-three-year-old schoolteacher, Theodosia Warner, and her twenty-six-year-old first cousin and husband, Hiram Asa Park, a soldier in the Union army. At the end of the war, the Parks moved to Red Wing, Minnesota, a Mississippi River town forty miles south of Minneapolis, where Hiram Park would become a locally prominent wholesale grocer. Robert spent his first eighteen years in Red Wing, taking notice of the local Indians and making friends with the children of the town's Swedish and Norwegian immigrants. Upon graduation from high school in 1882, Park attended the University of Minnesota for one year and then transferred to the University of Michigan, from which he matriculated with a Phi Beta Kappa key and a Ph.B. degree in philology in 1887. Among the professors who influenced him there were Calvin Thomas, a Germanist, and John Dewey, the philosopher.

From the time of his graduation until 1898, Park worked as a journalist on various newspapers in the Midwest and in New York City. He had, he would recall in 1929, "made up my mind to go in for experience for its own sake, to gather into my soul as Faust somewhere says 'all the joys and sorrows of the world.' "[7] He completed but was never able to publish a novel, *The Isle of Enchantment*, about the social classes of Manhattan, and with Franklin Ford and John Dewey tried but did not succeed in bringing out a new kind of newspaper, *Thought News*. In 1894, Park married Clara Cahill with whom he would father four children between 1895 and 1902. In the fall of 1898, he enrolled at Harvard for an M.A. in philosophy, studying primarily with William James, George Santayana, and Hugo Münsterberg. One year later, he and his family moved to Berlin where Park registered at the Friederich-Wilhelm University. During his second year there, he took three courses with the man he would later call "the greatest of all sociologists," Georg Simmel. It was during the second year of his graduate studies in Berlin that Park wrote and published his analysis of the new German army, the paper that is the subject of the first chapter of the present volume. Although it provides a virtually "Weberian" analysis of class, status, and military power in Germany and adumbrates his later writings on the rise of what Harold Lasswell would call the "garrison state," Park's study of General von Moltke's organizational reforms has never been treated by sociologists as anything but journalism. Park journeyed from Berlin to Strassburg (later Strasbourg) and, soon after, to Heidelberg, where in 1903 under the supervision of Wilhelm Windelband he completed a doctoral dissertation entitled *"Masse und Publikum: eine methodologische und sociologische Untersuchung."* It is a testimony to the neglect of Park's early work that this study was not translated into English and published until 1972.[8]

Returning to the United States in 1903, Park accepted a one-year position as an assistant to William James in Harvard's department of philosophy. One year later, he became secretary of an international protest group, the Congo Reform Association, whose American branch he had co-founded with Thomas Barbour, secretary of the American Baptist Missionary Society. After a quick but intensive study of the situation then prevailing in Belgian King Leopold's Congo Free State, Park ghosted one essay for Booker T. Washington[9] and under his own name in 1904, 1906, and 1907 published in *The World To-Day* and in *Everybody's Magazine* four articles, entitled, respectively, "Recent Atrocities in the Congo State"; "A King in Business: Leopold II of Belgium, Autocrat of the Congo"; "The Terrible Story of the Congo"; and "Blood Money of the Congo." These essays form what I believe is an embryonic theory and critique of capitalism and imperialism that proceed from a perspective that I have called "Gothic." Although these essays have never been subjected to a thoroughgoing sociological analysis—and the first one does not appear on any published bibliography of Park's works—here it will be argued that they form and illustrate a transition in sociological thought.

As sociology moved out from its possible location in German romantic philosophy[10] and toward becoming the rational and excessively positivistic social science that is represented today by its mainstream professionals, it had to come to terms with the existence of evil in the world. At the time Park wrote his Congo essays, American Social Gospel sociologists had begun the formulation of a secular theodicy that would at one and the same time transvalue Protestant thought into a seemingly objective and positive science of social reconstruction and create a new academic discipline.[11] Working outside the academy and skeptical of the efforts of religiously inspired social reformers, Park, even when he was working in cooperation with the Baptist missionaries who made up the corps of the Congo Reform Association's field investigators, formulated a far more complex perspective on modernity's modes of evil. In effect, as will be elaborated in the second chapter of the present book, he developed a basis for a philosophical sociology of horror[12] that combined a critique of the political economy of capitalist imperialism with a *geisteswissenschaftliche* Gothic outlook on both the Protestant ethic and the personification of wickedness. That outlook analogized the capitalist form of imperialist exploitation of labor to that of the preternatural vampire, who must roam the earth in search of its source of life-giving sustenance, human blood, and in the process turn its victims into its soulless followers. The emerging sociology of modernity and values might gain much by considering Park's thought on the subject as one alternative to that of Marx.[13]

Upon completion of his work for the Congo Reform Association, Park accepted Booker T. Washington's offer to become the already renowned Tuskegee principal's private secretary, research analyst, and amanuensis. For the next seven years Park roamed through the American South's "Black Belt," which he described as "a strange country with a strange people . . ." He went on to observe that, "[V]ery few of us . . . have much real knowledge either about the Black Belt, or the people who inhabit it."[14] With Washington, Park also toured Europe in quest of what the Tuskegeean called "the man farthest down," i.e., a people living under socioeconomic conditions as bad as or worse than those affecting America's blacks,[15] and, uncredited, Park coauthored a two volume history of America's blacks.[16] Under his own name, Park carried out and published a study of the black settlement at Winston-Salem, North Carolina, another study of the domestic standard of living in African-American homes, and a thoroughgoing analysis of Booker T. Washington's agricultural extension program in Macon County, Alabama.

In these studies—which are treated in the third chapter of the present book—Park presents an empirical analysis of what I choose to call the benevolent face of Booker T. Washington's applied variant of the Protestant ethic.[17] In other words, when read together, Park's Congo and Black Belt studies form themselves into a comprehensive portrait of the double-sided moral character and socioeconomic effects of the Reformation. The Protestant ethic was the fount from which flowed both the preternatural horrors of capitalist imperialism in Africa and the beneficent incentives to chastity, honesty, frugality, and hard work in rural Southern black settlements in America. No previous analysis of Park's work has formulated the matter in this way. But, of course, no previous analysis has bothered to evaluate Park's "pre-Chicago" writings from a sociological perspective.

After resigning from his position at Tuskegee in 1912, Park accepted W. I. Thomas's invitation to become a teaching member of the faculty at the University of Chicago. Park offered his first course in the fall-winter quarter of 1913–14 and until 1920 in the annual summer sessions. He signaled his assumption of professional identity by joining the American Sociological Society in 1914, becoming its national president a decade later. Park served as president of the Urban League chapter in Chicago and played an important role in the Chicago Commission on Race Relations.[18] For the next two decades Park became a principal guide and mentor to the graduate students at the University of Chicago and thereby established what has become his generally recognized place in the development of American sociology.[19]

But, read in the light of his pre-Chicago works, Park's academic writings can be seen as a further elaboration of his conception of the civilizational process and its effect on race relations and the development of a civil society. Civilization, Park believed, "is a consequence of contact and communication," while "races are the products of isolation and inbreeding." In Park's sociology, the city is the locus of civilization, the place in which "the forces which have been decisive in the history of mankind . . . have brought men together in fruitful competition, conflict, and cooperation."[20] In light of this formulation of the matter, it should be observed that Booker T. Washington's bi-racial ruralization program for the nation's blacks—much as it did to train them in the racial etiquette necessary for survival in the Redemptionist South and to shield them from the more virulent aspects of ubiquitous white racial prejudices—had also kept them isolated in the countryside and, hence, had held them back from participation in the inevitable rough and tumble of a democratic, urban, but racist civil society.

Once out of the black South, Park took a greater interest in America's urban blacks, seeing in their literary, artistic, and musical works, as well as in such movements as that for black civil rights, for Marcus Garvey's back-to-Africa program, and in the several racially conscious protests against their neglect by historical and humanistic scholars, the development of a sense of peoplehood, history, and culture.[21] That emerging sensibility, he argued, transcended and would eventually overwhelm their identity as a merely physical presence, i.e., as a race. Rather than remaining abject subjects of a "natural history," Park came to recognize that the "new Negroes" would be active participants in a social history, much of which would be of their own making.

As such, Park observed at the end of his life, they would nevertheless still have to fight for their civil rights and long-deserved equal status.[22]

During and after his academic years at Chicago, Park continued his travels all over the world. By the late 1920s, he had come to see that the dynamic of the "melting pot" applied to the whole world, that America was no longer the sole locus of that process—indeed, that by closing its "racial frontier on the Pacific"[23] to the peoples of Asia, the United States had become retrogressive with respect to the global trend toward assimilation of every people into the vortex of an industrial, commercial, meritocratic, and mass-oriented civilization. Yet, that civilizing movement generated its own atavistic regressions. From the 1920s on, Park took increasing notice of the character, scope, and direction of American racial prejudices, of the social, economic, and political implications of the rise of Italian Fascism, German Nazism, and Soviet Communism, and of the concomitant decline of Christianity as an inner-worldly moral force.

During the late 1930s and early 1940s—already retired from the University of Chicago and, after 1936, ensconced at Fisk University—Park continued to address the sociology and social psychology of the race question in global and military-geopolitical, as well as national and local, terms. Although his former place of inspiration, Tuskegee, had not yet shown an interest "in adapting its program to the new frontier of American and Negro life,"[24] Park had. Among the hundreds of his students and followers, it is to be noted that many of those who were non-white adopted a broad, supranational, and often worldwide perspective. Samuel C. Adams, for example—who matriculated under Park at Fisk in 1940, went on to earn a Ph.D. at Chicago in 1952, entered the Foreign Service, serving in twenty-seven countries, and became United States Ambassador to Niger—claimed that one reason he held his first teacher in such high esteem was that Park had "had the art of knowing that the world around him was filled with secrets, waiting to be understood."[25] St. Clair Drake (1911–1990), who in 1945 had co-authored *Black Metropolis* with Park's former student, Horace Cayton,[26] joined with Kwame Nkrumah in establishing a post-colonial Ghana, analyzed the race problem in terms of its international scope and effects,[27] directed the African and Afro-American Studies Program at Stanford University from 1969 to 1976,[28] and, at the end of his life, authored a new interpretation of the history and meaning of the African diaspora.[29] In reconsidering the meaning of the years Park had spent with Booker T. Washington, Drake cast doubt on the claim made by Park's detractors that his interest in "Negroes stemmed only from a desire to study them, to use them as data for his intellectual ruminations." Park's "preoccupation with Africa and the New World diaspora," Drake pointed out, "suggests that his interest ran far deeper than that."[30] E. Franklin Frazier (1894–1962) not only empirically tested Park's theory of the race relations cycle with respect to black American lifeways and, finally, came to reject it as either descriptive or prescriptive, but also developed a variant of Park's approach to study the character and predict the likely outcome of race and culture contacts in the post-colonial world.[31] Although conventional, American, mainstream sociologists conceive Park's interest in "human ecology" to be applicable exclusively to the study of neighborhoods and cities, we have no less than the testimony of Werner Cahnman—who had received his Ph.D. from the University of Munich in 1927 and served as instructor and Julius Rosenwald fellow at Fisk University during Park's final years—that "Park had expressed the desire to see the principles of human ecology fortified by the methods of geopolitics and applied to the problems of the international scene."[32]

At the time of his death (February 7, 1944), Park's concerns about the world of races, cultures, and civilization must have seemed to him to have come full circle. Germany's military might—which, he had pointed out in 1900, had achieved the pinnacle of modern organizational development under Bismarck's field marshall chief of staff, Helmuth von Moltke—had under Nazi direction so alarmingly challenged Western civilization that the field marshall's grand nephew had become a secret plotter against the regime.[33] Hitler's proposed Aryan racial order, his holocaust involving the destruction of Jews, Gypsies, homosexuals, and other "undesirable" elements, had shown Park that, contrary to conventionally held linear theories of state development, the modern polity could coexist with, even be motored by, the atavistic horde, and that civilized public spiritedness could be overwhelmed by charismatically inspired, mindless crowd behavior. However, not only had Germany's and Japan's garrison states become the agency of a global totalitarian threat, but also the exigencies of the latter had evoked comparable militaristic developments in non-totalitarian societies that, as L. L. Bernard pointed out in 1944, boded ill for the postwar world.[34] Moreover, the modern city, once conceived as the place where freedom, civil society, and social and personal idiosyncrasy might not merely coexist but flourish, was now "like the civilization of which it is the center and focus, a vast physical and institutional structure in which men live, like bees in a hive, under conditions such that their activities are considerably more regulated, regimented, and conditioned than is likely to appear to the spectator or be perceived by the inhabitant."[35]

In such a civilization it would be possible for the horrors of Hitlerism, even more than Leopold II's depredations in the Congo, to be routinized beyond the power of Gothicism to provoke an outcry. The lesson about the dangers of Gothicism that was explicitly drawn in Park's "terrible story of the Congo" had not yet been learned—in Europe or in America. The recognition of the individual worth of each human being, regardless of race, color, culture, or creed, had been repudiated by the Nazi regime and was still only an ideal in America—honored on occasions of patriotic self-congratulation but disregarded in the institutional practices affecting the lives and livelihoods of the country's African-Americans, Asians, Hispanics, and Amerindians.

Park's final talk to his erstwhile colleagues at Chicago pointed to this discrepancy between public policy and national purpose.[36] It harked back to one of his earliest statements and might very well be his epitaph: "We must not lay down as a principle and apply to others what we do not want them to apply to us."[37] This book is dedicated to reminding us of the sociological relevance of that statement for our own time.[38]

ACKNOWLEDGMENTS

Portions of the argument of this book were presented at the following roundtables, academic conventions, convocation lectures, colloquia, and meetings of professional associations:

"The Writings of Robert E. Park: Militarism, the Garrison State, and the Sociology of Conflict," Gregory Stone Symbolic Interaction Symposium, Arizona State University, Tempe, Arizona, March 16–19, 1989.

"The American Garrison State and Race Relations During the Second World War: A Sociological Perspective," convocation lecture, Lake Forest College, Lake Forest, Illinois, April 4, 1989.

"A Gothic Theory of Capitalism and Imperialism," Humanities, Arts, and Social Sciences Research Seminar, Florida Atlantic University, Boca Raton, Florida, January 23, 1990.

"Reconsiderations of Robert E. Park," roundtable, annual meeting, American Sociological Association, Washington, D.C., August 11–15, 1990.

"Accomodations to Evil: The Conflict and Fusion of Race, Religion, and Culture in Late Nineteenth- and Early Twentieth- Century America," Humanities, Arts, and Social Sciences Research Seminar, Florida Atlantic University, Baca Raton, Florida, September 5, 1990.

"Re-reading Robert E. Park: Toward a Gothic Perspective on Capitalism and Imperialism," annual meeting, Mid-South Sociological Association, Hot Springs, Arkansas, October 24–27, 1990; annual meeting, Gregory Stone Symbolic Interaction Symposium, San Francisco, California, February 7–9, 1991.

Portions of theses presented in this book appeared as essays in the following:

"Park and Realpolitik: Race, Culture and Modern Warfare," *International Journal of Politics, Culture, and Society,* Vol. 3, No. 4 (Summer 1990), pp. 565–86.

"Robert E. Park Reconsidered: The Early Writings," *The American Sociologist,* Vol. 21, No. 4 (Winter 1990), pp. 342–51.

"Civilization, Culture, and Color: Changing Foundations of Robert E. Park's Sociology of Race Relations," *International Journal of Politics, Culture and Society,* Vol. 4, No. 3 (Spring 1991), pp. 285–300.

"Robert E. Park's Congo Papers: A Gothic Perspective on Capitalism and Imperialism," *International Journal of Politics, Culture and Society,* Vol. 4, No. 4 (Summer 1991), pp. 501–16.

"Rereading Robert E. Park: Toward a Gothic Perspective on Capitalism and Imperialism," *Explorations: The Age of Enlightenment,* Special Series, Vol. IV (1990), pp. 29–107.

✦ ✦ ✦

The essays by Robert E. Park were originally published in the following journals:

"The German Army: The Most Perfect Military Organization in the World," *Munsey's Magazine,* XXIV:3 (December 1900), pp. 376–95.

"The Yellow Press," *Sociology and Social Research,* XII:1 (September 1927), pp. 3–11.

["Sombart on Sociology"*], an untitled review essay of *Die Drei Nationalökonomien,* by Werner Sombart, (München und Leipzig: Verlag von Duncker & Humblot, 1930), *American Journal of Sociology,* XXXVI:6 (May 1931), pp. 1071–77.

"Recent Atrocities in the Congo State," *The World To-Day,* Viii (October 1904), pp. 1328–31.

"A King in Business: Leopold II of Belgium, Autocrat of the Congo and International Broker," *Everybody's Magazine,* XV (November 1906), pp. 624–33.

*Title supplied by Stanford M. Lyman.

"The Terrible Story of the Congo," *Everybody's Magazine,* XV (December 1906), pp. 763–72.

"The Blood-Money of the Congo, *Everybody's Magazine,* XVI (January 1907), pp. 60–70.

"A City of Racial Peace," *The World To-Day,* IX (August 1905), pp. 897–99.

"Agricultural Extension Among the Negroes," *The World To-Day,* XV (August 1908), pp. 820–26.

"Negro Home Life and Standards of Living," *Annals of the American Academy of Political and Social Science,* XLIX (September 1913), pp. 147–63.

"Letters Collected by R. E. Park and Booker T. Washington" by Robert E. Park, *Journal of Negro History,* VII:2 (April 1922), pp. 206–22.

"The Conflict and Fusion of Cultures with Special Reference to the Negro" by Robert E. Park, *Journal of Negro History,* IV:2 (April 1919), pp. 111-133.

Untitled review essay by Robert E. Park of *Die Drei Nationalökonomiwn,* by Werner Sombart, (München and Leipzig: Verlag von Duncker & Humblot, 1930), *American Journal of Sociology,* XXXVI:6 (May 1931), pp. 1071–77, permission obtained from James Redfield, the grandson of Robert E. Park.

Reprinted from *Social Forces* xx:1 (October 1941). "Methods of Teaching: Impressions and a Verdict" by Robert E. Park. Copyright © The University of North Carolina Press.

The author would like to thank Arthur J. Vidich and Marvin B. Scott for their encouragement and critical advice throughout the course of the preparation of this book. The author also benefited from the advice and commentary of Patti Adler, Peter Adler, David Altheide, Peter Bacho, Carl Backman, Michael Banton, James E. Blackwell, Kenneth Bock, Richard Harvey Brown, Ying-jen Chang, Frank Chin, Randall Collins, Norman Denzin, Jack Douglas, Carolyn Ellis, Arthur Evans, Reynolds Farley, Andrea Fontana, David Franks, Ronald Glassman, Cecil Greek, David Harvey, Richard Helmes-Hays, Herbert Hill, Gisela Hinkle, Roscoe Hinkle, Gordon Hirabayashi, James Hirabayashi, Lane Hirabayashi, Jon Huer, Everett Hughes, Won Moo Hurh, John Johnson, Danny Jorgensen, Tetsuden Kashima, Shuichi Kato, Lewis Killian, Illsoo Kim, K. C. Kim, Peter Kivisto, Joseph Kotarba, Him Mark Lai, Ivan Light, William Liu, Dennis Lum, George McCall, David Maines, Ira Mandelker, Peter Manning, Jitsuichi Masuoka, Tom Morrione, Victor Nee, Guy Oakes, Virginia Olesen, Michael Omi,

Vincent Parrillo, Robert Perinbanayagam, John Shelton Reed, Julian Roebuck, Peter Rose, Ahmad Sadri, Mahmoud Sadri, Paul Shapiro, Ronald Takaki, Susan Takata, Stephen Turner, Pierre van den Berghe, Ling-chi Wang, Carol A.B. Warren, Charles Willie, Charles Choy Wong, and Shawn Wong.

Stanley Tang provided yeoman service in the hunting and gathering of manuscript materials.

The index was prepared in his usual masterful fashion by Dr. Paul Cantrell.

Without the aid of Joan Schilling, who not only typed and retyped the many versions of this manuscript, but also maintained relevant records, diskettes, and correspondence, and cheered the author on, this manuscript could not have been completed.

The faculty, staff, and administration of Florida Atlantic University have provided me with a fine setting for research and writing.

I have dedicated this book to the faculty in Sociology and Social Institutions at the University of California, Berkeley, 1951–1961, from whom I first learned of Robert E. Park and received the inspiration to pursue my lifelong studies in sociological thought. I should especially wish to extend my appreciation to Reinhard Bendix, Herbert Blumer, Kenneth Bock, Kingsley Davis, Wolfram Eberhard, Cesar Graña, William Kornhauser, Seymour Martin Lipse, H. Franz Schurmann, Philip Selznick, and Tamotsu Shibutani.

The drawing of Robert E. Park that serves as a frontispiece is taken from *Robert E. Park: Biography of a Sociologist*, by Winifred Raushenbush, published by Duke University Press, Durham, 1979. Reprinted with Permission of the publisher.

The staff and editorial board and the very fine art director of the University of Arkansas Press have once again proved themselves to be outstanding members of their profession.

War, Race, and
Modern Civilization:
A Sociological Perspective

Introduction

Shortly before his death on February 7, 1944, Robert Ezra Park mailed a review essay of *Jews in a Gentile World*, a compilation of eighteen social scientific papers that had been put together by Isacque Graeber and Steuart Henderson Britt in response to the calamitous situation then threatening that people's survival, to its senior author. Park's essay eventually found its way into print in the *American Sociological Review*.[1] It is worthy of note that in that paper, as in others published in the same period, Park addressed unresolved aspects of the central theme that had been the basis of his investigations, researches, and writings for more than four decades. The relations among peoples, nations, races, and states—the sources of conflict and the grounds for accommodation—constituted Park's conception of modernity's fundamental problem.

At the turn of the nineteenth century, Park had conceived of the matter in terms of the necessity for Christianity's "Golden Rule" to become universal: "We must not lay down as a principle and apply to others what we do not want them to apply to us. Yet, this is the state of international relations today."[2] In 1944, however, having recognized the declining significance of religion for the enforcement of public morals, as well as having noted that the long history of the "Jewish problem" made it, perhaps, the quintessential exemplar of the world's inability thus far to deal with the fact of its human diversity, he reformulated the issue: The "problem of the Jew, whatever it may have been in the past, is at present identical with the problem of Democracy."[3] But the latter problem had itself moved out from its geopolitical boundaries in such post-Enlightenment state societies as the United States of America. Nevertheless, although "Democracy . . . [was] no longer a local or a national problem . . . [and had become] a world problem, . . . [it remained], before anything else, an American problem."[4] America was the situs of the world's problem of democracy because "if there is any place on the planet where people of different races and religions are destined to live and work together in peace and understanding, it is here."[5] To Park, the civil ordering of a democratic society was illustrated in and tested by its capacity to institutionalize liberty, equality, and fraternity within a modern, secular, political economy.

What Park called the problem of democracy was integral to the apparent triumph of *civilly ordered* state societies over all previous types, a triumph that seemed likely to become worldwide in the twentieth century. Civil societies would find their ideal form in the *cosmopolis*, as social thinkers from Lester Ward to Stephen Toulmin have noted. To Ward, the cosmopolis would arise only after the process he called *social karyokinesis* would have completed a worldwide racial and ethnic amalgamation.[6] To Toulmin, belief in a coming cosmopolis calls for supporting the victory of Reason (despite its various and sometimes contradictory meanings from the sixteenth to the nineteenth centuries) over divine, magical, and other non-rational bases for ordering a polity.[7] Although Toulmin shows that protagonists of the cosmopolis idea found in it a justification for the nation-state, Park eventually came to see that nationalism, racial chauvinisms, and other claims on polity that are based in what Max Weber called the "mystery of blood"[8] were survivals of a premodern *Zeitgeist*. Yet, as Park had already observed, these anachronisms and atavisms had not disappeared in the face of modernity. Rather, they remain embedded in its only seemingly rational and scientifically justified institutions and laws. They are the discontents that disturb—and threaten to destroy—the coming of a truly civil society.

For Park, World War II constituted a terrifying test of civilization. "Both the Axis Powers and the Allies recognized the necessity of an international authority capable of maintaining international peace," he observed in 1942, "but they have different notions of the form that this 'new order' should take, how authority should be administered, and who should exercise it."[9] Moreover, as Park sardonically remarked, "The Axis Powers have a program which has the advantage of being pragmatic rather than ideal. They propose to conquer the world and impose over as much of it as each is able to hold in effective subordination, an order that is at once economic, political, and eventually religious and cultural."[10] Against this totalitarian illusion of a new age, the "Allies . . . are seeking to improvise a social order which will insure not merely international order but international freedom and equality."[11] However, the Allies' project was "less a program than an ideal."[12] America, Park asserted in 1943, precisely because it was the model for this project, would have to discard its own racist ideologies and discriminatory practices,[13] but he held out little hope that this could occur without a possibly violent struggle.[14] The world cosmopolis, built around the guarantees of peace, freedom, and equality "must remain a consummation to be hoped for, an article of faith, something that can be measurably achieved only in the course of an historical process to which we can as yet set no limits."[15]

✦ ✦ ✦

The present volume is a study—in some parts, a hermeneutic; in others, a meditation—of the early papers of Robert E. Park. It has long been a convention among American sociologists to disregard or pass lightly over those writings of Park that preceded his appointment to the faculty of the University of Chicago. Academic sociology has seemed to require that its founders and great contributors be academics as well. Yet, Park, who was born in 1864, only one decade after the first book-length treatise on sociology in America (in fact, in the world) had been published,[16] was in a not uncommon situation for early sociologists when—during the first fifty years of his life—he chose journalism, muckraking, and a private secretaryship to a race leader as ways of pursuing a knowledge of society. The Southern Comteans, for example, that quartet of slavocratic antebellum sociologists—three of whom continued to write and publish for many years after the Civil War had ended—all had varied backgrounds and wide experience. The first, Henry Hughes (1829–1862), premier formulator of the theory of society as a social system,[17] served as a lawyer, journalist, state senator, and volunteer in the Confederate forces. Another, George Fitzhugh '(1806–1881), who wrote *Sociology For the South* (1854)[18] and *Cannibals All!* (1857)[19]—and in his later years proposed development of a phenomenological sociology[20]—was very much the private scholar.[21] Still another, George Frederick Holmes (1820–1897), whose *Science of Society*[22] appeared in the same year as Lester Ward's *Dynamic Sociology*, spent his life as a professor of history and economics at the University of Virginia.[23] The last of them, Joseph LeConte (1823–1901),whose ideas would influence Josiah Royce's theory of the philosophy of loyalty,[24] spent the most productive of his scholarly years as a professor of natural history and geology at the Berkeley campus of the University of California.[25] When Park joined the faculty of the University of Chicago in 1913, he had had an enormous amount of field experience in the rural South, in the international politics of reform in Africa, and during the years of his doctoral studies in Berlin and Heidelberg, in modern, militarizing Germany. His early papers constitute ethnographies of these experiences as well as adumbrations of his subsequent theories of race relations and civil society.

PARK'S STUDY OF THE GERMAN ARMY

"I submit," writes James Alfred Aho, one of the few sociologists who have reconsidered American sociology in relation to German ideas of *Realpolitik*, "that sociology received its initial impetus and early formulation in the German slough of romantic despondency, and that at least its original theories of social discord . . . were written within the same tradition of political cynicism that informed the world views of the most outspoken apologists for German military conquest—Treitschke, Moltke, and Bernhardi."[26] Although Aho does not analyze Park's essay, "The German Army: The Most Perfect Military Organization in the World," published in *Munsey's Magazine* in December 1900, he treats Park's sociology as exemplary of the German romantic tradition. Aho's unilateral complaint is not wholly justified by the facts, but, nevertheless, it directs those concerned about the lasting effects of sociology's beginnings to the original scholars of social conflict—Ludwig Gumplowicz, Gustav Ratzenhofer, and Franz Oppenheimer (about whom Aho has written extensively[27])—and, more particularly for our purpose, to the intellectual influences attending Park's essay on the German army. Like other Americans who received their advanced education in Germany at this time, Park did not shrink from immersion in the social thought and intellectual fashions that enlivened his German sojourn. However, his searching and critical spirit did not desert him when he undertook to write about what his studies and experiences had taught him.

Park's approach to German *Realpolitik* stemmed in part from his early interest in the territorial basis of all organized social life. He would later assert that "[E]very student of sociology should have to know geography, human geography particularly, for after all, culture is finally a geographical phenomenon."[28] For Park, as well as for his student, Everett C. Hughes, human geography constituted a vital part of the environment affecting "the relations between peoples." Because some peoples moved more often and over greater expanses of territory than others, they "occupied land in an active way by conquest, trade, and the like. . . . These were all cases of the relations of . . . races as races then [were] conceived."[29] As Park conceived of the matter, the peculiar case of German militarization was an instance of that nation's geopolitical position; it arose out of that country's vulnerable occupation of the space at the center of Europe: "The old Prussian army, with which Frederick the Great had hewn an empire out of central Europe, went to pieces under the blows of the French battalions at Jena. . . . The catastrophe of 1806 impressed upon the minds of the men of that day one important fact, namely, that Prussia, from the very nature of her geographical position, was likely to be called upon from time to time to fight for her very existence as a nation."[30]

Park's emphasis on the importance of geopolitics and human geography for sociology did not enjoy widespread support among his contemporaries nor did it become germane to later practitioners of that discipline in the United States. Although Lester F. Ward would assert that migration, invasion, conquest, and forced assimilation were fundamental aspects of the world-historical acculturative process that he called "social karyokinesis,"[31] and Everett and Helen Hughes would author a seminal study of where peoples meet,[32] there occurred a constriction of breadth in the main concern of American sociology. After the First World War, human geography and, more especially, the cultural and historical implications of territorial configurations on the political and social order were taken up by the University of California's iconoclastic scholar, Frederick Teggart, and his disciple, Nicholas Spykman,[33] but when, in 1946, that curriculum was transformed into Berkeley's Department of Sociology and Social Institutions, the special attention paid to the sociological approach to geopolitics faded.[34]

Park never ceased reminding his colleagues and students that human geography could inform a world-encompassing socio-cultural analysis and enhance domestic civic practice. "The history of the expansion of Europe offers abundant material for the study of the growth of civilization," he wrote in a paper not published until after his death.[35] And, as the Second World War cast doubt on the possibility of the world ever achieving peaceful relations among nations, he urged, "We shall need, as never before, to know human geography, and, perhaps, geopolitics. . . . We must have institutes, such as they have long had in Germany, France, and England, for the study of the languages and cultures of the peoples outside of Europe, in Asia and Africa. We must . . . prepare ourselves as never before to live not merely in America but in the world."[36] Park's advice, still not taken, is still good.

PARK'S PAPERS ON THE CONGO QUESTION

During his stint as international secretary of the Congo Reform Association, Park ghosted one essay and under his own name published four papers on King Leopold II's depredations in the Congo Free State.[37] Usually treated as unsociological in both character and content, these papers are regarded as pieces of "muckraking" journalism. They are charged with being unduly biased—investigative reports in service to a cause: that of arousing public outrage over Belgian King Leopold II's reign of terror in what was supposed to be his benevolent stewardship over an African territory. Certainly, the manifest intent of Park's essays was to bring about such an arousal, as well as to encourage appropriate and lawful action that would bring an end to Leopold's unconscionable atrocities. The Belgian monarch had converted his trusteeship over the Congo Free State into a satrapy, its people into his victims, and its lands into his private preserve. Nevertheless, despite their ostensible intent,

Park's Congo essays cannot be consigned solely to their rightful place in journalism's early annals.[38] Nor can they be dismissed as exemplars of Park's prescientific writings, unworthy of serious consideration by students of sociological theory. A closer and, admittedly, interpretive reading of them— more intense than has heretofore been given—will yield more than mere adumbrations of Park's later work.

It will be argued here that the Congo essays constitute a case study in what might be called a Gothic sociology of capitalism. The latter is a critical as well as explanatory perspective that had its elementary but unacknowledged formulation in the early writings of Karl Marx, and would be further refined in selected works of Max Weber, Georg Simmel, and Albion Small. But it has not yet been fully developed in its own right. Park's contribution to this matter is largely empirical; he took his point of departure directly from the Gothic metaphor and focused critical attention on the macabre and malevolent aspects of monarchical, capitalist imperialism. Read in this way, Park's Congo writings may assist in the much-needed reconstruction of sociological thought on capitalism and its discontents.

It is the usual first resort of writers on Park's contributions to dismiss his four signed essays on the Congo as pre-sociological and to neglect his ghosted essay altogether. Park's critical if laconic recollections of his service to the Congo Reform Association, (CRA), may have contributed to the tendency to dismiss their importance. Most chroniclers of Park's life and work do not even mention their existence or pass over the matter lightly. A good example of this unfortunate neglect of an important part of his *oeuvre* is to be found in a recent essay purporting to evaluate Park's ideas about inequality in relation to his ecological formulations. Richard C. Helmes-Hayes correctly observes that Park's social thought was pervaded by "a fatalism that runs as a dark thread through his work and that sparked an uncertainty in him regarding humanity's capacity to understand and control the social problem of inequality."[39] However, Helmes-Hayes, who cites nothing written by Park before 1915, and seems to have been unaware of Park's political and economic studies of the Congo, holds—quite incorrectly—that "Park's . . . relative deëmphasis on the explanatory importance of political and economic power was typical of American liberal thinking of the period," adding that "[s]tudies of national systems of economic and political power did not become common until after 1955."[40] Another recent critique of Park's work acknowledges the existence of the latter's Congo essays obliquely and without citation of the original publications,[41] fails to recognize Park's conceptualization of an emerging monarchical-capitalist-imperialist-complex affecting modern world politics, and asserts, again quite wrongly, that "Park was not inclined to seriously consider the current increase in monopolies an impediment to a more equitable resolution of differences between groups."[42] One of Park's biographers, Fred H. Matthews, treats the Congo essays as part of the "prehistory" of the sociologist's intellectual development.[43] Matthews describes the "tone" of Park's writing on the topic as "controlled hysteria" and asserts that, syntactically and substantively, they are in sharp contrast to his later "deliberative, ruminative style." Moreover, he believes that the Congo essays embody "an interpretation of events in terms of personal volition which Park came to regard as superficial and unscientific."[44] Seeing but not grasping the Gothic orientation at work in Park's Congo essays, Matthews asserts that Park described King Leopold II as a "corrupting capitalist superman" and, mistakenly, believes that Park's point of view on the matter expresses "a personalized, devil-figure theory of history" which the academic sociologist would later reject.[45] However, one erstwhile student of Park sees the issue quite differently. Helen MacGill Hughes believes that Park's stint with the Congo Reform Association "changed the focus of his career."[46] Although he was "writing public relations pieces on Belgian atrocities in Africa," she writes, ". . . his generalizing bent persisted." Indeed, Hughes comes closest to recognizing the embryonic elements of a Gothic theory in Park's Congo studies, observing that he "grew curious to learn the sequence of change which sets in when Europeans invade tribal villages, turn local raw materials into commodities, and wring from the land products for world trade, with, as a rule, the involuntary labor of primitive peoples." She goes on to point out that he "noted the constant disposition of Westerners to identify commerce with soul-saving and, willy-nilly, to slip from economic contacts into moral relationships, typically confused and contradictory."[47] The disparity among these interpretations, as well as the widespread belief that Park's Congo studies are "pre-sociological," have contributed much to their neglect as contributions to that discipline's development.

PARK'S PAPERS ON THE RACE QUESTION IN THE SOUTH

Park was one of the few post-bellum sociologists to take up the race question in the United States and Africa and to treat it as both a national and a world problem. Although William Graham Sumner (1840–1910)—who coined the term ethnocentrism[48] and supervised the first sociological study of lynching[49] in America—had asserted that the federal government's failure to intervene on behalf of the black victims of the South's virulent Negrophobia was indicative of the fact that the United States of America had not yet reached the point in its socio-cultural development that would permit it to be designated as a civilized society,[50] Lester Frank Ward (1841–1913), Sumner's opponent on a host of issues affecting the nature and evolution of both social science and civil society,[51] seemed ready to justify the Southern practice of first emasculating and then immolating black men accused of taking an untoward interest in white women as part of what he called the natural "philosophy of rape."[52] Other of Park's contemporaries regarded the ex-slaves and their progeny with considerable antipathy. Nathaniel Southgate Shaler (1841–1906), for example, the Harvard professor of geology and paleontology whose books *The Neighbor: The Natural History of Human Contacts* (1904)[53] and *The Individual: A Study of Life and Death* (1905)[54] would have a certain amount of influence on Park's general conceptualization of the processes entailed in human relations,[55] considered the black race to be constituted of "a lowly variety of man," the mulatto as merely a "third something which comes from the union of the European with the African," and went on to credit American slavery (which, he acknowledged, was morally reprehensible) with having "lifted a savage race nearer and more rapidly towards civilization than had ever before been accomplished."[56]

Negative, patronizing, and disdainful evaluations of the ex-slaves and their descendants also came from the leading feminist sociologist of that period, from racialist theorists, and from all too many preachers of the Social Gospel—a religious movement that had inspired the post-bellum reinvention of the new science of sociology. (In the antebellum era, sociology had been associated with the Southern Comteans' justification of Negro slavery,[57] or with a few Northern anarchist sex radicals, who advocated communal experiments, free love, and the abolition of marriage.[58]) Charlotte Perkins Gilman (1860–1935), a self-proclaimed disciple of Lester F. Ward,[59] who would become the "Marx and Veblen" of the woman's movement in America,[60] maintained a lifelong aversion to both blacks and Jews[61] and, in 1908, contributed "A Suggestion on the Negro Problem" to the *American Journal of Sociology* in which she proposed the following: "Let each sovereign state carefully organize in every county and township an enlisted body of all negroes below a certain grade of citizenship. Those above it—the decent, self-supporting, progressive negroes—form no problem and call for nothing but congratulation."[62] Gilman's "suggestion" in effect entailed—although she seemed unaware of the fact—a revival of Henry Hughes's program for what he called "warranteeism with the ethnical qualification,"[63] i.e., a seigneurial socialist administration of black labor under the control of a white master class.[64] Like Hughes, Gilman insisted her plan did not involve ownership of blacks: "This proposed organization is not enslavement, but enlistment."[65] And, again similar to Hughes's idea of a Southern pastoral utopia,[66] Gilman proposed that those members of her army of blacks old enough to work be trained for and concentrated in agricultural pursuits on self-supporting "model farms, under the best management, furnishing experiment stations, and bases for agricultural instruction, as well as the food for the whole army and its officials."[67] Other blacks might be "enlisted" to work "in mills and shops belonging to the undertaking, [and] would make clothing, uniforms, etc. for them all."[68] That "whole body of negroes who do not progress, who are not self-supporting, who are degenerating into an increasing percentage of social burdens or actual criminals," Gilman insisted, "should be taken hold of by the state."[69] Moreover, she made their compulsory "enlistment," what Hughes would have called a "warrantable" calling, into a public service: their "direct service to society would be in meeting the crying need of the whole South for better roads, harbors, river banks, and the general development of the country."[70] As Gilman—who was a knowledgeable political economist—noted, "Applied labor is wealth."[71] Further, "enlisted" blacks offered an untapped resource that, properly exploited, could "add millions to the value of southern land, and all within the independent power of each state."[72] Park's skepticism about social reformers and government programs, his service to the self-help program of Booker T. Washington, his probable knowledge of the latter's secret fight for the blacks' civil rights, as well as his own emerging tragic vision of civilization are certainly of a different order of the sociological imagination than that of Ms. Gilman.[73]

However, Park's writings on the race situation in Africa and in the American South must also be read against those of a rising chorus of scientific race experts who developed various theories on the social and behavioral effects of human anatomical and color differences. In Park's day, much of the science of anthropology was devoted to demonstrating what Harvard University's demographer, John Cummings, scornfully called "racial phrenology,"[74] and, it should be noted, Park's early writings appeared before Franz Boas's assault on his fellow anthropologists' scientific racism had won the day.[75] It is true (although little known even among today's sociologists) that Max Weber, in his capacity as a founder and principal editor of the *Archiv für Sozialwissenschaft und Sozialpolitik*, had published his former student W. E. B. DuBois's essay, "Die Negerfrage in den Vereinigten Staaten" in 1906.[76] Additionally, in 1910 in his fierce debate with Dr. Alfred Ploetz—a race scientist who would later serve the Hitler regime[77]—Weber had pointed out in reply to Ploetz's claim that America's Negroes compromised "Yankee" standards with their "uninhibited morals, . . . defective intelligence, and . . . foolish behavior" that "Nothing of the kind is proven." "I wish to state," Weber had gone on, "that the most important sociological scholar anywhere in the Southern States in America, with whom no white scholar can compare, is a Negro—Burckhardt DuBois."[78] Unlike most of that generation's students of the race question, Weber attributed antipathies toward blacks to "mass beliefs" that had arisen outside of the realm of "facts and experiences."[79] Weber scorned such beliefs in the face of what might be discovered by a truly scientific sociology:

> But does there exist even today a single
> fact that would be relevant for sociology—
> a single concrete fact which in a truly
> illuminating, valid, exact and incontestable
> way traces a definite type of sociological
> circumstance back to inborn and hereditary
> qualities which are possessed by one race or

another? The answer is definitively—note
well—definitively no![80]

However, Weber's remarks notwithstanding, there remained the published
writings of such significant figures as France's Georges Vacher de la Pouge
(1854–1936) and his American disciples, Carlos Closson and William Zebina
Ripley, forceful advocates of the anthropo-sociological, cephalic index school
associated with Germany's Otto Ammon.[81] In 1897, Closson insisted that
he had established the validity of the following formula: "In point of energy
and capacity, *Homo Europaeus* stands first, *Homo Alpinus* second, and the
Mediterranean third, in the hierarchy of European races."[82] Two years later
de la Pouge insisted that in determining the answer to the question, "Of the
races present among the Aryan peoples, which race was socially predominant,
to which ought the civilization to be attributed?" a scientist would have "to
distinguish between the element which counts and that which does not
count, between that which is influential and that which simply exists within
the society without playing any active role."[83] Not only did de la Pouge
immediately banish "the Mongol," the "Indo-Chinese, "the Chinese type . . .
originating in Kashgaria," and the "Indians of the United States" from the
races contributing to Aryan civilization—Africans were not even worthy of
consideration or mention—he also designated no less than ten human types
(some of them composed of racial mixtures) that had once, "six thousand
years before our era," resided in central Europe and the "British-Scandinavian
region."[84] From these, he winnowed out "the dolichocephalic blond, *Homo
Europaeus*" and selected it as "the dominant class among the primitive Aryans.
. . ."[85] Sure that the "civilization of a people is the creation of the master
class," de la Pouge granted to a white, blond, unmistakably proto-American
variant of that type the authorship of Occidental civilization.[86] "As regards
physical type," he observed, ". . . the image evoked by the name Aryan dif-
fers according to the author that one reads. . . ."[87] "In my view . . .," de la
Pouge concluded, "the dominant classes among them, the builders of the
Aryan civilization, were of the type of 'Uncle Sam,' or, to use the terminology most suitable from the anthropological point of view, were of the race *H.
Europaeus*."[88]

Of all the movements that affected the development of late nineteenth- and
early twentieth-century sociology in America, none had so great an influence
on its interests, paradigms, and direction as the Social Gospel. Rooted in the
conception that America was the redeemer nation[89] and that its societal, economic, and spiritual ills would have to be treated systematically and scientifically before its divine mission could be fulfilled, Social Gospel advocates
moved from the church pulpit to the academic platform, from the study of
texts to the service of people, from interpreting the casuistries of theology to
preaching a theodicy of social ills.[90] However, the race question confounded
and compromised the Social Gospel message. Influenced by conceptions of

Aryanist, Teutonic, and Anglo-Saxon superiority,[91] Social Gospel–inspired community settlements concentrated their programs of uplift on the plight of newly arrived Europeans,[92] ignored (with rare exception) or opposed altogether the immigration of Asians,[93] expressed profound ambivalence on the Jewish question,[94] and adapted their ministries to blacks to the prevailing fears about mixing the races.[95] Robert Park's animadversions about religiously zealous social reformers might have stemmed in part from what he heard and saw of the latter's Eurocentric ideology and segregationist practices. Nevertheless, in Booker T. Washington's program of education and only apparent accommodation to Southern "redemptionist" elements, Park seems to have perceived a practical way out of the quagmire of the American racial dilemma. As shall be argued in the pages to follow, Park's analysis of and participation in the Tuskegee experiment speaks to his conception of but one of the contradictory faces of the Protestant ethic, the other being its Gothic countenance, revealed in his Congo papers.

Once Park had left the service of Booker T. Washington and, like so many blacks and poor whites during the same period, moved to a major metropolis in the North, he seemed to depart from his emphasis on a "natural history" approach to the black situation.[96] Taking notice of the "new Negro" represented in an emergent and race-conscious literature, music, and art, Park came more and more to acknowledge a new perspective on race history: A social history of their own making would in the future guide the fortunes of America's blacks. By the time of World War II, Park no longer took the Southern caste order and its bi-racial organization as an effective model for America's race relations, but he worried over whether the burgeoning garrison state that he saw rising over the nation's not-yet-developed egalitarian and civil society would recognize its duty to fulfill the mandate of the Thirteenth Amendment—the abrogation of all of the badges and incidents of slavery.[97] Park's papers on German militarism, the horrors of the Congo, and the black American effort in the Redemptionist South provide both a guide to study and a warning. America has yet to understand or to realize their full import.

German Militarism,
the Garrison State, and Total War

Aspects of Robert E. Park's Sociology of Conflict

INTRODUCTION

In December 1900, *Munsey's Magazine* published Robert E. Park's first and only essay on the character and organization of the German army.[1] Subtitled "The Most Perfect Military Organization in the World," Park's essay seemed to celebrate the tactical effectiveness, strategic philosophy, and national chauvinism of the new Reich's armed forces. A superficial reading of the essay might have led a reader to suppose that Park shared some of the militant ideas of Heinrich von Treitschke, or that, more generally, he had been excessively influenced by the German school of national-historical thought associated with such figures as Johann Gustav Droysen and Leopold von Ranke. However, a closer reading reveals that Park's essay is a macro-sociological study; it can neither be relegated to the historical dustbin, nor treated as merely an American scholar's representation of the imperial German *Zeitgeist*. It contains the latter, but also transcends it. Not only does Park carefully analyze the process whereby the once feudal German officer corps was democratized, he also pinpoints the social psychology that animates the *Reichswehr*. In so doing, Park forewarns us of the dilemmas and contradictions that would plague all forms of militant and militarized ethno-nationalism and anticipates the fundamental political reorganization that would come to haunt and horrify the twentieth century—the rise of the garrison state and the extension of international conflicts to total war.

Park's essay on the German army may be read today in a double context: As an early attempt at preparing Americans for living in a multi-national, multi-cultural world that, he foresaw, would be inescapably fraught with perils; and, as an instance of Simmel's ideas about the conflict and tragedy of culture. Fred H. Matthews, a biographer of Park, believes that the thirty-six-year-old former journalist found in both the officers and ranks of the new

German army "an example of that dedication, that will to victory, and readiness for sacrifice which he had looked for in vain in modern America."[2] Perhaps this is so, but the larger context of Park's essay is to be found in its analysis of the emerging militarization that was attending the rise of ethnonational states. That militarization, in turn, had been amplified by technological advancements in transportation and communication, facilitated the bureaucratic reorganization of political, economic, and socio-cultural life, and in later decades would lead to conflicts over the extension of citizenship and the spread of democracy. The historicism of Treitschke, Droysen, and Ranke was an intellectual strand of these developments and became, in effect, an implicit topic of, as well as an explicit resource for, Park's later observations on the militarization of modern state societies. Ultimately, Park seems to have glimpsed the darker implications of the rising militarization: war's emergence from the limitations of cultural and moral constraints; indeed, war's "liberation" from its constraining forms so that it might fulfill its ultimate mission, annihilation.

RANKE, TREITSCHKE, AND PRUSSIAN ETHNO-NATIONALISM

Germany's establishment as a bellicose national-state, conceived in Bismarck's *Kulturkampf* of "blood and iron," found both its historical voice and its *raison d'être* in the writings of its so-called "liberal" historians.[3] Of these, Leopold von Ranke (1795–1886) stands out over all the others.[4] Ranke had proposed a remarkable "universal history" in 1880, but had nevertheless insisted that "Universal History would degenerate into mere fantasy and speculation were it to desert the firm ground of national history."[5] Park would later point out that Germany's national identity had been forged in the collective will characterizing its national history; in the process, national identity and will had been fused and then mobilized for the defense of its borders.[6]

The defense of the state was Ranke's ruling ethos. The state, Ranke had insisted, "is obliged . . . to organize all its internal resources for the purpose of self-preservation." This "supreme law of the state" required a shift in the priorities affecting its reconstruction: "I thought," he wrote, "more of making a state great and powerful than [of making] its citizens wise and good."[7] And this in turn seemed to call for a new kind of war: "Previously wars were waged with the excess of forces, with the people who could be spared, with money either found in the treasury or at least raised elsewhere . . . Now the nations, armed as they are, fight almost man for man, with all their might. . . . One must be prepared for a struggle for life or death."[8] For Ranke the history of the state was likened to the biography of a powerful individual. "In the end," historian Raymond J. Sontag noted in his summary of Ranke's outlook, ". . . the peculiar needs of each state would reassert their strength, and European history would again become the biography of states, each seeking to live and to grow in accordance with its own law of life."[9] The task of German history, Ranke had once asserted, should be to strive "to provide body for an otherwise vague national consciousness, to reveal the content of German history, and to experience the effective, vital spirit of the nation in it."[10] As Park conceived of the matter, this task had received its impetus and major manifestation in von Moltke's military reorganization.

However, it was Heinrich von Treitschke (1834–1896) more than Ranke who gave substance and support to a conception of reason that emphasized the Teutonic national will. That will not only superseded the will of the ordinary citizen, but also exerted absolute authority over the latter. Friedrich Meinecke, a student of Treitschke's thought, points out that the German variant of Europe's "classical liberalism" arose from a proposed synthesis of instrumental reason and military force. Among Germany's classical liberals, Meinecke regarded "Heinrich von Treitschke [as] . . . perhaps their greatest, at any rate their most influential, representative."[11]

Six years after Park published his essay, Meinecke—who had been born two years before Park and who would live ten years longer than the latter—had voiced a cautious optimism about the reforms made in Germany before the rise of the classical liberals, during the first decades of the nineteenth century. "If in the first decade of the twentieth century men can regard the state as more than a cold and oppressive force, and the nation as more than a primitive racial concept, if both seem to offer spiritual clarity and warmth, an atmosphere in which the free individual can breathe, then in Germany it is due largely to the Prussian reformers," who, he insisted, had responded to the exigencies of the Napoleonic era.[12] This sanguine assessment overlooked the arrogantly nationalistic and virulently anti-Semitic interpretation of these reforms that would be made by Treitschke; it was a failure of judgment that Meinecke, who had succeeded Treitschke as editor of the *Historische Zeitschrift* and who regarded the latter as "the man who surpassed all of us, young as well as old,"[13] would—all too late—deplore.[14] "Out of the anti-Semitic feeling [that Treitschke and his followers had begun in the 1880s]," Meinecke lamented in 1946, "it was possible for an anti-liberal and an anti-humanitarian feeling to develop easily—the first steps toward National Socialism."[15]

Treitschke had elaborated on his peculiar brand of ethnocentrism, in the process denigrating both Jews and African Americans. He regarded Jews as not only a deservedly stateless people, but also as a threat to the burgeoning Prussian hegemonism that he and his fellow historians were championing. "In plain words," he exhorted his readers, "The Jews have always been an 'element of national decomposition'; they have always helped in the disintegration of nations."[16] Although Treitschke allowed that a "certain number of

European Jews have, as a matter of fact, succeeded in really adopting the nationality of the people among whom they live . . . it is equally certain that in Berlin, and eastwards from that city, there are many Jews who are inwardly real Orientals, in spite of the language they speak."[17] Holding that in antiquity, Jews had played "an essential role" in the Alexandrian and Roman Empires, and that later, in "the early Middle Ages . . . Jews [had] controlled the trade of the world," Treitschke believed that "the Jews [had] ceased to be indispensable" with the onset of the age of national state building.[18] Once having lost their indispensability, he hinted, they had become expendable.

Not content to encourage an anti-Jewish, inhumane, and generally ethnocentric national struggle in behalf of Prussian domination of German culture, Treitschke turned his vitriolic pen onto the situation affecting freedom in the United States of America in the aftermath of that nation's Civil War. Holding to his premise that "When several nations are united under one State, the simplest relationship is that the one which wields the authority should be the superior in civilization,"[19] Treitschke pointed to what he regarded as the absence of civilization altogether among black Africans and Afro-Americans: "The black races have always been servants, and looked down upon by all the others, nor has any Negro State ever raised itself to a level of real civilization."[20] Treitschke's version of Aryan supremacist history led him to ignore altogether such once-flourishing African kingdoms as Songhay and Mali. Instead, Treitschke's racial and national views led him to connect genetic peoplehood to nationality, nationality to state, state to patriotism, and patriotism to war. In all of this, as we shall see, Park did not only *not* follow him, but hotly opposed Treitschke's tendentious reasoning.

PARK AND REALPOLITIK

Nowhere in Park's essay on the German army does he mention the name or present the perspective of Treitschke; rather, the latter's racialist and bellicose historicism haunts the thematic of Park's study. Park's depiction of the collective conscience that gave German militarism its patriotic esprit de corps is that developed by Helmuth von Moltke the Elder (1800–1891), chief of the German army's general staff from 1857 to 1887.[21]

Moltke, as Park described him, personified not only the German nation at war preparedness, but also the modern type of authoritarian technocrat that national states of the twentieth century would demand as their own military leaders. "Every organization," Park observed, "—and the German army is a striking illustration of the principle—presents a double aspect. On the one side, it is a machine, a tool, and on the other it is what I may call an organized experience, a will."[22] As a machine and tool, Moltke had understood, the soldiers in the ranks had to be completely obedient to the orders that were formulated by the general staff and the officer corps and embodied in the will of their commander. Hence, while the national army, after its reorganization on the basis of universal military conscription, might offer the hitherto stratum-bound son of a *bauer* a path to social and economic advancement, it could not be governed according to the principles of democracy. The "machine-like automation that one finds in a well drilled army," Park pointed out, depends on a "centering of control" in the "leadership element."[23]

Park's interest in Germany's new militarism arose out of his conviction— derived intellectually from his studies with Simmel and personally from his many and varied experiences in the knockabout world—that the many forms of conflict are a general feature of social life. It is not accurate to say, as James Alfred Aho has written, that "there is little question but that realpolitik permeates Park's social theorizing."[24] Park regarded war as "a crude form of social competition" that had "as its goal . . . the suppression of the opponent."[25] In 1916, two years after Europe had become embroiled in what was to be designated as the First World War, Park would note in a letter to his daughter how "the simplest problems . . . are world problems, the problems of the contacts and the frictions and the interactions of nations and races." Park reported that he hoped to do a study of war posing the following questions: "Why do we, irrespective of specific causes, have wars? Why do men fight? What is the function of war? Is war one way, one necessary way, of getting on in the world? Is it part of the cosmic process of evolution, part of the struggle for existence? Are human beings so made that the world would be worse off if these tremendous struggles did not exist? In short, is war founded in the nature of human beings?"[26] Such questions do not arise in the mind of one steeped in realpolitik.

Although Park's other studies diverted his attention from these questions, he never ceased his interest in the study of war in particular and more generally in ferreting out the bases and consequences of bellicose conflicts and the grounds for their peaceful accommodation.

THE GERMAN ARMY, THE GARRISON STATE, AND TOTAL WAR

State Militarization

In 1922, Park prophesied that "When the final history of the World War comes to be written, one of its most interesting chapters will be a description of the methods and devices which were used by the armies of both sides to destroy the will to war in the enemy's troops and among the peoples behind the lines."[27] He was not only echoing an observation he had made two decades earlier in his study of the German army, but also elaborating upon the Treitschkean model of a German national will to war. In 1900, Park had taken cognizance of a development in Germany that would usher in a new era: the century of total war. It was General von Moltke, Park pointed out, who had come to the conclusion that future wars would "be waged with the railway and telegraph," i.e., that "modern science had given to a capable leader the means of concentrating and putting in action an army larger than had ever before been dreamed of, an army that was nothing less than a nation in arms."[28] Park had delineated the policies and programs whereby imperial Germany had accomplished the institutional reconstruction requisite for converting itself into a militarily prepared and fully garrisoned national state, a Treitschkean war-state.

However, Park had been misled about the much-vaunted upward mobility said to have "democratized" the German officer corps. Despite his citation of Bismarck's good-natured complaint—that his own son had not been promoted from the ranks as rapidly as other conscripts from less-favored lineages—as a telling piece of evidence of the elimination of aristocratic privilege in the new German army,[29] we have no less than the authority of Friedrich Meinecke revealing that, despite the liberal reforms, "the tradition of the officer corps as a corporation held together by unique attitudes and qualities was not abandoned." Meinecke observed that "In the course of time this development carried the officer corps back to its aristocratic, old-Prussian roots, and former qualities reasserted themselves more than the reformers had wished."[30] Hans Kohn has been even more emphatic, locating the source of Prussian aristocratic predominance in the very workings of the system of universal conscription that Park had described: "Whereas in Germany the 'common man' served three years," Kohn pointed to the fact that "the high-school graduate, then always a member of the upper classes, had to serve only one year, and at the end of the year if he chose to stay *in the reserves* as an officer was generally commissioned as a second lieutenant." Such a system, Kohn concluded, "helped to preserve the strict class character of the German army."[31]

Although Park was sure that the "rule which treated all alike had an inspiring effect upon the rank and file of the soldiers,"[32] he had failed to notice a feature of the universal military conscription program that would make his assertion about all of Germany being a "nation in arms"[33] a far more formidable prophecy. That feature would be noticed by Hans Speier in his 1932 study of German white collar workers—a monograph suppressed by the Nazis. Pointing to the fact that the "veteran of twelve years of army service . . . was especially favored for placement" in the civil service, Speier documented the very high percentage of veterans holding positions in the *Reichsverband der*

Zivildienstberechtigten and observed that "the special rights of the veteran . . . guaranteed the militarization of the lower bureaucracy."[34] Moreover, it was Speier who pointed out that Hitler had completed the egalitarianization of the army that had only been begun by the National Liberals:

> When Hitler reintroduced universal military service, he abolished the privilege of shorter service in the army which boys with a high school education had enjoyed under the kaiser. In this respect and also with respect to promotion from the ranks the military system of this modern despot is more egalitarian than was that of Imperial Germany. . . . With this resolution to liberate destructive techniques from humanitarian fetters and to sacrifice any tradition to military efficiency he has brought to a head the martial equalization of society that began in eighteenth century Prussia but required the rise of modern political mass movements to become truly effective.[35]

Although Park had been mistaken about its democratization, he had correctly noted the enlargement of the German general staff, its division into specialized departments, and its adaptation of advances in science and technology to military purposes. "In 1857," he pointed out, "when Moltke became chief [of staff], the personnel of his bureau was composed of sixty-four officers, a number . . . increased [later] to eighty-three. . . . In 1867 his subordinates numbered one hundred and nine. . . . At . . . present . . . there are two hundred and seven officers in the general staff."[36] Moreover, Park saw the relationship of this division of labor to the institutionalization of the Treitschkean will to war. He likened this steadily enlarging staff to the "brain" of a giant organism that, he said, was the essence of the army; the men in the ranks served that "brain" as a "corresponding automatism."[37]

Park's shrewd observations about the implications of the resurgence of German militarism focused on the fundamental reconceptualization of warfare that Moltke had formulated and introduced to the public. In effect, Park pointed out how Moltke had not only proposed to end those self-imposed restrictions that most modern states had recently adopted, but also ushered in an era of virtually unconditional war. In a speech to the Reichstag that Park quoted, the chief of staff had asserted, "I do not agree with the declaration made at St. Petersburg, that the weakening of the enemy's forces constitutes the only proper method of warfare." And, as Park took care to report, Moltke wished to convert warfare into an all-out assault on the enemy's military bases, natural resources, and civilian population. "[W]e should," Moltke insisted, "direct our attack against all the means and resources that the enemy possesses—against his finances, his railways, his food supply, even his prestige."[38] Having adopted Moltke's program, reconstructed its armed forces, fixed authority in the hierarchy of the general staff, centralized control in the commander in chief, and girdled the country with military fortifications, Germany stood poised with its army standing, in Park's words, "upon its own soil, silent, observant, calm, in an attitude of formidable defense."[39] But, as Park hinted in the conclusion of his essay, Moltke's military philosophy was not limited to justifications for wars in *defense* of the realm. "'Eternal peace,' said he, 'is only a dream, and not even a happy dream . . . Without war the world would fall into decay, and lose itself in materialism.'"[40]

Park's observation that *fin de siècle* Germany's social organization had taken on a new form—an entire nation in arms, motored by constantly improved military technology and molded by militaristic indoctrination—portended a frightening future, one wherein wars would become indiscriminate in their infliction of casualties and unrestrained in their assaults on people and property.

Park and the First World War

Park returned to the analysis of total war at the end of the First World War, devoting thirty-five pages of his study of the immigrant press in America to the character and effectiveness of Germany's wartime campaign of propaganda.[41] Noting that "the leaders of the German people realized the power of propaganda earlier and more completely than the peoples of other nations," Park recounted the activities that would, in effect, fill out Moltke's vision of an all-out war: Germany's leaders had made "detailed studies of the sources of actual and potential unrest in all the countries with which they were likely to come in conflict;" had been "active in establishing cultural colonies in every part of the world to which German commerce and German immigration had penetrated;" and, in the United States, had kept "alive the German spirit . . . under the auspices of the Deutsch-Amerikanischer Bund . . . [whose] national charter . . . , [according to the *Alldeutsche Blatter*, held its 6,500 local societies] 'together in the bonds of Germanism.'"[42]

Despite the German military's dedication to making war on every element of the enemy's resources including its prestige, Park was dubious about both the conspiratorial origin and the social effectiveness of the German campaign. Although he was aware that there "is evidence . . . to show that Germany had foreseen the political and military as well as the commercial advantages of promoting German *Kultur* abroad," and that "long before the war, plans had been broached for converting the New York *Staats-Zeitung* into an English [language] newspaper . . . to counteract the influence of England in American affairs," Park cautioned against "attributing omniscience to the German General Staff."[43] As Park observed, "It is not necessary to assume that all this extension of German influence had taken place merely to serve the military ambition of Germany."[44]

Germany's aim of assaulting the "prestige" of the enemy had taken a special direction in the case of its assault on the neutrality of the United States in the years from 1914 to 1917. In his analysis Park treated propaganda of the deed as well as that of the word, calling attention to that nation's agents' attempts to "prevent the shipment of munitions to the allies; . . . to spread pacifism; . . . to convert American public opinion to the German point of view; and . . . to promote dissension among various elements of the population."[45] In reviewing all of this, Park proceeded to indicate what was involved in the confrontation of Germany's all-encompassing attack by America's long-standing but still precarious commitment to the values that support freedom of speech and of association.

Although Park mentions in passing such acts of German sabotage as "incendiarism and blowing up munitions ships,"[46] he concentrates attention on the various agents' attempts to shape the conscience, consciousness, and public opinion of the American people. It would be otiose to detail Park's discussion. Suffice it to say that after presenting the facts related to Germany's propagandists' program of organizing fronts to exploit the already aroused peace sentiment, purchasing or influencing major American newspapers, distributing pro-German films, and, finally, trying to "promote dissension among the heterogeneous elements of the American population,"[47] Park inquired critically into the American response. In so doing he took note of both the laws and policies enforced by the United States Postal Service to counter enemy propaganda and of the postwar raids and round-ups of foreign "radicals" designed to suppress dissent.

Park acknowledged that the limited program of immigrant press censorship imposed by the United States Postal Service had been effective, but he believed that it was still the case that "Of all the liberties guaranteed by a free government, freedom of speech and of conscience are undoubtedly those most cherished by the people of the United States."[48] For this reason Park was far less sanguine about the ethics or effectiveness of Attorney General Palmer's postwar forays into immigrant ghettoes in search of foreign radicals and political dissenters. Not an admirer of the radical press himself, Park remarked acidly, "[T]here is reason to believe that the raids of the Department of Justice, the sensational arrests, and the deportations of radicals since the armistice, have been a great stimulus to the publication of new radical papers."[49]

Park's personal admiration for Hugo Münsterberg (1863–1916), one of his mentors at Harvard, as well as his recognition of the right to freedom of conscience, might have led him to omit from his analysis of German propaganda any consideration of the scandal that had erupted when Münsterberg enraged significant portions of American academia by openly engaging in highly publicized activities in behalf of Germany's cause in the war. When, in 1922, Park presented in stunning detail the pro-German activities of Louis N. Hammerling, chief executive of the American Association of Foreign Language Newspapers, of Charles J. Hexamer, president of the German-American Alliance, of Drs. Heinrich Albert and Bernard Dernberg, officers of the German High Commission in the United States, of M. B. Claussen, publicity agent of the Hamburg-American Line, and of six front organizations and several newspapers founded or infiltrated by German agents to foster sentiment in behalf of American neutrality in the war taking place on the Continent,[50] he studiously avoided mentioning Hugo Münsterberg's attempts to provide intelligence to the German Foreign Office and, more significantly, to discourage Americans from sympathizing with England's aims in the war.[51] Yet, in certain significant ways, Münsterberg's outlook illustrated one aspect of the German conflation of building up a national will with entering into a total war, the very process that Park's essay of 1900 had portended.

In eschewing a discussion of Münsterberg's pro-German efforts, Park missed an opportunity to compare and contrast his own views on German militarization with those presented in Münsterberg's book, *The War and America*.[52] In addition to Münsterberg's accusations that Russia and France had started the war[53] and that England's primary interest in entering it was to defeat its only serious industrial, commercial, and imperial competitor in the world market,[54] Münsterberg had warned his American readers that "If Russia wins to-day and Germany is broken down, Asia must win sooner or later, and if Asia wins, the achievements of the western world will be wiped from the earth more sweepingly than the civilization of old Assyria."[55]* Having wrapped the Kaiser in the mantle of protector of Occidental civilization, Münsterberg went on to charge what he regarded as the misinformed, duplicitous, and secretly pro-English media in the United States with having "whipped the millions of peaceful American readers ruthlessly and shamefully to the passionate attack against their best friends, the Germans."[56] But Münsterberg went even beyond these fulminations. Not only did he employ virtually all of the techniques that Park would designate as propagandistic

---

*Not until after the war did a revisionist perspective on the origins of the First World War begin to affect the outlook of certain important American sociologists. During the war, Columbia University's preëminent sociologist, Franklin Henry Giddings, had adopted an uncritical pro-American, anti-German stance, encouraging an ethnocentric patriotism that culminated in his support of Columbia University's president, Nicholas Murray Butler, and Butler's draconian policy against those professors who dissented from the war, which Giddings expressed in his statement about the rights of minorities to dissent: "One reservation must be made. In time of war the liberty of minorities and of individuals is inevitably curtailed. In time of war the state rightly demands the loyal and active cooperation of all citizens. . . . While war lasts things cannot be or continue 'as usual,' whether business, or pleasure, or freedom of speech. . . . Open or disguised obstruction [of the war effort] may not be tolerated." Franklin Henry Giddings, *The Responsible State: A Reexamination of Fundamental Political Doctrines in the Light of World War and the Menace of Anarchism* (Boston: Houghton and Mifflin, 1918), pp. 76–77. After the war, Harry Elmer Barnes, at one time an admirer of Giddings, and a scholar much-influenced by Sidney Bradshaw Fay's *magnum opus* of revisionism, *The Origins of the World War*, 2d rev. ed. (New York: Macmillan, 1936), would become a lifelong opponent of American involvement in world wars and a major revisionist thinker. See William L. Neumann, "World War I Revisionist," in Arthur Goddard, ed., *Harry Elmer Barnes, Learned Crusader: The New History in Action* (Colorado Springs, Colo.: Ralph Myles, Inc., 1968),pp. 261–87.

persuasion devices in behalf of the Kaiser's cause, he also elaborated on the national-militaristic psychology that had been given voice by Treitschke and Moltke.

Park might have selected Münsterberg's diatribe of 1914 as a sequel to and, perhaps, a logico-historical extension of the triumph of the Treitschke-Moltke vision over that of its Christian opponents. Unfortunately, he took no notice of Münsterberg's version of the German spirit. It is worthy of note that in 1904, four years after Park had published his German army essay, Ernst Troeltsch, who had attended Treitschke's lectures on history in Berlin in 1886, addressed the *Evangelisch-Sozialer Kongress*, an association of theologians, social scientists, pastors, politicians, civil servants, and church officials, on the subject of "Christian Ethics and Contemporary Society." He presented a thesis not too dissimilar from that argued by Simmel three years later in his monograph on Schopenhauer and Nietzsche. Troeltsch pointed out how little ethics had come to mean in the Empire, how the ideals of Kant, Fichte, and Hegel had been set aside, how the present German state lacked any true moral foundations, and how the new and much-vaunted Teutonic nation had descended into an expression of super-patriotic collective egoism. He went on to tell how the once prominent natural-rights principles of justice and equality had become the exclusive property of the Social Democrats, while the German people's habitual devotion to the legitimating capacity of historical authority had been corrupted, becoming the guiding precept of the chauvinistic Prussian ruling class.[57]

Unlike Troeltsch, Münsterberg had taken over for himself the stance of the Prussian elite. The German national will, which Park had observed being enshrined in Moltke's conception of the nation's armed forces, was given even greater charismatic credit in Münsterberg's polemic fourteen years later. "When future historians study the underlying conditions and factors of this European war," he prophesied, "they will, no doubt, recognize that [the] . . . superiority of the German army . . . does not result from a merely outer professional war technique, but comes because the German army is the embodiment of the national soul with all its intellectual and moral energies."[58]

Park's observation that *fin de siècle* Germany's militarized social organization portended a frightening future, one wherein wars would become indiscriminate in their infliction of casualties and unrestrained in their assaults on people and property, adumbrated an argument that Münsterberg would make in 1914. But, when Münsterberg sought to justify Germany's aerial bombardment of Paris and Antwerp and its widely condemned invasion of Belgium, a neutral state,[59] as well as the underground mining of open fields by the forces of both sides, he not only claimed that each of these acts was within the provisions of accepted international conventions governing the conduct of nations at war, but also reminded his American readers of Civil War General William Tecumseh Sherman's enunciation of a perspective on war not dissimilar from that of von Moltke. Münsterberg pointed out that Sherman had stated as part of an official report, "I should not hesitate to burn Savannah, Charleston, and Wilmington if the garrisons were needed. Of necessity in war the commander on the spot is the judge and may take your house, your fields, your everything and turn you all out helpless to starve. Our duty is not to build up; it is rather to destroy both the rebel army and whatever wealth or property it has founded its boasted strength upon."[60]

In effect Münsterberg seemed to be respecifying the nation to which blame ought to be assigned for first expanding the concept and enlarging the scope of warfare. Recent scholarship has lent a measure of support to Münsterberg's claim that America's militarization during its Civil War constituted the actual beginnings of total war.[61] By not attending to Münsterberg's monograph on the war—or, more to the point—by not investigating Münsterberg's allegation that the American Civil War General William Tecumseh Sherman had inaugurated the practices that would come to be associated with the conception of total war, Park missed an opportunity to develop even further the thesis that he had presented in his essay on German militarization and to relate that thesis to the military threat to non-European peoples. In a confidential dispatch to General H. W. Halleck, dated September 17, 1863, Sherman had enunciated his practical theory of unconditional warfare:

> I would banish all minor questions, assert the broad doctrine that as a nation the United States has the right, and also the physical power, to penetrate to every part of our national domain, and that we will do it . . . that we will remove and destroy every obstacle, if need be, take every life, every acre of land, every particle of property, everything that to us seems proper; that we will not cease till the end is attained; that all who do not aid us are enemies, and that we will not account to them for our acts. If the people of the South oppose, they do so at their peril; and if they stand by, mere lookers-on in this domestic tragedy, they have no right to community, protection, or share in the final results.[62]

Sherman later not only put forward a military reorganization program for the post–Civil War United States that was, *mutatis mutandis*, not dissimilar in motivation from that of von Moltke's,[63] but would also employ the totalistic practices, tactics, and strategies of general annihilation that he had perfected in his assaults on Atlanta, Wilmington, and Savannah[64] in the United States' wars against those trans-Mississippi Amerindians who dared to resist America's conquering advance to the Pacific coast.

During the quarter century that separated the ending of the Civil War and the closing of the frontier—the years of Park's youth—American military operations were almost exclusively confined to the winning of the West. Although Park apparently took no notice of the fact, the totalistic war conceptions that had figured so significantly in the Union victory were turned against the aboriginal peoples who lived beyond the Mississippi River.

Indeed, Minnesota, the site of Park's childhood and adolescence, was one of the bloodiest arenas of the new warfare.[65] A territory in 1849, Minnesota had been granted statehood nine years later, its white population having risen to 150,000, while its less populous Indian tribes had been forced to cede title to 28 million acres of land in exchange for a restricted reservation life and a paltry and much-abused annuity. In 1862, two years before Park's birth, militant factions of the Santee Sioux had risen in rebellion against the thoroughly corrupt federal Indian agency and its aborigine pastoralization program. Commissioned a colonel in Minnesota's rapidly mobilized state militia, Henry A. Sibley, a trader who profited from the agency system, proclaimed, "My heart is steeled against them, and if I have the means, and can catch them, I will sweep them with the besom of death."[66] After defeating a Sioux war party at Wood Lake, Sibley captured over 2,000 Indians and had 303 of them tried, convicted, and sentenced to hang. President Lincoln commuted the sentences of all but 38 of these, but also ordered both Sioux and Winnebago peoples removed from the state altogether and placed on even less hospitable reservations in the Dakota Territories.[67] The few Indians whom Park had known in his youth must have been among those who had escaped or avoided this draconian policy in some other way.

That Park devoted almost none of his sociological studies of war or race relations to the situation of the American Indians speaks much to the compartmentalization of peoples that would become *de rigueur* in American social science. Indians came under the control of the Bureau of Ethnology and, thereby, under the aegis of anthropology;[68] the social problems of blacks, Asians, Hispanics, and European ethnics fell to the theoretical and empirical investigations of sociology. By the time Park reached Chicago, race and ethnic problems were defined in terms of the socioeconomic condition of blacks, Asians, Italians, Poles, Russians, and Jews.[69] Assimilated whites belonged to history and the study of civilization. Thus did a separate and unequal division of disciplinary labor facilitate a massive failure of the sociological imagination.

America's nineteenth-century Indian pacification program coincided with Europe's partition of Africa among its imperial powers. In both cases policies were put forward to subjugate—or remove altogether—an aboriginal obstacle to white continental hegemony. Although put forward in the name of a progressive and beneficent policy of civilization,—and manned by Protestant (and a few Catholic) missionaries,[70] unscrupulous traders, and corrupt political lackeys[71]—American "manifest destiny" and European imperialism in Africa were secured all too often by military force. In the case of the Belgian depredations in the Congo, Park would be foremost among sociologists in analysis and critique. In the instance of America's Indian wars, he—like so many others of his profession—remained silent.

The aims, strategy, and tactics of those wars were derived from and commanded by Civil War generalship. As chief architect of the postwar regular army, General William Tecumseh Sherman fashioned an approach to the

"Indian question" that with rare and occasional exception treated the aborigines as rebels and traitors;[72] his replacement on the frontier, General Philip H. Sheridan, opposed the peace policy inaugurated but hardly implemented under Grant's Administration and conducted marauding military expeditions designed to kill as many Indians as possible, destroy their homes, camps, provisions, and ponies, and in general annihilate the aboriginal peoples altogether.[73] Successful presidential candidate and Civil War hero Ulysses S. Grant promised a reporter that the westward migration of white settlers would be protected even if it meant the extermination of every Indian tribe.[74] Despite the professions of the Quaker-based "Grant Peace Policy" toward the Indians,[75] wars of a near-genocidal character were carried out in the central, southwestern, Pacific, and northwestern regions of the trans-Mississippi West until 1890.[76] Although it is beyond the scope of the present study to explore all of the ramifications of America's post–Civil War military reorganization, suffice it to say that Park's failure to become sociologically sensitized to his former teacher's (Münsterberg) admittedly propagandistic attempt to lay the blame for the cruelties of modern warfare on the Union generals' Civil War strategy and tactics—or to look back on the region of his youth as a strategic research site for studying the relationship of warfare to race and ethnic relations—was an unfortunate departure from his usual astuteness.

Had Park looked into the matter, he might have seen that America's policy of acculturating the Indians—with its curious mixture of god-fearing piety and Gatling gun fire power—had some elements in common with Bismarck's *Kulturkampf* and, more significantly, corresponded to the "coercive" form of social assimilation that had been described in the essay series by Sarah E. Simons in *The American Journal of Sociology* in 1901–02,[77]—the years immediately following publication of his own essay on German militarization and four years before his first essay on the black community of Winston-Salem, North Carolina. Simons cited as one example of an ineffective program of coercive assimilation Bismarck's cultural policy toward the Danes of North Schleswig, a territory that had been ceded to Austria in 1864 but that had fallen into Prussian hands in 1866 as a prize of victory in the Austro-Prussian War. "The culture of the two nations is so similar," Simons observed, "that assimilation would be easy if the proper method were adopted. If the German government were to treat the Danes as the equals of the Germans, and show respect for their civilization and consideration for their customs, adaptation would naturally follow."[78] But the American Indians were not Danes. When Simons turned her attention to the policies and processes seeking to effect the assimilation of Indians in the United States of America, she scrupulously avoided mention of Grant's, Sherman's, and Sheridan's military forays into their territory; of the official scorn heaped upon native-American customs, language, and lifeways by congressmen, officials of the Indian bureau, and not a few missionaries; and of the uncensured exploitation, unalloyed corruption, and unredeeming humiliation inflicted upon the tribes that had been corralled on reservations. Taking her point of departure from an uncritical reading of the lofty aims of the Dawes General Allotment Act of 1887 and the Severalty Act of 1891,[79] Simons asserted that "The United States . . . is now employing the same method in assimilating the Indian that she uses in the assimilation of the immigrant."[80] However, she seemed to have sensed that something was amiss, that elements of the earlier nakedly hostile attitude still prevailed, that a people whose every member had first been considered "a barbarian and an infidel" could not be absorbed as easily as Germans, Danes, or Britons. "It is not unlikely," Simons concluded, "that *a remnant* of the Indian race may, by becoming assimilated, fit themselves *to survive* in open competition with the whites."[81]

Park was not unaware of Simons' analysis of assimilation—in 1921, together with Ernest W. Burgess, he would reprint the opening three paragraphs of her monumental series of essays on the topic.[82] Nor was he likely to be unaware of Münsterberg's role in trying to keep America from allying itself with England in its war against Germany and of the latter's thesis about America's Civil War Generals' role in the modernization of warfare. Yet, he did not re-analyze his thesis about the originality of von Moltke's reforms and eschewed the opportunity presented by Münsterberg's challenge to investigate the effects that Civil War military reorganization had had on the Indian frontier wars or on America's move toward garrison statehood. Had he done so, he might have discovered—as a young historian, Robert Allen Wooster, did in 1988[83]—that as a result of the ineffectiveness of Civil War methods of warfare when employed against Cubans, Puerto Ricans, Spaniards, and Filipinos in the Spanish-American War of 1898–1900,[84] United States Secretary of War Elihu Root determined to scrap the Sherman reforms and, in their stead, to institute an Army War College, establish a general staff, and replace the position of commanding general with that of a chief of staff.[85] Like von Moltke's, the new American general staff was ordered to develop strategic planning on a systematic basis. Its chief was to be an adviser to the civilian secretary of War. And in lieu of garrisons scattered on the far-flung frontier, thousands of troops were to be stationed in the overseas areas that became the strategic front line of America's empire in the Pacific.[86] When, in 1927, Park would begin to reformulate his cycle theory of race relations on the basis of an investigation of "Our Racial Frontier on the Pacific,"[87] he did not make the connections that he might have on the one hand to his German army study and his critique of Leopold II's atrocities in the Congo, and, on the other, to Münsterberg's thesis about America's role in the invention of total war and its imperial policies against Indians, Hispanics, Asians, and Pacific Islanders. It is a thesis that has yet to be fully elaborated.

The Second World War and the Treitschkean Fulfillment

It would not be until the eve of America's involvement in the Second World War that Park would set down on paper his pessimistic observations about how advances in the means of destruction and the techniques of propaganda had led to the repudiation of the few jurisprudential restraints on the conduct of war that still existed.[88] Noting in 1941 that neither scholars nor statesmen knew "whether to regard war as a natural phenomenon, like an earthquake or a pestilence, or to classify it as a social phenomenon, like a political contest, or an elementary form of judicial procedure like the ancient trial by battle,"[89] Park pointedly challenged the current applicability of Treitschke's assertion that "Between civilized nations . . . war is the form of litigation by which states made their claims valid."[90] Park pointed out that the "so-called 'laws of war'" had been undermined by "the rapid advances in the technology of war [that had] . . . assumed ever vaster proportions and achieved an ever more terrible efficiency"[91] in the decades after Treitschke had written those words. Moreover, Park went on, "International politics . . . [have] become more realistic and more cynical."[92] Ultimately, he concluded, "Under these conditions it is difficult to conceive of war as a form of judicial procedure even as elementary as the ancient trial by battle. It is even doubtful whether it can any longer be regarded as it once was, as an 'institution recognized by international law.'"[93] War had burst the bonds of its own self-restraints. "It is an institution—a political institution—in process; an institution whose function has not been defined, whose structure is not yet fixed in custom and in tradition."[94]

Park had earlier proposed that the state, the modern form of geopolitical unity, be conceived as the endpoint of an evolutionary trajectory. That trajectory could be depicted as moving through successive stages of collective group formation, beginning in the crowd and becoming, sequentially, the caste, the sect, the class, and, finally, the state.[95] Although in 1904 Park had supposed that there was "progressive social differentiation and increasing stability from stage to stage," in his later writings he constantly compared the state to the crowd. However, by 1942 he had come to regard the failure of reason to have deterred the development of Hitler's Third Reich as, in effect, a refutation of Hegel's dictum that, as Park had earlier paraphrased the German philosopher, "The general will assumes the self-conscious form of reason only within the State."[96] Two years before his death, Park called attention to the fact that, "Most of us have been astounded, and some of us have been terrified, by what Herr Hitler and his associates have accomplished in recreating, in so short a time, the German army and transforming the disorganized German Empire into the most powerful military and political machine the world has ever known."[97] But, more significantly, Park, in an essay written about the same time, called attention to the fact that Hitler and his junto had organized and manipulated a mass psychology of fascism and taken it through all the stages of political development without ever divesting it of its essentially irrational character. The calamitous spectacle of a modern state society in the throes of a fanatical charismatic atavism, destroying the gains in rationality supposedly ensured by the Enlightenment gave Park pause. "[I]t suggests," he wrote, "the relativity of worlds in which men are actively alive and for whose orderly existence they are in some way personally respon-sible."[98] The Nazis had made a shambles out of the relationship of personal responsibility to state action and democratic values. Energized by its sectarian rites and urged on by the racialist creed contained in its "Bible," *Mein Kampf*, the Nazi movement had earlier found "in Hitler its prophet, if not its God . . ."[99] As soon as the Nazi movement captured control of the state it had "attempted to suppress every form of dissent with all the fervor and fanat-ical vigor of a newborn religion."[100] Moreover, "Herr Hitler and his associates seem to have inspired the army, if not the people, with an invincible faith in their mission and destiny . . . and . . . have sought to support that faith by rit-ual, by myth, and above all, by ceremonies that revive . . . the atmosphere and . . . mood of exaltation in which it was originally conceived."[101]

Park had once remarked, with regard to Sumner's discussion of the mores, that "It is . . . only in a political society, in which a public exists that permits discussion, rather than in a society organized on a familial and authoritative basis, that rational principles tend to supersede tradition and custom as a basis of organization and control."[102] However, the establishment of the Nazi state in Germany and its subsequent war program that intended to dominate the entire world had ushered in something entirely new, an aggressive state-society that seemed to have burst both the traditional restraints of custom-bound orderliness and the deliberative rationality and legal controls of constitutional republics.* "World War II," he observed, "which began with the assumption

---

* Taken together, Park's German army essay, his doctoral dissertation, and his writings on war and fascism in the 1930s and 1940s adumbrate and reinforce those of the then-promi-nent journalist and columnist, Dorothy Thompson (1893–1961), who had interviewed Hitler in 1931. In "This Book," her introduction to a volume of her newspaper columns entitled *Let the Record Speak*, (Boston: Houghton Mifflin, 1939), Thompson had written:

> [Nazism] is a repudiation of the whole past of western man. It is . . . a complete break with Reason, with Humanism, and with the Christian ethics that are at the basis of liberalism and democracy. . . . In its joyful destruction of all previous standards; in its wild affirmation of the "Drive of the Will"; in its Oriental acceptance of death as the fecundator of life and of the will to death as the true heroism, it is darkly nihilistic. Placing will above reason; the ideal over reality; appealing, unremittingly, to totem and taboo; elevating tribal fetishes; subjugating and destroying the common sense that grows out of human experience; of an oceanic boundlessness, Nazism—that has been my con-sistent conviction—is the enemy of whatever is sunny, reasonable, pragmatic, common-sense, freedom-loving, life-affirming, form-seeking and conscious of tradition.

Quoted in Peter Kurth, *American Cassandra: The Life of Dorothy Thompson* (Boston: Little-Brown, 1990), pp. 163–64.

that its purpose was to revise the treaties with which World War I was concluded, is now proclaiming itself a world-revolution. . . . It is rather an ideological war—a war to establish a new order based upon a new political
philosophy and a new philosophy of life."[103] That new order and philosophy
of life would embrace and intertwine "total war" with "the garrison state."

TOTAL WAR AND MODERNITY:
THE GARRISON STATE

There is a foreboding imagery in Park's commentaries on the relation of
war to the perils of modernity. Writers on the history of war have disagreed
with one another on the precise date—or even the precise era—that marks
the onset of truly *modern* warfare. For Park, however, it was the German
General Erich Ludendorff, that "Faustian genius of war," and "military
fanatic" as Michael Geyer has called him,[104] who had formulated the societal
praxis that was the concomitant of *total* war. In 1936 there had appeared an
English translation of Ludendorff's military philosophy. Park quoted the thesis
that Ludendorff had enunciated—"A totalitarian policy must put at the disposal of . . . a war the strength of the nation and preserve it. . . . [O]nly a
conformity to the fundamental racial and spiritual laws will succeed in weld-
ing nation, conduct of war, and politics into that powerful unity which is the
basis of national preservation."[105] Park concluded that Ludendorff's philosophy had added validity to George Herbert Mead's assertion that "as a policy
for adjudicating national differences, [war] is utterly discredited."[106] The total
destruction that Ludendorffian conceptions of modern world wars seemed
about to bring forth would, in Mead's words, leave "nothing to be adjudi-
cated, not even the enemy nations themselves."[107]

Park did not develop a comprehensive theory of total war or of the garrison state. The former term he pointedly associated with Ludendorff; the latter
is a product of the fertile interdisciplinary mind of Harold Lasswell, a social
scientist who had spent some time at the University of Chicago. A deeper
understanding of the relationship of the garrison state to total war and to the
larger dilemmas and contradictions in values that the rise of German militarism had evoked has been presented by Hans Speier, a German emigré
scholar.

Were today's political sociologists to study the writings of Robert Park,
they might recognize that long before they had sought to "bring the state
back in" Park had become aware of a specific instance of the structuring of
relationships that they think they are the first to have discovered. "A nation,"
Park had observed, "includes within its wide embrace all ordinary forms of

association with which we are familiar, i.e., local, familial, economic, political, religious, and racial."[108] Park had then gone on to note that the problem
for any state seeking to weld these potentially disparate elements into an
enthusiastic, cooperative, uncritical, and tractable body of civil subordinates
had been resolved in Hitler's Germany by adoption of the policy known as
Gleichschaltung: National morale had "been achieved by coordinating, subor-
dinating, and eventually fusing every local and minor loyalty into a totalitarian
loyalty to the national state."[109] Speier's and Lasswell's further analyses of total
war and of the garrison state have brought considerable amplitude to Park's
observations. They also have contributed new understandings of the nature
and types of state societies and, in effect, had brought the state "back in" a
half century before Theda Skocpol and her colleagues claimed to be about to
do so.

By 1941, Park had reconsidered von Moltke's epistolary comment,
"Perpetual peace is a dream and not even a happy dream." From this and
other statements Park now supposed that the Prussian militarist, whose sol-
dierly skills and organizational genius had brought about the military successes
of the Second German Reich, had actually believed that war is "one of the
instruments of God's mysterious providence designed not to settle international disputes but (1) to purge society of a political regime and a social order
which were decadent and doomed to destruction and (2) to supersede these
with forms more vigorous and fit to live."[110] In effect, Park seemed to be saying that Hitler and the Nazis had carried von Moltke's vision to its most
deadly conclusion, creating and exploiting a mass movement more characteristic of a religious sect than of a secular political party, one that would burst
asunder the moral restraints on war. Von Moltke's grand nephew had come
to a similar conclusion. A leader of the anti-Nazi opposition group known as
the Kreisau Circle who would forfeit his life in service to his ideals, Helmuth
James Graf von Moltke (1907–1945) observed, "For us, Europe after the war
is less a problem of frontiers and soldiers, of top-heavy organizations or grand
plans, but Europe after the war is a question of how the picture of man can
be re-established in the breasts of our fellow-citizens."[111] Graf von Moltke
supposed that this might be accomplished with the aid of Christian evange-
lism; Park, however, had already lost much of his earlier faith in the moral
power of salvational religions to ameliorate the human condition.

"Generally speaking," Park once observed, "one may say that war is politics."[112] The garrison state was the product of the amoral and inextricable
coalescence of war with the total political reorganization of a society. Four
years after he had coined the term, Lasswell conceived of a new and terrifying
world order: "Consider the possibility that we are moving toward a world of
'garrison states'—a world in which the specialists on violence are the most
powerful group in society."[113] As early as 1941, Lasswell had believed that a
transition to garrison statehood was possible, indeed, probable for all of
the major world powers. The central question was, merely, "What is the

probable order of appearance—Japan, Germany, Russia, United States of America?"[114]

The garrison state heralded the onset of a kind of total war previously unimagined. By 1941, Lasswell had noted how the "growth of aerial warfare . . . has tended to abolish the distinction between civilian and military functions . . . and . . . [pointed out] that . . . in some periods of modern warfare, casualties among civilians may outnumber the casualties of the armed forces."[115] In such a situation, the ethical and juridical limitations that protected violence from becoming "absolute" would lose their force, and the older conception of wars as codified forms of combat would become obsolete.

In the same year, Park observed that what was now being called "'total warfare' . . . is limited neither to the heavens above nor to the waters under the earth." Moreover, he went on to note, "[W]ith the advent of the 'new strategy of treachery and terror,' war has invaded the realm of the spirit."[116]

THE GARRISON STATE, TOTAL WAR, AND
THE RESURGENCE OF RACISM

The rise of garrison states in the modern world shifted the central attention of their political elites toward problems and policies of internal loyalty and national security. Park had taken special notice of this shift during World War I, while conducting his studies of United States governmental agencies' attempts to censor the writings and keep surveillance on the activities of immigrant peoples and alien leaders and associations.[117] Despite several attempts by Germany's supporters and spokesmen to propagandize Americans toward neutrality or toward sympathy with the aims or philosophy animating the Central Powers, as well as such occasional acts of outright sabotage as the Black Tom explosion reportedly carried out by the Kaiser's secret agents in New York City and New Jersey,[118] Park advised against America sacrificing its world status as a democratic republic that stood for ethnic toleration and freedom of speech by succumbing before the fear-mongering advocates of the suppression of dissent. Although he was generally satisfied with Woodrow Wilson's wartime programs for securing the nation against espionage, sabotage, or disunifying propaganda, Park feared that postwar suspicions about Italian anarchists, Japanese invaders, and other alleged subversives of America's national interest would undermine the moral basis of America's Enlightenment. Of the several national minorities in the United States whom Park took special notice, none aroused his concern more than the Japanese.

Park's most general theory about America's modern urban civilization prophesied that the various folk cultures that made up its ghetto enclaves would eventually disappear, the peoples having become fully acculturated to and assimilated within its industrial, civic, and mass society. However, Park had been quick to notice that fears of military invasion by peoples of different color and alien culture were likely to inflame deeply rooted racial prejudices and, thus, retard the otherwise "natural" motion of these socio-cultural processes. One people so stigmatized was the Japanese immigrant. In 1913, Park had dolefully predicted that "The Japanese, . . . is condemned to remain among us an abstraction, a symbol, and a symbol not merely of his own race, but of the Orient and of that vague, ill-defined menace we sometimes refer to as 'the yellow peril.'"[119] The latter epithet had first been popularized by the German Kaiser in 1900, who may have sought to turn Europe's and America's attention away from the threat presented by his own country's militarization and toward the Far East and its "gelbe Gefahr."[120] As America moved slowly toward its own development of garrison statehood, Park noticed the growth of what he regarded as an atavistic trend of racialist hostility toward Japanese who had settled on the Pacific coast.

Park first voiced his fears about America's hostile policies and prejudicial attitudes toward the Japanese in 1926, as he was coming to comprehend the limits of the national state for encompassing the concomitant global processes of economic interdependence and intercultural adjustment. Although America's racially restrictive policies—on immigration (the omnibus immigration act of 1924 had halted virtually all emigration from Asia to America); on naturalization (the 1922 Ozawa case had judicially reserved the right to American citizenship for free white persons and persons of African descent); and on ownership of land and the formation of corporations (California and ten other states had enacted "alien land laws" prohibiting persons classified as ineligible for citizenship, i.e., Japanese and other Asians, to own land or form corporate enterprises)—had created a situation in the United States that Park believed was "distinctly racial" in character, he pointed out that throughout the world "races and peoples are coming out of their isolation, whether it be geographic, economic or political."[121] America's racially restrictive legislation, Park went on to assert, took no notice of these new global processes: "It is as if we had said: Europe, of which after all America is a mere western projection, ends here."[122] Such an anachronistic perspective, he suggested, constituted evidence of the American people's failure to realize that evolution toward the formation of ethnically homogeneous state societies no longer described the trend of civic development. "In a world in which every event, every significant gesture, reverberates around the globe, the concept of national independence . . . becomes a legal fiction."[123] Moreover, Park concluded, even if "America was once in any exclusive sense the melting pot of races, it is [such] no longer." "The melting pot," Park proclaimed, "is the world."[124]

Nevertheless, as it became clearer to him that global reformation was occurring in defiance of economic interdependencies and in behalf of garrisoning the several competitive world powers, Park began to reconsider what form the final outcome of intercultural associations would take. Until the late 1930s, Park had supposed that a worldwide cycle of race and ethnic relations would culminate in assimilation after passing through three consecutive stages of contact, competition, and accommodation.[125] However, the situation affecting the Japanese in America had caused him to begin to have second thoughts: "The position of the Japanese in America [has] been completely undermined by the passage of the Alien Land Law. . . . [T]he undertow of public sentiment, [is] carrying the Japanese in the United States, in spite of every effort to conciliate public opinion, into the same sort of social ghetto in which the Chinese before them had found refuge."[126] But it was not until 1937, in a commentary on the larger implications of Romanzo Adams's study of interracial marriage in Hawaii—the farthest frontier of America in the Pacific; the place where, in 1926, Park had supposed that "all the races of the Pacific meet and mingle on more liberal terms than they do elsewhere"[127]— that Park gave up his conviction about the ultimate assimilation of everyone.

Adams had predicted that the already developed harmony and growing assimilation of the various peoples making up the population of the island territory would continue so long as Hawaii did not become a focal point for international economic competition or aggressive conflict. If, however, "a military government were to be set up in place of the territorial [one]," he wrote, "it is probable that in respect to race relations there would be a reversal of practice. . . . If there should be a war it would modify the character of social relations temporarily and, maybe, for a long time."[128] Park, reflecting on this statement as well as on other global developments, concluded that, with respect to race relations, "it is not possible to predict with any certainty the final outcome. . . ."[129] Park noted the apparent finality of the caste system of India; the seemingly complete assimilation of foreigners in China; the likely relegation of Jews to permanent minority status in Europe. But he said nothing about the form the final stage of the race relations cycle would take in the United States of America. Making no prediction about the American outcome suggests that Park had lost confidence in what he had once regarded as the inevitability of the social process. Hawaii's and the rest of America's emerging garrison statehood would begin four years later, when the island territory would be placed under military rule.

After the outbreak of the Second World War, America's fears about its own national security took the form of a distrust of the loyalty of certain ethnics among its own citizenry. The nation's sociologists were divided over the extent or even the existence of a problem. Talcott Parsons worried about the depth of patriotic commitment of all those who were not white Calvinists;[130] Herbert Blumer, on the other hand, urged that an ubiquitous desire to get the job over with constituted a sufficient incentive for Americans of all colors and creeds to carry on the war effort effectively.[131] Park's earlier concerns over the treatment of America's racial minorities during a time of great patriotic revival proved well founded. In accordance with President Franklin D. Roosevelt's Executive Order 9066, issued on February 19, 1942, all persons of Japanese descent residing in those portions of the Pacific coast under the command of Lieutenant-General John L. DeWitt were incarcerated in specially constructed places of detention originally called "concentration camps" but soon cosmetically redesignated "relocation centers."[132]* Park's son-in-law, anthropologist Robert Redfield, echoed his father-in-law's worries when he wrote, "The justification for talking about the impact of war on the Japanese Americans lies rather in consideration of what has happened or may happen to all the rest of us as a result of the evacuation and confinement of the Japanese Americans and in the larger issues which [this] smaller problem illustrates."[133] An official apology and a Congressional vote of financial compensation to the survivors of the incarceration program would not occur until more than four decades had passed.

Among the larger issues that Park addressed was the revival and reinforcement of age-old racial prejudices that accompanied America's assumption of garrison statehood but violated American principles of equity and freedom. Although the Japanese Americans were the only group to suffer wholesale arrest, detention, and suspension of their constitutionally guaranteed civil rights,[134] other peoples were also subjected to draconian policies or became victims of a collective paranoia that patriotic and xenophobic fears encouraged. For example, President Roosevelt, in collaboration with FBI Director J. Edgar Hoover, fought an unsuccessful battle throughout the war years to suppress, stifle, or censor the black press in America.[135] In the same period, Mexican Americans, derogated as "pachucos," were made the victims of numerous racist imprecations and were the objects of violent assaults, the worst of which was a mob attack, led by servicemen on leave, that came to be known as the Zoot-Suit Riot of 1943.[136] In the same period, the shortage of migratory farm laborers occasioned by the incarceration of the Japanese-Americans led the United States government to import Mexican laborers from their home country and to overlook their exploitation as "braceros" by the forces of agribusiness.[137] Some American Indian tribes resisted the government's offer to extend citizenship to those who would enter military service under the terms set in Washington, D.C.: the Iroquois, for example, claiming their rights as a separate nation, declared their own war on the Axis powers;[138]

---

* The terminology appropriate to designating the places of forced detention of the Pacific Coast Japanese Americans was still a matter of bitter debate in 1990. In August of that year, a California assemblyman introduced a bill that would require the State's public schools to teach that the prisons were "relocation centers" and not "concentration camps" and that the detention was justified by "military necessity," not race prejudice. Katherine Bishop, "Descendants of Japanese Fear California Bill," *New York Times*, August 28, 1990, p. A14.

"The Tunica, among other Louisiana Indians, objected to the military draft during World War II, claiming that only the tribe held sovereignty over its manpower and refus[ing] to let Tunica youths be inducted into segregated units, [but] virtually all the young men of that tribe went to war as volunteers."[139]

Racist practices also marred the organization and policies of the U.S. military forces. Black American troops in the European theater of operations were segregated into battalions largely used for labor; when employed in combat situations, they were regarded—in the words of a postwar *Time* magazine article about the all-Negro 92d Division—as having the "handicap of less-than-average literacy and more-than-average superstition;"[140] while the efforts of the all-black 332d Fighter Group—The "Tuskegee Airmen"—went unsung.[141] On the home front, Benjamin O. Davis, Sr. (1880–1970), the first African American to become a general in the United States Army, and the commander of the all-black 99th Pursuit Squadron, spent considerable time investigating the complaints of the unfair promotion policy, segregated quarters, and prejudicial treatment meted out to Negro troops.[142] The all-Nisei 442d Regimental Combat Team—that would emerge from the war with more military decorations than any other unit and with "The Purple Heart Battalion" as its *nom de guerre* because of its 9,486 dead and wounded members—was attached to the otherwise all-black 92d Division when it began its participation in the invasion of Italy;[143] another unit of Japanese-American inductees became so demoralized over their fellow Nisei's treatment by the United States government that it was regarded as unfit for combat and kept on American soil throughout the war;[144] still other Nisei fought unnoticed under the command of the non-racist General Joseph Stilwell on the China-Burma-India front;[145] while eighty-five Nisei at the Heart Mountain internment camp went to prison as draft resisters, refusing to fight for a society that didn't trust its own citizens enough to allow them to live freely and openly in the places where they had settled.[146]

Reviewing the racial situation in the United States in 1943, Park asserted that it could "all be summed up in one, or at least two phrases: 'This is a white man's country' [and] 'The Negro is all right in his place.'"[147] But, taking special note of how the wartime fears had exacerbated racialist sentiments, he went on to point out how the antipathies and distrust of the Negro in the South had spread into the North and been extended to apply to other so-called "colored peoples." "The difference is," he observed, "that in the South the Negroes have a place, if only they would stay in it; in the North, as far as there is any racial doctrine that could be described as orthodox, the Negro, the Indian, and the Asiatic have no place at all. They are merely more or less tolerated aliens."[148]

FROM CONFLICT TO COLD WAR

The focus of Park's analysis had come full circle. Beginning with a study of the implications of Germany's military modernization for that state's social development and for world peace, he laid the foundation for understanding the ensuing century's total wars and uncovered the character of what would become the garrison state. Germany's *Kulturkampf*—shorn of its enforcement in "blood and iron"—soon became an unacknowledged model for Park's and other American sociologists' theory of how America might absorb and incorporate its several immigrant and minority peoples.[149]

The process of assimilation—what Park once defined as a coordination of sentiments[150]—promised to bring about a national unity that would insure a common front in the face of international crises. However, as militarization and preparation for and participation in international wars came to take precedence over other issues, the trustworthiness that Park supposed should be granted to the peoples not yet fully a part of the much-vaunted national consensus was withheld. Persons of alien culture and non-white color came to be especially suspect. In the Second World War, the United States entered the conflict reluctantly, ostensibly to preserve and protect the "Four Freedoms" and, in later statements of its war aims, to extend those freedoms to all the peoples in the world.[151] Sadly, the aroused fears about disaffection, disunity, and disloyalty led not only to a suspension of those freedoms for select minorities,[152] but also to a climate of distrust that in the postwar years would find outlet in an anguished quest for absolute national security.

While concern for the loyalty of racial minorities diminished somewhat in the postwar years—the FBI's suspicions about Chinese Americans during the Korean War and its dogged pursuit of black civil rights leaders and racial dissidents during the 1960s and 1970s standing out as remarkable exceptions[153]— fears about communists, liberals, intellectuals, students, and homosexuals seemed to deny any claim that the idealized ethno-national consensus had at last taken place. Instead, a seemingly permanent condition of American garrison statehood—one that would not be challenged until the "deconstruction" of the Soviet satellite states in Eastern Europe and Soviet Union President Gorbachev's proposed domestic reforms seemed to presage an end to the cold war—tended to encourage a continuation of surveillance over the thoughts and deeds of whatever portions of the citizenry seemed about to disattend, depart, or dissent from the putatively prevailing national ethos. Ironically, events occurring in the 1990s in South Africa, China, the Middle East, Eastern Europe, and the Soviet Union, as well as in the United States, indicate that a peaceful conclusion to the cold war will not bring with it an end to ethno-national struggles. Indeed, in the Soviet Union and eastern Europe it seems to have revived much of the long-buried nationalistic fervor that had troubled that part of the world before 1914. Neither America nor the world can reasonably look forward to a near time when there will occur a complete loss of racial or ethnic distinctiveness, or to a future global society in which a meltdown of the individuals of all nations has forged a new and uniform race of humankind.

✦ ✦ ✦

PARK'S SOCIOLOGY OF WAR AS A TRAGEDY OF CULTURE

One reading of Park's sociological observations about war would interpret them as an uncompleted exemplar of Simmel's theses on the conflict and tragedy of culture. To engage this reading we must briefly explore Simmel's ideas about the cultural process. Simmel, Park's only mentor in the discipline of sociology, had formulated a dialectical theory of culture, a cyclical dynamic that described the never-ending struggle of the effervescent stream of *life* against the *forms* which its spirit creates to enclose its content and encompass itself with order. "We speak of culture," Simmel observed, "whenever life produces certain forms in which it expresses and realizes itself: works of art, religions, sciences, technologies, laws, and innumerable others."[154] However, Simmel went on to point out, "Left to itself, . . . life streams on without interruption; its restless rhythm opposes the fixed duration of any particular form."[155] Thus it is the case that the true dynamic motoring the history of culture manifests itself as a dialectic of struggle: "Each cultural form, once it is created, is gnawed at varying rates by the forces of life."[156] Ultimately, life strives after release from all forms of itself.

In some respects, Park's sociology of conflict appears to follow Simmel's dialectic of culture. War, in Park's understanding of it, is one of the *forms* of conflict—a crude form, Park notes with bitterness, and one that "has as its goal . . . the drive for domination that causes a nation to test its power in war against other nations."[157] In perfecting that test, the avant-garde among the makers of war—military geniuses such as von Moltke—seek to liberate war from the rules of proprietary and humane conduct that constrain its fullest expression. By endowing war with the elementary characteristics of the sacred—Park pointed out that it was von Moltke who said that in war "the most noble virtues of men find their expression—courage as well as abnegation, fidelity to duty and even love and self-sacrifice"[158]—the new German military radicals had hoped to place it beyond the restraints imposed by the morality that appreciated a common humanity. These restraints had been codified in the international conventions that limited the technics and tactics of combat to those necessary for fighting against the enemy's armed forces. Demanding the right to burst the bonds that thereby held warfare back from realizing its own freedom of destructive action, von Moltke proclaimed the right to extend the field of combat to encompass the enemy's civilian population, culture, morale, and, in effect, every aspect of the enemy's basis for existence. War, the destroyer of life, would, in von Moltke's vision of it, become the agent of a statist *Kulturkampf* and, in utterly annihilating the forces opposed to it, would realize a new ideal—that of the state conceived as "an individual . . . [with] a destiny which its actual existence serves to realize."[159]

The emancipation of war from the rules of war had led on the one hand to the concept and the reality of total war and, on the other, to the reconstitution of the state as an instrument devoted to the realization of its own destiny through warfare. In such a state, patriotic self-sacrifice becomes not only the highest duty a citizen can perform, not only the exhibition of the noblest of national virtues, but in fact the veritable epitome of a sacrament. The freeing of war from the limits imposed on it by a commitment to humane morality was in effect signaled by von Moltke's mundane designation of the state as the earthly communion of God and, as such, the proper object of the citizen-soldier's innerworldly faith—the thing for which he would sacrifice his life. Patristics had given way to patriotics: "War," said von Moltke, "is an institution of God, a principle of order in the world."[160]

Park had completed his doctoral dissertation in 1903. Four years later, Simmel, confronting the philosophies of Schopenhauer and Nietzsche, noted that in the pre-modern epoch Christianity's vision of the "salvation of the soul and the kingdom of God . . . became an offer of absolute value for the masses, a definitive goal beyond the meaninglessness of an individuated and fragmentary life." But, he went on to point out, "in recent centuries, Christianity [had] lost its appeal to and power over innumerable people." The decline of Christian faith, however, had deprived "life" of its "deep desire for an absolute goal . . ." The unfilled gap of Christianity's heritage is "a need for a definitivum of life's moment, which has continued as an empty urge for a goal which has become inaccessible."[161] Park, who abjured philosophical abstraction, had already seen that the transvaluation of Christianity had, in Germany, taken the form of a sacralization of the militarized state, and that this transmogrification had introduced into the twentieth century a new entity, the warfare state.

Park did not live to see the end of the Second World War nor to record its effects on the changes in state formation that America's victory would entail. That he had a dark premonition of the unhappy shape of things to come was indicated three-and-a-half months before the attack on Pearl Harbor, when he explained to Louis Wirth about the qualms he had over signing a petition relating to the war: "I am . . . unreservedly in favor of supporting the President and the policy of the government in the crisis . . . I am in favor of militarism in the United States, not only for the present emergency but for all the other emergencies I see looming up."[162] However, Park worried over the implications of that militarism for America's moral order and its place in what he supposed would be a cockpit of postwar nations at odds with one another. In 1943 he would warn America of the dire necessity of solving the race question in terms of a recognized equality of all peoples and a granting of the full panoply of civil rights to its non-white and non-Anglo minorities. Moreover, he warned, America should not presume too much about the benevolence of the world, nor should it seek allies in its restricted world mission. In 1941, he had told Wirth that he did not "favor . . . any permanent or temporary alliance with England or Russia which will impose on us the necessity or the moral obligation of enforcing terms of peace that require us to police the world."[163]

As a sociologist with a world outlook, Park could analyze America's foreign as well as its domestic policies and processes. In 1939, he observed that "the whole world is living in a kind of symbiosis; but the world community is at present, at least, quite incapable of collective action."[164] Although Park believed that "the web of life which holds within its meshes all living organisms is visibly tightening, and there is in every part of the world . . . a growing interdependence of all living creatures . . .,"[165] he pointed out that "[o]n the political level the freedom and competition of individuals is still further limited by the express recognition of the superior and sovereign interests and rights of the state. . . ."[166] For Park, the struggle for a free and interdependent life uniting all the peoples of the world—a struggle that seemed about to complete itself as "the incorporation of all the peoples of the earth in a world-wide economy"—had "laid the foundation for the rising world-wide political and moral order. . . ."[167] But this new world society would not—or, in Park's view, ought not—be organized as a victor's spoil of a worldwide war nor should it be policed by the United States.

Simmel had once paraphrased Kant to the effect that "every war in which the belligerents do not impose some restrictions in the use of possible means upon one another, necessarily, if only for psychological reasons, becomes a war of extermination."[168] However, the post–World War II era seemed to offer an exception to such a deadly finality. According to Harold Lasswell, the onset of the cold war and the likelihood of a long period of world bipolarization meant "a continuing high level of expected war"[169] and continued militarization. Although Lasswell did not make the point, it soon became clear that the cold war was prevented from becoming a total war by the tacit agreement of the two superpowers to abide by the self-restrictions imposed by the kind of military technology that had devastated Hiroshima and Nagasaki in 1945. War, having been unleashed from the restraints of international conventions and the moral law, had enclosed its makers in an iron cage of mutually assured destruction should either adversary employ nuclear weapons against the other. The lives and societies of civilized humankind would be preserved so long as each of the leading states refused to countenance national suicide as the price of its own victory. What Simmel had seen, abstractly, as the conflict and tragedy of culture had not yet reached its ultimate end, had not yet brought humankind to its grave. In 1942 Park had observed, ironically, that "the fact that men still make war to insure the perpetuation of a way of life, or to impose upon the world a new social order, suggests that it is not as Spengler suggests, either declining, or finished."[170] Park's irony is compounded when we realize that the "it" in the sentence just quoted is contextually ambiguous: Does "it" refer to humankind or merely to the Occident?

Park's Congo Studies

Toward a Gothic Perspective on Capitalism and Imperialism

CAPITALISM, IMPERIALISM, AND
GOTHIC SOCIOLOGY—AN INTRODUCTION

Sociology—the discipline which Park had studied under the guidance of Georg Simmel—seems to owe its origins to the Enlightenment, to the aftermath of the French Revolution, and to the epoch in which rational and increasingly corporate capitalism began to flourish in the Occident. The two leaders of what we now recognize as German socioeconomic thought—Karl Marx and Max Weber—insisted, each in his own way to be sure, that capitalism institutionalized the very quintessence of rational, calculating thought and conduct. Yet, again in his own way, each of these scholars' analyses of capitalism evoked or turned upon darker themes stemming from pre-scientific and even occult thought.

At the very time (ca. 1880–1914) that social science began to compartmentalize itself into separate disciplines in Europe and America, there also occurred a new "sleep of reason" in literature, journalism, and the style of the essay.[1] Out of this sleep came dreams and nightmares, fantasies that visualized a Manichean world in which the positive claims of progress were desublimated, seen as shrouds and shibboleths of a hidden atavism and a banal evil that were together creeping over the modern world. Gothic discourse captured this mood most clearly, and it was given an unintended impetus by Max Nordau (1849–1923) and his mordant attempts to thwart modernism's spread in real-world culture.[2] A self-appointed disciple of Italy's biosocial criminologist, Cesare Lombroso, Nordau sought to extend the latter's studies of the constitutional degeneracy of "criminals, prostitutes, anarchists, and pronounced lunatics" so that they would apply to "authors and artists . . ., [those] degenerates in literature, music, and painting . . . [who had] in recent years come into extraordinary prominence, and are revered by numerous admirers as creators of a new art, and heralds of the coming centuries."[3] Railing against the pessimistic but popular intellectual philosophy of the *fin de siècle*, Nordau sought to allay the desolate and debilitating fears that, he insisted, had "arisen in more highly-developed minds . . ." These apprehensions included "vague qualms of a Dusk of the Nations, in which all suns and all stars are gradually waning, and mankind with all its institutions and creations is perishing in the midst of a dying world."[4] Nordau diagnosed these shadowy but powerful ideas of his age not as mere illusions of fancy, but rather as symptoms of a biosocial degeneration that would have to be combatted by an act of will, accompanied and inspired by a conscious critical, religious, and somato-scientific intelligence.

It is not our intention in the present work to elaborate upon or critically appraise Nordau's peculiar sociobiologistic philosophy.[5] Rather, here it is relevant to see how in setting up his problem, Nordau admitted the degree to which a Gothic thematic had penetrated the scientific as well as the literary mind of his day. To Nordau, Lombroso was, in effect, the post-Frankensteinian doctor-saviour who had uncovered the natural basis for unnatural conduct. As Lombroso's prophet, Nordau sought to lay the degenerative spirit of a modern malaise that, he was sure, had entered the bodies and souls of the urban intellectual classes. To this extent Nordau was a veritable Dr. Van Helsing—and, in fact, is cited by the fictional doctor as one source for his own estimate of the degeneracy of Count Dracula*—in his employment of a religiously rooted scientism against the specters and harbingers of civilizational decay. Just as Van Helsing, the fictional opponent of the arch-fiend of Gothic literature, the vampire Dracula, sought to oppose that leader of the undead with both the supramundane power of the Cross and the earthly potency of positive ballistic science, so Nordau, as the real-life opponent of the "degenerate" artistry of late nineteenth-century Europe (i.e., the mystics, pre-Raphaelites, symbologists, Tolstoists, the "Richard Wagner Cult," "Parnassiano," "Diabolists," Nietzsche, Zola, and a host of other assorted "aesthetes" and "decadents"), proclaimed the power of modern science, when combined with the moral discipline associated with Calvinism, to be the effective therapeutic for what he regarded as Europe's "severe mental epidemic; . . . a sort of black death of degeneration and hysteria . . ."[6] First, however, also reminiscent of Dr. Van Helsing's call for a band of dedicated vampire killers to aid him in his crusade, Nordau proposed that there be established a "Society of Ethical Culture" to annihilate both the decadent creatures and dismal texts of the *fin de siècle*:

> Whoever believes with me [he wrote at the conclusion of his major work, *Degeneration*] that society is the natural organic form of humanity, in which

---

* "The Count is a criminal and of criminal type. Nordau and Lombroso would so classify him, and *qua* criminal he is of imperfectly formed mind. Thus, in a difficulty he has to seek resource in habit." Bram Stoker, *Dracula* (New York: Modern Library, n.d. [1897]), p. 378.

alone it can exist, prosper, and continue to develop itself to higher des-
tinies; whoever looks upon civilization as a good, having value and deserv-
ing to be defended, must mercilessly crush under his thumb the anti-social
vermin. . . . There is no place among us for the lusting beast of prey. . . .[7]

For Nordau, the watchwords of the day—"freedom," "modernity," "progress"
and "truth"—had been degraded by those who popularized them: "They
wish for self-indulgence; we wish for work. They wish to drown consciousness in the unconscious; we wish to strengthen and enrich consciousness."[8]
The true protagonists of freedom, modernity, progress, and truth, he asserted,
could be "distinguished from impostors calling themselves moderns
. . . [by] this: Whoever preaches absence of discipline is an enemy of progress;
and whoever worships his 'I' is an enemy to society."[9]

Despite the fact that he was a Jew and a Zionist, Nordau's idea of society
was Pauline, and, like that of the American philosophers Josiah Royce[10] and
Nathaniel Shaler[11]—scholars whose work influenced Park—took "as its first
premise, neighbourly love and capacity for self-sacrifice."[12] His idea of
progress, however, was a variant of the Christian Gothic: "[P]rogress is the
effect of an ever more rigorous subjugation of the beast in man, of an ever
tenser self-restraint, an ever keener sense of duty and responsibility."[13] What
Nordau would not, indeed, given his predilections, probably could not,
acknowledge was the possibility that modern European society, with its
preëminent corporate personification in the form of the Protestant-inspired
but now secularized economic enterprise as its driving force for progress, had
become the very beast of prey that must be subjugated if a truly neighborly
social order was ever to be established.* That perception, with varying
degrees of emphasis and different kinds of interpretation, would be made by
Marx, Weber, and—belatedly—Albion W. Small, and empirically studied by
Park in his essays on the Congo.

"The Gothic novel," George E. Haggerty tells us, "finds its most fruitful
mode of evocation in delineating an imaginative response to the objective
world that is grounded in the emotions."[14] A Gothic sociology, by contrast,
expresses itself in depicting the architectonic paradox of the supposedly objective world—viz., the natural preternaturalism that has contributed to the
world's construction. Where Gothic fiction instructs its horrified readers in

---

*In terms of the thesis being presented here, it is worth recalling that Nordau became
involved in the debate over European colonization of Africa when the Zionist movement,
to which he was passionately attached, momentarily settled on Uganda as the proposed site
for a Jewish homeland. Nordau denounced the Uganda scheme, holding, among other
objections, that it would do nothing for the moral regeneration of the Jews if they were led
to a "Promised Land" whose development required the exploitation of blacks. See Ernst
Pawel, *The Labyrinth of Exile: A Life of Theodor Herzl* (New York: Farrar, Straus and
Giroux, 1989), pp. 494–95 *et passim*.

the unreal horrors attendant upon a realistically imagined fictional world, Gothic sociology teaches its readers about the actual horrors that produce and prevail in the social construction of modernity. Where Gothic literature offers "scientifically objective terminology and clearly empirical observation as a means of establishing intensely private, subjective experience,"[15] Gothic sociology employs preternatural imagery and occult fantasy to evoke in the reader an intellectual understanding of the actual world and to inspire a praxiological response to it. Hence, in what is an apt conclusion to a piece of Gothic sociological writing, Robert E. Park, in an essay on the Congo that he penned for Booker T. Washington, detailed the atrocious practices of the mercenary "Zapo-zaps" and showed them to be central aspects of Leopold's "humane and noble" Congo project; then he closed the matter circumspectly: "Certainly the whole subject demands careful investigation and swift action."[16]

Marx

Gothic elements had begun to appear in the early approaches to a sociology of capitalism. In Marx's and Weber's studies, capitalism cannot be entirely disentangled from the uncanny, the forbidden, and from its challenges to God and His creative uniqueness. For the early Marx,[17] capitalism was inextricably related to a surplus value that found its most naked expression in the personal possession and alchemical use of money: "Money," he noted in 1844, "since it has the property of being able to buy anything, and to appropriate all objects to itself, is thus the object par excellence." Elaborating on Shakespeare's analysis of money in *Timon of Athens*, Marx supposed money to be nothing less than the long-sought philosopher's stone, capable of transforming anything—including social character and human anatomy—into something else:

> Thus what I am and what I am capable of is by no means determined by my individuality. I am ugly, but I can buy myself the most beautiful women. Consequently I am not ugly, for the effect of ugliness, its power of repulsion, is annulled by money. As an individual, I am lame, but money can create twenty-four feet for me; so I am not lame; I am a wicked, dishonest man without conscience or intellect, but money is honoured and so its possessor is good. Money relieves me of the trouble of being dishonest; so I am presumed to be honest. . . .

With the discovery of money's creative and transformative powers, Marx supposed, religion, and especially its supramundane justifications for earthly morality, ceased to have any great significance—except as opiates for the masses who could not obtain large amounts of money. Money had become, Marx said, both the "visible god-head" and "the universal whore." It was now, he continued, "the universal means and power, exterior to man, not issuing from man as man or from society as society, to turn imagination into reality and reality into imagination." As capitalism's unique transubstantial substance, Marx seemed to say, money had made the most terrifying Gothic fancy possible as a mere mundane experience.

Weber

How, in the modern world, money might issue not from man as man or society as society was part of Max Weber's contribution to a preternatural sociology of the emerging rational social order in the Occident. Central to Weber's discussion of this problem is his insistence that capitalism brought about a distinction between greed and profit.[18] "The impulse to acquisition, pursuit of gain, of money, of the greatest possible amount of money," he wrote, "has in itself nothing to do with capitalism. . . . Capitalism *may* even be identical with the restraint, or at least a rational tempering, of this irrational impulse." Capitalism was something new, Weber insisted, and was to be identified with a new and different pursuit. "[C]apitalism is identical with the pursuit of profit, and forever *renewed* profit, by means of continuous, rational, capitalistic enterprise." Occidental capitalism, which, according to Weber, had its roots in Protestantism, separates the greedy pursuit of gain from the ascetic pursuit of profit. However, to accomplish this remarkable feat, Western capitalists had resorted to what can best be described as an occult and blasphemous art: They had created their unit of enterprise in the form of an immortal being—the corporate firm.

As Weber is at pains to demonstrate, the instrumentality for the separation of greedy vice from innerworldly virtue, for extinguishing the demonic avatar of wealth in favor of the secular saint of industry, is the *firm*. Obliged to heed the divinely inspired inner voice that called them to act in its pursuit, but enjoined against laying up treasures on earth, the Puritan pioneers of capitalism formed repositories for holding and disposing of their monetary gains, non-somatical bodies, appropriately called corporations. These impersonal entities are recognized as legal persons. As such, however, they not only remove their Calvinist creators from the temptation to engage in sinful excess, but also outlive them, coming to have a functionally autonomous life of their own. Indeed, their *elan vital*, their strength and length of life, is determined wholly and exclusively by their engorgement of the material equivalent of blood—profits. As Weber observed, "In a wholly capitalistic order of society, an individual capitalistic enterprise which did not take advantage of its opportunities for profit-making would be doomed to extinction." And, in avoidance of that doom—as Park would demonstrate—corporate entities moved out beyond the Occident, ever in search of new sources of life-sustaining profits.

Crucial to the character of the corporation is its immortality. This impious miracle, creating intramundane everlasting life, is performed in the first instance through a Gothic activation of the sin of pride. That sin reaches its epitome when humans arrogate to themselves God's power to create beings that have the characteristics of persons.

The specifically sinful aspects of such a creation were imaginatively fictionalized in 1818—the year of Marx's birth, nearly a half century before Weber's or Park's—by the twenty-year-old Gothic novelist Mary Wollstonecraft Shelley (1797–1851) in her novel *Frankenstein, or the Modern Prometheus*. Her tale unfolds a horrifying story in which an eighteenth-century doctor of natural philosophy—whose curiosity and ambition have been fired by reading the esoteric works of Henricus Cornelius Agrippa of Nettesheim (1486–1535), Theophrastus Bombastus von Hohenheim, better known to students of the occult arts as Philippus Aureolus Paracelsus (1493?–1541), and Albertus Magnus (1193?–1280)—determines to create life in a laboratory. The being he brings to consciousness is fearfully ugly, and, having been rejected by both his creator and all of humanity ("I ought to be thy Adam; but I am rather the fallen angel, whom thou drivest from joy for no misdeed."[19]), wreaks a terrible vengeance on Dr. Frankenstein, his wife, family, and friends. Truly a modern Prometheus, the good doctor from Geneva had assumed the role of God ("Frightful must it be;" wrote Mrs. Shelley in the introduction to the third edition of her novel in 1831, "for supremely frightful would be the effect of any human endeavor to mock the stupendous mechanism of the Creator of the world"[20]).

Just as the fictional Dr. Frankenstein creates his proto-human fiend by combining the hermetic arts of the medieval mystics with the experimental sciences of the emerging age of Enlightenment, so in their innovative catechism combining commerce with Christianity, the early capitalists created their own version of a soulless being. By synthesizing the ideas of medieval corporatism with those of an anthropomorphic legalism that was arising in the era of burgeoning entrepreneurship, the Puritans created the enduring agent of their economic actions, the firm. And, just as the Swiss doctor's blasphemous creation would turn upon its maker, making him into its anguished victim, so the corporation's escape from its progenitors' virtuous constraints on excess, had, in Weber's words, enslaved their successors in an "iron cage" of enervating effort that would likely continue "until the last ton of fossilized coal is burnt."[21]

In Gothic terms, the corporation belongs to that category of uncanny entities known as the undead. Such entities are represented in that genre's fictional literature by the vampire.[22] Although vampiric literature had found representation before the middle of the eighteenth century,[23] it is relevant to our thesis that the most significant forms of that Gothic sub-genre were published in the nineteenth century, beginning with John William Polidori's *The Vampyre; A Tale* in 1819,[24] and finding its fully developed form in Bram

Stoker's *Dracula* in 1897.[25] The vampire serves macabre literature as a san-guinary eidolon of repressed sexual horror, but it provides the Gothic sociol-ogy of capitalism with its demonological symbol: corporate enterprise's world-roaming drive for its life-sustaining substance, abject labor power. The fact that such African-American publicists as George Washington Williams and Booker T. Washington, as well as Robert E. Park, chose to designate Leopold II's officers in the Congo as vampires speaks loudly to the power of metaphysical horror that this symbol possesses.

PARK'S ANTECEDENT: GEORGE WASHINGTON WILLIAMS

Park was not the first American scholar to turn an abiding intellectual curiosity into an activist investigation of the situation in the Congo. His immediate predecessor in this endeavor—although apparently unknown to Park—was George Washington Williams (1849–1891), whose biographer describes this all-too-neglected African-American historian as a "soldier, cler-gyman, editor, lawyer, legislator, historian, diplomat, lecturer, and world trav-eler."[26] Whereas Park gravitated from his Congo studies to a life-long interest in the position and prospects of America's blacks, Williams's intellectual and participatory odyssey moved in the opposite direction. The author of what was at the time of its publication in 1883 a definitive *History of the Negro Race in America*,[27] as well as *A History of the Negro Troops*,[28] published five years later, in 1889 turned his attention to the problem presented by King Leopold II's intrusion into the Congo.

Williams's earlier works were by no means mere narrative histories; they were infused with a sociological outlook and dedicated to employing histori-cal and anthropological knowledge to overthrow the prejudices, myths, and stereotypes that, then as now, contribute to the demoralization of the American Negro, reduce that people's self-esteem, and restrict their individ-ual and collective life chances. Like other students of culture and society in his day, Williams was guided by deep religious convictions, and, like most of the sociologists who would constitute the first post–Civil War cohort of the makers of that discipline's tradition,[29] he had studied at a theological school (Newton Theological Institution) and been ordained a (Baptist) minister of the gospel.[30] Williams's Congo papers extended his socio-historical concerns for African Americans to the descendants of their forebears living in contem-porary Africa. Taken as a whole, Williams's works constitute what should be recognized as the beginning of a project for African-American studies, one that has yet to be fully developed.

Williams, a true Calvinist, subscribed to a belief in a mysterious divine plan for humankind's salvation. The deity had preordained the happenings that his own historical researches had uncovered. This supramundane force, he believed, would continue to guide the events to come, an unfolding of the munificence contained in the Christian promise.[31] Theorizing on the basis of this perspective, Williams insisted on the following as a priori assumptions of his researches that monogenesis described and defined the beginnings of humankind:[32] that the religious interpretation so prominent after the Sixteenth Century in Europe and America,[33] holding that the biblical curse of Ham and Canaan had been visited upon the first Africans and upon their descendants, producing an ineradicable inferiorization, was incorrect— (Williams noted, "We find that Cush . . . [is] the oldest son of Ham, and the father of Nimrod . . . , [who] founded the Babylonian empire. . . . These wonderful achievements were of the children of Cush, the ancestor of the Negroes. It is fair to suppose that this line of Ham's posterity was not lacking in powers necessary to found cities and kingdoms, and maintain government"[34])—and that the "antiquity of the Negroes as a distinct people was a certainty."[35] The latter assumption was illustrated by facts that great civilizations had flourished in ancient Africa, such as that of the Ashantee,[36] and of Ethiopia, from which, Williams asserted, classical Egypt, Greece, and Rome had borrowed so much.[37]

The deity, in Williams's hermeneutic on the relationship of ethnology to ethnography, had made high culture and a civil ordering of polity and economy a free gift. ("It is fair to presume that God gave all the races of mankind civilization to start with. We infer this from the known character of the Creator."[38]) Ultimately, he held that the civilizing inheritance, that had lapsed in Africa because of the peoples' forgetfulness of God,[39] would find its way back to its place of origin through the agency of a divinely guided corps of black American evangelical missionaries:

> The future work of the Negro is twofold: subjective and objective. Years will be devoted to his own education and improvement here in America. He will sound the depths of education, accumulate wealth, and then turn his attention to the civilization of Africa . . . touching at the Grain Coast, the Ivory Coast, and the Gold Coast. America will carry the African missionaries, Bibles, papers, improved machinery, instead of rum and chains. And Africa, in return, will send America indigo, palm-oil, ivory, gold, diamonds, costly wood, and her richest treasures, instead of slaves.[40]

For Williams, the promised barter of Africa's agricultural and mineral resources in return for America's material and moral enlightenment constituted a more than fair exchange: "Tribes will be converted to Christianity; cities will rise, states will be founded; geography and science will enrich and enlarge their discoveries; and [with] a telegraph cable binding the heart of Africa to the ear of the civilized world, every throb of joy or sorrow will pulsate again in millions of souls."[41] In his perspective, the Protestant ethic would reproduce on the "Dark Continent" not only the spirit of capitalism but also the stimulation of science and the sensibilities of civil society. "In the interpretation of History," Williams urged, "the plans of God must be discerned. . . ."[42] Divine providence went hand in hand with progress. Years later, Robert Park would point out that, even as a young man, he had come to a quite different and sadder conclusion: "I knew enough about civilization even at that time," he would recall, "to know that progress . . . is a terrible thing."[43]

Williams's exposé of the nefarious scheme of Leopold II speaks, implicitly, to his belief in the cunning of the divine historical design. In his commencement address at Newton Theological Institute in 1874, Williams had treated the three centuries of the African slave trade as only *seemingly* an unmitigated disaster inspired by activated evil. Once emancipation had ended chattel slavery in the United States, he asserted, the Negroes had been transformed into "human beings; no longer bondsmen, they are free men, with almost every civil disability removed. . . ." Moreover, he proclaimed that the entire era could now be re-evaluated, showing that God's positive plan for Africa had utilized the evil purposes of European and American whites to accomplish a greater good: "The Negro of this country can turn to his Saxon brothers, and say, as Joseph said to his brethren who wickedly sold him, 'As for you, ye meant it unto evil, but God meant it unto good. . . .'" And what was that good for the sake of which God had permitted Africa to be "robbed of her sable sons"? It was, Williams asserted, "'that we, after learning your arts and sciences, might return to Egypt and deliver the rest of our brethren who are yet in the house of bondage.'"[44]

Fifteen years after delivering this address, Williams embarked on a mission that would combine his religious convictions with his already demonstrated skills as a shrewd investigator. He attempted nothing less than to liberate the Congolese people from the Belgian monarch who had obtained a trusteeship over their lands by promising them "fostering care," "benevolent enterprise," and an "honest and practical effort" to "secure their welfare."[45] Although Williams did not live long enough to carry his mission to completion, he might well have supposed that his encounter with Leopold II—whom he first had admired—and his proposal to recruit black American students as worker missionaries in the Congo was another part of God's unfathomable prescience.

Williams firmly subscribed to the practical as well as the spiritual ideals of the Protestant ethic, to the inextricable connection of commerce to soul saving. More specifically—and despite the transformation of what had begun in 1877 as Leopold II's "l'Association Internationale du Congo" into what had become in 1885 "l'Etat Independent du Congo," a personal possession and colony of the King of the Belgians—Williams was convinced that there could be promoted in that unhappy place another part of God's plan for the redemption of Africa. After carefully tracing how Leopold had meretriciously managed to win the support of the United States in engineering his nefarious scheme, and how Henry Morton Stanley, the newspaperman-turned-explorer-and-imperial-advance-man, had exaggerated the economic value to be obtained from exploiting the Congo's natives and natural resources, Williams nevertheless reaffirmed his faith in a properly administered Congolese mission. This could be accomplished through the introduction into Africa of an ethically inspired regimen of labor; such a regimen would grow out of the inspiration provided by truly dedicated Christian missionaries. Ultimately, he envisioned the establishment of a post-colonial, multi-racial, and independent nation-state in the Congo: "I indulge the hope," he wrote to President of the United States Benjamin Harrison in 1890, "that when a new Government shall rise upon the ruins of the old, it will be simple, not complicated; local, not European; international, not national; just, not cruel; and, casting its shield alike over black and white, trader and missionary, endure for centuries."[46]

Before that local, international, just, and enduring government could be instituted, however, Williams believed that there would have to be two developments: First, a full-scale public exposure of the nefarious character of Leopold's Congo administration; second, the establishment of a reconstituted industrial missionary program in the Congo, a mission best staffed by Christianized African Americans from the Southern states of the United States. In carrying out the first of these, Williams gave expression to his belief that the spirit of an imperial capitalism in Africa might be given its major impetus by the newly energized Protestant ethic to be found among the recently emancipated black Americans. In proposing the second, Williams re-enforced "African zionism," an idea that had sparked occasional back-to-Africa movements among American Negroes since the late eighteenth century, and one that would influence such otherwise disparate religious and secular Africanist orientations as those of Booker T. Washington, W. E. B. DuBois, and Marcus Garvey in the twentieth century.

Williams's exposure of Leopold II's venture reveals the disappointment of an erstwhile true believer in the avowed aims of Belgium's sovereign as well as the unshakeable faith of a convinced Calvinist in God's inscrutable plan.[47] When reporting in 1890 to Leopold II on the latter's twelve major failings as king and proprietary owner of the Independent State of Congo, Williams acknowledged that he had at first aided Leopold in obtaining American recognition of the Congo Free State because he had been "inspired by . . . your publicly declared motives and aims. . . ." Leopold II had professed to be carrying forth the "work of Christian civilization for Africa." Indeed, Williams conceded that he had been "led to regard your enterprise as the rising Star of Hope for the Dark Continent. . . ." and that "[a]ll the praisefull things I have spoken and written of the Congo country, State and Sovereign" had been predicated upon "the firm belief that your Government was built upon the enduring foundation of *Truth, Liberty, Humanity and Justice*."

The aforementioned virtues were inextricably bound up with Protestant Christianity in Williams's perspective. Thus, when his own on-the-spot investigation of the matter had proved that Leopold's regime was utterly devoid of redeeming value—viz., that it was "deficient in moral, military, and financial strength necessary to govern a territory of 1,508,000 square miles, 7,251 miles of navigation, and 31,694 square miles of lake surface;" that the "black Zanzibar soldiers," hired to watch over the fifty military posts established in the Congo, were expected "not only to sustain themselves, but to raid enough to feed the garrisons where the white men are stationed"; that "Your Majesty's Government is guilty of violating its contracts made with its soldiers, mechanics and workmen, many of whom are subjects of other Governments"; that the "laws printed and circulated in Europe 'for the protection of the blacks' in the Congo, are a dead letter and a fraud"; that "Your Majesty's Government is excessively cruel to its prisoners, condemning them, for the slightest offences, to the chain gang, the like of which cannot be seen in any other Government in the civilised or uncivilised world"; that "Women are imported into your Majesty's Government for immoral purposes" and that "Whenever children are born of such relations, the State maintains that the woman being its property, the child belongs to it also"; that "State soldiers patrol many villages forbidding the natives to trade with any person but a State official, and when the natives refuse to accept the price of the State, their goods are seized by the Government that promised them 'protection'"; that "Your Majesty's Government has been, and is now, guilty of waging unjust and cruel wars against natives, with the hope of securing slaves and women, to minister to the behests of the officers of your Government"; that "Your Majesty's Government is engaged in the slave-trade, wholesale and retail"; that "Your Majesty's Government has concluded a contract . . . for the establishment of a line of military posts . . . [along] territory to which your Majesty has no more legal claim than I have to be Commander-in-Chief of the Belgian army"; that "Mr. Henry M. Stanley, the man who was your chief agent in setting up your authority in this country, has grossly misrepresented the character of the country" and that his very name "produces a shudder among this simple folk" of the Congo; and, finally, that "by firing upon native canoes; by confiscating the property of natives; by intimidating native traders, and preventing them from trading with white trading companies; by quartering troops in native villages when there is no war; by causing vessels . . . to be visited and [compelled to] show their papers; by forbidding a mission steamer to fly its national flag without permission from a local Government; by permitting the natives to carry on the slave trade, and by engaging in the wholesale and retail slave-trade itself," Leopold's policies had "violated the General Act of the Conference of Berlin," i.e., the conference

that had granted, recognized, and legitimated his rule in the Congo—
Williams admitted to having become "disenchanted, disappointed and dis-
heartened." But he did not abandon his faith in Africa's ultimate Christian
redemption.

For Williams, the Congo's "vampires"—a term he used to refer to the
mercenaries in the employ of King Leopold II—could be vanquished by the
cross, i.e., only if they were confronted by dedicated missionaries espousing a
gospel of virtuous labor. The terrible conditions of bare subsistence that he
found in the unfertile and non-arable parts of the Congo region would not be
relieved unless and "until the native shall have been taught by the European
the dignity, utility and blessing of labour."[48] In behalf of this thesis, Williams
presented his own analysis of the situation of the West African Kroomen—a
seacoast people, used to a livelihood earned by fishing, but recruited to labor
on the railway under construction in the Congo.[49] He contrasted their condition with that of their compatriots working outside of the authoritarianism of
Leopold's regime. Although the "Kroomen belong to the sea; and when they
no longer behold its blue bosom nor smell its sweet waters, they droop and
die . . . , wherever they appear along the African continent in factories or
upon steamers, their labour has proved invaluable and their reputation for
fidelity is unquestioned." Yet in the Congo, where they are paid but one
shilling per day, fed on a deficient diet, "worse quartered than the natives,"
and "are beaten and kicked by their overseers upon the slightest provoca-
tion," they run away and break their contracts. More to the point, Williams
observed that the Kroomen demonstrated the validity of his thesis by the fact
that they worked conscientiously only for those who had been kind to them.
"These black Irishmen of the West Coast," Williams noted in an apt comparison, "have no flag to cover them, no language, no Government, but every
year 5,000 of their number go from home to work with a united determination to serve their friends and shun their enemies." What Africa needed,
Williams concluded, was "the blessing of a practical labor system which, while
it addresses itself to the soul, will not ignore the body, its earthly temple; and,
while inculcating spiritual truths, will not fail to teach the native the primal
lesson of human history: *For in the sweat of thy face shalt thou eat thy bread*."[50]

Implicit in Williams's reports on the Congo is a sociobiological theory
relating enhancement of a people's physiques and moral character to
Christianization and contact with the right kind of representatives of
Occidental culture.[51] Examining the anatomies as well as the attitudes toward
labor of nine tribal groups located in the Congo, Williams called attention to
those inhabiting the Lower Congo, "where the natives have been in contact
with Europeans for centuries, [and had] felt the shock of the slave-trade
and the degrading influence of rum. . . ." These unfortunate people were
"diminutive in form, obsequious, deceitful, untrustworthy, unmanly, and
unreliable." Further inland, Williams claimed to have noticed "a slight

improvement." A pastoral tribe dwelt in the Cataract Region; "and yet these
. . . people are surely falling under the destructive influence of poisonous
liquor . . . , the old people looking older, and the young men weary and pre-
maturely decaying; and villages, formerly the scenes of content and activity, at
present rent by brawling disorders." Even further inland, Williams found
what he regarded as far less civilized peoples. "From Iringi until some distance
above Upoto, the natives are in a deep state of degradation." He took special
notice of their "cutaneous" diseases, their "revolting" scars, their custom of
inserting a piece of ivory or iron through a perforation in the nose or lip,
their tattoos, and their practice of human sacrifice and cannibalism. Each of
these peoples had certainly suffered from an unmodified adherence to their
autochthonous, "savage" life styles, but, Williams believed, they had been
hurt even more by the fact that they had not yet had any effective contact
with European or American bringers of the true gospel.

On the other hand, Williams was quick to point out how a combination
of sufficiency of food and carefully conducted Christian endeavor could effect
a powerful incentive to work upon peoples not yet ruined by their own
degradation or by the imperialist depredations of amoral Europeans.[52] "I have
noticed, he wrote, "that wherever the African has sufficient food and labor,
he presents a splendid type of man, tall, well and closely knit, muscular, agil[e]
and cheerful. He is also less cruel and superstitious." Along the shoreline connecting the mouth of the Aruwimi River with that of the Lumani, Williams
came upon such a people, "a people without a country or a village." These
were boat people—he called them "water-gypsies"—who fished and traded
with the landed natives. Untouched by the barbarities of their land-locked
trading partners, and apparently able to keep themselves away from the worst
effects of the commerce with Europeans, these people were "strong, healthy
and contented. . . , taking pleasure in their work, and with spirit to fight
when assailed by the more warlike tribes inhabiting the river-towns."
Moreover, Williams claimed that "as I continued my journey up the river, I
noticed the native type improving in feature, size, complexion and even in
character." Where the natives could not obtain liquor, this advocate of
Christian temperance "found an industrious and prosperous people." But he
worried about their prospects for the future. "Among the people around
Bolobo, Bangala and Equator I beheld the most splendid types of physical
manhood I had seen in any land or among any people I have travelled," he
exulted; "I found them [to be] brave, frank and generous; but how long they
will be able to keep this character if rum is once introduced among them, I
cannot say." These peoples had already come into contact with white men,
and these favorable meetings had evoked in the natives an eagerness for more
trade and for continued peaceable relations. Williams believed that contacts
with abstemious traders and with non-exploitative representatives of the
Christian Occident were crucial to their future welfare. "And with practical

missionary work, or industrialism," Williams promised, "these people would soon become civilized."

THE AFRICAN MISSION TRADITION
IN AFRO-AMERICAN THOUGHT

Elaborating on a theme that had been enunciated for nearly two centuries before he wrote, Williams proposed that the practical missionary work necessary for the enlightenment, salvation, anatomical enhancement, and redemption of Africa be undertaken by black Americans.[53] As early as 1714 a proposal had been put forward that male Negro slaves be manumitted by their masters and financed by the latter as missionaries to their homeland, but nothing came of this idea. In 1773, two Negroes, sponsored under Rev. Samuel Hopkins's and Ezra Stiles's plan that the Congregational Church of Newport, Rhode Island, educate blacks for the mission field, departed for Africa as the vanguard of a scheme whereby manumitted slaves would be repatriated as missionary-colonists. The Revolutionary War brought this project to an end. On June 10, 1809, Paul Cuffe (1759–1817), the son of an African father and an Indian mother, residing in Westport, Massachusetts, had proposed "to make a voyage to Sierra Leon[e] in order to inspect the situation of the country. . . ." Cuffe claimed to be "feeling a real desire that the inhabitants of Africa might become an enlightened people and be so favored as to give general satisfaction to all those who are endeavouring to establish them in the true light of Christianity."[54] To this end, after personally exploring the terrain in 1810–11, Cuffe had outfitted a ship and sent thirty-eight free black Americans to Sierra Leone in 1815. Promising to send even more African-American settler-missionaries after the first group—two thousand free blacks reportedly had expressed an interest in the venture—Cuffe did not live long enough to complete his self-proclaimed mission. His death in 1817 brought a halt to the endeavor but not to the dream that had inspired it.[55]

Forty-three years after the abortive Sierra Leone expedition, Dr. Martin R. Delany (1812–1885), born in Charleston, Virginia, to a Mandingo mother and a Golah father, proposed and carried out an exploration of the Niger Valley in the hope of establishing a colony of black American settlers and achieving thereby "The Moral, Social, and Political Elevation of Ourselves, and the Regeneration of Africa." The latter project could, he insisted, only be effected by "men of African descent."[56] Of the latter, he acknowledged that "a part of the most enlightened of that race in America design to carry out these most desirable measures by the establishment of social and industrial settlements . . . , in order at once to introduce in an effective manner, all the well-regulated pursuits of civilized life." Holding that Christian morals, democratic politics, and laissez-faire commerce were linked together and that in combination they contributed to the advance of civilization in Africa as elsewhere, Delany had "determined that the persons to compose this new element to be introduced into Africa, shall be carefully selected in regard to moral integrity, intelligence, acquired attainments, fitness, adaptation, and, as far as practicable, religious sentiments and professions."[57] However, Delany's Niger plan was frustrated by the responses of the African kings with whom he had negotiated treaties that were soon unilaterally repudiated, by British missionaries who opposed the competition his endeavor would give to their enterprise, and by the American Civil War in which he served the Union and abolitionist cause—Delany mustered out of the Union army in 1865 as a major. No lasting African-American settlement in the Niger Valley took place.[58] A similar project proposed by Henry Highland Garnet (1815–1882), grandson of a Mandingo prince, Delany's rival in such ventures, and, later, United States minister to Liberia, came to naught.[59] Nevertheless, as the career of Alexander Crummell (1819–1898), a leading African-American intellectual, missionary to Liberia, and founder of the American Negro Academy, illustrates—Crummell believed that a backward, degraded, and unenlightened Africa could be redeemed through the agencies of "Commerce, Christianity, and Civilization"—the idea of black American missions to and colonization schemes in Africa did not die out.[60] As late as 1924, Alain Locke, the first black American Rhodes Scholar and the philosophical leader of the Harlem Renaissance movement, complained that "Except from the point of view of religious missionarism, it has been until recently almost impossible to cultivate generally in the mind of the American Negro an abiding and serious interest in Africa."[61] Africa seemed destined for missions.

Black American religious and educational institutions expressed interest in missions to Africa long before and for at least three decades after Williams's exposés of King Leopold's malfeasances. However, by the turn of the century there began to develop a contradiction within the spiritual quest and a slight but noticeable separation of missionary endeavor from commercial development and from some of the European powers' colonialist aims. John Chilembwe, a Nyasaland native brought for religious instruction to America by the white Australian missionary to Africa Joseph Booth, was ordained a Baptist and in 1900 returned to British Central Africa not only as a missionary of the all-black National Baptist Convention, but also as the future leader of the politically abortive but symbolically significant Nyasaland Rising of 1915, the first anti-colonial outbreak in Africa.[62] Some black American missions to Africa associated themselves with "Ethiopianism," the Pan-African movement that took as its motto "Africa for the Africans." Among these were Chilembwe's Providence Industrial Mission and the various African missionary endeavors of the African Methodist Episcopal Church, U.S.A., under its "Ethiopianist" leader, Bishop Henry McNeal Turner (1834–1915). A sometime civil rights advocate in America, Turner had despaired over the chances for freedom and justice for America's blacks after "Redemptionist" policies had legitimated the freedmen's disenfranchisement and enacted segregation statutes.[63] Turner's followers aroused the suspicion and hostility of South Africa's white rulers, and they sought to restrict A.M.E. activities in the colony.

Williams, Turner, and other African–American Ethiopianists espoused an African dream that was, in effect, a black American variant of the Protestant dream for America: It sought to lead Africa out of its supposed darkness by imposing on Africa the Christian and commercial aspirations that had already inspired the recently emancipated freedmen and women once they had left the slave plantation's house of oppressive bondage. The dream offered Africa a Protestantized black American subculture that would replace Africa's own varied civilizations and cultures.[64]

However, in what began as the "native pastorate controversy," some Christianized Africans began to suspect that the British, and perhaps the other European and American missionaries as well, harbored Eurocentric and racist sentiments toward their African charges, sentiments expressed most directly in the reluctance to ordain natives as pastors.[65] In at least one instance, Edward W. Blyden, born in the Danish West Indies, an early advocate of American Negro settlement in Liberia, and a leader in the movement to "civilize" Africa by establishing Christianized self-governing republics throughout the continent, came to appreciate the effects of the Muslim religion on the self-esteem of the Africans. Blyden advocated what one British bishop fearfully called "a scheme for a godless West African University under Government and Negro control," and as early as 1873 he espoused a secular, or, at the least, a religiously plural pan-African nationalism.[66] By the 1930s, a threefold dichotomization could be observed: race consciousness detached itself from its earlier exclusivist religious moorings;[67] African independence came to the fore as political movements for national self-determination in opposition to European colonial regimes;[68] and civilization and progress came more and more to be perceived as secular processes and socio-cultural desiderata that could be dissociated from racial or spiritual parochialisms.[69] However, as, in effect, a contribution to this trend, the joint and separate efforts of Booker T. Washington and Robert E. Park in Africa would provide important modifications.

BOOKER T. WASHINGTON,
ROBERT E. PARK, AND TUSKEGEE IN AFRICA

George Washington Williams's protests about Leopold's atrocious conduct in the Congo had little immediate effect on developments in that colony. The quest for appropriate and effective black American efforts in Africa—e.g., missionary advocacy of a Christian variant of Ethiopianism, like that of Henry McNeal Turner in 1900 and the years thereafter;[70] Afro-American settlements, proposed as a pleasant and productive refuge, like "Chief" Alfred Charles Sam's abortive project for Oklahoma Negroes in Sierra Leone in 1914;[71] participation in Pan-African Congresses and hortatory support for an Afro-American role in the African liberation movement, like that of W. E. B. DuBois in 1900 and subsequent years;[72] or gospel-inspired technical assistance programs designed to promote agricultural and industrial development in German Togo and other European colonies, and in Liberia, the program Booker T. Washington supported in the first decade of the twentieth century[73]—continued their irregular pace well into the twentieth century.

Once Park took an interest in these matters, however, the issue was reconceptualized as a basic problem affecting the modern capitalist world civilizational process. Although not *in haec verba*, Park formulated the basic elements of a Gothic and idealist critique of advancing capitalism that, had it been continued and fully developed, might have challenged the preëminence of the materialist one developed so prominently by Marx and his followers. Leopold's Congo, in effect, became the setting for the embryonic elaboration of a perspective that has not yet been brought to maturation or test. After completing his service to the Congo Reform Association, Park went to Tuskegee, Alabama, to work for Booker T. Washington, serving as his private secretary and ghost writer for seven years and modifying themes Park had addressed in his Congo essays.

Like others inspired by the commercial as well as the salvational promise of Christian redemption, Booker T. Washington formulated his "Tuskegee idea" not as a critique of capitalism, but, rather, around the moral and material virtues associated with and presumed to emanate from the Protestant ethic. Preaching a gospel of hard work, thrift, abstinence, temperance, and success through vocational efforts, Washington—who feared that emancipation had suddenly thrust millions of black men, women, and children into an emerging free market of industrial labor without the basic wherewithal necessary to survive in it—sought simultaneously to protect his compatriots from the ravages of modern life and to empower the freedmen and women by educating them in the agricultural and lesser industrial arts. Moreover, in his famous Atlanta Compromise address of 1895, Washington seemed virtually to surrender to the unyielding power of the New South's white supremacists, turning the black Americans' agenda away from demands for the full panoply of civil, political, and social rights guaranteed by the postwar amendments to the Constitution and toward acquiescence to their separate and unequal condition. He urged black Americans to oblige themselves to self-help, to acknowledge a willingness to perform civic and economic duties, and in social and political matters to accommodate themselves to the demands of the segregationists.[74] Although W. E. B. DuBois scorned Washington's public obeisance to the white power structure and opposed the Tuskegeean's all-too-meek withdrawal from the public struggle for equal rights, it is worth noting that he did not altogether dissociate himself from Washington's educational curriculum: "So far as Mr. Washington preaches Thrift, Patience, and Industrial Training for the masses," wrote the Harvard- and Berlin-trained scholar-leader, "we must hold up his hands and strive with him. . . . But so far as Mr. Washington apologizes for injustice, . . . does not value the privilege and duty of voting, belittles the emasculating effects of caste distinctions, and opposes the higher training and ambition of our brighter minds—so far as he, the South, or the Nation, does this—we must unceasingly and firmly oppose them."[75] In fact, it is now known that Washington engaged in a subtle, covert, and largely clandestine program to halt the worst abuses of Negroes and to effect some of the civil rights of black Americans[76] at the same time that he sought to spread his gospel of success-through-virtue-and-agricultural-and-mechanical-training throughout the African-American scene and to the African continent. However, as Ras Makonnen—a Pan-Africanist from Guyana who was educated in America and Denmark and who would play a significant part in both the anti-colonial movement of the 1920s and 1930s and in the post-colonial politics of Ghana and Kenya—would later point out, the skills that Washington sought to impart to both American Negro and black African youths "were already being outdated by the technology of the new land-grant colleges."[77]

Washington's ventures in uplifting Africa can be distinguished according to whether they constituted a general application of the Tuskegee principle to such places as German Togo, Anglo-Egyptian Sudan, the Union of South Africa, or Liberia, or whether they served the cause of the Congo Reform Association, of which he was a vice-president at the same time that Robert Park worked as its recording secretary. Beginning in 1900, Washington offered his school's services to various European colonial authorities, adopting a remarkably uncritical stance toward the German colonial policies in Togo, Morocco, and East Africa. These policies had been adopted in the 1870s and 1880s as elements of Bismarck's *Mittelafrika* plan, a course of action designed to forge a "tool to counter the political fragmentation that was beginning to appear as the main problem of German national politics."[78] One specific aim of *Mittelafrika* was to convert Germany's recently acquired protectorate, Togo, into a colony of independent cotton farmers that would service the metropole's burgeoning textile industry and at the same time act as an entering wedge for a German sphere of influence extending into the mineral-rich Katanga region of the Congo Free State.[79]

In 1900, the same year that Park would take note of the new German army and its implications for the world, Washington became an unwitting technical assistant to the *Mittelafrika* component of the Reich's *Weltpolitik*. Washington had been approached by Baron Herman of the *Kolonial-Wirtschaftliches Komitee* (*KWK*) and asked whether Tuskegee could supply black Americans to train Togolese farmers in cotton production. Asked if these technical assistants would acquiesce to the colonial authorities, Washington assured his new client, "I do not think in any case that there will be much if any difficulty in the men who go from here treating the German officials with proper respect. They are all kindly disposed, respectful gentlemen." Moreover, Washington added, "I believe at the same time they will secure the respect and confidence of the natives."[80] Of the nine Tuskegeeans who went to Togo between 1901 and 1909, four died and another four left within two years. The last remaining member of the original team, John W. Robinson, a true exemplar of Washington's philosophy of humility and industriousness—in 1904, he wrote George Washington Carver, the agricultural "wizard" of Tuskegee who advised Washington's missionaries on such matters as cross-pollination and the elimination of insect pests, "I feel that my future is sealed up in these cotton stalks, then why should I run away from it?"—drowned in 1909.[81] The *KWK*'s Togo project failed, not so much because of the cotton production levels, but rather because the German importers rejected the several varieties of staple-length cotton produced by the Tuskegee-trained Togolese[82] and because the areas of major cotton growing increased their own productivity, causing a downturn in prices and the virtual ruin of marginal producers like those in Togo.[83]

These events did not deter Washington from continuing to spread overseas his gospel of success through virtue and industry. His writings were translated into many languages, and, as a result, according to his biographer, Louis R. Harlan, "All manner of men, American missionaries, European colonialists, African nationalists, Buddhist reformers, and Japanese modernizers sought to enlist his aid."[84] The Tuskegeean orientation spread over much of the African-Asian continents. Its message—together with the autobiography of its originator—inspired some who would never meet Washington or receive his imprimatur. A fine exemplar of the latter is Shen Zonghan, Republican China's leading agronomist, whose life story of early poverty, conversion to Christianity, abstemious living, dedicated effort, and educational attainment (at the Georgia State College of Agriculture and Cornell University) could serve as a positive testimony to Washington's program. Early in his life, Shen had been impressed by the autobiographies of the Tuskegeean, as well as those of Benjamin Franklin and Abraham Lincoln. However, his Tuskegeean-inspired efforts came to an ignominious denouement when his Rockefeller-funded project to eliminate pests from China's rice fields failed to win either popular or governmental backing.[85] Despite its setbacks, however, Washington's philosophy of Christian faith and agricultural endeavor would continue to serve as a beacon of practical enlightenment not only for the South's black peasantry, but also for much of the non-Occidental world.

Washington caused an article on "Industrial Education in Africa" to be published in 1906 under his name—although it was probably ghosted by Park—and reiterated his conviction that a Protestant ethic would insure civilizational advance. Having "very little faith in the success of any effort to educate or to increase the economic value of the native Africans that is not conducted by those who have confidence in and a disinterested desire to improve the condition of the people intrusted to their care," Washington asserted, ". . . I am disposed to believe that no attempt to educate the native peoples of Africa or to lift them to a higher plane of industrial efficiency, will have any permanent success that does not go hand in hand with the teaching of the Christian religion, or at least with a devotion and desire to help the people similar to that which has inspired the work of the missionaries in Africa."[86]

Washington apparently believed that the German colonialists shared his vision. While visiting Berlin in 1910, he praised the "wholesome and constructive manner" in which they carried out their African policies. "They do not seek to repress the Africans," he insisted, though he had not visited German Togo to ascertain what actually had occurred, "but rather to help them that they may be more useful to themselves and to the German people." So impressed was Washington with the Reich's colonial policy and practice that he enthused, "Their manner of handling Negroes in Africa might be taken as a pattern for other nations."

Washington also sent Tuskegeean agricultural advisers and teachers to the Anglo-Egyptian Sudan and to South Africa. In the Sudan, they were intended to facilitate the work of Leigh Hunt, an American venture capitalist who hoped to pioneer experimental cotton farming on a large tract of Nile coastland at Zeidab; in South Africa, Tuskegee's men were expected to educate the natives so that they might become "skilled laborers in agriculture, mining and the trades."[87] The export of a Tuskegeean agricultural and mechanical training program resonated not only with the exploitative interests of Occidental colonialists in Africa, but also expressed the pastoral, virtually preindustrial ideology that permeated Washington's overall perspective toward the non-industrial world. The principal of Tuskegee had become convinced that urban life was detrimental to the South's blacks, to Asia's peasantry, and to Africa's natives.

However, as Louis R. Harlan has taken care to point out, "Washington became involved in a more congenial African role as defender of mistreated Negro people in King Leopold's Congo Free State."[88] This exception to his otherwise supportive attitude toward European imperialism in Africa stems from his role as a vice-president of the Congo Reform Association, (CRA), the organizational arm of an international movement formed by those who protested Leopold's atrocities.

In America, a chapter of the CRA had been established under the auspices of the Massachusetts Commission for International Justice by Robert E. Park, who became its international secretary and published his first report on the matter in October 1904.[89] On January 15, 1905, Park had written to the former George Edmond Pierre Achille Morel-de-Ville (1873–1924)—the Paris-born journalist who had been naturalized a British subject in 1896, adopted the name E. D. Morel, and, on the basis of his expert knowledge of West African affairs, in March 1904 formed the Congo Reform Association[90]—saying: "I agree perfectly . . . that this is not a fight against the Congo State alone, it is against slave labour in tropical Africa. It is simply the race issue in its most concrete form, that is, in the case where you have not merely the race but its appropriate environment, the soil on which it lives as an element in the problem."[91] Morel's other correspondent in America, Thomas Barbour, a Baptist missionary to the Congo, had recruited Washington to become a vice-president of the CRA. The Tuskegeean, in turn, had won the support of the National Baptist Convention[92] to the cause.[93]

Park's association with Washington deepened because of their joint work for the CRA and laid the basis for their subsequent collaboration. When one of King Leopold's agents attempted to bring Washington to Belgium to lecture at a proposed international congress on economic expansion, Park urged him to go, but warned him, observing that "the king of Belgium hopes to win you over to his theory of dealing with the Blackman." And, Park went on, pointing to the venal character of the Belgian monarch, "It is part of his cynical view of things in general that everyone can be purchased with money or flattery."[94] Park hoped that Washington would use the occasion of a visit to Brussels to contrast American with European colonial policies: "The difference between our colonial system and others," he wrote to the Tuskegeean leader, "consists in the fact that we are preparing the peoples we govern for citizenship, either in the United States or as independent states; other countries are interested only in the *economic development* (a vague term, which may be interpreted in many ways) of their possessions. . . ."[95] Washington, however, declined the invitation to address the international congress; about nine months earlier—in what would be the beginning of a ten-year association—he had persuaded Park to ghost write his article on "Cruelty in the Congo Country" for *Outlook Magazine*.[96]

That essay, appearing on October 8, 1904, under Washington's name, is the first sustained effort in Park's Congo writings. Without enunciating any theoretical stance, it provides, inferentially and empirically, a Gothic basis for understanding Leopold's machinations in the colony.[97] The essay begins by distinguishing those of Leopold's policies that are the product of ignorant folly from those that stem from knowing knavery. Noting that, in 1884, the

United States had recognized the king of Belgium's claim to have established a legitimate government in the Congo basin, Washington/Park point out that it was supposed to consolidate "an independent confederation of free negroes" in equatorial Africa, much like the "negro State of Liberia . . . [which] had been established in Africa as a result of the philanthropic people of the United States." However, the principal policy "error in judgment" undertaken by the new government was its decree that all of the Congo's vacant lands belonged to the state. Having not yet perceived that modern capitalism's corporate firm was like the dreaded fictional Transylvanian vampire in that its immortal soullessness required it to roam the earth in search of its peculiar form of life-renewing blood, i.e., land and labor, Washington/Park at this time regarded Leopold's property-appropriation measure as a neutral if unwise decree that had had deleterious but unintended consequences. "This decree," they wrote, "worked great injustice to the natives." The chief effects of the Belgian king's new law had been to take from the Congolese people "at one stroke all the natural wealth of the country, with which they might have been able to purchase the products of civilization."

Without an incentive to obtain wealth or advancement, and robbed of the opportunity to live on the subsistence of the rubber- and plant-rich usufruct of the land, the natives had in effect sunk lower than they had been in the scales that equate personal morality with productive effort. Reduced so much that "From this time on we hear the complaint that the West African will not work," the natives were subjected thereafter to a consciously planned and evilly intended program of government-sponsored terrorism. That program was designed to frighten them into abject submission and unalloyed acquiescence to forced labor in the rubber forests. Here vampirism—the archetypical anthropomorphosis employed by the Gothic perspective—becomes literal as Washington/Park, drawing upon the on-the-spot reports of the black American missionary, Rev. W. H. Sheppard, detail how a special force composed of members of one cannibalistic tribe, known as the Zapo-zaps, engage in what are virtually officially encouraged "rubber raids." The raids consist in the killing and eating of recalcitrant natives. Afterwards, the Zapo-zaps turn in to the government the severed right hands of the dead men. The hands serve as proofs of the Zapo-zaps' service and as documents that determine the amount of their pay. Reverend Sheppard's grisly descriptions illustrated local gustatorial nuances—"The men who have young children do not eat people, but all the rest ate them."—and practical cephalic innovations—" 'Where is the man's head?' I asked. 'Oh, they made a bowl of the forehead to rub up tobacco and diamba in.'" All in all, the missionary's reports indicated that the Congo had become victim to a government-sanctioned depravity that was beyond redemption, and that Leopold's much-vaunted mission of civilization had reintroduced and reinforced savagery.

Washington/Park were convinced that "the native is not the only victim of this system." They took care to summarize the effects that Leopold's atrocious program was having "upon the white men who are condemned to perform this degrading work." The Congo had truly become a heart of evil darkness, for "all reports agree that these [European] men almost invariably give themselves over to the worst vices, if for no other reason than to escape from the melancholy which their isolation breeds." The train of evils carried out in bloody pursuit of Leopold's Congo Free State had virtually corrupted the souls of the colonial authorities: "Some of these men, it is said, condemned on account of their crimes for long service in the interior, give themselves up to despair and kill themselves or commit horrible crimes." Yet, despite the enormity of the abominations in the Congo, the white functionaries employed to wreak this moral havoc had fared better—even in their punishments—than the natives. "What a comment on the whole situation," remarked Washington/Park, "is the single fact that only a few months ago an officer of the Government was condemned to fifteen years' imprisonment, after he had been convicted of killing one hundred and twenty-two persons!" Such horrors required civilized humanity in general, but as Washington/Park pointed out, the people and authorities of "our own country" in particular, to rouse themselves "to bring about such action as will in any manner modify or improve the present state of affairs."

ROBERT PARK'S CONGO—A GOTHIC ANALYSIS OF CAPITALIST IMPERIALISM

"Everywhere in the nineteenth century," observed Park (and Burgess) in 1921, "we find a double preoccupation with the past and with the future. . . . The imagination of the age was intent on history; its conscience was intent on reform."[98] In 1905–06, when he wrote three of his four signed essays on the Congo, Park was himself acting as a muckraking publicist, seeking to awaken the public conscience so that outraged Americans would demand that action be taken to halt Leopold's oppression of the natives of the Congo. To succeed in his endeavor, Park employed much of the rhetoric that would resonate with the newly popular interest in Gothic occultism and its demonological war against Christianity. The very term muckraker—which had been introduced into journalistic discourse in President Theodore Roosevelt's address to the Gridiron Club on March 17, 1906—had had its origins in John Bunyan's Pilgrim's Progress, a Restoration text of Christian redemption. As would prove significant, Park's efforts in behalf of the Congolese people had the backing of the American Baptist Convention. For Park, who would later attest to the importance of arousing non-rational beliefs as springs to action,[99] employment of the fantastical imagery of Gothic imagination, especially as that imagination pitted the forces of religiously inspired virtue against the powers of preternatural satanic evil, served the purpose for which his reformist writing was intended—to expose the dark and unconscionable activities of a real-life human vampire masquerading as a civilized and Christian monarch.

"A new figure looms large on the horizon of Europe! A figure strange, fantastic and ominous—the king who is capitalist, *le roi d'affaires*; the man who unites in himself the political and social prestige of a reigning monarch with the vast material power of a multimillionaire."[100] So opens the first of Park's three truly Gothic essays on the Congo. (Park's 1904 essay, "Recent Atrocities in the Congo State," published in the popular magazine *The World To-Day* in October of that year, is largely reportorial, but it adumbrates the theme he would develop in the later essays when he notes "that the tales that have reached us from there have usually been listened to and dismissed with a shudder as one of the incidents of that terrible process of civilization whose results, as we see them under our very eyes, are often melancholy enough."[101]) And, as the text unfolds, Park's Gothic methodology reveals its muckraking intent. He has a threefold purpose: to remove from the imperial ruler of Belgium the mask of Christian piety with which he cloaks his nefarious crimes against Congolese humanity; to expose to the destructive rays of factual light the real-life vampire-king who is literally and figuratively sucking the lifeblood out of the hapless natives of Central Africa; and, lastly, to show how the modern devices of propaganda and publicity are employed to cover up the atrocities that are so rampant on a continent that, in the throes of a religiously inspired imperialism, is nevertheless being kept in darkness. In the process, Park utilizes Gothic imagery of the kind found in the classics of that literary genre—e.g., *The Castle of Otranto*, *Melmoth the Wanderer*, and *The Vampyre*—to challenge not only King Leopold II of Belgium's claim to trusteeship over the Congo, but also to question the legitimacy and morality of the entire, modern enterprise of capitalist imperialism. As a new figure on the land and seascapes of the world, the "strange, fantastic and ominous" Belgian monarch seemed to require an analysis that would be both responsive to the conditions of his appearance and a warning to the people of the world of its far-reaching consequences.

Park's essays follow the general pattern of presentation that is to be found in the earliest versions of the classical Gothic novels.[102] In the latter, a serious crime committed in the past has gone unpunished and, in some instances, unnoticed. The criminal has succeeded not only in escaping justice but also in becoming a murderous usurper of the hero-victim's rightful place in the socio-political order. At the time of the action of the story, the victim of the malefactor's usurpation is in abject circumstances and, perhaps, without the knowledge of his true identity. Persecuted still by the as yet unexposed evildoer, the victim seems to be unable to understand his own situation and, worse, powerless to remedy it. But a chain of events and circumstances, some of them preternatural, works to reveal the true character of the villain, who is eventually overthrown. In the *denouement* of such fictional romances, the victim's stolen patrimony is returned to him, and, by implication, the legitimate hierarchy of power and authority is restored. However, in Park's rendition of the real-life-and-death sociological Gothic of the Congo, the villain, King Leopold II, is depicted more like those of the later Gothic fiction. In Park's Gothic, Leopold II, like his evil-doing counterpart in *Melmoth the Wanderer* (1820) or *Dracula* (1897), has evoked a Mephistophelian fascination about himself, that of a veritable preternatural but noble arch-villain of the modern world. However, he is not yet overthrown, and his victims remain in a state of misery that, absent Park's morally inspired polemic and an aroused public intervention, will go on indefinitely.

Like the Gothic mysteries which they so much resemble, Park's first two Gothic Congo essays (as well as the essay he wrote for Booker T. Washington) proceed as a slow but steady unmasking of the villain. First, he reveals the "crime" committed before Leopold's Congo venture. Insulated by a carefully cultivated cloak of false Christian piety and the belief that he reigned over a tiny and powerless kingdom, Leopold had converted these only apparent weaknesses into international imperial assets. Even the press's exposure of his less than Puritanical private life—viz., as that "of the jaded pleasure-seeker, pursuing a new sensation in the purlieus of the Parisian boulevards; the royal sport, lending a vogue to the gaming-tables at Ostend, in which he was, it is charged, a secret partner; the domestic tyrant, driving his wife into retirement by the brutalities of his scandalous life, imprisoning his daughter in an asylum because she rebelled against a marriage without love or respect; the miserly libertine, who after squandering money lavishly on his mistresses, robbed his wife of her fortune while she was living, and cheated his daughters out of their heritage after she was dead"[103]—had been worked to his advantage. His infidelities and vices pandered to the popular taste for royal scandals, shielding rather than penetrating the imperialist arcanum wherein his true and enormous villainy resided. "Leopold," Park observed, "is less the avaricious adventurer, philanthropist [philanderer?], and satyr than a cynical man of the world, who sees through, even while he enjoys the pretty, visible, trivial world of sport, fashions, and affairs."[104] The popular press, in seeking to portray him as a petty participant in the promiscuities of the demimonde had unwittingly given him another mask under which to hide his real evildoings.

As Park is at pains to show, Leopold's carefully promoted counter-image— an abstemious old man who rises each day at 5 A.M., drinks only water or warm tea, eats sparingly, disposes of his early morning correspondence while taking moderate bodily exercise, goes on three or four solitary walks a day, is punctilious about time and appointments, has "an extraordinary sense for details," and is "abrupt with his employees, dry with his orderlies, and inflexible with his ministers"[105]—is closer to the truth. But it too serves to mask his intentions, even better than all the vice- and sex-ridden stories reported about him. For

Park, Leopold personifies the new man of power in the modern world, the bureaucratic monarch-manager, and his actions foreshadow the new modes of evil—modes that Hannah Arendt would more than fifty years later characterize as "banal"[106]—that were beginning to shape and shake the foundations of the twentieth century.

The earlier "crime" of Leopold—one that would adumbrate as well as set in motion what Park called "The Terrible Story of the Congo"[107]—consisted in his having abandoned even a show of the traditional constraints against money grubbing that were supposed to attend European nobility. As a king in business, Leopold went "openly into the money markets." Although Park conceded that other members of European royalty had had "more or less illicit relations with the stock-market" and acknowledged without either assent or denial the gossip "that half the thrones of Europe are indirectly allied with the Standard Oil Company," the fact that Leopold had "put himself at the head of the Belgian group of financiers and [had] led the crusade for foreign concessions"[108] made him the personification of the emerging character of what I am here calling Gothic capitalism—a roaming over the earth for new economic lifeblood to replenish that of the undead-but-not-soulfully-alive corporate entity.

Showing how the financial manipulation of the European scramble for foreign concessions could make even "a little country, with an insignificant army" into one that had "no less than fifty concessions in China," that had become economically "established in Siam, in Persia, and in Morocco," and that in the form of a Franco-Belgian syndicate "owns more than half the debts of Santo Domingo," Park detailed the intricate manner in which Leopold had succeeded as financier-king. Employing stratagems in effect equivalent to those used by Polidori's "vampyre," Lord Ruthven, to secure and maintain his sanguinary hold over the depraved and déclassé women of Europe, the Belgian monarch had achieved such great world financial power "that there is not [now] a spot on the globe where the weakness or rottenness of local government has cast the scent of concessions on the air that Belgians are not already settled, or hovering about expectantly."[109] Once begun, Leopold's quest to secure markets for Belgium's manufactures moved over the undeveloped world of Asia and Africa like that of the vampire bat in Stoker's and others' Gothic fiction*—seeking out the weak persons and institutions in the world, finding just those whose socioeconomic jugular he might pierce, thereby making them into the craven servants of his malevolent scheme for a worldwide colonial empire.

---

*The association of bats with vampirism is itself a product of the European advance into the non-Occidental world: ". . . [T]he bat transformation is recent. During the Spanish conquest of Mexico the conquistadores found a bat (Desmodus rotundus) that seemed to drink blood, and returned home with the story. Actually, they do not drink blood; they remove a small plug of skin and lap the blood, but too late—the image by the nineteenth century was already in place." James B. Twitchell, Dreadful Pleasures: An Anatomy of Modern Horror (New York: Oxford University Press, 1985), p. 311n. 9.

In Park's description of his machinations, Leopold operates much like the villainous characters in Gothic fiction. Noble in birth but outwardly seeming to be little more than a powerless potentate among the great Powers of Europe, King Leopold II—in what Park designates as "a testimony to his genius"—turned "every one of these weaknesses to his own and Belgium's advantage." Just as Polidori's impoverished nobleman-vampire, Lord Ruthven, makes himself the mysterious but somehow attractive companion to the wealthy, but naïve and decadent gentleman, Aubrey—poisoning the youth's soul, destroying his body, marrying his sister, sucking out her blood until she is lifeless, and then making off with the fortune that he has inherited as the widower and sole surviving heir to the family's fortune—so Park's Leopold, precisely because "Belgium was feeble and neutral and, to all appearances, a mere international inconvenience, . . made of himself the middleman of the [European] Powers, engineering projects and conducting negotiations for them which, because of international jealousies, they did not think it advisable to carry on in their own names." Thereby, Leopold eventually secured for himself and his coterie of venture capitalists a venomous control over many of Europe's colonial possessions, concessions, and foreign investments, a control that none of the Powers had anticipated.

Park's close analysis of Leopold's nefarious scheme involving the construction and control of the Pekin-Hankow railway is a veritable Gothic case study, involving a weak, abject, and decadent Chinese government, the fierce and rivalrous diplomacy of the less-than-honorable British, French, and Russian concession seekers, Belgium's calculating brokerage service offered to all parties to the struggle, and, again reminiscent of Polidori's tale, a conclusion in which the only seemingly benevolent evil-doers win out not only over their jealous but inept opponents but also over the Occident's innocent (or ignorant) bystanders. Park concluded, "China has since bought back, at considerable profit to Belgian as well as American investors, the concessions that she [had] granted to Americans alone. As a result of the whole transaction, American prestige in China has been severely shaken, and the American tradesman is the sufferer."[110]

With his abilities at foreign venture capitalism already recognized, and while his true intentions were still unknown to the imperial leaders of Europe, Leopold hatched a scheme whereby he could take control over Central Africa. Again, like a fictional Gothic figure, he masked his true aims, in the instant case, behind a cloak of Christian missionary endeavor. True to his task of ripping away the layers of masquerade that covered Leopold's most horrific villainies, Park tears off Leopold's veil of virtue, revealing the monarch's—and by extension, modernity's—true nature. Leopold, Park shows, in five bold strokes had put himself at the head of "the most unique government on earth, a commercial monopoly farmed by an autocrat"[111]—first, with his formation of the International Association for the Exploration and Civilization of Central Africa in 1877; second, by sponsoring Henry

Morton Stanley's explorations of the region through another cover group, The Society for Studies of the Upper Congo, in 1881; third, by engineering his own appointment as international guardian of the neutral Congo territory at the Berlin conference of 1884; fourth, by taking advantage of loopholes in the international agreements made at the Brussels Antislavery Conference of 1890 to revoke free trade and levy import duties in the Congo; and, last, by supplanting Congolese trade with taxation and a parceling out the territory of the anomalously named Congo Free State "among stock companies, who pay fifty per cent of the profits to the state for the privilege of assessing and collecting these taxes."[112] Hidden behind the persona of a religious and progressive "royal Captain of Industry," Leopold had succeeded in obtaining absolute and cruel sway over the Congolese people, and, as Park indicates, he did so with the support of most of the heterogeneous elements—Catholic and Protestant, Germanic and Gallic—who made up the business-minded Kingdom of Belgium. And the *denouement* of this drama of deviltry has been an unexampled reign of ruin disguised as civilizational progress and justified by capitalist gains. "Leopold," Park notes, "says that the results are civilization. The missionaries say they are hell. *But everybody admits that they are profitable.*"[113]

An unfeeling bureaucratic control over and a callous oppression of dependent peoples for the purpose of garnering ever-greater profits constitute the elementary forms of Gothic capitalist imperialism. Precisely by interposing a soulless corporate being—i.e., the firm—between themselves and their objectives, imperialist capitalists had imparted a banality to their evil practices that would both cloak and characterize their atrociousness. Belgium, Park points out, had become a country immersed in business in the early years of capitalist development. But, Park notes, when Leopold, who in the beginning was expected by the Powers merely to reign rather than rule, insured that the Congo stocks earned enormous dividends on the Antwerp market, took the lead in the formation and aggrandizement of the country's foreign concessions, and opened up Africa and Asia for Belgian manufactures, he virtually converted what would ordinarily be regarded as a pre-capitalist monarchical role into that of a business corporation's general manager and turned his Continental subjects into his loyal national stockholders. The king had become both the personification and the chief executive officer of the imperial corporation.

The transformation of king into corporate manager had inured Leopold against both accusations of moral default and most of the obligations and ethics traditionally associated with monarchy. ". . . [W]e expect personal dignity, intelligent consideration, justice, and the like from a king," Park observed. "We ask only one thing of a General Manager—dividends."[114] The Belgian public and the ministers of the Belgian government, Park went on to point out, had shown "an otherwise incredible subserviency to a king whose private life has been a public scandal, and whose public career a shameless and unscrupulous clutching after gold. . . ."[115] They had become so conscienceless about and insensitive to the sufferings of Leopold's Congolese victims "because," Park concluded, "they recognize in him the General Manager." "Those who have not bowed to the prerogative of the king have yielded to the imperious necessities of business."[116] And those necessities had dictated a royal carnage in the Congo. King Leopold was, as Park put it presciently, "the crowned incarnation of the aspirations of a business people and a business age."[117]

The cruel usurpation of the Congo people's land, Park indicated, had been followed by a murderous exploitation of their labor. It was Park's point that it was the supposedly progressive practices of modern civilization, justified by a wedding of commercialism to Christianity—and not Africa's alleged heathenism or the atavistic practices attributed to the Congolese people—that had brought all this about. It was, Park pointed out, the civilized world, "shocked and startled into protest by tales of the atrocities of the Portuguese slave-trade along the Congo and in the adjacent territories," that had convoked the Brussels convention of 1876, and, he went on to show, it was his manipulation of that meeting that had started the wily Leopold on the course that led to his present position as a most heartless autocrat of the Congo.[118] Park's refusal to add his voice to the chorus of support for Joseph Conrad's imagery of Africa—e.g., Conrad's descriptions of the continent as "the other world," of a voyage up the Congo River as a trip "back to the earliest beginning of the world," of the Congolese male as a "prehistoric man . . .[,] cursing us, praying to us, welcoming us . . .," and of the white man as one who might recognize only a "remote kinship with this wild and passionate uproar"[119]—not only testifies to his unusual departure from the conventions of thought of his age,[120] but also speaks to his perception that the true heart of darkness was to be found in the dominant political and economic institutions of western civilization.

Park epigrammatized "The Terrible Story of the Congo" with British M.P. Herbert Samuels' question, "If the administration of the Congo Free State is civilization, what then is barbarism?"[121] And, along with his own text, he caused to have printed photographs (supplied by the Congo Reform Association and the American Baptist Missionary Union) showing "cannibal sentries set over native villages by the King's agents,"[122] "a [one-handed] boy of Illinga, mutilated by State soldiers during a rubber raid,"[123] and "Nsala, of Wala, and the remains of his five-year-old daughter. Both wife and child were eaten at a cannibal feast."[124] And, as Park makes indisputably clear, "This is the Congo Free State as Leopold, the Philanthropist, has made it."[125]

It is in the second essay, "The Terrible Story of the Congo," that Park employs a full-blown Gothic discourse. The horrors committed in the name of Leopold's version of civilization more than match those envisioned by the writers of macabre fiction. Pointing out the awful fate of a Congolese village that has failed to meet its state-imposed quota in taxes, rubber, or copal, Park observes, "The offending village is raided by the [King's] soldiers. Men, women, and little children are either dragged away as 'hostages,' . . . or are shot down like dogs, and their right hands cut off and turned over to the State as evidence of duty done." Although Belgian authorities would continue to attribute the mutilations of the Congolese to traditional native customs, adding that the cutting off of hands was conducted only upon the dead, Park noted in refutation that "missionaries will tell of living people, maimed in ways beyond all healing; and [that] missionaries and students alike bear witness that no study of native life has shown the slightest trace of any such 'custom'" to exist among the natives. In fact, Park asserted, these and other atrocities were "solely one of the evidences of philanthropy and civilization."[126] And, after detailing the reports of "[m]utilation, outrage, and degradations unspeakable, death by shooting, by starvation, by the lash, and by the halter, . . . visited by armed black soldiers, at the instigation of a handful of whites, upon unarmed and helpless natives . . . ," Park rips off the final mask—Leopold's claim that his regime of terror in the Congo has, if nothing else, benefited Belgium's economy and enhanced the Congo's development:

> There is no trade in the Congo. There is, instead, forced production, extortion, and an organized system of plunder.
> There has never been freedom; there is, and always has been under Leopold's rule, virtual and absolute slavery.
> The supply of ivory is practically exhausted; in certain districts the yield of rubber has nearly ceased.
> The land is being depopulated at the rate of 15,000,000 in twenty years; vast stretches of country are devastated; from these districts the natives who have escaped slaughter have fled into the depths of the forests, miserable, outcast, and hopeless.[127]

In Stoker's fictional account of *Dracula*, the eponymous arch fiend of the undead is killed by an outraged band of Occidental young people who, guided by a benevolent scientist of the occult, administer the ritually appropriate lethal weaponry. In Park's account of Leopold's atrocities in the Congo, however, the monarch of murder and pillage has aroused only "faint stirrings of conscience . . .; there are resolutions, and discussions, and cries of pity and shame." Against such assaults—as Park's third essay, entitled "The Blood-Money of the Congo,"[128] documents so clearly—the predatory Leopold is virtually invulnerable because of the effectiveness of his own "huge machine—his gigantic Press Bureau— . . . a machine grinding tirelessly, night and day, that its owner may pose as the Philanthropist, and not be exposed as the Vampire."[129] Unless more is done, unless the mundane equivalent of the nemesis of this real-life *Nosferatu* can be found, he and his system will develop even more terrible variations on what Park denotes as "the most highly perfected business methods of the twentieth century."[130] Meanwhile, as Park dolefully concludes, "The Vampire sits sucking the lifeblood of the victim that has slowly ceased to struggle."[131] Gothic capitalism had for the moment escaped its just deserts.

The limitations of Gothic discourse as a critique of modernity are suggested by both the fate of Park's foray into Gothicist muckraking and by its abandonment as a perspective by his disciples' subsequent sociologies of black Africa.* Park would later complain that he was used unfairly by the Baptist Mission Society, and acknowledge that through his work with the Congo Reform Association he had been inveigled, at first unwittingly, into taking sides in a jurisdictional dispute between Belgian Catholic missions in the Congo Free State, who were favored by King Leopold, and rival English and American Baptist missions to the Congo that had the support of the CRA.[132] "I didn't take much stock in their atrocity stories,"[133] Park recalled, perhaps retrospectively rebuking himself for having presented in graphic detail such a horrifying sight as that relayed to him by the Reverend E. V. Sjöblom of the American Baptist Missionary Union: "The mother was shot and the right hand taken off. On one side was the elder child, also shot, and the right hand also taken off. On the other side was the younger child, with its right hand cut off, but the child, still living, was resting against the mother's breast."[134] However, Park did not repudiate the general conclusion about progress that he had reached in his earlier studies. "I discovered . . . ," he would later write, "that conditions in the Congo were . . . what they were certain to be whenever a sophisticated people invades the territories of a more primitive people in order to exploit their lands and, incidentally, to uplift and civilize them." By the time he had completed his Congo studies, Park claimed he "knew enough about civilization . . . to know that progress . . . is a terrible thing. It is so destructive and wasteful."[135]

Park's complaint about the missionaries' exploitation of the Congo Question speaks to a fundamental weakness in his own and the CRA's usage of a Gothic perspective. The Gothic is embedded in a subterranean Christian (indeed, largely Catholic) outlook. As Dr. Park reveals the truly evil character of the king of the Belgians, he makes himself into a character not unlike Dr. Van Helsing in Stoker's fictional account of the exposure and death of another preternaturally evil nobleman, Count Dracula. The vampire, according to Montague Summers, "is one who has led a life of more than ordinary immorality and unbridled wickedness; a man of foul, gross and selfish passions, of evil ambitions, delighting in cruelty and blood."[136] When Park has shown Leopold II to be just such a being, he has reached the intramundane limits of action of the vampire hunter. His "band of brothers," i.e., the members of the international CRA who had joined together to extirpate the evils committed by King Leopold and his minions, the real-life equivalent of Van Helsing's compatriots in the struggle against Dracula, relied on the power

*See appendix at end of chapter

of an aroused Christian conscience to put down the veritably preternatural power of the tyrant of the Congo. But, if that source of morality was already dead, or if it was in its final throes of strangulation, choking on the shards of a commercial civilization that had been fatally lodged in its preachers' and practitioners' throats, a reliance on the Christian homiletic would appear to have been unpromising.

In fact, Park's essay appeared at a time when traditional Christian faith was under assault from science and other elements of modernity. For his own part, Park had from the beginning viewed the matter politically, a point he made when first writing to CRA founder E. D. Morel, requesting the right to turn the Massachusetts Commission for International Justice into the American branch of the Congo Reform Association: "There is nothing in the world that a man of your temperament or of my temperament would rather do in this world than fight just such iniquity as this in the Congo State. . . . To my way of thinking, politics, I mean politics of just the sort that you and I are engaged in, is the real business of human life."[137]

Unfortunately, what Park regarded as the real business of human life, despite an unstinting publicity campaign,[138] may have done less to relieve the Congo from the worst features of its oppressive condition than the death—from natural causes—of its evil monarch on December 17, 1909.[139]

Park's subsequent disaffection from the efforts of Protestant missionaries to expose the horrors of Leopold's regime in the Congo seems in retrospect to be an instance wherein he himself might have fallen victim to the Belgian king's carefully orchestrated disinformation program. Leopold had conducted a wide-ranging propaganda campaign designed to discredit the opponents of his Congo policies.[140] Central to that campaign had been the king's co-optation of English and American Catholic opinion in behalf of his claim that Protestant missionaries had falsely accused him and his agents of atrocities in order that they might usurp the mission field from their Catholic rivals. By threatening to expel the Catholics should they join in the chorus of protest emanating from the Presbyterian, Baptist, Disciples of Christ, and other Nonconformist denominations, and then pointing to the former's silence as a defense of his policies, Leopold had hoped to turn the international movement for Congo reform into an inter-church squabble. In fact, as Morel would come to observe, Protestant missionaries had not rushed forward to publish their own observations of Leopold's maladministration, fearful of the king's revenge, and had had to be persuaded by secular reformers to speak out. When Park ruefully disavowed his credulity with respect to the CRA missionary reports, he seems, unwittingly, to have succumbed before the very giant propaganda machine operated by the preternatural monarch he had sought to expose.

Despite the demise of the Congo Question as a public issue, the questions it had raised about international ethics and colonial domination remained unanswered. The CRA officially disbanded on June 16, 1913, claiming its efforts had brought an end to atrocities, slavery, rubber taxation, restraint of trade, and the corruption of capitalist commerce and Christian civilization in the Congo.[141] But depredations in the Congo had not come to an end, nor would the memory of Leopold's reign of terror soon fade away. More than a half-century after the Belgian king's death, a group of Italian airmen were murdered at Kindu. "The reports said that a large crowd of Congolese who witnessed the massacre . . . dismembered the bodies and tossed the pieces in the Lualaba River. The Congolese were said to have mistaken the Italians for Belgians."[142] The fundamental issue—to which the Gothic discourse had been addressed—remained unresolved.[143] It was boldly stated in 1920 by E. D. Morel, still seeking after justice in colonial Africa: "The real problem is to insure that a material relationship, which is inevitable, shall not preclude just, humane, and enlightened government of tropical African peoples by European States."[144]

CAPITALISM AND GOTHICISM: SMALL AND PARK

How to infuse Europe's capitalist imperialism with a conscience remains a problem for the moral and social sciences to the present day precisely because of that system's institutionalized invulnerability to a humane orientation. The Gothic perspective permits one to see that, by first establishing the corporate firm as a legal and veritable person, and, then, by interposing this soulless and profit-devouring zombie between the capitalist and the human sources of their profits, the builders of capitalism had created the conditions for commerce with a cold-blooded face. Hence, unsecularized Gothic sociologists— the last of whom was Albion W. Small (1841–1926), Robert Park's colleague at the University of Chicago—would continue to seek victory over the devil-ridden corporate structure of the Occident by implanting the cross in the board of directors' conference rooms:

> In one aspect [Small would write in 1920], a corporation is a deathless superpersonal selfishness vested by the state with superpersonal powers. This monster is commissioned by the state to exercise its superpersonal powers within the society of plain persons. Thus we have unconsciously converted our property system from a protection of similar natural persons against one another, into a licensing system of supernatural persons. . . . The invention is not, and cannot come to, good, unless the society of plain persons can either endow corporations with souls, with souls' liabilities, or create and operate in its own interest an adequate super-personal enginery of corporations.[145]

Park himself came to regard the more egregious effects of imperialism as an inevitable incident in the history of modern Europe's attempt at world hegemonism. His subsequent writings on Africa—chiefly in the form of book reviews[146]—did not utilize Gothic imagery; rather, they emphasized one consequence of Europe's imposition of its civilization on the native races of Africa—the arousal of nativistic nationalism. "The race problem as it exists today," Park wrote in 1925, "is primarily a product of the expansion of international trade and the improvement of transportation and communication."[147] Gothicism, we should note, precisely because it was a part of the religious outlook that Europe had inherited from the Middle Ages (the epoch Park referred to as "'the age of faith'") and "from a society that was at once feudal and catholic," seemed no longer serviceable as a discourse for modernist criticism. "The trouble with Europe," Park pointed out in 1935, "is not merely that it is divided economically and politically, but that it has outgrown its traditional and religious faith."[148] In fact, he went on, echoing an earlier observation of Simmel,[149] "With the rise of modern industrial society, . . . and the incidental secularization of all the forms of life, the inherited religious beliefs are no longer in accord with the practices of commercial and plutocratic society."[150]

The nineteenth-century imperial quest for the domination of Africa had been guided by a supposition that Christianity and commerce were the conjoint moral basis of Europe's world-historical destiny—a supposition that had inspired black American as well as white European missions to Africa.[151] The horrors of the Congo affair had not undermined all faith in this innerworldly eschatology; rather, as Park observed, "The ultimate source of the disorders and discontents of . . . the modern world is the fact that Europe and the modern world have lost faith in themselves."[152] In the process, capitalism had been freed from the ethical constraints on the sin of greed that its Puritan originators had hoped to impose upon its agents and instrumentalities.[153] As Park came belatedly to see, the competition for a harvest of African souls had caused all too many missionaries to compromise their faith and to come to terms with the innerworldly and soulless devil-corporation. Missions, thus, could not restrain capitalist greed by preaching homiletics about Christian mercy. "Capitalism," Park concluded, "which is the ultimate product of a free and individualistic society, has many apologists, but no prophet."[154]

GOTHICIST SOCIOLOGY:
BETWEEN RELIGION AND POSITIVISM

Unwilling to adopt for himself the Marxist critical stance on capitalism—a disillusioned and disunited Europe, Park acknowledged in 1926, "is at a disadvantage in its struggle with a new, communist imperium, supported by a new and fanatical faith"[155]—Park was also unable to elaborate further upon the essentially Christian-Gothic critique of capitalist imperialism that had suffused his Congo essays. "Bolshevism," Park would observe in a critique of the writings of Karl Kautsky, "has followed fatally the path of Christianity. What was a movement of liberation in its origin has evolved an institution for the suppression of liberty."[156] With both Christianity and communism having evolved into their opposites, Park moved toward rejecting both religious perspectives and philosophical systems in favor of searching out "a knowledge that is instrumental and empirical, if not experimental; a knowledge that justifies itself by its ability to bring about the effects it predicts."[157] However, his pessimism and his idealism—each of which had been manifested in his Gothic essays on the Congo—and his ambivalence about how a sociologist should sort out his roles as citizen and scientist, participant and observer, led Park to a healthy skepticism about the then-emerging school of American positivism. Although he asserted, on the one hand, that "No social experiments, . . . have ever been based on a philosophy of history,"[158] Park also admitted that, "Personally I share the opinion of the Chinese philosopher, Lin Yutang, who thinks that there are certain things—among them personality and culture—that cannot profitably be described in mathematical terms."[159] Caught on the horns of this dilemma, Park called attention to how Werner Sombart's methodological orientation toward a theory of capitalism—a *magnum opus* that had taken the German scholar twenty-five years to complete—had shifted focus from either naturalistic description, historical explanation, or ethical prescription to a morally eviscerated game framework.[160]

In effect, Park's analysis of Sombart's *Die Drei Natiönalokonomien* announces the emergence of a sociology that had—like the corporation before it—been relieved of its soul. Sombart contrasts three modes of carrying out social scientific research: *die richtende*, i.e., judging, evaluating, and assessing what, under the circumstances that are present, ought to be done; *die ordnende*, i.e., discovering what is the case factually and rendering the findings in a scientific argot, that is, statistically; *die verstehende*, i.e., inquiring why such a state of affairs has come about. Although Sombart opts for a special variant of *die verstehende sociologie*—*Wesenwissenschaft*—that seems to combine what today we call functionalism with a form of game analysis, American sociology would opt in the main for *die ordnende* approach.

Although in the 1920s Park was under a certain amount of pressure from his colleagues at the University of Chicago[161] to acquiesce to the American variant of *die ordnende* approach—quantification, mathematical measurement, and statistical procedures (and though he even undertook a quantitative study of newspaper circulation as an index of urbanization,[162] perhaps to show his insistent colleagues that he knew how to calculate)—he could not subscribe to the positivists' demand for the reduction of the complexities of human conduct to numbers and equations—to the transmogrification of morals into methods. Nor could he wholly accept the variant of functionalism that he apprehended in Sombart's *Wesenwissenschaft*, likening the processes of life as moves in a chess game, i.e., guided by the impersonal rules of jurisdiction and juridicality that constrain conduct.[163] For Park, who had both learned from and been chastened by his Congo studies, morals would always be more than mathematics could measure or metaphysics meditate upon. As he told an audience in Beijing, China, in December 1932, while on one of his trips to escape from the deadening effects of the new sociology in America, "Men are so constituted that, as they become aware of other men,—that is, aware of them as persons,—they are disposed, just in the degree that this acquaintance becomes intimate and personal, to act toward them—as Kant's fundamental law of ethics prescribes—as if they were fellow creatures like themselves."[164] In effect, Park tells us that if we sociologists are to be faithful to the nature of our subject matter, we too must render our statements about human conduct, its causes, conditions, and effects, as if the actors are fellow humans, too. We must cease our support of the undead, insist that all of the qualities of humanity be attributed to each and every one of our "others," and act as if we are all brothers and sisters under the colors of our skin. But we must also tell others how such a point of view can become institutionalized.

APPENDIX:
SOCIOLOGIES OF BLACK AFRICA AFTER PARK

Despite the pioneering effort of George Washington Williams and the potential for further studies emanating from his and Park's essays on the Congo, few American sociologists took the peoples, societies, and cultures of Africa as topics for investigation in the eight decades following the publication of Park's analysis of the situation there. (Such is not the case, however, with French sociologists. Interest in the Congo and other parts of Africa are well represented in two works by Georges Balandier, *Daily Life in the Kingdom of the Kongo: From the Sixteenth to the Eighteenth Century*, trans. by Helen Weaver [New York: Pantheon, 1968]; and *The Sociology of Black Africa: Social Dynamics in Central Africa*, trans. by Douglas Garman [New York: Praeger, 1970]. The penetration of African cultures into the Americas has been analyzed by two works by Roger Bastide, *African Civilizations in the New World*, trans. by Peter Green [New York: Harper Torchbooks, 1971]; and *The African Religions of Brazil: Toward a Sociology of the Interpenetration of Cultures*, trans. by Helen Sebba [Baltimore: Johns Hopkins University Press, 1978]). Just as black American historians would have to struggle for years before the professional historians would recognize that peoples from Africa had a viable history worthy of investigation and critical awareness (cf. William Leo Hansberry, *Pillars in Ethiopian History*, African History Notebook, Vol. I, ed. by Joseph E. Harris [Washington, D.C.: Howard University Press, 1981]; *idem*, *Africa and*

Africans As Seen By Classical Writers, African History Notebook, Vol. II, ed. by Joseph E. Harris [Washington, D.C.: Howard University Press, 1981]; Lorraine A. Williams, ed., *Africa and the Afro-American Experience: Eight Essays* [Washington, D.C.: Howard University Press, 1981]; August Meier and Elliott Rudwick, *Black History and the Historical Profession, 1915–1980* [Urbana: University of Illinois Press, 1986]; Darlene Clark Hine, ed., *The State of Afro-American History: Past, Present and Future* [Baton Rouge: Louisiana State University Press, 1986]), so black American sociologists who turned to socio-historical, cultural, or political-economic studies of the supposedly "Dark Continent" found few fellow social scientists interested in the subject. Nevertheless, there remained among certain of the students of Robert Park a sufficient interest in the past and present of Africa and its relationship to Americans of African descent to encourage a modest number of empirical investigations, cultural analyses, and critical commentaries. Although it is beyond the scope of the present work to treat these works thoroughly, their place in continuity and discontinuity of Park's studies is worthy of notice.

The African writings of three of Park's African-American students— St. Clair Drake, E. Franklin Frazier, and Charles S. Johnson—stand out. However, none of them employed a Gothic perspective. Reflecting on Park's influence on sociological studies of race and ethnic relations, St. Clair Drake (1911–1990) appears to accept George Fredrickson's term "romantic racialism" (George M. Fredrickson, *The Black Image in the White Mind: The Debate on Afro-American Character and Destiny, 1817–1914* [New York: Harper and Row, 1971], p. 327) as an apt designation for Park's philosophical perspective, but also notes that by the 1930s Park had abandoned his biosocial ideas about hereditary racial temperament (St. Clair Drake, *Black Folk Here and There: An Essay in History and Anthropology* [Los Angeles: Center for Afro-American Studies, University of California, 1987], Vol. I, pp. 49–59). Drake's interest in Africa is enmeshed with his association with Ghana's first premier, Kwame Nkruma, with his critical attitude toward the latent lingering biologisms in Aime Cesaire's and Leopold Senghor's conceptualization of *Negritude* (St. Clair Drake, "Hide My Face? On Pan-Africanism and Negritude," in *Soon, One Morning: New Writing By American Negroes, 1940–1962*, ed. by Herbert Hill [New York: Alfred A. Knopf, 1963], pp. 77–105), his thoughtful support for study of as well as commitment to an Africa-conscious African American cultural identity (St. Clair Drake, "The Relations of the American and the African Negro in the Context of Pan-Africanism," Address before the Fourth Annual Meeting of the American Society of African Culture, New York City, June 23–24, 1961. *Summary Report*. Fourth Annual Meeting, American Society of African Culture, [New York: ASFC, 1961], pp. 4–12), and his shift from a strictly sociological perspective on Africa's place in world affairs (St. Clair Drake, "The International Implications of Race and Race Relations," *The Journal of Negro Education*, XX [Summer 1951], pp. 261–78; "The 'Colour Problem' in Britain: A Study in Social Definitions," *Sociological Review*, III, n.s. [December 1955], pp. 197–217) toward development of an interdisciplinary approach to the study of Africa and African Americans. In light of Drake's special interest in and service to Ghana, it is perhaps worth noting that a 1976 report on the development of sociology in that country fails even to mention his name or to cite his works and relies primarily on the influence of British social anthropology (Max Assimeng, "Sociology in Ghana," *Universitas: An Inter-Faculty Journal*, V:2, n.s., [May/November 1976], pp. 100–25).

In addition to his well-known studies of American Negro urban, familial, and middle class life, E. Franklin Frazier (1894–1962) extended, elaborated, and modified Park's idea of the race relations cycle, applying it to Africa and to the global situation. Ultimately recognizing that Park's famous cycle was only a logical and not a chronological formulation (E. Franklin Frazier, "The Theoretical Structure of Sociology and Social Research," *British Journal of Sociology* IV [December 1953], pp. 292–311), Frazier ruled out its unilinear and evolutionary character and reformulated its major features in relation to the demographic, economic, political, and social factors that would affect its dynamic (E. Franklin Frazier, "Racial Problems in World Society," in *Race Relations: Problems and Theory*, ed. by Jitsuichi Masuoka and Preston Valien [Chapel Hill: University of North Carolina Press, 1961], pp. 38–51). As Frazier envisioned the matter in 1957, the world cycle of race relations would culminate in three great "islands" of racially distinctive peoples: Euro-America, Asia, and Africa. Africa, with its multiplicity of peoples, nations, tribes, religions, languages, and post-colonial states would likely ground its continental unity on the commonality of race (E. Franklin Frazier, *Race and Culture Contacts in the Modern World* [New York: Alfred A. Knopf, 1957; Boston: Beacon Press, 1965], pp. 327–38). However, unlike Williams, DuBois, Washington, Park, and Drake, Frazier believed that neither the black American masses nor the African-American intellectuals would have anything significant to give to the newly developing post-colonial ethnonational or racial situation in Africa. Convinced that American Negroes have "never been taken seriously," "have never been free, physically or psychologically," and that for "the great masses of Negroes the fact of their origin has been regarded as a curse," Frazier believed that impoverished, undereducated, demoralized, and politically impotent black Americans could offer neither capital, skills, nor leadership to the self-determining nations of the new Africa. Moreover, Frazier, who had just completed a scathing indictment of the life styles of the black middle classes in the United States (E. Franklin Frazier, *Black Bourgeoisie: The Rise of a New Middle Class in the United States* [Glencoe: The Free Press and Falcon's Wing Press, 1957]), was even more pessimistic about the role that American Negro professionals and intellectuals might play in the spiritual and cultural invigoration of Africa: "Their general outlook is dominated by the provincial and spurious values of the new Negro middle classes. They live in a world of make believe and reject identification with the cultural traditions of American Negroes as well as with their African origin. They seek acceptance by white Americans at the price of losing all their racial and cultural identity and of being swallowed up in white America. Their attitude towards the future is that of the gladiators and slaves in the Roman arena, who cried, 'Hail, Caesar, we who are about to die salute you.'" (E. Franklin Frazier, "What Can the American Negro Contribute to the Social Development of Africa?" in John W. Davis, ed., *Africa Seen By American Negro Scholars*, a special edition of *Presence Africaine* originally published in Dijon, France, in 1958 [New York: American Society of African Culture, 1963], pp. 263–78). For Frazier, the socio-cultural doom of the black American had been sealed by the special effects of Park's race relations cycle—contact, competition, accommodation, assimilation—on their lives and situation. "On the other hand," he concluded, "the African has a future in this world and has a place in shaping a new world as an African."

Whereas Park had concentrated his critical attack on the situation in the Congo, black Americans usually concentrated their interests on Liberia, the republic that had been established by manumitted slaves from America in 1821. By the 1930s, however, Liberia had proved to be something of an embarrassment to those blacks who had hoped that an enlightened American-bred Americo-Liberian elite would shine a beacon of light on colonial-dominated Africa—governing justly, admitting the aborigines into full political and economic equality, and eschewing the debilitating effects that European imperialism had imposed on the Congo and other colonies below the Sahara. In 1933 W. E. B. DuBois—who in 1897 had corresponded with Paul Hagemans, Belgium's consul general in Philadelphia, to inquire whether the emigration of American Negroes to the Congo Free State was feasible and desirable (W. E. B. DuBois, "On Migration to Africa [1897]," in *idem, Against Racism: Unpublished Essays, Papers, Addresses, 1887–1961*, ed. by Herbert Aptheker [Amherst: University of Massachusetts Press, 1985], pp. 43–49)—published an account of Liberia's woeful world debt situation, its unsuccessful attempts to obtain foreign loans, and its ultimate exploitation, begun in 1926, by the Firestone rubber company and its patron, the United States of America. Labor was supplied for Firestone's ventures through contracts made with various tribal chiefs. When this only seemingly voluntary labor force became scarce, the Liberian government allegedly entered into the slave trade to meet the company's demands, in turn engendering a series of reverses: intervention by the League of Nations, an American proposal that the League appoint an "adviser" to manage Liberia's affairs, the repudiation of the Firestone Loan, and an American attempt to restore Firestone's preëminent position in the Liberian economy. DuBois's final question on the Liberian matter echoes Park's critical stance toward Leopold II's capitalist exploitation of central Africa: "Are we starting the United States Army toward Liberia to guarantee the Firestone Company's profits in a falling rubber market or smash another Haiti in the attempt?" (W. E. B. DuBois, "Liberia, The League and the United States," *Foreign Affairs* [July 1933]; reprint, in Davis, ed., op. cit., pp. 329–44).

Robert Park's student, Charles S. Johnson (1893–1956) undertook a full-scale study of the Liberian situation in 1930 and revised it in 1948. In the course of his investigation, Johnson discovered the same kinds of ruthless exploitation, deprivations of land, and cruel tortures that Park and the Congo Reform Association had discovered in Leopold's Congo. Like Williams and DuBois, Johnson believed that a resolution of the dilemma arising out of Liberia's need for outside aid and its understandable reluctance to accept white instruction or controls could be achieved by instituting a system of "native administrators trained in other colonies, or through American blacks who can share their outlook and concern for continued autonomy." For Johnson, America had more than a political, economic, or historical interest in Liberia. America, in effect, was or ought to be the nemesis of the terrible Gothic imperialism that had turned Liberia's once promised land into a bitter Canaan. "America," he wrote, "cannot escape its spiritual obligations to these exiles from its own institutions, even though their descendants have bowed down before strange idols in a Canaan stripped of illusions." (Charles S. Johnson, *Bitter Canaan: The Story of the Negro Republic* [New Brunswick, N.J.: Transaction Books, 1987], p. 226). The bitterness of Liberia's "Canaan" has continued to the present day. In March 1988, the present author lectured in Monrovia and was invited to introduce a museum exhibit of, and describe the cultural elements that made up, the Afro-Americans' artistic works of the "Harlem Renaissance" of the 1920s. It is worthy of note that the greatest interest in the subject that was brought to my attention came from the French cultural affairs officer, Paris of the same era having been a haven for black American intellectuals, dancers, and musicians. Much of the middle class element of the Americo-Liberian population had fled the country in the wake of Samuel K. Doe's coup a few years earlier. In 1990 a revolt against Doe's regime and the Krahn and Mandingo tribes resulted in massacres carried out by governmental troops against the peoples of the Gio and Mano tribes and in similar atrocities by the forces of Charles Taylor and Prince Johnson, the respective—and opposed—leaders of the two rebel groups. President Doe was eventually killed, and, at the time of present writing, an international group of African states is attempting to restore order in Liberia and to resolve the separate and opposed claims of the rival rebels, Taylor and Johnson.

Accommodations to Evil

The Conflict and Fusion of Race, Religion, and Culture in Park's America

INTRODUCTION

Park's Gothic perspective on Leopold II's depredations in the Congo may be read, in a larger sense, as part of a more general transition in Occidental socio-cultural thought—a movement away from medieval and toward modern conceptions of evil. The medieval conception—the last literary stand of which was presented in the era's Gothic fiction—held that evil was the antithesis of all that is good, that it encompassed all that is morally depraved, thoroughly bad, unambiguously wicked, and plainly vicious. Modern social scientific conceptions have eviscerated this conception,[1] reducing it to references to "deviance," or to that which causes discomfort, pain, unpleasantness, offense, harm, and disagreeableness. The evil recognized in modernity is less a phenomenon than a condition; its personification is factored, deconstructed, decentered, and decomposed.[2] And, even when it is personified, it is relieved of its original sense of horror, terror, and condemnation. Hence, to capture the true wickedness of Adolf Eichmann's contribution to the Holocaust, Hannah Arendt found it necessary to coin the phrase, "banality of evil,"[3] not only linking the Nazi horrors to a thoroughgoing bureaucratization of civil life and society, but also, curiously, intending "to counteract a culturally and politically harmful demonization of Hitlerism."[4] Park seems to have intended the opposite—i.e., to demonize Leopold's atrocities in order not merely to shock the conscience of the world but to characterize modern imperialism.

In light of the fact that most modernists have supposed that the concomitant rise of capitalism, science, and bourgeois civilization rendered the medieval conception of evil obsolete, it is possible to locate Park's Congo essays, as well as his subsequent studies of black life and labor in Winston-Salem, North Carolina, and Tuskegee, Alabama, as significant signposts on the road to social science's transvaluation and deconstruction of wickedness. Insofar as modernity has been a collaborator with the shift of culpability for all that happened to hurt humanity, or select portions thereof, first from a personified devil to an anthropomorphized satanic surrogate, and, following that, to a depersonalized complex of institutionalized societal elements, Park's conception of Leopold II as "a king in business" who extracts "blood money from the Congo" and conducts his worldly monarchy in the manner of a terrifying vampire can be said to combine pre-modern with modern orientations: the anthropomorphosis of evil is brought together with the bureaucratization of the evil deeds. Before what was once supposed to be preternatural in origin could be thoroughly banalized, it had first to be given a human face.

However, there is an even more complex vision of morality's countenance in Park's early sociology. Protestantism—that genitor of modernity's spirit—is conceived as two-faced. Its positive persona is revealed when one examines Park's studies of black communities in the post-Redemptionist South. In effect, Park showed that the Protestant ethic—which had been suborned, desublimated, and exploited by Leopold II to overwhelm central Africa's pre-capitalist economy and undermine the traditional moral basis of Congolese society—could also be benevolent. In the hands of a true practical ethicist it could introduce the sons and daughters of African-American slaves to values, attitudes, habits, and ways of life that would facilitate both their material success and their moral development in a not yet fully industrialized America. In the philosophy and praxis of Booker T. Washington, Park found the positive face of a Janus-headed Western civilization—a Protestantism that was both ethical and practical, that could produce a countryside of pastoral production and a city of racial peace.

Leopold II personified the deviltry in development for Park; but, in stunning contrast, he regarded Booker T. Washington as the principal representative of the practical goodness that could flow out from the same religious fount. As Park put it, Washington, "whom I knew longer and from whom I learned more than from any of my teachers," shared his own perception that "the problem of the American Negro was merely an aspect or a phase of the native problem in Africa; . . . a problem which, like slavery, had arisen as an incident in an historical process and as a phase of the natural history of civilization." The historical process might proceed inevitably and as a "natural" matter of course—for Park, however, it moved like a locomotive down the track of a merciless progress, wiping out local, traditional, and folk cultures, absorbing people into classes, masses, and individuations, and, at the same time, piling up its discarded human junk along the side.[5] Thus, the civilizational process was punctuated and interrupted by social problems. For Park, it was Booker T. Washington, rather than William Graham Sumner (whose social philosophy Park openly admired[6]), who taught him "how deep rooted in human history and human nature social institutions were, and how difficult, if not impossible it was, to make fundamental changes in them by mere legislation or by legal artifice of any sort."[7] To Park and Washington, the move into civilization was conditioned by human nature.

Washington seemed to approach[8] the Negro question from the vantage point of a unique African-American variant of human nature, rather than as a problem whose solution depended on changes in public policy or political administration. As such, the race problem could be resolved by the methods and programs that chastened and socialized that nature. A practical Protestantism seemed most appropriate to bring the conduct of the progeny of slaves into alignment with a society whose spirit was increasingly capitalistic.

MORAVIAN MORALS AND RACIAL ACCOMMODATION IN EARLY AMERICA

"Special circumstances have, perhaps, contributed to put the two races in Winston-Salem on terms of mutual good will," wrote Park in his brief but careful study of racial accommodation in the North Carolina town he called "a city of racial peace."[9] Written one year after the first essay of his series on the Congo and eight years before his even more comprehensive analysis of the bi-racial caste and class stratification that prevailed among blacks in the same area,[10] Park's first Winston-Salem study designates as one of the more important "special circumstances" that contributed to the town's racially tolerant character the fact that "Salem, founded in 1752, is an old Moravian settlement."[11] Thus did Park, in synchronization with the major German scholarship of his day[12]—which he was no doubt familiar with from his studies in Berlin—attribute peaceful progress, social development, and economic advance to the effects of one of the sects preaching a variant of the Protestant ethic. "Salem," Park went on, "is one of those many communities that the missionary enterprise of Count Zinzindorf [sic] and his followers have scattered over the earth, in which thrift and industry have united with pure religion to give the world a true example of the 'Simple Life.'"[13]

The debate over the innerworldly effects of the Protestant Reformation constituted a principal element of late nineteenth-century German social science. In addition to disagreeing over the particulars of what would later come to be called the "Weber thesis," i.e., the thesis emphasizing Protestantism's contribution to the development of a capitalistic spirit,[14] the major German philosophers, economists, sociologists, and theologians disagreed over whether and to what extent the respective casuistries of Lutheranism and Calvinism affected economic, social, and political developments in Europe and America. Max Weber (1864–1920) placed his emphasis on the *inner-*

weltliche Askese and the emotional pietism found in such Protestant denominations as the Quakers and the Baptists, and he founded his conception of a Protestant ethic on an ideal-typification of the innerworldly casuistries of Calvinism, Puritanism, Pietism, Methodism, and the beliefs and practices of the Anabaptist sects.[15] Wilhelm Dilthey (1833–1911), on the other hand, credited Martin Luther and Ullrich Zwingli, and more especially the "Germanic" personalities that each epitomized, with forging the theological weaponry whereby the Catholic church hierarchy's "demonic mechanism preventing the free access of the soul to God" might be overcome, and he insisted that Lutheranism had been the first to elevate everyday occupations to their place in God's structure of "callings."[16] Georg Simmel (1858–1918), the one German sociologist with whom Park had had a direct relationship, came closer to recognizing the declining innerworldly effectiveness of an ascetic Christianity that—with its conceptions of the "salvation of the soul and the kingdom of God . . . [providing] an offer of absolute value for the masses . . . [and giving them] a definite goal beyond the meaninglessness of an individuated and fragmentary life"—at one time had provided "the absolute meaning to life." That meaning, Simmel went on to observe, "was needed after life itself had been lost through its multiplicities and formalities in a labyrinth of means and relativities." However, Simmel pointed out, "in recent centuries Christianity [had] lost its appeal to and power over innumerable people."[17] Its residue remained, nevertheless, as Christianity's bequest to modernity.

For Park, it was the religious ideas of the original Moravians—(the eighteenth-century Oxford Methodist Benjamin Ingham likened their first missionaries to the American colonies to "Primitive Christians," claiming they had retained "the Faith, Practice, and Discipline delivered by the Apostles" and lived by the precepts of "perfect Love and Peace"[18])—that had left their imprint on the moral lives and industrial habits of the blacks of Winston-Salem. In so doing, he believed, this pietistic sect had contributed significantly not only to the growth of "one of the most prosperous manufacturing towns in the South,"[19] but also and more important to the development of an accommodative resolution of the race question.

Park did not elaborate on the precise relationship of the Moravian praxis to socioeconomic progress in race relations, but a brief analysis of that sect's mission in America is helpful in understanding how Park had come to his perspective on the matter. Park was not alone in recognizing the significance of the Moravians for modern economic developments. Moravians are frequently alluded to by Max Weber in his analysis of the worldly implications of the Protestant ethic. Weber noted that, at first, much of Pietism retained its connections with Protestant orthodoxy, and "[o]nly the faction dominated by Zinzendorff, and affected by lingering Hussite and Calvinistic influences within the Moravian brotherhood, was forced, like Methodism against its will, to form a peculiar sort of sect."[20] In the form associated with its principal exponent, the Saxon nobleman, Nicholaus Ludwig, Count von Zinzendorff

(1700–1760), pietistic Moravianism "led away from the doctrine of predestination."[21] Nevertheless, Weber is at pains to point out that "Zinzendorff's conception of his own religious position, even though it vacillated in the face of attacks from orthodoxy, tended generally toward the instrumental idea." Furthermore, although Weber characterizes Zinzendorff as a "remarkable religious dilettante," he also observes that the Saxon nobleman had "followed the Puritans in expressing to John Wesley the opinion that even though a man himself could not, others could know his state of grace by his conduct."[22] Combining an anti-rational with an emotional religious expressiveness, Weber showed that Zinzendorff and his followers had decreed a "connection between morality and the forgiveness of sins . . . [that] is part . . . of his fundamentally eudaemonistic ideal of having men experience eternal bliss (he calls it happiness) emotionally in the present. . . ."[23] However, as Weber also emphasizes, "the practical rationalization of life from the standpoint of utility was very essential to Zinzendorff's philosophy."[24]

Although it extolled the pious sincerity that led to apostolic poverty and encouraged a selfless missionary endeavor to all those who felt the call to that vocation—and seemed thereby to lead its followers away from an individualistic quest for material gains—the Moravian Brotherhood was nonetheless not only "a great missionary centre, [but also] at the same time a business enterprise."[25] Originally, its spirit of business enterprise had found expression in Zinzendorff's advocacy of a communitarianism conditioned by noblesse oblige. The Moravians' great interest in missions to the unsaved aborigines and Afro-Americans of the New World represented one significant variant in the benevolent but seigneurial point of view that described its leader's basic socioeconomic perspective. Zinzendorff's "whole religious attitude," Weber noted, "is influenced by nothing more strongly than the fact that he was a Count with an outlook fundamentally feudal."[26] Zinzendorff looked upon work as that for which life should be lived—"One does not only work in order to live, but one lives for the sake of one's work, and if there is no more work to do one suffers or goes to sleep,"[27] he once said.

THE MORAVIAN MISSION TO AMERICA

It is pertinent to a more complete understanding of Park's emphasis on the practical ethics espoused by the Moravians to point out that in the era that followed the emancipation of America's black slaves it was not only the descendants of Count Zinzendorff's Herrnhutterites who worried that the suddenly masterless freedmen and women would leave off of their labors and sink into somnolent sloth.[28] Zinzendorff had subscribed to the doctrine that the blacks' bondage was the legacy of God's curse on Ham,[29] and, as such, it neither prohibited Moravians from owning slaves nor imposed upon them a religious commitment to abolitionism. To Zinzendorff, slavery was a God-ordained system of compulsory labor.[30] In the nineteenth century, America's first sociologists—i.e., the Southern Comteans Henry Hughes (1829–1862), George Fitzhugh (1806–1881), George Frederick Holmes (1820–1897), and Joseph Le Conte (1823–1901)—had justified the Southern system of slavery in part by asserting that it had institutionalized and secularized the Christian obligation of stewardship over the less-than-civilized blacks, who had not yet absorbed the most elementary lesson of the Protestant outlook on inner-worldly life, viz., in Hughes's words, that "To consume and not to produce, either directly or remotely, is wrong. Every class of society has its economic duty. If it does not do it; if it violates its duty; that is criminal."[31]

When the ratification of the Thirteenth Amendment to the Constitution ended legalized slavery in America, these pro-slavery sociologists worried over and sought various means to assure the industrializing society that the emancipated blacks would still comply with the larger society's demands for stewardship over their abject labor power. George Fitzhugh, certain that the freedmen and women did not possess the social and cultural qualifications for participating in a *laissez-faire* economy, proposed that Congress legislate a vast system of paternalistic but regulatory laws that would at one and the same time coerce African Americans to remain employed in America's menial and unskilled job sector, provide for their care, feeding, health, and maintenance in old age, and insure that they would not enter into the competitive struggle for skilled occupations, the learned professions, or the seats of economic, political, or social power that he believed ought to be reserved permanently for white males.[32] By 1882, George Frederick Holmes had become convinced that "the passion for work, and the exaggerated commendation of it," were peculiar to modern times in the Occident. It was in fact confined to the char-acterology of white men, who, fired by a "lust of gain, the greed of wealth, [and] the jealous and feverish craving for the means of commanding luxury and power," had produced in themselves "a furious earnestness of work. . . ." By contrast, he argued, "the Transmutation of slavery into what has been humourously [sic] termed Free Labour has been a very slow, very gradual, and very agitated process."[33] Seeking a peaceful conclusion to that agitation, and convinced that unsupervised black workers would not labor efficiently or productively, and that an endogamous African-American people would breed itself into biological extinction, Joseph Le Conte proposed that a means be found to mate blacks with what he called the "lesser whites" so that a new and more progressive labor force would be available for a rapidly mechanizing America.[34]

In postwar North Carolina, where, four decades later, Park would claim to have found a Moravian-inspired situation of interracial peace and progress, the fears about the free Negro matched those found elsewhere; an observer of the situation there wrote to Thaddeus Stevens, the Radical Republican champion of the blacks' civil rights, that in that state the freedman "was sneered at by all and informed daily yes hourly that he is incompetent to care for himself—that his race is now doomed to perish from off the face of the Earth—that he will not work—that he is a thief by nature[,] that he lies more Easily and naturally than an honest man breathes."[35]

Despite the fact that from 1861 to 1890 the American Missionary Association (AMA) engaged in a comprehensive program of black education aimed at preparing emancipated Negroes for full and equal citizenship in the United States—including the establishment of universities designed to matriculate Afro-American doctors, pharmacists, lawyers, ministers, teachers, bookkeepers, businessmen, civil servants, and politicians, as well as homemakers, farmers, and ordinary workers—a combination of unfortunate events and circumstances, not the least of which was the Ku Klux Klan's violent and incendiary opposition to their efforts,[36] led to that movement's decline in favor of Booker T. Washington's far more modest and less demanding program. It was to the latter educator's idea—steeped in a racially restrictive vision of the economic advancement open to blacks inspired by the Protestant ethic—that Park both subscribed and seemed to see in progress at Winston-Salem.

In his Atlanta Exposition address of 1895, Washington, a pious Protestant (but not a Moravian) had in effect adapted the noblesse oblige of Count Zinzendorff's attitudes toward practical life to his own philosophy of race and labor.[37] Unlike the AMA's civil rights advocates, who had tried to build up an educational program equal to that available to white students, or W. E. B. DuBois, who had demanded immediate enforcement of all of the provisions of the postwar Constitutional amendments, Washington cautioned his fellow black Americans not to "permit our grievances to overshadow our opportunities," and he prophesied that "we shall prosper in proportion as we learn to dignify and glorify common labour and put brains and skill into the common occupations of life; shall prosper in proportion as we learn to draw the line between the superficial and the substantial, the ornamental gewgaws of life and the useful."[38]

One year after Park had visited and reported on Winston-Salem, Washington edited a volume of autobiographical essays written by graduates of his Tuskegee Normal and Industrial Institute in Alabama. Although he included pieces by a college president, a country school principal, a lawyer, a school treasurer, and a druggist, he also saw to it that *Tuskegee and Its People* would be seen to have matriculated a shoemaker, a blacksmith, a wheelwright, a carpenter, a farmer, a teacher of cooking, and a Sunday School instructor.[39] In his contribution to this anthology, Roscoe Conkling Bruce, director of Tuskegee's Academic Department, presented a thesis relating agricultural and mechanical training to both moral uplift and a spirit of industry that is reminiscent of Moravian casuistry and praxis: "The Negro needs industrial training in eminent degree, because the capacity for continuous labor is a requisite of civilized living; because, indeed, the very first step in social advance must be economic; because the industrial monopoly with which slavery encompassed black men has fallen shattered before the trumpet-blast of white labor and economic competition; and finally, because *no instrument of moral education is more effective upon the mass of mankind than cheerful and intelligent work.*"[40]

What most impressed Park upon his investigation of the black situation in Winston-Salem was the Slater Industrial and State Normal School for Negroes, begun by S. G. Atkins, a teacher who had pioneered the establishment of "Columbia Heights," the black quarter of the city in 1891.[41] Park—who would later recall that he had come to work for Booker T. Washington after becoming convinced that "if there was any solution of the Congo problem it would probably be some form of education" and after the black educator had invited him to see Tuskegee rather than investigate the industrial school for natives established at Lovedale in South Africa[42]—placed considerable emphasis on the fact that the white Moravians of Winston-Salem had "given Professor Atkins from the outset, not only material aid, but what is even more important, their counsel and continued moral support."[43] Here was the kind of Christian spirit that Park and Washington most admired.

The Moravian settlement at Winston-Salem in fact constituted one of the few successful examples of that sect's missionary endeavor in America. Its origins date back to 1735, when Augustus Gottlieb Spangenberg (1704–1792) and twenty-four German-speaking Moravians, seeking to re-invigorate the Hussite order *Unitas Fratrum* and extend its efforts out from Count Zinzendorff's center at Herrnhut in Saxony to the American colonies, joined with a group of Anglican ministers, including John and Charles Wesley, to spread the gospel to the aborigines of James Oglethorpe's Trusteeship, Georgia.[44] However, the interests of the Anglican Society for the Propagation of the Gospel in London and those of the Saxony-based Herrnhutters were not the same, and, in addition, each had its difficulties with the Georgia Trustees, the several Indian tribes in the area, and the Anglo-Spanish-French rivalry that characterized the diplomatic and military situation in eighteenth-century North America. Moreover, as staunch opponents of armed aggression, the Moravians constituted a troubling and anomalous element to all of the contenders in the struggle for domination of the North Atlantic American settlements. Within five years the Moravian mission to Georgia had failed; in 1740 the Herrnhutters shifted their center of activities to Pennsylvania and established missions in the colony at Nazareth and Bethlehem. From there, the followers of Count Zinzendorff sent the mission that eventually would settle Winston-Salem.[45]

Despite their origins in Hussite pietism,[46] the Moravians, as Ernst Troeltsch pointed out, "felt a closer affinity with Calvinism than with Lutheranism."[47] And, Troeltsch went on to observe, their Calvinistic tendencies were "strengthened by the fact that . . . the community . . . became limited essentially to active members who were engaged in trade, and also by the fact of the necessity of meeting their own expenses, particularly those connected with their mission work. . . ."[48] However, as Weber observed, economic enterprises that arise from a new religious orientation might still be carried on in a traditionalist fashion.[49] In the case of the Hernhutterite settlements in North America, Count Zinzendorff, who for three years (1740–1743) came to lead the Moravian congregations at Bethlehem, sought nothing less than to foster not only an extension of his program of economic communalism to America, but also to establish an ecumenical union of Pennsylvania's several Protestant denominations under his own spiritual guidance. His efforts came to nothing. After 1748—despite the Saxon nobleman's successful mission to England where, in 1749, he obtained formal parliamentary recognition for the *Unitas Fratrum* as an ancient Protestant Episcopal church—the American Moravians went their own separate way.

Among the issues that made for disharmony in and between the several post-Reformation sects contending for hegemonic jurisdiction over Protestant American Christendom, perhaps none seemed to arouse as much controversy as the religious truth supposedly embodied in the Moravian semicommunistic economic formations. At Nazareth and Bethlehem their communities boasted more than thirty cooperatively administered industries and several communal farms; while their practice of reinvestment of the surplus in missionary expansion in America and Europe aroused the resentment of their competitors in soul saving.[50] As missionaries to the Indians and, to a lesser extent, to black Americans, the Moravians combined preaching a pietistic gospel with practical training in handicraft, manual skills, trade, and commerce.[51] Their version of the Protestant ethic hoped to develop a spirit of collective enterprise within communities that would remain endogamous and keep themselves spiritually isolated from the non-Moravians with whom they necessarily would have to engage in trade and commerce.

CONTRADICTIONS AND DILEMMAS IN AMERICA'S PROTESTANT HERITAGE

The Moravian-influenced "city of racial peace" that Robert Park studied less than five years after he had designated General von Moltke's reorganized German army as "the most perfect military organization in the world"[52] in effect highlights the contradictory legacies that descended on America from the Reformation in Germany. On the one side is an anti-democratic orientation that, more than forty years after Park had called attention to Germany's developing war machine, would lead Harvard University's foremost sociologist, Talcott Parsons, to warn that Americans of "Lutheran background . . . are apt to be partial to a political authoritarianism and old-fashioned legitimist

conservatism"[53]; on the other is the spiritually benevolent and materially progressive heritage of peace, prosperity, and hard work that such pietistic sects as
the Moravians sought to implant among Indians and Afro-Americans in the
colonial settlements along the Atlantic coast and in the interior of North
America.

Although he would become jaded about the relationship of civilization to
progress and would learn to be suspicious of missionaries and other "do-
gooders" largely because of his experiences with the Congo Reform
Association, Park never divested himself entirely of his admiration for the
pietistic missionary spirit and its effects on the downtrodden peoples of the
world: "What the missionary activity inevitably does accomplish," Park
observed in 1924, "whether it expressly wills to do so or not, is to bring the
world measurably within the limits of a single moral universe."[54] When, in
1909, Booker T. Washington published under his own name the two-volume
history of the Negro that he had in fact co-authored with Park, the authors in
effect pointed to the single moral universe that had found expression in a
"number of quiet, clean, thrifty little Negro communities that are growing up
everywhere in the South at the present day." Among these, they singled out
Winston-Salem where "the coloured people . . . have . . . prospered greatly."
Washington/Park gave credit for this advancement "in a large part to the
assistance and encouragement the coloured people have received from the
white people of that city, particularly from the descendants of the Moravians
of Salem."[55]

The theology of spiritually enforced peace and communal enterprise that
had been both preached and practiced by the original followers of Count
Zinzendorff in America gradually became compromised or eroded in the face
of the realities of the American situation. Caught up in the deadly European
competition for colonial hegemony in the Americas, attempting to remain
neutral in the wars among the several Indian tribes, and refusing to volunteer
for military service in the American Revolution, the Moravians earned the distrust and disapproval of virtually all parties to these struggles. Although the
armed forces of the Cherokee and Catawba tribes, having been permitted in
1758 to march unmolested through the Herrnhutter settlement at Bethabara—
a town on the 100,000-acre Wachovia Tract, purchased by the Moravians in
1753 and named in honor of Count Zinzendorff's estate in the Wauchau
Valley—praised "the Dutch Fort, where there are good people and much
bread,"[56] the pledge to non-violence to which the Moravian missionaries
bound their Indian converts put the latter at a distinct military disadvantage in
their wars with other tribes.[57] Later, when Moravians in Pennsylvania resisted
enrollment in General Washington's revolutionary army, the Brethren earned
the enmity of Benjamin Franklin;[58] the Wachovians further aroused the envy
and contempt of their independence-minded neighbors when they agreed to
pay a triple tax in lieu of taking up arms against the British.[59]

During the course of the nineteenth century, however, their opposition to military service began to erode. By the time of the Civil War, the North Carolina epigoni of Count Zinzendorff's preachments of peaceful conduct had become staunch supporters of the Confederacy. Never in fact having been unalloyed pacifists—during the French and Indian War, the Wachovian Brethren had been willing to arm themselves in self-defense against what they called "murdering Indians"—they had willingly joined the North Carolina county regiment after 1831.[60] Thirty years later, not only did the Salem congregation musical ensemble become "the regimental band of the 26th North Carolina Infantry, C.S.A . . ., "[61] but also "dozens of young men marched out of Salem to fight for the Confederacy, while four hundred miles to the north their Brethren in Bethlehem donned blue and marched out to meet them."[62]

Opposition to taking part in offensive wars was not the only aspect of the Moravian creed that fell in the wake of the American experience. During the "Great Awakening" of the 1740s, the doctrines preached by Count Zinzendorff himself, as well as those espoused by his disciples in America, were subjected to a severe assault by that religious movement's principal leaders, Samuel Finley and Gilbert Tennent. Tennent accused the Moravians of "antinomianism," berated them for bringing in "damnable heresies"—among which the most serious seemed to be "to pretend to *know* certainly who are *gracious*" and thus "to assume an incommunicable Prerogative of God"—and, perhaps most important, belittled their claim of unworldliness, i.e., the Moravians' communal economism. Tennent likened the Moravian practice of holding goods in common to that of the "begging Friars among the Papists," who, he pointed out, also gave up "all their worldly goods." He went so far as to credit Judas, the betrayer of Jesus, with a comparable practice.[63] In attacking their egalitarian basis for community life, Tennent and other Great Awakening preachers not only checked the excesses of enthusiasm so dear to the Pietists, but also set the terms for refusing to countenance a Christian American social organization built around Zinzendorff's brand of seigneurial socialism and the collective ownership of property.

By 1905, the year Park came to survey Winston-Salem, the Moravian mission to America had become, in Sydney Ahlstrom's words, "a relatively static movement . . ." Its membership had grown but slowly, "numbering about 3,000 in 1775, 8,275 in 1858, [and had only risen to] about 20,000 in 1895 . . ."[64] Its errand into the wilderness of America's aborigines had not been able to keep up with the white settlers' steady dispossession of the Indians' lands,[65] or with the vigorous competition mounted against its mission to the brown-skinned "heathen"—especially to the Cherokee tribe and its subdivisions[66]—by the more aggressive Methodist and Baptist denominations; its potential for regional domination of Virginia and the Carolinas had been brought to a halt by synodical factionalism;[67] and its anti-military and anti-capitalist philosophies had all but disappeared.[68]

Those who have assessed what survived of its original program describe a legacy wherein agricultural techniques, mechanical innovations, and ritualistic practices became attenuated from their spiritual origins. Thus, according to Robert Henry Billigmeier, "One of the most enduring heritages . . . [Moravians] left was in the tradition of their husbandry: the careful choice of farm land, the preservation of soil through crop rotation, use of meadowland, careful exploitation of woodlands, deep ploughing, and the replenishing of fertility by the careful spreading of animal manure."[69] Robert Calhoun observed, "Although communalism ceased in the early 19th century and Moravians reluctantly became a Protestant denomination, the churches in North Carolina preserve a wide range of rituals and cultural observances dating to Zinzendorff's practices in Moravia—among them the arrangement of the cemetery into four separate 'choirs' for men and women, married and unmarried, using identical flat grave markers; an Easter sunrise service held in the old Salem burial ground every year since 1772; lively traditions in Christmas cooking and decorating; and an important musical heritage of brass music and hymnology."[70] As Park and Washington saw the matter, however, what had survived after more than a century-and-a-half of Moravian settlement in America was an ethically rooted, bi-racial, capitalist spirit.

Park claimed that "[o]ne of the motives which led to . . . [Winston-Salem's] establishment was the [Moravians'] desire to carry Christianity to the Indians and negroes."[71] Indeed, not only was Park informed that the first person baptized in eighteenth-century Salem had been a slave,[72] but he and Washington later would call attention to the fact that among the figures represented in a painting of eighteen of the United Brethren's first converts to Christianity at Bethlehem, Pennsylvania, "are Johannes, a Negro of South Carolina, and Jupiter, a Negro from New York."[73] Nevertheless, Park observed that "comparatively few negroes have been taken into the [Moravian] church," but at the same time, "a large number of negro children, who have subsequently joined other denominations, have been educated in the Moravian Sunday schools."[74] The Moravian spiritual program emphasized the moment of conversion, its songs put its stamp of disapproval on the miser, the braggart, the beggar, and the clown,[75] but its practice was to discourage racial integration.

WINSTON-SALEM AND
THE CONCEPT OF ACCOMMODATION

Park conceived Winston-Salem as the community where "to a greater degree, perhaps, than in any other city in the South, that solution of the negro problem has been taken to heart, that Mr. [Booker T.] Washington first publicly urged upon a southern audience of whites and blacks ten years ago at the Atlanta Exposition."[76] Washington's solution became in Park's reconceptualization of it the bi-racial, i.e., segregated, organization of the community. In fact, bi-racialism, without being designated as such, had been consistent with Herrnhutter attitudes toward the enslaved Africans as well as the Indians in the eighteenth-century Southern colonies. Count Zinzendorff not only subscribed to the belief in a rigidly structured universe, and a "Great Chain of Being" on which God had designated a niche for every person, but also to a God-ordained racial-caste hierarchy in which blacks occupied a place lower than whites.

The questions of the relationship of conversion to manumission and to whether blacks (or Indians) should be owned by Moravians and compelled to labor for them had been sources of occasional anxiety in the North Carolina communities established by the disciples of Count Zinzendorff. Although the Southern Herrnhutters could ill afford to purchase slaves, a few had been brought to the Wachovian Tract by pious migrants from Bethlehem. A few years later, in spite of their apprehension that the "heathen" traditions of the African slaves would likely corrupt the morals of their white masters, the devout conduct of "Sam," a slave whom they had purchased for £120 and converted in 1771—as well as a growing need for menial laborers—led the leaders of the communal *Oekonomy* to purchase four more blacks.[77]

However, the slavery question would eventually undermine the Moravian mission to the Indians, compromise their commitment to neutrality in wartime, and bring about the death of one of their own missionaries. Having never opposed the practice of slavery that was carried out in sight and knowledge of their mission to the Cherokee Nation, the Moravians were unable to respond effectively to the rise of an anti-slavery element within that Indian tribe. When, after the outbreak of the Civil War, the abolitionist Keetowah Society (commonly called the "Pins" or "Pin Indians" because of the crossed pins they wore) opposed the pro-slavery elements among their fellow Cherokees who wished to ally with the Southern Confederacy, the Moravians were caught off guard. Their missionary, Sam Ward, although married to a Cherokee, aroused the enmity of the "Pins" when he brought his slaves to the mission school at New Spring Place in the heart of the Cherokee Nation and put them to work on the same farm that taught the aboriginal student converts the Moravian way of agriculture. Ward was murdered by an outraged Pin who became a Northern Baptist preacher after the war.[78] The race-slavery-conversion question had never been fully resolved.

With the end of slavery, however, all ideas about a bi-racial community organization would have to respond to the presence of blacks who were no longer in bondage. Within the cities emerging in the New South, Washington/Park observed the rise of what they called "race towns." Such a racially restricted development of the urban landscape permitted each racial group to build up a division of labor among its own members and to distinguish among the latter by economic class and social status. "Whatever one may be disposed to think of this segregation of the white and black races which one sees going on, to a greater or lesser extent, in every section of the country," wrote

Washington/Park in 1909, "it is certain that there is a temporary advantage to the Negro race in the building up of these 'race towns.'"[79] Columbia Heights, the black section of Winston-Salem was one such "race town," and in it Washington/Park thought they saw a situation wherein "the masses of the [black] people . . . find a freer expression to their native energies and ambitions than they are able to find elsewhere, and at the same time . . . [they obtain] an opportunity to gain that experience in cooperation, self-direction, and self-control, which it is hard for them to get in the same degree elsewhere."[80]

For the black denizens of Columbia Heights, however, that opportunity had been fostered by two institutions that Park thought owed their origins to the Moravian ethic—the Slater Industrial School and the R. J. Reynolds Tobacco Company. The former, as mentioned earlier, provided vocational training for blacks and had received material and moral support from a prominent scion of "one of the old Moravian families"; the latter, an industrial harbinger of the "New South," had hit upon the idea of employing black workers in the production of its popular product, and, by the time Park visited Winston-Salem, had more than 3,200 male and female Negroes on its payroll, "working side by side, performing the same tasks and receiving the same wages" as its white workers.[81] However, although the Reynolds Company's black workers might have labored on the same factory floor as its white employees, they were required to reside in separate communities. Park, nevertheless, took hope for the future of race relations in the South from the facts that black-owned commercial establishments had begun to prosper inside the racially restricted Columbia Heights neighborhood, and that a few black professionals had already "earned the entire respect of their white neighbors."[82]

The larger context of Park's discussion of the possibilities for black advancement in America is to be seen in his growing realization that in the civilizing process that he credited as modernity's central tendency, a new and all-encompassing moral universe would eventually supersede all of the traditional world's folk cultures, drawing the peoples of the earth into new non-ascriptive forms of association. These forms would be based on the acquired criteria that counted for calculating one's membership in the emerging class order. Moreover, the forces of modernity moved all whom they touched toward individuation, urbanization, and an alienation from custom-bound associations and conduct. For blacks and other peoples of color and non-European culture, Park believed Christianity, especially mission-inspired Protestantism, would act as a most significant corrosive solvent to their premodern ways of life and, in so doing, bring them into civilization with all of its attendant characteristics—including its discontents.

RELIGION, THE RACE RELATIONS CYCLE, AND THE CIVIL ORDERING OF CONFLICTS

In an autobiographical note that was found after his death, Park stated that he had, finally, become convinced that in his researches on blacks in the South, he had in fact been "observing the historical process by which civilization, not merely here but elsewhere, has evolved, drawing into . . . its influence an ever widening circle of races and peoples."[83] In its broadest sense, Park's sociology of race and ethnic relations takes the civilizational process as its central concern. His well-known formulation of the four stages through which a race relations cycle would pass—viz., contacts, competition, accommodation, assimilation[84]—though not without considerable difficulties as a theory describing the order and direction taken by the several races' actual experiences,[85] nevertheless postulates the ultimate victory of modern market civilization over all traditional modes of social organization. As Park conceived of the matter, modern societies—with their centers in multi-racial and multi-ethnic cities—are characterized by "changes of fortune [that] are likely to be sudden and dramatic," by an "atomization" in which "every individual is more or less on his own," by "[s]ocial forms [that] are flexible and in no sense fixed," and by a *polis* in which "[f]ashion and public opinion take the place of custom as a means and method of social control."[86] These modern "mobile societies," as Park called them, have an inexorable tendency to attract to themselves the still tradition-oriented peoples and, in the event, to convert them from their custom-bound ways of life into civic-minded citizens of a new Occidental socioeconomic order. That order, in turn, would shift them away from their membership in collective, family-based primary groups and move them into individuated, impersonal, and secondary associations of persons who must struggle for necessarily scarce material and spiritual rewards in a society built around commerce and competition. ". . . Occidental, and particularly modern and American, culture," he told delegates to an Institute of Pacific Relations conference at Hangchow, China, in 1931, "may be said to have had their origin and to have found their controlling ideas in the market place, where men come together to barter and trade, and by the exchange of commodities and services . . . to improve— each for himself, and according to his own individual conception of values— his condition of life."[87]

How America's blacks fitted into this universal process became a matter of special significance to Park and proved to be the most difficult and ambiguous instance of the operation of his postulated race relations cycle. As Park saw the matter, much but not all of the assimilation process for African Americans had already taken place during their 225 years of enslavement.[88] However, the incorporation of the Negro into the lifeways, economy, culture, and polity of both slave and post-slavery America had proceeded unevenly and selectively.

A household slave, for example, "very soon possessed himself of so much of the language, religion, and the technique of the civilization of his master as, in his station, he was fitted or permitted to acquire," but the "assimilation of the Negro field hand, where the contact of the slave with his master and his master's family was less intimate, was naturally less complete."[89] Moreover, in such regions of the South as "the Sea Island plantations off the coast of South Carolina," regions, that is, that had been "less touched . . . by the white man's influence and civilization," or on those large plantations where class distinctions within the enslaved group had reduced master-slave contacts to a minimum, "the assimilation of the masses of the Negro people took place more slowly and less completely. . . ."[90] Nevertheless, Park pointed out, by 1860, although only one out of eight blacks were free while the great majority, numbering nearly four million, were still in bondage, "it is safe to say [that] the great mass of . . . Negroes were no longer, in any true sense, an alien people."[91] But, Park was quick to add, "They were, of course, not citizens. . . . It might, perhaps, be more correct to say that they were less assimilated than domesticated."[92]

For the emancipation of the slaves to proceed beyond domestication and toward the kind of assimilation appropriate to a modern, industrial society, Park perceived, the black Americans would have to be incorporated into what was veritably a new social order, a society undergoing a fundamental and rapid reorganization, a society that was more and more coming to be characterized by impersonal relations, the drive for individual achievement, and the sequestration of affective feelings and familism to the arena of private life. During the period of slavery, as Park conceived of the matter, assimilation had occurred in great measure as a byproduct of the intimate and personal relations among masters and (house) slaves. While aspects of these patronizing but primary relations continued in force after the Civil War, especially for those ex-slaves who continued to live near or work for their former masters, emancipation had opened the hitherto rural-bound blacks to the opportunities of moving around, of migrating north or west, of going to the cities, or, in a few cases, of becoming pioneers of a liberated Africa or of other opening frontier areas. Their mobility, in turn, had fostered individualizing tendencies. Except for the supervening fact that the Southern Redemptionist forces had imposed on the newly freed blacks a caste structure to replace the old and discredited slave system, these individualizing tendencies might have encouraged freedmen and women to develop their aptitudes and talents and, hence, to participate directly and fully in the incorporating process.[93] But such had not been the case. The return of "home rule" to the former Confederate states, the abrogation of Emancipation's promise in the form of black codes, Negro disfranchisement, and a host of new segregation practices had in effect erected a formidable barrier to the assimilation of the Negroes.

In the face of these developments, for Park's vision of a complete assimilation of America's blacks to come about, some agency of progress, individuation, and initiative would have to be activated within their own ranks. It is not the case that Park discounted the effects that a dedicated implementation of the provisions of the Thirteenth, Fourteenth, and Fifteenth Amendments or a vigorous enforcement of the Civil Rights Acts of 1866 and subsequent years would have had on black assimilation; rather, he developed his outlook on the matter after that option had been foreclosed by the victory scored after 1876 by the retrogressive white supremacist forces. "As it turned out," he would recall in 1935, "the interests of race and caste triumphed over the interests of class and party." Prescient as he so often was, Park at that time looked to the courts of the twentieth century to carry out the mandate of the Radical Republican Congress of 1866. In effect, to build on and to paraphrase Sumner, Park eventually came to encourage the use of what might be called "courtways" to bring "mores" into alignment with "stateways": "The courts must complete the work of the legislature," he observed almost twenty years before *de jure* segregation of public schools would be declared unconstitutional, "and until the law, as interpreted and enforced, has brought about what the psychologists might describe as a 'reconditioning' of the people for whom it was enacted, one cannot say the political process is complete."[94]

However, in the period of Park's early studies, the era, that is, immediately following one that Rayford W. Logan would characterize as producing the nadir of civil rights and black opportunities in America,[95] Park looked to the African Americans themselves—and to what benefits they might derive from adapting a Protestant orientation to their own conduct and ethics—for progress along what he then knew to be the obstacle-filled course toward their eventual assimilation. It is in this sense that his comprehensive picture of a highly stratified bi-racial community in Winston-Salem and other communities in 1913 attests both to the positive change in "Negro home life and standards of living" that had already occurred in the half-century since slavery had been abolished, and to the role played in that advancement by the practical ethicism espoused in Booker T. Washington's program of Negro uplift.[96]

Park's second Winston-Salem study in fact depicts the peculiar structure of socioeconomic stratification that had occurred in several cities of the South and is the most comprehensive empirical picture he would provide in support of his observation—fifteen years later—that the character of race relations in the twentieth-century South had begun to assume a new and more complex form: "With the development of industrial and professional classes within the Negro race," he pointed out in 1928, "the distinction between the races tends to assume the form of a vertical line. On one side of this line the Negro is represented in most of the occupational and professional classes; on the other side of the line the white man is similarly represented."[97] Whereas the laws and customs of antebellum America had permitted the development of only "two classes of Negroes in the United States, namely free Negroes and slaves," with the abolition of slavery there had emerged a class of black peasants comprising eighty percent of the race and, above them, "a small class composed in part of free Negroes, in part of a class of [formerly] favored slaves. . . ." The latter element, ". . . all those . . . [to] whom education, opportunity or natural ability had given material advantages and a superior social position,"[98] had taken over the leadership of the race in the years after the Civil War, but had become divided over how to ameliorate the condition of the unlettered black peasantry and the unemployed and unskilled members of the urban black *lumpenproletariat*. Park fell in line with the program put forward by Booker T. Washington.

In 1913, Park was at pains to show that in the half-century since Emancipation the non-rural body of the black people, though still a statistical minority of the race, had become far more differentiated in both class and status. By that year matters had changed such that he could count a rising professional element—viz., "lawyers, physicians, teachers, musicians, playwrights and actors . . . [as well as] missionaries to Africa, secretaries of Young Men's Christian Associations, social settlement workers, and so forth"—among non-rural blacks. In addition, Park pointed out, "there has grown up in recent years a vigorous and pushing middle class, composed of small contractors, business men of various sorts, bankers, real estate and insurance men . . . [and] a small class of plantation owners."[99] Lastly, Park noted that although "[l]abor unions have almost invariably sought to keep Negroes out of skilled trades . . ., [i]n those occupations . . . in which the Negro has shown his ability to compete and has managed to gain a sufficient foothold to compel recognition, . . . labor unions have made earnest effort[s] to bring Negroes [in] . . . and have thus insured for them the same wages and ultimately the same standards of living as prevail among white artisans of the same class."[100] Such had been the development of bi-racial socioeconomic organization in the South by 1928 that Park—who believed that this new form of race-caste structure was unique to the United States—proposed a new diagram of the occupational situation:[101]

White	*Colored*
Professional Occupation	Professional Occupation
Business Occupation	Business Occupation
Labor	Labor

Despite his careful delineation of urban jobs, occupations, and professions among post-Redemptionist blacks, Park's explanation for the admittedly only partial advancement of the Negro into full-fledged incorporation within the citizenry of the United States emphasizes the stimulus that frugality, faithfulness, and the pursuit of farming had given to the aspiring blacks. In this sense, Park came to believe that property ownership in the form of a farm or homestead—and the values and attitudes associated with such ownership—would be crucial, a virtual precondition for the further advancement of the black masses into modern America. Property encouraged its owner to settle down and assume responsibility for its maintenance. Acquiring property required one to scrimp and save until the purchase price—or at least a down payment—could be made. Although very few blacks had been able to enter the large-scale landholding class of the South by 1900,[102] Park and Washington looked forward to the development of a mass of black smallholders. The philosophy of work that Park perceived arising out of the teachings of Booker T. Washington constituted a basis for a practical, homestead-oriented wisdom that, in the face of the racist hostility that was all around them, Park supposed might inch the black man and woman forward—or, at least, shield them from American racism's worst excesses.

For himself and for those who were likely to become fully incorporated into modern urban life by the operations of America's commercially spirited civilization, Park believed the city would serve as a stimulating and exhilarating environment. However, for the first steps of advancement of the mass of America's blacks, who in the early decades of the twentieth century had little more culture and survival skills than their heritage of 225 years of rural slavery had provided, Park and Booker T. Washington favored the countryside and an agricultural life. "The city," Park would later observe, "is, finally, the natural habitat of civilized man."[103] The South's black masses, though Park believed that they had been divested of virtually all elements of their African past except its hereditarily fixed temperament,[104] were still not sufficiently possessed of enough of the perquisites of an Occidental civic culture to thrive in a modern metropolis. Although he was quite aware that the small number of successful black artisans and prospering professionals had managed to adjust effectively to city life, Park noted in 1913 that "There are, particularly, in every large city as well as in every small town in the South, multitudes of Negroes who live meanly and miserably." These blacks, he went on, "make their homes in some neglected or abandoned quarters of the city and maintain a slovenly, irregular and unhealthy sort of existence, performing odd jobs of one kind or another."[105] The black man's first ambition, according to Park, is "to build himself a comfortable home," and while his own researches showed that the middle, professional, and upper classes of African Americans could and did do so in the city,[106] both he and Washington believed that a wholesome home life for the black farmer and farm worker was more likely to be achieved in the countryside.

"There is no part of the South, perhaps no part of the United States," Park noted, "where the small Negro farmers are more independent and prosperous, or where the two races get on better together, than, . . . in the region around Christiansburg, Va."[107] The symbolic significance of Park's having selected a city named in honor of the religion whose missions he supposed would hasten "the attainment of a common culture in which [different] races and peoples may share,"[108] and, in the same endeavor, introduce pre-modern peoples into civilization, should not be overlooked by those seeking to comprehend the full meaning and implications of his sociology. Nor should the fact that Park emphasized the importance that the rural way of life would exert on the movement of blacks toward assimilation. Although in the cities he observed that the "number of really cultured Negro homes is, as might be expected, small," Park pointed out that, "Wherever one meets a colony of Negro landowners and wherever one meets a Negro who has risen to the position of farm manager, one invariably finds improvement in the character and condition of the Negro home."[109] The fact that "the number of Negro landowners is increasing throughout the South about 50 percent more rapidly than the white," that "[w]henever a good school is established it is usually the center of a group of thrifty Negro farmers," that "a large proportion of colored farmers in Macon County [where Tuskegee Institute was located] live at present in neat four- and five-room cottages . . . [and that the] standard of living has been appreciably raised in this and neighboring counties" provided Park with the evidence for his conclusion that "Ownership of land invariably brings with it an improvement in the stability and the comfort of the [black family's] home."[110] However, improvements in black rural life could not depend on the unaided efforts of the Negro peasantry; rather, they were catalyzed by what Park regarded as the modern equivalent of the old Moravian mission, Booker T. Washington's errand into the black countryside.

Park supposed that the most modern expression of the original Protestant missionary spirit was to be found in the university settlement movement.[111] That movement had sprung up in late nineteenth-century America out of emulation of the activities of the English Christian Socialists in London,[112] but in the United States it took on a distinctive character of its own, becoming the instrument of a new revival, the spreading of the "Social Gospel."[113] In the Northern cities, a new sociology became its voice,[114] and the Social Gospel was spread via such college and university slum settlements as Andover House in Boston,[115] the Neighborhood Guild and Rivington Street Settlements in New York City,[116] and Hull House in Chicago.[117] The clientele of these errands into the wilderness of city slums were for the most part the urban poor and the impoverished and unacculturated new immigrants from southern and eastern Europe.[118] But, after blacks began migrating into the industrial cities of the Northeast and Midwest, settlements were also established to minister to their needs. However, in the North the Social Gospel leaders divided over virtually all of the issues that made up the "race question": viz., whether settlement houses ministering to Negroes should be segregated or interracial; whether a drive for integration and a vigorous quest for equal justice should take precedence over working to meet the special needs of the Negro poor and recognizing that it might be counterproductive to "force personal relations across racial lines;" and over whether its main message to the blacks ought to be that "Negroes, like members of other racial groups, must make their way into favor by their productive capacity and their ability to command respect."[119] As two of the foremost leaders of the movement noted in 1922, "Negroes present the particularly difficult problem of delayed assimilation."[120]

For Park and for Booker T. Washington the delay in the assimilation of America's blacks called not only for special measures of self-help to be cultivated with reference to the actual conditions of black life, but also for the unassimilated blacks to seek their futures in the very region of the United States where they or their ancestors had once been slaves. In his Atlanta address of 1895, Washington had urged blacks to stay in the South, to cultivate friendly relations with Southern whites, and, he added, "when it comes to business, pure and simple, it is in the South that the Negro is given a man's chance in the commercial world."[121] However, although Washington had at first urged his racial compatriots to seek their fortunes in the South "in agriculture, mechanics, . . . commerce, . . . domestic service, and in the professions,"[122] he soon came to see that if a spirit of individualism and an aptitude for free enterprise were to prevail among the masses of them, it would most likely arise from farming and in homesteading. Cities, North and South, might be places of progress for a few skilled black artisans and unusually gifted professionals, but, by the first few years of the twentieth century, both Washington and his opponent in so many aspects of the race question, W. E. B. DuBois, had become convinced that the city was no place for the black proletariat.[123]

When the Social Gospel sent its missionaries into the South, their preachments lent support to Washington's conclusions. The Gospeler's right wing, in the form of the Woman's Home Mission Movement of the Methodist Episcopal Church, urged that the time had not yet come when Christian whites could cease helping to develop this "backward race," but that its future would depend on the leadership of the few "exceptional negroes" among them;[124] its "left wing," in the person of Washington Gladden (1836–1918), while not willing to accept Washington's thesis wholeheartedly,[125] eventually came to blame the problem faced by the Southern Negro on the rapidity with which the Reconstruction governments had granted the freedmen and women their liberties: "To invert the natural order of society, and give to the ignorance of the community the supremacy over its intelligence," Gladden observed in 1916, "was an infatuation to which rational legislators ought not to have been subject."[126] Washington, who once admonished whites that they too often overlooked "the fact that geographically and physically the semi-barbarous Negro race has been thrown right down in the centre of the highest civilization that the world knows anything about,"[127] decided to make sure that Macon County, Alabama, the site of Tuskegee Institute, would develop as a Negro farming area and that agriculture would become the base from which his people would slowly rise to the upper echelons of that "natural order."

"The greatest mission station in the world," Park proclaimed in 1908, ". . . is situated in a little country village in the 'black belt' of Alabama—

Tuskegee."[128] Conceiving Washington's agricultural, mechanical, and normal school at Tuskegee as a mission station permitted Park to place its operations squarely within the assimilating endeavor of Protestantism's practical social gospel. Max Weber seemed to agree. When, in 1904, Weber paid a visit to Washington's educational institute at Tuskegee he reported: "At Tuskegee no one is permitted to do only intellectual work. The purpose is the training of farmers; *"conquest of the soil"* is a definite ideal. An enormous amount of enthusiasm is generated among the teachers and students, and Tuskegee is the only place with a socially free atmosphere. . . ."[129]

Washington had insisted that all the elements of assimilation that Park summed up in his term "incorporation," and that, a half-century after Washington's death, Talcott Parsons would designate as "full citizenship"[130]—viz., the right to vote economic independence, and the respect of his fellow Americans—would "come to the Negro, as to all races, by beginning at the bottom and gradually working up to the highest possibilities of his nature."[131] The "bottom" was in unskilled labor and in agriculture, but the former had brought blacks too close to hostile, urban, white workers and their racist organizational practices, and in the first two decades of the twentieth century Washington and Park both placed considerable emphasis on farming and rural residency as desiderata for aspiring blacks. Indeed, in the letters collected by Park and Washington from and about Tuskegee graduates, care was taken to discover all who had chosen farming as a vocation and, by publicizing this choice, to encourage others to follow in their footsteps.[132] When, in 1913, as Washington's representative, Park toured fifteen "Tuskegee schools" established as agricultural training branches of the Macon County stem, he particularly criticized the sloppy operations of the Snow Hill school, and Washington threatened to withdraw his support lest the school's inadequacies undermine the Tuskegee mission.[133]

Although a transition from enslaved field hand to independent farmer-with-forty-acres-and-a-mule had been envisioned for the freedmen by Northern abolitionists, the actual practices employed to redistribute confiscated Confederate lands had subverted the aim of that project.[134] By the turn of the century all too many of the freedmen and women had been reduced to peonage, sharecropping, or to becoming itinerant farm laborers.[135] A century after the issuance of the Emancipation Proclamation, Gunnar Myrdal—the Swedish social economist whose prognostications about what in 1944 he had called the inherent contradictions of the "American Dilemma" had begun to supplant Park's promissory paradigm of an inexorable race relations cycle[136]—would lament the fact that during the Reconstruction Era there had been "no real preparedness to undertake large-scale social and economic reform . . . and . . . in particular . . . land reform."[137] Moreover, fourteen years later, Lawrence Goodwyn, in his careful study of the populist-inspired agrarian revolt in *fin de siècle* America, would assert that, "In the South of the 1890s, there was almost no public way black Americans could 'see themselves' experimenting in democratic forms" or cooperating with the generally white supremacist farmers' alliances being formed all around them.[138] Writing in the midst of the situation that had developed in the aftermath of these less than promising developments, Park took heart from the facts that in the farming district that Tuskegee Institute served, "blacks already outnumber the whites five to one and Negro immigration is steadily increasing that ratio . . . ; [that] the land is frequently poor, but it is for that reason easy to buy . . . ; [that the] Negro farmers . . . found Macon County . . . a good place in which to live . . .; [and that] there are schools here, and, quite as important, racial peace."[139] Tuskegee, in Park's vision of it in 1908, was a quiet oasis situated in, but isolated from, the desert of racism that had already begun to dessicate the New South.

Park's analysis of the Tuskegee agricultural mission forms one part of his empirical study of racial accommodation, the penultimate stage in his race relations cycle. That stage was characterized in the case of the Southern Negro by the build-up of a generalized racial caste order, a bi-racial urban social organization, the operation of a rigid color line in virtually all formalized black-white relationships, and the relative isolation of the mass of black peasants and rural workers. The latter group could, if guided by Christian leaders who both preached and showed them how to live in accordance with a practical theology of moral abstemiousness, personal hygiene, domestic simplicity, hard work, and vocational instruction, move the race a step closer to the kind of respect that was a *sine qua non* for full-fledged incorporation into the larger society.

Neither Washington nor Park believed that a public show of abject acquiescence before the many kinds of racist victimization heaped upon them would by itself win a victory for blacks in their struggle. In fact, in the year following the publication of Park's essay on Tuskegee's agricultural mission station, Washington began secretly to help fund and organize the ultimately successful litigation of Alonzo Bailey, a black farm worker who sought to have the United States Supreme Court declare Alabama's notorious contract labor law an unconstitutional violation of the Thirteenth Amendment.[140] Although they would not support the South's imposition of legalized white supremacy, both Washington and Park shared the point of view presented by Ray Stannard Baker—himself the author of a muckraking exposé of the condition of the African American in the so-called Progressive Era[141] and a fundraiser for the Alonzo Bailey case—who noted in relation to the victory achieved in the Bailey case that as long as "so many negroes are densely ignorant and poverty stricken, and while so many white men are short-sighted enough to take advantage of this ignorance and poverty, so long will forms of slavery prevail."[142] For Washington and Park, the elimination of poverty and ignorance among the black masses constituted in effect a continuation of the centuries-long fight against slavery.

In Park's description of it, the Tuskegee program for black farmers appears to operate much like the early Moravians' missions to the Indians. Just as the Moravians liked to establish their settlements in isolation from those of other European settlers and soul savers, so Tuskegee is situated in what at first seems to be "a vast unbroken forest, green and waving, . . ." but on closer examination turns out to be the site of "farms and the [black] farmers, twenty thousand people in an area of 650 square miles."[143] And, in a manner reminiscent of that by which Moravian and other early missionaries cultivated the indigenous leaders of the Indian tribes as both models and messengers of the Gospel, Washington organized the first of what would become the educational arm of his outreach program, the Tuskegee Negro Conference: He invited to the foundational meeting of his institute the leaders of the small black churches that had become the centers of Afro-American life in the years just after the Civil War.[144] Further, like fundamentalist Protestants who have been "born again" and wish to "witness" their wonderful experience to others, the successful black farmers of Macon County were encouraged by Washington "to tell how they had done it . . ., [showing] the difficulties and the human nature in the situation; . . . [and revealing] the heroism in the struggles of these obscure and narrow lives. . . ."[145] These first "witnesses," in turn, were sent back to their own communities, from which, eventually, their "stories . . . were . . . repeated in all the dark corners of the county and state."[146]

From such modest beginnings by 1908 there had developed a local newspaper and an attendant rise in literacy, a monthly educational meeting to which black farmers were invited, and, as early as 1904, an Institute-sponsored short course of lectures and practical instruction in crop science and other matters that would eventuate in the establishment of the "Agricultural Wagon." The Agricultural Wagon referred to a pedagogical project in which a horse-drawn vehicle "was fitted out with specimens of the best modern machinery, including a revolving churn, butter molds, diverse cultivators, cotton choppers, and various sorts of fertilizers, milk testers, cream separators and a number of charts and other demonstration material" and brought "directly to the farmers, [providing them] with the instruction which the school had to offer. . . ."[147] The success of the Agricultural Wagon had in turn inspired the General Education Board of New York to fund the establishment of demonstration farms "carried on under the direction of a graduate of the school acting as field agent of the Agricultural Department at Washington."[148] In all of this Park saw much more than material aid being given to an impoverished and neglected black peasantry. The advances in farming made possible by Tuskegee's mission station had been a "moral tonic," and—as illustrated in the story told by an old Negro farmer of how, because he had improved his situation with the aid of Washington's agricultural extension service, he was no longer addressed as "Old Giles" but as "Mr. Hill"—a builder of individual and collective character.[149] ". . . [I]n the final analysis," Park observed, "it is character, character in the individuals and character in the communities, that industrial missions are seeking to build up."[150]

CHARACTER, CHRISTIANITY,
AND RACIAL TEMPERAMENT

Modernity, as Park conceived of it, had as one of its central characteristics that the more significant aspects of racial assimilation would occur in secondary relationships rather than in primary groups. The content and quality of this modern mode of assimilation would necessarily be different from that which occurred among "primitive peoples." Park noted that although the latter are often found to have considerable differences in external appearance, their societies exhibit "a monotonous sameness in the mental attitudes of individuals." In cosmopolitan societies like the United States of America, on the other hand, assimilation presents itself as "a superficial uniformity, a homogeneity in manners and fashion, associated with relatively profound differences in individual opinions, sentiments, and beliefs."[151] Thus, although Park did not make this point, assimilation of the latter kind could occur without any racial integration, interracial amalgamation, or even the assurance of peaceful relations among the several races in question preceding it or following suit.

However, the differences in opinions, sentiments, and beliefs that might lead some assimilated blacks and whites to maintain considerable social and personal distance from one another could also be mitigated by the development of a common interest or a cluster of such interests. Interests, Park insisted, rather than feelings, constituted the social cement that bound members of a cosmopolitan civilization together. As new technology entered into the daily lives of peoples living in backward, traditional, or transitional sections of such a society, the interests in it that were generated thereby could result, if only for a brief instant, in interracial cooperation. Park cited one such instance from his Tuskegee investigations. The Agricultural Wagon had been drawn up at Mount Zion, a segregated community of black landowning and tenant farmers about ten miles north of Tuskegee. The usual black audience was suddenly joined by a few whites who "had come up to see what there was to learn." Soon, after the black agricultural agent had explained the advantages of alfalfa over the locally used cow-pea as a fertilizer, "we were all, white or black, engaged in a lively discussion of the merits and the possibilities of the new legume. . . ." Although he could not help but notice that the "race distinctions were there, to be sure," Park was more impressed by the fact that, at least "for the moment, because we had found a common interest, the race problem was solved."[152]

However, Park was not altogether sanguine about the chances for common interests to overcome deep-seated racial prejudices, or for the message of Protestant Christianity and its innerworldly economic ethic to impress itself on those who needed most to hear and internalize it. Just as his student, Herbert Blumer (1900–1987), would later dispute the claim made by more than one school of sociological thought that the introduction of industrialization and a money economy would inevitably dissolve racial prejudices and substitute class struggles for racial disputes,[153] so Park began to notice how the common interests that the introduction of a technologized society ought to have aroused among white and black farmers or white and black workers were often blocked—not only by an ever-resilient host of race prejudices, but also by the racial temperament that each racial group possesses by dint of its heredity. Even more significant for Park's increasingly unsanguine outlook on assimilation was his observation that any racial group's temperament would necessarily influence the manner in which its individual members would absorb and be able to express the values, customs, ideas, beliefs, and sentiments of the society into which, as an alien and a stranger, he or she had been brought.[154]

Park's claims about the existence and effects of a racial temperament are the most controversial of his ideas about race relations. In an essay written in 1944 but not published until 1964, the black novelist Ralph Ellison took the occasion of his review of Myrdal's *American Dilemma* to denounce Park's designation of a racial temperament—and, more pointedly, the latter's depiction of the Negro as "the lady among the races"—as "a descriptive metaphor . . . so pregnant with mixed motives as to birth a thousand compromises and indecisions . . ., uncomfortably close to the preachings of . . . Dr. Goebbels. . . ."[155] In a defense of Park, Morris Janowitz claimed that, with respect to the phrase that had so outraged Ellison, "Park regretted it again and again," but then Janowitz went on to justify the general context in which Park had employed the phrase as having formed one part of Park's and W. I. Thomas's quest for a way to eliminate "biological racism" and develop in its place "a new vocabulary of intergroup relations."[156]

It does not seem, however, that Janowitz's defense has been widely accepted. More recently, some sociologists have sought to bury the issue as far as sociological discourse is concerned. Thus, the late César Graña (d. 1986), in a wide-ranging discussion of the sociology of literature that also commented on the literature of sociology, treated the matter, ever so briefly, as indicative of the "perplexity, grim suspicion, or simply alarm and indignation" that characterizes "the response of [such] literary men [as Ralph Ellison] to American sociology." Graña went on to note that Ellison had not referred to Park "as the 'social ecologist' with whose works every graduate student must sooner or later become familiar," but rather as "the man . . . responsible for deflecting black political energies towards the tamer fields of educational self-improvement, and as the amiable social theorist who believed in the innate voluptuous artistry of black folk."[157] Even more recently, Barbara Ballis Lal acknowledged that "Park's characterization of Afro-American temperament now sounds pejorative and patronizing" and appeared to deprecate the fact that he had "emphasized those traits that would impede the attainment of goals he himself thought important, such as occupational success." But Lal thinks that it is also worth remembering that Park's depiction of the Negro's innate temperament "does suggest an appreciation of qualities absent from native, white, middle-class Americans, [and is] not unlike those mentioned by . . . W. E. B. DuBois." Ultimately, however, Lal concludes that because the "theme is mentioned in very few of his publications . . . and . . . [because] the influence he accorded to racial temperament was very limited . . . , Park's discussion of racial temperament is of little consequence."[158] However, none of these critiques, excuses, elaborations, or justifications treats the relationship of Park's discussion of racial temperament and its relation to his larger discussion of assimilation and the problems attending the modern civilizational process.

Although Park's conception of assimilation in cosmopolitan societies seems to permit the phenomenon to become fully accomplished without any serious undermining of the modern, pluralist, socio-cultural order—(In the words of James A. Geschwender, "Park believed that there was a long-term trend toward assimilation and the elimination of national minorities as such . . . , that minorities were taking on many of the characteristics of the dominant society, . . ." Nevertheless, Geschwender credits Park with the thesis that such minorities might "still retain some distinctive features . . . sufficient to allow for recognition, but not so great that . . . [they] would impede interaction within a class hierarchy."[159])—in the period of his early writings, Park was far less optimistic about the absorption of racially distinctive peoples in American society and greatly concerned over the limitations on acculturation that such a people's hereditary racial temperament would impose. In 1914, Park pointed out that such apparently immutable features as black or yellow skin color, or the shape of a people's eyes, insofar as these traits had been biologically determined, might act as impediments to assimilation. "The fact that the Japanese [or the Negro] bears in his features a distinctive racial hallmark, that he wears, so to speak, a racial uniform, classifies him. He cannot become a mere individual, indistinguishable in the cosmopolitan mass of the population, as is true, for example, of the Irish and, to a lesser extent, of some of the other immigrant races."[160] Moreover, the capacity to become a "mere individual, indistinguishable in the cosmopolitan mass of the population" was also limited by the manner and form that each group's racial temperament permitted it to absorb the larger society's fund of common cultural materials. In 1918, addressing the annual meeting of the American Sociological Society, Park laid out the fundamental issue. "The question . . . resolves itself into this: How far do racial characteristics and innate biological interests determine the extent to which one racial group can and will take over and assimilate the characteristic features of an alien civilization?"[161] He was not altogether sure of the answer to that question.

The "racial characteristics" to which Park referred consisted of two elements—the external marks, i.e., the skin color, eye shape, hair texture, and other visible features that make up the "racial uniform," and the "subjective, historic and ultimately perhaps racial and temperamental factor . . . which makes it difficult, though not impossible, perhaps, to transmit political and religious institutions to people of a different racial type and a different social tradition."[162] The "offensive rather than the pleasing traits [of racially distinctive peoples] . . . impress us," Park observed. "These impressions accumulate and reinforce natural prejudices."[163] Although the intensification of intimate associations across the color line that had been erected as the main bulwark of the South's racial caste order might yet induce whites to have a heightened respect and esteem for their black fellow citizens, the impersonal character of modern forms of civil association tended to discourage such. Further, Park did not believe that interracial marriage—forbidden by law to blacks at one time or another in thirty-nine of the States of the United States[164]—would likely resolve the race-culture issue. Offspring of such unions, Park pointed out in 1931, were commonly classified as Negroes in the United States, and though a mulatto differed in color, culture, and consciousness from unamalgamated blacks, and was likely to be "disposed to escape from the racial coil in which his origin and his history have involved him . . . , the vigor with which the racial line has been drawn against him has compelled him . . . to throw in his fortunes with the black and make the Negro's cause his own."[165] Park supposed that racial intermarriage was more likely to take place "where . . . custom is relaxed and the traditional distinctions of class and caste [are] not rigorously enforced."[166] The South of his early writings was certainly not such a place, and, Park concluded, "Where races are distinguished by certain external marks[,] these furnish a permanent physical substratum upon which and around which the irritations and animosities, incidental to all human intercourse, tend to accumulate and so gain strength and volume."[167]

The "innate biological interests," on the other hand, constituted a more complex problem for Park's sociological analysis. Janowitz is incorrect insofar as his commentary on Ellison's critique implies that Park's discussion of racial temperament was aimed at eliminating altogether the hereditary component of any social scientific analysis of the race question. Rather, what Park seems to have been doing in his invocation of a racial temperament is attempting to respecify, in as exact a way as his knowledge and observations would allow, precisely what amount of the Negro's character and personality was biological in origin, what amount a survival of African culture, and what amount the product of acculturation in America. Furthermore, Park sought to get at the effects that the internalization of this tripartite and emergent compound of constitutional elements, cultural survivals, and acculturative adaptations would have on the incorporation of African Americans into an ever-modernizing United States of America.

In this respect, it is important to see that Park subscribed rather strongly to the thesis that very few Africanisms could have survived the assaults on culture that occurred as matter-of-fact concomitants of the Middle Passage, the "seasoning" of captured Africans in the West Indies before their settled enslavement on the plantations of the colonial South, and the Negroes' subsequent 225 years of enforced, slavocratic "Americanization."[168] ("My own impression," Park wrote in 1919, "is that the amount of African tradition which the Negro brought to the [Atlantic colonies of North America that would later become the] United States was very small. In fact, there is every reason to believe, it seems to me, that the Negro, when he landed . . . , left behind him almost everything but his dark complexion and his tropical temperament."[169]) Temperament, which Park took to consist in "a few elementary but distinctive characteristics, determined by physical organization and transmitted biologically,"[170] had played and would continue to play a considerable—but, as he was ultimately forced to concede, incalculable—role in the Afro-American's response to America's Eurocentric society and culture. Indeed, Park was at pains to distinguish the blacks from European and Asian immigrant peoples in precisely this respect. "The fact that the Negro brought with him from Africa so little tradition which he was able to transmit and perpetuate on American soil, makes that race unique among all peoples of our cosmopolitan population."[171] That uniqueness cried out for further investigations of racial temperament and its consequences.

Park found evidence of the continued operation of a "tropical temperament" in such things as the African American's "genial, sunny, and social disposition," in his and her "attachment to external, physical things rather than to subjective states and objects of introspection," and—most important for the argument being presented here—"in a disposition for expression rather than enterprise and action."[172] In the latter statement is contained what Park seemed, perhaps not consciously, to be implying—viz., that there is an inherent contradiction, on the one hand, in exhorting blacks to take to the kind of hard-working, abstemious, and self-directed life style associated with a dedicated adherence to the Puritan ethic, and, on the other, in recognizing that in the unique instance of the Afro-American, racial temperament would likely dictate a quite different mode of response to Puritanism's innerworldly casuistry. Hence, Park observed:

> Everywhere and always the Negro has been interested rather in expression than in action; interested in life itself rather than in its reconstruction or reformation. The Negro is, by natural disposition, neither an intellectual nor an idealist like the Jew, nor a brooding introspective like the East Indian, nor a pioneer and frontiersman like the Anglo-Saxon. He is primarily an artist, loving life for its own sake. His metier is expression rather than action. The Negro is, so to speak, the lady among the races.[173]

And Park certainly saw, if only obliquely and without further elaboration, the implications of his analysis for racial policies and for any proposals for socially cognizant solutions to the race problem: "[I]f these things are true," he wrote, referring to his carefully worded differentiation of the temperament of the Jew—who "just because of his intellectuality is a natural born idealist, internationalist, doctrinaire, and revolutionist"—from that of the Negro—who "because of his natural attachment to known, familiar objects, places and persons, is preadapted to conservatism and to local and personal loyalties . . . ,"— "we shall eventually have to take account of them practically."[174] Indeed, one possible practical conclusion to be reached from Park's discussion of the importance of the effects of their in-born "tropical temperament" on black Americans is that the Protestant ethic's and Social Gospel's reliance on instilling into them attitudes of diligence, thrift, sobriety, and prudence as prerequisites to economic and social advancement and the awarding of full citizenship might be to little avail. As an "artist" who loved "life for its own sake," the Negro might respond to a different inner call. Although Park did not say it in these words, his suggestion that the operation of Negro temperament is analogous to "the role of the *wish* in the Freudian analysis of dream life"[175] comes close but—because of the qualifications of situation and opportunity that, Park admitted, also affect the Negroes' future—does not quite reach the claim that temperament is destiny.

Park's discussion of the societal effects of a racial temperament should be read in relation to his studies of religion among black Americans and to his thesis that Booker T. Washington's rural Tuskegee Institute was in fact a modern mission station like that of the urban Social Gospel settlements. "The first, and perhaps the only distinctive institution which the Negro has developed in this country is the Negro church," Park observed.[176] And, although he claimed that "it is in connection with his religion that we may expect to find, if anywhere, the indications of a distinctive Afro-American culture," Park regarded the African part of that culture as temperamental rather than cultural in its origin, while he held the American aspect of it to be the result of acculturation. Carefully distinguishing the type of Christianity that developed on the slave plantations from that preached in "the first separate denominational organization of Negroes"—i.e., Richard Allen's and Absalom Jones's African Methodist-Episcopal Church of Philadelphia, and its congregations established in other cities—Park held the latter to be "in all essentials faithful copies of the denominational forms . . . in the [white Protestant] churches of that period," while he supposed that "the religion of the Negroes on the plantation was then, as it is today, of a much more primitive sort."[177] In the unusual religious practices of the remote Sea Island Negroes of South Carolina, Park thought that he had found "the nearest approach to anything positively African . . . [i.e.,] the characteristics of primitive ritual."[178] Nevertheless, he insisted that even these ceremonies, as well as the Sea Islanders' institutional separation of the church from the "praise house," were not survivals of African *culture*; rather, they—like the Voodoo songs whose spiritual meaning, in Park's estimation, had become attenuated from their musical rhythms[179]—were expressions of the African *temperament*. "I assume, therefore," he concluded, "that what we find in the most primitive form of Negro Christianity is not the revival of an older and more barbaric [African] religion[,] but the inception of a new and original form of Christianity."[180]

If it was true to say that "On the whole the plantation Negro's religion was a faithful copy of the white man's," Park nevertheless found it necessary to point out that "It was content rather than the form which suffered sea change in the process of transmission from the white man to the black."[181] Beset by the seemingly irrevocable condition of their enslavement, Park asserted, early Afro-American Christians had turned their religious expression in an other-worldly direction: toward heaven and toward the eternal life they would lead there after shuffling off their mortal coil. The spontaneously composed spirituals and folk songs of the slavery era—in which, Park insisted, "music and expression are everything . . . , [while the] words . . . represent broken fragments of ideas, thrown up from the depths of the Negro's consciousness and swept along upon a torrent of wild, weird and often beautiful melody"[182]—might probably have had "their origin in the excitement of a religious assembly"[183] but, more significantly, they served as "a free and natural expression of their [i.e., the slaves'] unfulfilled desires." "In fact," Park concluded, "these ecstatic visions of the next world, . . . portrayed with a directness and simplicity that is at once quaint and pathetic, are the most significant features of the Negro's songs of slavery."[184]

In effect, Park seems to be saying that the enslaved black man was not likely to adopt for himself the innerworldly attitude toward effort that went with the Calvinist version of the Protestant ethic in Europe and New England because, unlike the white Christians, he was "a constant spectator of [a kind of] life in which he could not participate."[185] Moreover, it was precisely because he was "excited to actions and enterprises that were forbidden to him because he was a slave . . . , [that] the Negro . . . readily and eagerly took over from the white man his heaven and apocalyptic visions. . . ."[186] These other-worldly aspects of Protestant Christianity, Park noted, not only "met the demands of his peculiar racial temperament . . . [but also] furnished relief to the emotional strains that were provoked in him by the conditions of slavery."[187]

Park supposed that slavery's inhibiting effect on the spirit of action and enterprise would recede once that institution and its enervating effects had been obliterated. Indeed, in 1919 Park held out hope for the assimilation of the Afro-Americans because he perceived "[n]ew ideals of life . . . expressed in recent Negro literature" and noticed that "slowly and imperceptibly those ideas are becoming institutionalized in the Negro church and more particularly in the cultural ideals of the Negro school."[188] But could these new ideas and ideals overcome whatever debilitating effects the Negro's tropical temperament might have on their activation in a race-ridden society? Park was not sure. The message preached by the Tuskegee station seemed to be effective, i.e., to produce a goodly share of thrifty, provident, hard-working successes among its graduates. But the racial temperament does much to "determine what elements in the cultural environment each race will select, in what region it will seek and find its vocation, in the larger social organization;

. . . [while] technique, science, machinery, tools, habits, discipline and all the intellectual and mechanical devices with which the civilized man lives and works remain relatively external to the inner core of significant attitudes and values which . . . rests ultimately upon a complex of inherited characteristics, which are racial."[189]

In the end, the precise weight that should be assigned, respectively, to hereditary and acculturative factors eluded Park. He suggested that miscegenation might initiate a "breaking up of the complex of the biologically inherited qualities which constitute the temperament of the race,"[190] but by 1923 Park was pointing out how the rapid rise of a new race consciousness among black Americans and the widespread recognition that racial hybrids would still likely be officially classified as Negroes had effectively undermined the confidence that sociological meliorists could place in that panacea.[191] Moreover, "other factors"—Park mentioned "individual competition, the formation of classes, and especially the increase of communication"—"cooperate to complicate the whole situation and to modify the effects which would be produced by racial factors working in isolation."[192] At that point Park could only call "for more complete analysis and further investigation."[193]

COLOR, CULTURE, AND CIVILIZATION IN PARK'S SOCIOLOGY, 1914–1944

Although its basic assumptions remained the same, Park's outlook on the race question underwent considerable modification after he left the service of Booker T. Washington. Most significantly, he came more and more to regard the issues entailed in the debates over the Southern race-caste system, the prohibitions on Asian entry into the United States, the quota restrictions on non–Anglo-Protestant immigration embodied in the Omnibus Immigration Act of 1924, and the rise of black, Chinese, and Japanese ghettos in America's major cities, together with the growth of race consciousness, not only as qualifying events in the race relations cycle, but also as incidents in the "natural history" of a worldwide civilizational process. Modernity would usher in the discontents associated with progress: Some races and many cultures would die, dissolve, or become deformed; economic development would complicate, modify, but not altogether obliterate the several racial caste structures; and America's response to its internal race problem would become a part of, as well as a contribution to, a new civilized global order. Qualifying all of these matters was Park's growing apprehension about the rise of fascism and Nazism and the retrogressive effects these ideologies and their attendant programs and policies would have on the evolution of race relations.

Park's earlier emphasis on the ameliorative role played by such mission stations as the one established at Tuskegee became less important to his theorizing as he took notice of the decline of the Social Gospel movement, the migration of Southern blacks to the cities of the North and West, the sociocultural and economic features common to the situation of blacks, Asians, and Jews in America and elsewhere, and the growing importance of a new-found racial identity to a rising generation of Afro-Americans. With Booker T. Washington's death in 1915, the new leaders and researchers at Tuskegee took notice of black migration—and tried, albeit unsuccessfully—to halt the movement of Southern blacks to the cities of the North by reinvigorating the school's agricultural extension service to black farmers[194] and, at the same time, by publicizing in the white media how the region's humiliating racialist practices were costing it a valuable human resource.[195]

In the same period, the settlement house phase of the Social Gospel mission to immigrants and blacks in the cities began to wind down.[196] As black city dwellers—including such erstwhile followers of Washington's philosophy as William Pickens (1881–1954), who became a field secretary for the NAACP, the organization whose civil rights philosophy the Tuskegeean had assiduously opposed[197]—shifted their attention from abject accommodationism toward political activism and social protest, the white Protestant churches and social settlements continued to preach the gospel of self-help, to teach Victorian urban folkways to Negro newcomers, and to practice racial separation in their parishes and conferences.[198] As a result of these changes in the status, station, and situation of the African Americans, Park increasingly turned his critical attention onto the "New Negro," and onto the rapidly increasing black urban proletariat and its fate in America's cities and the world's civilization.

As early as 1915, Park had come to see and to critically appraise the actual character of the much-vaunted "New South Creed" as it applied to blacks. As part of his review of Thomas Pearce Bailey's *Race Orthodoxy in the South and Other Aspects of the Negro Problem*, Park pithily summed up its central message, using Bailey's own words:

> 'Blood will tell'; The white race must dominate; The Teutonic peoples stand for race purity. The Negro is inferior and will remain so. 'This is a white man's country'; Let there be no social equality; no political equality. In matters of civil rights and legal adjustments give the white man as opposed to the colored man the benefit of the doubt. In educational policy let the Negro have the crumbs that fall from the white man's table. Let there be such industrial education of the Negro as will fit him to serve the white man. Only Southerners understand the Negro question. Let the South settle the Negro question. The status of peasantry is all the Negro may hope for, if the races are to live together in peace. Let the lowest white man count for more than the highest Negro. The above statements indicate the leadings of Providence.[199]

Although Park allowed that "This statement of the Southern Creed is practically the common opinion of the South" and went so far as to claim that "Race orthodoxy in the South is . . . the most candid statement of the race problem . . .," he pointed out that its advocates were for the most part dogmatists who could not and would not offer a way out of "the moral cul-de-sac into which it has forced the Southern people. . . ."[200] However, in the new migration of blacks to urban areas, in a renewed quest for their African roots, in a new race-conscious Afro-American literature, in the rise of social and political protest movements, and in the transformation of the hitherto caste-bound race into a contemporary nationalistically oriented minority, in all of these developments taken together, Park thought he perceived blacks finding their own way out, and, in the process, entering into another stage, taking another step forward in the inexorable cycle of race relations.

Central to this new conception of the changing black experience in America was Park's recognition that a secular race consciousness and the development of a people's collective identity as a national minority are necessary developments in the march toward assimilation in a modern cosmopolitan society.[201] The old-time religion receded in its effects on conduct in the face of these modern developments. Hence, Park pointed to the cultural discontinuity that he thought he perceived emerging out of the literary, artistic, and musical productions of the younger, urban, black generation of the 1920s. "The modern Negro folk songs, 'the Blues,' . . ." he observed in 1928, "are secular and mundane rather than sacred. . . ."[202] Moreover, the facts of the black experience in America showed that the diachronic linearity of progress supposed to operate for all peoples in the process of cultural development had been replaced by a nomothetic juxtapositioning of stages.

Rather than participating in a chronological movement from a stage of primitive to one of modern culture, Park now asserted that America's blacks had been unique. "No other people, in the United States at least, have compressed into a career so brief so many transfigurations of their racial life. . . ." This remarkable fact, in turn, had led to the present peculiar cultural situation of the Negro, viz., that "no other racial group . . . [could] count among its living members representatives of so many grades of culture, ranging from the primitive peasant of southern plantations to the sophisticated singers of the Harlem cabarets and the radical poetry of the so-called 'Negro Renaissance.'"[203] And the temporal co-presence among America's blacks of all these otherwise sequential stages of culture meant, as Park came to see, that, for the emerging future at any rate, the African American's own consciously directed efforts would contribute to and alter that people's "natural history." "In a sense," Park observed in 1923, "it may be said that Negroes did not begin to have a history until Emancipation. . . . It was only after Emancipation, finding themselves in the middle of an intolerant and hostile society in which they were forced to fight for recognition and status, that black folk began to have a tradition and a history quite their own." When members of a living people, such as the Afro-Americans, regard themselves and are regarded by others "merely as representatives of a race, i.e., a species or variety of mankind, it is hard to understand how there could be any history of the[m] . . . , except a natural history."[204] Race consciousness, as Park saw it, would operate on a race with something like the effect that class consciousness, in Marx's vision of that phenomenon, would have on aggregates of workers, i.e., it would turn them into conscious members of, and active participants in, their own life conditions and futures.

However, Park became ever more pessimistic as less than ameliorative racial relations unfolded in the three decades that followed his departure from Tuskegee. As he pointed out in 1928, "The modern Negro folk songs . . . record, on the whole, . . . the Negro's disillusionment." The "Blues seem to be . . . the reflection of a life that is ineffectual and unsatisfying, 'flowering into song.'"[205] In 1925, Park had applied Ray Stannard Baker's phrase—the very same phrase that he and Booker T. Washington had previously used to entitle their 1913 study of impoverished Europeans[206]—to the situation of the contemporary black American: "The black man in America . . ., 'the man farthest down,' the man most removed from the understanding and sympathy of the larger world in which he lives . . ., is now engaged in a mortal struggle to attain actually, within the American community, the status which he has legally."[207] And in that same year he hinted at the reformulation of his race relations cycle that so many recent events—the comparable situations of the Jew and Negro, the unusually well-documented racially separatist thesis of W. D. Weatherford,[208] the brilliant cultural pluralist argument advanced by William James's disciple, Horace Kallen,[209] and, most ominously, Park's own comparison of the preachings of the Ku Klux Klan with the propaganda of the Nordic supremacists—seemed to suggest:

> The Negro race, as Booker Washington used to say, is a nation within a nation. For somewhat different reasons the Jews in this country are in a similar situation. The Jews are seeking to preserve their culture while accommodating themselves in other respects to the conditions of American life. Different as they are in other respects, the Negro and the Jew are alike in this. . . . The Jew and the Negro are . . . the two outstanding illustrations of the impending cultural pluralism so interestingly advocated by Horace Kallen. What Mr. Weatherford proposes for the Negro, Mr. Kallen proposes for all the races and language groups in America. He would add to the federation of states the federation of races. The American people have not fairly faced this issue. But the Ku Klux Klan and the Nordic propaganda are unquestionably preparing the way for such a new constellation of the forces in the cultural life of America.[210]

As Park was to warn in 1927 (in a critical discussion of fellow sociologist Jerome Dowd's book-length meditation on thirty years of social scientific literature about the race question), "In view of recent developments—the movement of the Negro to the industrial societies of the North, the new race consciousness of the Negro as reflected in the new Negro literature [and, he might have added, the revival and spread of the Ku Klux Klan into parts of America outside the South and the rumblings of racist fascism in Europe]—the benevolent mood in which [Professor Dowd's encyclopedic volume] is written, strike[s] one as rather antiquated and out of date."[211]

Park's recognition of the recent rise of a race-and-history-conscious nationalism among America's urban blacks was attended by four interrelated concerns: 1) his realization that a market-based industrial civilization, the successor meta-culture to all systems of pre-modern belief and practice with which it comes in contact, had become a global phenomenon, displacing America's preëminence as the "melting pot" and making assimilation a worldwide rather than a society-centered process; 2) his conviction that American culture was much too pragmatic to give sincere recognition to black people's claims to a history of their own; 3) his belief that while Africanisms had not survived among blacks, both Africa and its overseas peoples had become part of modern world history; 4) his fear that totalitarian fascism not only threatened Western progress with an atavistic retrogression, but also bid fair to undermine the movement to extend democracy to the colonialized and the caste-exploited peoples of the emerging world order.

Civilization

"Civilization," Park once observed in a paper not published until after his death, "is built up by the absorption of foreign ethnic groups, by undermining them, and by secularizing their cult and sacred order."[212] Although Park held to the thesis that "civilization is always a territorial affair,"[213] he did not hold to the view that the boundaries of national states, or any other kind of politically organized unit, would necessarily be coextensive with those of civilization. In this sense, Park's conception of civilization bears a certain resemblance to that of Emile Durkheim and Marcel Mauss, who sought to establish a new science of social morphology that would take as its central concern those cultural phenomena that could not be contained within geopolitical state formations.[214] In Park's case, however, the modern civilizational process is associated with the growth of cities and the fact that such growth is concomitant with the rise of a money economy, the rationalization of life activities, and the coming together of racially and culturally distinctive peoples. Thus, to Park, the contact, conflict, accommodation, and assimilation of races is both incidental and integral to the civilizational process.

However, the fact that that process had moved out from its once central locus in the United States, out even from the Occident, and had proceeded to envelop the entire world introduced a new era in race relations. "The race problem as it exists today," Park observed in 1925, "is primarily a product of the expansion of international trade and the improvement of transportation and communication."[215] As such, the problem could be resolved if the race relations cycle were to be completed in a general assimilation that would dissolve all racial groups in the solvent of market interests and within a world market-society. However, as Park was at pains to assert, the civilizational character of this modern form of assimilation would have to overcome both the aspiring nationalisms of racial and ethnic minorities as well as the racially biased ethnocentrism of such already established state societies as the United States. As he put it in 1926, "If America was once in any exclusive sense the melting pot of races, it is so no longer. The melting pot is the world."[216] But, as Park was quick to see—he pointed to the erection of immigration restrictions and other new barriers to immigration set up at "our racial frontier on the Pacific"[217]—few had recognized this fact or its implications.

An Ahistorical America

Park claimed that in moving out of the caste-ridden rural South and into the metropoli where mental life was both stimulated and altered, black Americans had passed beyond the stage wherein their situation could be depicted only in a "natural history." In fact, black urbanites had entered a new phase in their development in which their experience as participants in a peoplehood would have to be investigated in a "social history." During the 1920s, Park kept abreast of the new historical scholarship on both Africa and those of its people who had participated in the global diaspora emanating from that continent.[*] When, in 1917, Harvard University announced publication of

---

[*]Neither in his Congo papers nor when, in 1910, he accompanied Booker T. Washington on a trip through Europe on a quest for "the man farthest down," did Park take notice of Russia's concern with Africa—(See Edward Thomas Wilson, *Russia and Black Africa Before World War II* [New York: Holmes and Meier, 1974], esp. pp. 4–93)—or of the fact that a few American Negroes had been servants to the Czars of Russia from the reign of Alexander I to the abdication of Nicholas II (See Mina Curtiss, "Some American Negroes in Russia in the Nineteenth Century," *The Massachusetts Review*, IX:2 [Spring, 1968], pp. 268–96), or of the settlement of persons of African descent in the Black Sea area. Though they visited a Russian border village in that vicinity, Park and Washington missed a chance to see, perhaps even to "discover," the several Negro communities there, whose presence had been noted by travelers as early as 1884, and who would become a source of some public interest in 1913, after a Russian naturalist, V. P. Vradii, reported on their presence in *Kavkaz*, a newspaper published in Tiflis (Tbilisi). Ignored during the First World War, the Negro Caucasians of the Black Sea area were "rediscovered" in 1923, studied by Russian anthropologists and taken notice of in American publications in 1925 and 1931. Thought to be descendants of bond servants brought from the sixteenth to the nineteenth centuries by Turkish slavers into the Caucasus region, these blacks again became a topic for investigation in the 1960s, after most of them had become assimilated. (See Allison Blakely, *Russia and the Negro: Blacks in Russian History and Thought* [Washington, D.C.: Howard University Press, 1986], pp. 5–12.)

the first volume of its proposed series on *Varia Africana*, Park—despite his belief that very little of their homeland culture had survived the Atlantic crossing and slavery—held that "No study of the Negro in America will be complete which does not take account of the African background of the race." But he quickly added, "no attempt to assess the qualities and capacities of the native African, living in his isolated and primitive environment, will be adequate which does not take account of the Negro's progress under the conditions of a civilized environment."[218] While Park regarded the history of seventeenth-century Barbados—settled originally in accordance with a British imperial policy that used the island as a "dumping-ground for England's unruly and undesirable population . . ."—"[to be] the story of the failure of the white man to accommodate himself permanently to conditions of life in the tropics,"[219] he believed that Benjamin Brawley's interpretation of Afro-American history in 1922[220] depicted "a people who, out of their struggles to participate in the common life of America and the world, are slowly and painfully defining for themselves a common purpose, creating a common tradition, a common will and, by the very singleness of their racial purposes, making a contribution to the common life of America and of the World."[221] However, in order to overcome the widespread belief that black Americans had no history to which whites need attend, Brawley's positive perspective on the annals of America's blacks would have to alter the conventionalized attitude toward history that white Americans had already adopted. George Washington Williams and W. E. B. DuBois had tried to make white Americans recognize that the people of African descent had a history, that they were not merely a social problem. But their efforts had not been rewarded. Although Park himself had played an active role in the founding and early years of the Association for the Study of Negro Life and History,[222] a number of factors—not the least of which were his disagreements with fellow members of the Association—he was not sanguine about the capacity of white Americans to accept revisions in the cherished visions of their history. As he would point out in 1931, "Americans are notoriously lacking, as Europeans have frequently observed, in the historic sense."[223]

Africanisms in History and Culture

Whatever the historical attitude, however, Park insisted that the direction of history—including the history of Africa and overseas peoples of African descent—was toward the ultimate incorporation of all peoples, nations, and classes in a global system governed by the interests of commerce and industry. Such a system was the essence of modern civilization. Moreover, in facilitating this historical trend, Park believed that missions still had a role to play. Precisely because "the great missionary religions . . . have not been halted by political boundaries . . . [t]he function of missions . . . is . . . to create in an expanding world community a common understanding and a worldwide moral order, and by so doing to complete and humanize the new economic and political society which European imperialism has created." In Park's vision of the emerging global system, "the task of missions appears . . . as an integral part of the process by which a new world culture has come into existence and is rapidly superseding the earlier provincial and less inclusive types of civilization."[224] However, this greatly expanded vision of the role that a reinvigorated Protestant ethic would play was accompanied by Park's recognition that its Christian endeavor would have to compete with the claims on human sensibilities and social reconstruction presented by the rival faiths of ethno-nationalism, fascism, and communism.

Although Park seemed to accept the rise of racial and ethnic nationalisms in America and elsewhere as incidents in the natural history and progressive advance of universal assimilation—as early as 1914, he had asserted, "The fact is that nationalist sentiment among the Slavs, like racial sentiment among the Negroes, has sprung up as the result of a struggle against privilege and discrimination based upon racial distinctions. . . . [U]nder conditions of secondary contact, that is to say, conditions of individual liberty and individual competition, characteristic of modern civilization, depressed racial groups tend to assume the form of nationalities"[225]—he insisted that Africanisms, insofar as they were claimed as a vital part of the Afro-American minority's quest for a usable past, are both misconstrued and debilitating. Assuming as he did that both on the continent of their origin and among their present-day representatives overseas, "Africans are the only contemporaneous primitive people who have anywhere achieved race consciousness and civilization without losing their identity . . . ," Park had concluded that, as "a consequence almost every fundamental process and stage of civilization, from the most primitive to the most cosmopolitan . . ., is somewhere represented in the contemporary life of the Negro in Africa and America."[226]

Despite this claim—or, more accurately, to explain its foundations—Park insisted that it was their inherited tropical temperament rather than the few survivals of their African culture that had made it possible for African Americans to still exhibit exoticisms in their conduct. As for the eruption of nationalistic fervor among blacks in the United States and the Caribbean, Park asserted that this was nothing less than "another spontaneous manifestation of that unrest . . . which has found [its latest] expression in pan-Africanism and in the movement in this country headed by Marcus Garvey, whose program is Africa for the Africans."[227] When, in 1937, Melville Herskovitz suggested that his culture-conflict approach to understanding voodoo cults among Haitian villagers might also throw new light on the dilemmas and contradictions attending black life in the United States, Park dismissed the idea out of hand, asserting that "the amount of . . . [the American Negro's] African heritage must be very small, indeed . . . ," and going on to insist "that the African in the United States has, for reasons that

are obvious to those familiar with his history, retained less of his African heritage than is true of the Negro in any other part of the new world."[228]
Contrary to the claim of such Park apologists as Barbara Ballis Lal,[229] Park
maintained his belief in a tropical temperament and his opposition to the thesis of African survivals in the New World throughout his later years. Werner
Cahnman, who served at Fisk University in the early 1940s, would later
recall, "I was struck by Park's desperate opposition to Lorenzo D. Turner's
report about his findings among the Gullah Islanders on the South Carolina
coast, where he had encountered, in painstaking research, numerous West
African words, names, proverbs, tales, and usages. The evidence Turner presented was as clear as could have been desired, but Park refused to concede.
As he rose in the discussion, he attempted to explain away the Africanisms in
the language of the Gullah Islanders as an example of the universal habit of
'speaking in tongues.'"[230] To Park, black assimilation in America would not
proceed as a byproduct of the mutual give-and-take of an overseas African
culture.

Instead of concentrating their attention on the personal and social conflicts
engendered by the alleged presence of African survivals in black Americans'
daily life, social analysts of the Negro question might, in Park's estimation,
become better informed on the matter if they would examine the new cultural expressions emanating from "the centers of Negro urban life in the
North . . ." These included "a new, surprisingly vigorous, and radically independent literature, in which a new generation of Negro intellectuals have
sought to describe and interpret Negro life as they see and feel it, and to give,
at the same time, a new orientation and a more positive expression of
the Negro's rising race consciousness."[231] Park no doubt had in mind the
race consciousness represented by such "New Negro"[232] and "Harlem
Renaissance"[233] expressions as jazz music,[234] or such genre-defying novels
as Jean Toomer's *Cane*,[235] Countee Cullen's plaintive poetic ode to a lost
African culture, "Heritage,"[236] and the modernist depiction of black American
city dwellers' scenes and situations in the paintings of Aaron Douglas, Meta
Warrick Fuller, Palmer Hayden, and William H. Johnson.[237] But that race
consciousness did not arise out of any cultural legacy brought from Africa to
America. "My own conclusion," Park wrote in 1937, "is that all that the
Negro in the United States has retained is his temperament."[238]

Segregation, Racism, and the World Racial Order

Commenting on Hortense Powdermaker's pathbreaking study of the bi-
racial, segregated order that continued to prevail in Indianola, Mississippi, in
1939,[239] Park observed that "It was interesting to know that, in the long
period since emancipation, the caste system is still functioning in the region of
the Mississippi Delta much as it did sixty years ago, the chief differences being

that a Negro middle class has, in the meantime, come into existence and the topics of conversation in Negro society have become more worldly and sophisticated."[240] Park went on to lament Dr. Powdermaker's failure to describe the condition of the poor white sharecropper in the same community, because, "This seems the more important in view of the fact that the two most obvious examples of the neglected man, the Negro and the white sharecropper, though visibly antagonistic to one another, seem nevertheless so obviously bound together in a common destiny that the struggle of one to rise inevitably impedes the efforts of the other."[241] As people bound together in a mutually antagonistic destiny, the black peon and the white sharecropper illustrated the condition that had led Park to revise his prediction about the outcome of the race relations cycle three years earlier, and, two years after that to worry over the effects of the race cycle on the struggles among socio-economic classes. However, the problems presented by the caste order of the South were, in Park's estimation, a microcosm of those affecting the world situation—a point he had made, *sotto voce*, as early as 1924 by reviewing a study of the populist movement in Georgia side by side with one on the Fascist movement in Italy.[242]

The modern race problem, Park would assert in 1943, had arisen as a most significant incident in, as well as an effect of, the 450-year history of European civilizational expansion, a history that had first begun with Columbus's voyages in 1492. However, the quintessentially significant moment in that history has occurred only recently and could be realized through recognition of "the fact that within the last seventy-one years European expansion has finally reached the limits of the habitable world."[243] There had been, in effect, an enclosure of the racial frontiers of the world, and with it an evocation of new conflicts of consciousness and action that were bound to alter the shape of civilizational things to come. Whereas some had supposed that the four stages of his race relations cycle would always occur consecutively, in a chronological sequence, each succeeding the other and overturning its institutional arrangements and undermining its attendant attitudes, now it would likely be the case that the situations and sentiments appropriate to each stage would coexist in time and space with one another.

Slavery, Park argued in 1927, had been "an incident in the history of the plantation system, and the plantation system still survives."[244] Criticizing the applicability of the concept "oppression psychosis" to the struggles of liberation currently underway among races, nations, and classes, Park pointed out that it seemed to require holding to the validity of a prior, untenable, and "tacit assumption that conflict in some form—not necessarily war—is something less than the normal relation of social groups." In contrast to such an assumption, he went on to observe, it was in fact the case that "nationalities, like political parties, exist for the purpose of conflict."[245] The current "rise of race and national consciousness among the so-called 'oppressed minorities of Europe' . . . [had,] since the changes brought about by the war [of

1914–1918, taken the form of] . . . oppressing other racial minorities, some of whom were formerly their oppressors."[246] Indeed, by 1943, the cycle of imperialism, oppression, national consciousness, liberation struggle, and new oppression of minorities had become global, and Park was prepared to assert that, on the one hand, "Nationalism seems to be the normal reaction to imperialism," but, on the other, that "It seems also to be a stage in the evolution of the form which imperialism has assumed—that which it takes in totalitarian powers."[247]

In 1937 Park had succumbed before the thrust of events in Europe, Asia, the Pacific, and the United States, and he began to reformulate his estimate of what form the final stage of the race relations cycle would assume. At that time, the Asian issue seemed foremost in his mind. In 1931 Park had called attention to the cultural contradictions that were likely to engender conflict between the Occident and the Orient. "American civilization is founded typically upon the market place, where people come together for trade and barter; Chinese civilization, on the contrary, is founded on the family, where people come together for comfort, for security, and for moral support."[248] What forms would emerge, Park seemed to be asking, when a society whose most telling symbol was the ringing of the stock exchange bell came into contact, conflict, and an as yet undeveloped mode of accommodation with a civilization whose symbol of moral authority was a Confucian patriarch? "Chinese morality," Park had noted in 1927, the year that the Kuomintang split into nationalist and communist factions and began a civil war that would not end until 1949, "has not yet adapted itself to corporate management"; moreover, he went on to observe, "China . . . has had neither the experience nor the means for making the adjustments which the commercial and industrial invasion of Europe and America demands."[249] Moreover, the very principle upon which the Chinese polity had been founded stood in sharp contradiction to that which had engendered the Occidental state. In China, "[I]t is demanded of servants of the government not merely that they obey the commands of their superiors but that they be successful in carrying these commands into effect," Park pointed out.[250] And, he asserted, "It is only in respect to the principle of personal responsibility that the difference between Chinese and European legal conceptions finds its most obvious expression."[251] But these legal conceptions illustrated an age-old civilizational dichotomy: "There has always been, apparently, one law of the family and of the tribe, and another law of the market place."[252] The problem of the Pacific rim was, in effect, being exacerbated because, currently, there was occurring a collision of these two laws under conditions that gave little promise for the Chinese one to remain efficacious.

South Asia, and more especially, India, on the other hand, was being inducted into modernity and its civilizational complex more rapidly than China. "The 'passionate confusion' of present-day India," Park pointed out in 1926, "is part of the general unrest of Asia, and this pullulation of new life in these ancient civilizations is one of the significant facts of the modern world."[253] However, less like China, India had already undergone a considerable amount of industrialization. Indeed, Park noted, "India is not only the chief industrial country in the tropics, but the eighth greatest industrial country in the world. . . ."[254] As Park saw the matter, "the cycle of change which began with the extension of European trade to the Orient has, in the case of India at least, been completed."[255] Even though "its population of 320,000,000 [was still] mostly agricultural," Park pointed to the fact "that the cotton spinners in India are now in active competition with Lancashire, England, and the steel mills of Bengal are manufacturing steel plates and sheets in competition with the mills of Germany, England, and the United States."[256] Industrial development, Park concluded, "measures more accurately than anything else the extent and the character of changes in the life of India. . . . These changes touch every aspect of Indian life . . . [and] are . . . undermining the most characteristic feature of Indian civilization, mainly her caste system; . . . not to mention other and less obvious consequences they have created in a people speaking 222 distinct languages."[257] What was emerging in India was, "if not a nation, at least a nationality."[258]

However, for Park, the strategic site for following the pace and direction of the race relations cycle was Hawaii. "The Hawaiian Islands," he had claimed in 1926, "at the present moment have become a laboratory for the study of the race problem. In these islands all the races of the Pacific have come together in numbers and under conditions more favorable to the successful working of the melting-pot than are likely to be found elsewhere on the planet."[259] Eleven years later, the researches of his student Romanzo Adams on the extent and effects of interracial marriage in this territory of the United States, as well as the militarization of these islands in the face of the threat posed by Japan to American interests in the Pacific, led Park to reconsider the matter.[260] Race relations, he now proposed, occur in three dimensions—as adjustments, in long-term cycles, and fortuitously—that interpenetrate and complicate their pattern and movement. Yet, "[w]hat are popularly referred to as race relations ordinarily involve some sort of race conflict . . . [but] can best be interpreted if what they seem to be at any time and place is regarded merely as a phase in a cycle of change which, once initiated, inevitably continues until it terminates in some predestined racial configuration, and one consistent with an established social order of which it is a part."[261] Because of the varying character of the social orders extant in the world—because, in effect, Occidental civilization had not yet remade every society and culture into an analogue of itself—the final stage of the race relations cycle would also vary. "[W]hen stabilization is finally achieved," Park pointed out, "race relations will assume one of three . . . configurations. They will take the form of a caste system, as in India; they will terminate in complete assimilation as in China; or the unassimilated race will constitute a permanent racial minority within the limits of a national state, as is the case of the Jews in Europe."[262] It is noteworthy that in restating the character and terminal phase of the race relations cycle, Park made no prediction about the future status of blacks or any other of the non-white peoples in the American variant of that cycle.

WAR, RACE CONFLICT, AND
THE RACE RELATIONS CYCLE IN AMERICA

With the advent of the Second World War, Park—in one of his final papers—once again sought to reframe the issues entailed in American and global race frictions. "What the war has done thus far," he opined in 1943, "has been to make race relations an international rather than a local and national problem."[263] Nevertheless, there remained the deeply engrained attitudes, the apparently inflexible institutions, and the seemingly fixed opinions that in fact expressed racist ideologies. These ideologies had become embedded in the national culture and psyche and had had their own origin in the era of slavery. Although Park regarded the war to be, potentially at least, also a revolution in the ordering of humankind, he felt it necessary to point out that "Revolutions are the product not of changes in opinion but of changes in ideology. . . ." And he noted that "in the prosecution of the war and in the organization of the peace, [the] racial diversities of the American population will be either a national handicap or a national asset, depending on our ability to make our racial policies and our racial ideology conform to our national interests."[264] Park asserted that "A revolution in race relations in the United States may be impending, but it has not yet arrived,"[265] a thesis that the researches of his former student, E. Franklin Frazier, had already documented.[266]

Park ultimately came to apply his thesis about the ubiquity of conflict to the manner in which blacks would have to proceed as they moved along their own path to assimilation in America's market-oriented, class-based social order. Bi-racial social and economic organization had already produced parallel hierarchies of black and white professional, middle, and working classes, but the blacks' change in status from that of a caste to a minority group had been accompanied by a shift from their condition as a race buffeted about by an externally determined destiny to one in which they had assumed a certain degree of self-directed autonomy over the formulation of their own identity, interests, future, and leadership. The effects of a mounting pecuniary civilization had already taken their toll on the Southern black church—the one institution that had constituted the basis of the rural Afro-American life style in the Delta region of Mississippi, as Park's former student, Samuel C. Adams, Jr., would report in 1947: "The impact of civilization and the resulting changes in church, minister, and religious behavior in general can be summarized as follows: new forms of ridiculing ministers; declining rates of attendance; greater emphasis upon pecuniary and secular values than upon the spiritual life of the community; and, the substitution of other activities for the past all inclusive functions of the church. These factors indicate that the church is no longer the vital institution."[267] Adams's conclusion suggested that Park's post-Tuskegee perspective was finding a basis in the sociological theory of acculturation: "As the group becomes articulate in its protest against caste or other limitations, the members begin to create its own history and group loyalty."[268] This new mode of acculturation, however, would engender conflict and countervailing actions on the part of the white Anglo majority, as both Park and Adams pointed out.

Their rising status would encounter resistance from those whites determined to maintain the caste position under attack, but, as Park put the matter in a letter to his former student Horace Cayton, "If conflicts arise as a result of the efforts [of blacks] to get their place it will be because the white people started them." And, as he concluded in that epistolary statement, "These conflicts will probably occur and are more or less inevitable but conditions will be better after they are over."[269] The struggle for emancipation would continue, Park supposed, until that moment when race conflicts had disappeared altogether—only to be replaced by those of classes.[270] "One thing, however, seems certain," he wrote in 1943: "the races and peoples which fate has brought together in America and within the limits of the larger world economy will continue, in the emerging world society, their struggle for a political and a racial equality that was denied them in the world that is passing."[271] The struggle was inevitable even if its outcome was less certain.

Concluding Remarks

There have been many changes and paradigm shifts in sociology since Park's death—e.g., the rise and decline of the positivist-functionalist synthesis,[1] the challenges to the Columbia-Harvard disciplinary hegemony posed by such dissident schools as Herbert Blumer's symbolic interactionism, Harold Garfinkel's ethnomethodology, Levi-Strauss's structuralism, the varieties of European and American neo-Marxism, English (i.e., Giddens's) structurationism, the German (i.e., Habermas's) neo-Frankfurtian civic discourse school, and postmodernist French (i.e., Derrida's, Lyotard's, and Baudrillard's) deconstructionism[2]—but his original conceptualizations of social science and the sociological imagination he conveyed in his early as well as his later writings commend themselves to present and future scholars. Although one interpreter of American trends in sociology over the last century had concluded in 1978 that "Having gradually become institutionalized and largely professionalized . . . , having passed through a period of incubation during the years of Chicago dominance, sociology could embark on its mature career,"[3] other analysts have been far less sanguine. A discipline that for at least two decades has been said to be in crisis,[4] that has recently been characterized by two of its foremost younger theorists as embracing "an impossible science,"[5] that, in the words of one of its more iconoclastic emigré theorists and researchers, "seems to have missed every intellectually promising boat in the last half century,"[6] and one whose practitioners are said to be "as pressed now for reasonable sociological sense about the fundamental conditions of social life as they were nearly sixty years ago"[7] could certainly gain much by returning to its beginnings and reconsidering the writings and outlook of one of its most eminent contributors. More and more, it seems, it is time for sociologists to repudiate Robert K. Merton's adaptation of Alfred North Whitehead's dictum that "a science which hesitates to forget its founders is lost."[8]

Despite—or perhaps because of—Park's breadth of vision and range of interests, his legacy has been parceled out among his epigoni such that the parts fail to add up to the original whole that gave them life. Thus, claimants to a Parkian or "Chicago" discipleship define themselves as urban ecologists, sociologists of communication, race relations specialists, qualitative investigators, sociological ethnographers, or students of collective behavior. The one framework they do not select—indeed, one that has been virtually abandoned in contemporary sociology—is that of student of civilization and the civilizational process.[9] Park's early studies—of the German army, of King Leopold II's depredations in the Congo, of Booker T. Washington's program for black uplift in America—are not only investigations of significant substantive sociocultural and politico-economic issues, but also, and more importantly, prescient studies of what would later be called modernity.

The central characteristics of the trend toward modernity is seen in the movement of the *civilizational process*, i.e., the process whereby humankind's individuals are conducted—willy-nilly, or so it seems to some—toward a habitus within a *civil society*, toward a political identity as members of a *citizenry* of a *state society*, toward an economic condition within both a hierarchy of market-related *classes* and a *global political economy,* toward a social identity defined in terms of one or another *status* group, toward personal identity as attenuated parts of a *lonely crowd*, and toward restless if not anomic participation in the *mass*. However, those who travel along the road to modernity discover that it is not straight; it has its byways and detours, and it is strewn with rocks and obstacles. Park's early essays described some of these contours and impediments: the militarization of states with its attendant transformation of citizenship into patriotism; the industrial-capitalist thrust toward imperialism that placed peoples of darker color and different culture under the preternaturally evil sway of religiously inspired and morally arrogant Occidental authorities; and the racial ideologies that either denied full citizenship to non-Western peoples altogether or promised its benefits to them only after they had acquiesced to a long period of tutelage, subservience, and self-abnegation. Park's early papers not only engaged each of these impediments to modernity, but also set forth terms of discourse on the subject that continue to the present day to inspire research and trouble policy.

Indeed, Park's early papers and the problems he delineated and investigated are comparable in scope and intention—but different in approach—to the unfinished project of the contemporary civilizational sociologist, Benjamin Nelson (1911–1977), who wrote, concerning his own works: "I early became intent on investigating the central social and cultural structures and processes of the complex civilizational communities and societies in the specificities of their diverse histories as well as their *extra-domestic* encounters, expansions, and interdependencies."[10] Like Park, Nelson eventually came to be interested in both inter- and intra-civilizational encounters. But, where Nelson pursued his investigations via the written record and by means of what Park would have disparaged as "scholasticism,"[11] Park insisted that in his own case "think-ing is more fruitful when it is in touch, at least, with an empirical world, that is[,] a world of chance and change."[12]

Park's investigations of the German army, the Congo situation, and the operation of the Tuskegee idea were carried out in just such a world. His early papers were written in the first decade of an era that the historian John Milton Cooper, Jr., characterizes as "pivotal" for the development of American institutions.[13] That era began after one that is regarded as having witnessed the nadir of America's black-white relations.[14] In Park's estimation, achieving modernity was neither a pleasant nor a progressive experience; rather, it was merely inevitable and charted by "incidents"—slavery, segregation, imperial-ism, militarism—that seemed to make up a "natural history" but certainly boded ill for those who were its victims. Moreover, modernity, once achieved, would open up new bases for conflict for those who survived its coming into being.

It is fashionable today to criticize Park for not advocating a sociologically inspired socialism—that is, for not looking to the state to solve the many social problems or to ameliorate the social condition of the several peoples then in the throes of civilizational advance.[15] But, in the era in which he came to maturity, Park had good reason to distrust the politicians, judges, and bureaucrats who administered the state and guided the American nation in its march toward modernity. Indeed, his earliest memories portend his later skepticism: He "seemed to recall a vivid memory of [President Abraham] Lincoln's death—even though he was just fourteen months old at the time—and liked to recount how, as a small boy, he had been stopped and asked the way by a stranger who turned out to be Jesse James."[16] Remembering the first assassination of an American president and an early encounter with what later students of the frontier would call a "social bandit," Park's child-hood recollections suggest an early imprinting of an America undergoing a socio-political legitimation crisis. That crisis looms even larger in Park's later writings.

Like William Graham Sumner—upon whose ideas and concepts he often drew—Park was not sanguine about the efficacy, or the ethics, of ameliora-tive social movements or of state-sponsored programs for reconstruction, reform, or advance. In his eighteenth year, he would have read or heard about how the anti-Chinese movement, led by the trade unions that had organized white workers and developed the "white label" as a symbol of their racial group's emancipation,[17] had achieved its greatest success to date in the passage of the Chinese Exclusion Act of 1882.[18] By the time he was in his thirties, he had seen the Radical Republicans' program designed to advance the ex-slaves to full citizenship[19] scrapped in favor of the Redemptionists' policies of legalized inferiorization.[20] When he opted to work for Booker T. Washington and seemed to acquiesce[21] to the forces of white supremacy that had come to prevail in the South, he had had to recognize not only that there were no effective voices for full citizenship for the Negro in the corridors of American power, but also that such seemingly tolerant leaders as Theodore Roosevelt—who had once (December 1901) had Washington to dinner at the White House, but after complaints from Southern white leaders never again entertained a black man or woman there while he was president[22]—were also supporters of European imperialism in Africa. ("The English rule in Africa," Roosevelt would write in 1910, "has been of incalculable benefit to Africans themselves, and indeed this is true of most European nations. Mistakes have been made, of course, but they have proceeded at least as often from an unwise effort to accomplish too much in the way of beneficence, as from a desire to exploit the natives. Each of the civilized nations that has taken possession of any part of Africa has had its own peculiar good qualities and its own peculiar defects."[23]) If Park was skeptical of the efforts undertaken by W. E. B. DuBois, Monroe Trotter, and the NAACP to insure every jot and tittle of the African Americans' civil rights,[24] he had before him the terrible evidence of hundreds of uncensured lynchings in the South,[25] widespread popular and political support for continued segregation (e.g., Woodrow Wilson reintroduced segregation in the offices of his administration[26]), and a general fear of and hostility toward mixing the races that had led thirty-nine of the United States to pass laws forbidding marriage across racial lines.[27]

Although Park's global and civilizational outlook did not square with the prohibition on Asian immigration enacted by the United States Congress in 1924, he refused to remove the conclusion reached through his and his colleagues' researches on the racial situation along the Pacific Coast in 1926—that passage of the provisions for Oriental exclusion and strengthening of California's and thirteen other state's anti-Asian Alien Land Laws had for the moment reduced tensions in the area.[28] For Park, civilization manifested itself in only temporary accommodations among elements ordinarily antagonistic to each other. Racial accommodations in America were inherently unstable because that society was moving away from a racial caste order and toward one made up of open classes.[29] The modern American state and its racist public philosophy—insofar as it was a representation of the collective consciousness of the people in process of civilizational development—was part of the problem and certainly not the likely agency to carry forth a practical solution to the discontents attending modernization.

One problem implicit in Park's researches is how the civilizational process might overcome the ethno-national limits and religious exclusions that peoples and faiths put in the way of its advance. Civilization, as Emile Durkheim and Marcel Mauss used the term, refers to those cultural phenomena that somehow manage to transcend, leap over, burrow beneath, or muddle through established geopolitical and religio-cultural boundaries. Civilization to these two French thinkers had a tendency to become internationalized despite pressures toward national demarcation and geopolitical hermeticization.[30] For Park, the culture of individuation, achievement, and civil identity constituted the content of the modern civilizational process and was spatio-temporally located in the cities of the post-Feudal Occident. However, that process was everywhere modified by various attempts to restrict it within national, racial, or religious lines. In America—although Park did not make a point of this thesis, as well he might have—this tendency had been exacerbated by the fact that the white, Anglo-Saxon, English-speaking element in the eighteenth-century Atlantic colonies had taken the lead in liberating their people from the rule of the European seaborne empires and had established the United States of America as the first new nation-in-waiting, seeking to press its language, culture, and mores on other peoples—African, Asian, Hispanic, Amerindian, European—who had settled or would settle there. The fact that the four cultures of Albion[31] would eventually become more or less fused into a Protestant-oriented, white supremacist, and populist-inclined civil polity markedly influenced the playing out of the civilizational process in the ensuing centuries of America's national development.[32]

Park himself could not altogether liberate his sociologizing from the ethno-religious nationalization that had overwhelmed the civilizational process in America. In America—and in Europe—civilization was all too often uncritically equated in both the popular and academic mindwith the spread of Protestant Christianity. However, as Forrest G. Wood has recently shown, the leaders of the Social Gospel, the most prominent religious movement of the late nineteenth and early twentieth centuries—and the one that most influenced the development of American sociology[33]—nurtured dreams of an American-Anglo-Saxon/German-Teutonic axis that would dominate a world stratified in accordance with a permanent hierarchy of races.[34]

For Park—who in 1930 announced that he was "no longer interested in new faiths, either political or religious"[35]—missions of uplift embodied the contradictory effects that flowed from the activation of the Protestant ethic and its Catholic rivals. In the Congo they not only provided a rationale for some of the most horrendous atrocities ever committed against the flesh and faith of humankind, but also the basis for a bloody contest over the jurisdiction of souls. In the rural and small-town South, on the other hand, in the form of Booker T. Washington's educational program of Negro uplift, the Protestant ethic offered practical ways in which a much-beset people might realize a modicum of fruitful and secure opportunity. To Park, the universalizing principle inherent in Protestantism seemed to promise a fundamental ground for the breakdown of racial and ethnic parochialisms, but the actual practices of those engaged in its innerworldly missions all too often allied themselves with the prevailing racist ethos—the mystery of blood seemed all too often to prevail over the mystery of faith.

As a particular element of the civilizational process, the cycle of race relations that Park thought he had uncovered provided a "natural history" of race relations. Unfortunately, it could not be verified in fact or experience.[36] Yet, for most of his life Park charted its progress in terms of the impediments that seemed to block its advance to the final stage—assimilation. Hence, he could transvalue and sublimate Bismarck's Prussian acculturative program of "blood and iron"—the effects of which he had observed so closely during his stay in Germany—separating out the coercive elements and substituting in their stead an inexorable process that he thought he saw working silently and unobtrusively on the exotic and unacculturated peoples of the United States. Hence, he could explain the differences in black and Jewish adaptations to the American scene by positing the existence of an immutable, hereditary, racial temperament that modified these peoples' adjustment. Hence, he could insist that the cultures, languages, motifs, and arts of Africa could not have survived slavery and its acculturative powers. Hence, at the end of his life,[37] he could insist as a true American—steeped in the poetry of Walt Whitman[38] and the philosophy of William James[39]—that a public policy appropriate to the war against fascism required official recognition that the peoples of non-white color and non-Western culture in America deserved the full panoply of civil rights, social recognition, and chances to compete in the marketplace that were already granted to the majority element in the population.

Coterminous with the spread of civilization is the rise of the modern state and its powers. The state, moreover, bids fair to become the sole moderator of civil society, the agency that determines the nature and scope of the public and private spheres of everyday life.[40] For William Graham Sumner, the modern state found its quintessential form in the bureaucratic clerk, a personage, the Yale sociologist insisted, who exercised enormous power but deserved no respect.[41] For Park, the modern state reached its most dangerous form when it became a garrisoned national security entity—the kind foreshadowed in von Moltke's military reorganization and fully developed in Hitler's Nazi regime,[42] the kind he feared might envelop postwar America.

The predominance of state over all other forms of authority was, however, a concomitant of the erosion of all ascriptive sodalities and mediating communities in the face of the seemingly inexorable penetration of civic modernization. Park's race relations cycle—until 1937, when he gave it up—that promised the assimilation of peoples and cultures within the vortex of market economics and civil authority seemed to strengthen the arguments of all those who believed that the progress of both the state and civilization ought to be and, in fact, would be purchased at the price of private as well as quasi-public associations of hereditary kin and race groups. Park, who personally liked the élan and romance that a variety of vibrant cultures living cheek by jowl made possible, seemed to lament the dull enervating effect of the civilizational process, but he believed that its direction could not be changed nor its end result prevented.

✦ ✦ ✦

Virtually every one of Park's assumptions about slavery, race, and culture have been challenged in the scholarship undertaken since his death. To writers of the 1950s and thereafter, Park's emphasis on how the plantation slavocracy served the socio-cultural function of assimilation seemed to be all too dependent on the validity of the argument presented in the so-called Dunning school of historiography.[43] In Park's day, that school of thought had been reinforced by the writings of Woodrow Wilson,[44] Ulrich Bonnell Phillips (1877–1934),[45] and other supporters of the antebellum scene.[46] Since his death, revisionist scholars have challenged this school of thought and, in the process, turned attention toward different conclusions about the socio-cultural effects of slavery on the Africans' adjustment to America.[47] However, it should be noted that Park's approach to assimilation could, with but a few modifications, be made to resonate with Stanley Elkins' foreboding thesis that the kind of assimilation produced by the absolute authority structure of the South's plantation system was most similar to that of a Nazi concentration camp, and that both had fostered the development of the same character type—what stereotypists in America called the "Sambo," but what students of Nazidom's horrors called the infantilized personality.[48] No one has interpreted Park's thesis in this manner, however.

Park's belief in a hereditary racial temperament has not survived the rejection of biological determinism in much of contemporary sociology. But it—or some variant of it—could be resuscitated by those who take up the new interest in sociobiology.[49] Temperament has received serious consideration in the theories of society and personality developed by the Chicago-trained sociologist, Tamotsu Shibutani, but little has been done beyond the latter's shrewd and cautious usage of the concept.[50] At least one major critic of sociobiology, Kenneth Bock, has emphasized Park's socio-historical approach and pointed to his acknowledged debt to the iconoclastic opponent of hereditary explanations, Frederick J. Teggart, for what Park called the "catastrophic" theory of civilization. Bock treats Park's formulation of the "marginal man" idea as far more important than his thesis about racial temperament and as central to Park's general theory of civilization.[51] "Park's object," he notes, ". . . was to explain existing cultural differences among peoples, and he was convinced that racial and physical environmental theories [had] failed to do so."[52] As Bock summarizes the matter, the marginal man—a product of the collision of cultures but a full-fledged member of none of them (Park had adapted this conceptualization from Simmel's essay on the stranger[53] and put it together with both his German-Jewish mentor's discussion of the effects of the metropolis on mental life[54] and Teggart's belief that such collisions were the occasion for a release of certain persons from their slavery to habit and custom controls[55])—"is caught between a traditional orientation to life which he must leave and a new one of which he is not wholly trustful and into which he is not admitted."[56] And, as Bock concludes on this point, "It is in the reactions of marginal man that creativity may be observed."[57]

Bock's commentary provides an avenue by which one can link Park's early studies of Winston-Salem and Tuskegee to his and his students' later interest in the social and cultural life of blacks in American cities. In effect, Park's interest in the Tuskegee program evidences his investigation of an instance in which paternalistic guidance of the freedmen-and-women and their children and grandchildren, and Booker T. Washington's emphasis on agricultural and mechanical pursuits, acted as a brake on whatever deleterious and anomic effects their induction into urban civilization and its attendant tendency to marginalize them would have. On the other hand, once black migration out of the rural South to such cities as Chicago[58] had become a major demographic movement, Park and his followers could see both the creative possibilities and the disruptive consequences of such a change. In his student E. Franklin Frazier's studies of the urban African-Americans' family,[59] church,[60] youth groups,[61] and bourgeois elements,[62] and in the study of Chicago's black belt by St. Claire Drake and Horace Cayton[63], both students of Park, are charted the effects of the blacks' movement to the cities.

In the forty-seven years since Park's death, studies of the social, cultural, and economic conditions of America's black urbanites have in effect demonstrated Park's student Herbert Blumer's refusal to assure advocates of industrial, civil societies that urbanization would inevitably resolve America's race problem.[64] Bart Landry's analysis of *The New Black Middle Class* concludes that the latter group has learned that the old promise of "unilinear progress and unlimited growth" is no longer certain; that "in the 1970s and 1980s . . ., many detours and roadblocks" still remain; and that "[e]conomic equality . . ., even for the black middle class, now seems a long way off."[65] A recent multidisciplinary study of the social, economic, and political situation affecting living conditions for blacks in the urban South of the 1970s and 1980s concludes:

> Resistance to black economic and political parity with the larger society has not disappeared. Black southerners still encounter obstacles in . . . voting. . . . Black housing choices and ownership opportunities are limited because of institutional barriers. The issues surrounding school desegregation have not all been resolved. Black workers continue to be denied jobs and promotions because of their race. Discrimination has taken on a more sophisticated face, which makes it easy to practice but difficult to prove. Black residents in the South still have many hurdles to overcome.[66]

For those black men, women, and youths in the Northern inner-city, i.e., the slums and ghettoes that enclose the blue-collar and unemployed, matters are even worse. These African Americans constitute what William J. Wilson calls an "underclass" that is at one and the same time separated spatially and culturally from the black bourgeoisie and insufficiently skilled or educated to escape from their own plight.[67] Urban civilization has bred its peculiar discontent—a new class of the truly disadvantaged.[68]

Park's concern over what effects governmental intervention in the race problem might produce is still to be found in the opposed views of contemporary sociologists and socially conscious thinkers. Jack Douglas—a veritable intellectual incarnation of William Graham Sumner—observes: "It is precisely because our Western democracies have become ever more egalitarian politically and (less so) economically over the past two centuries that equality has become such a burning issue. The more equal we are, the more we compare ourselves to each other, and the more the ancient passions of shame, envy, resentment, and hatred are unleashed; and the more these passions threaten the very values, institutions, and forms of economic exchange which have produced our greater equality."[69] For Douglas, the "fundamental policy rule is the *conservative* rule. . . . It forbids [governmental] interference except when necessary because we are generally ignorant of all the major effects of such interventions."[70] However, K. Sue Jewell, who recently completed a comprehensive study of the institutional impact of America's social programs on the black family, holds to a different point of view about public policy. Recognizing that a number of analysts have concluded "that [government- sponsored] social and economic programs created more problems in the long term than they resolved;" that "liberalism created illusions of progress and gains that were only spuriously related to those achieved through open-market competition;" and that "liberal social policy dictated that certain cultural value systems be discarded so that black families could be totally integrated in all spheres of society," Jewell nevertheless is unwilling to jettison altogether liberal, i.e., state interventionist, policies designed to ameliorate the condition of America's impoverished racial minorities. "Ideally," Jewell writes, "social policy should be removed from the realm of partisan politics."[71] Her desideratum, however, is unlikely to become a reality. Park had despaired of the partisan politics of his day; but, in the absence of other resources for socioeconomic advance, the political process is likely to be the most utilized agency of any future human-directed push to fulfill a "natural history."

Of all of Park's ideas about the relationship of race to culture, none has aroused more debate than his assertion that little if any of the customs and lifeways of Africa could have survived the Middle Passage, the "seasoning" in the West Indies, and the two-and-one-quarter centuries of slavery. The issue has moved beyond its original post-Parkian formulation in the Frazier-Herskovitz debate.[72] New conceptualizations and innovative techniques of research—as well as the demands of black Americans that their cultural roots and ancient civilizations be given the recognition and respect that the academy's institutionalized racism has long denied—have not only produced evidence of a surprisingly large and varied body of African survivals,[73] but also shown—as in the recent work of Mechal Sobel[74]—that the character as well as the direction of acculturative borrowing moved back and forth across the racial lines. Even when these challenging researches fail to acknowledge

Park's contribution, they are testimony to the power of his early ideas and original observations to inspire nearly a century of debate, discussion, and scholarly investigation.

Park once said that he had entered into a Faustian bargain in order that he might see, experience, and understand the world as it really is. Were he alive today, I believe that he would recognize in the researches of both his disciples and his critics the works of those who also were willing to challenge cherished verities of thought, to smash the icons of an all-too-self-satisfied social science, and to open up new vistas and visions of the human condition. What, in 1941, he said of William Graham Sumner's legacy is equally applicable to his own:

> I believe that Sumner would be the last man to regard his contributions to social science as "ageless"—at least ageless in the sense that his ideas were to be preserved as embodied in the form in which they were originally presented. Rather, he would want the scientific spirit which animated him and the insights with which he reenforced that spirit to continue to inspire students and encourage them to further discoveries in the field in which he worked.[75]

Park has much still to recommend him as our mentor and guide.

NOTES

Preface

1. Robert E. Park, "The German Army: The Most Perfect Military Organization in the World," *Munsey's Magazine* XXIV: 3 (December 1900), pp. 376–95.

2. See four essays by Robert E. Park, "Recent Atrocities in the Congo State," *The World To-Day* VIII (October 1904), pp. 1328–31; "A King in Business: Leopold II of Belgium, Autocrat of the Congo and International Broker," *Everybody's Magazine* XV (November 1906), pp. 624–33; "The Terrible Story of the Congo," *Everybody's Magazine* XV (December 1906), pp. 763–72; "The Blood Money of the Congo," *Everybody's Magazine* XVI (January 1907), pp. 60–70.

3. See two essays by Robert E. Park, "A City of Racial Peace," *The World To-Day* IX (August 1905), pp. 897–99; "Negro Home Life and Standards of Living," *Annals of the American Academy of Political and Social Science* XLIX (September 1913), pp. 147–63.

4. Robert E. Park, "Agricultural Extension Among the Negroes," *The World To-Day* XV (August 1908), pp. 820–26.

5. For a comprehensive but incomplete bibliography of Park's published writings, see Edna Cooper, comp., "Bibliography of Robert E. Park," *Phylon Quarterly* VI (1945), pp. 372–83.

6. See Robert E. Park, "Methods of Teaching: Impressions and a Verdict," *Social Forces* XX (October 1941), pp. 36–46; "An Autobiographical Note," in Park, *Race and Culture*, The Collected Papers of Robert Ezra Park, Vol. I, ed. by Everett C. Hughes, Charles S. Johnson, Jitsuichi Masuoka, Robert Redfield, and Louis Wirth (Glencoe: The Free Press, 1950), pp. v–ix. Of the biographical accounts see Everett C. Hughes, "Robert E. Park," in *The Founding Fathers of Social Science*, ed. by Timothy Raison (Baltimore: Penguin Books, 1969), pp. 162–69; Fred H. Matthews, *Quest For An American Sociology: Robert E. Park and the Chicago School* (Montreal: McGill and Queen's University Press, 1977); Winifred Raushenbush, *Robert E. Park: Biography of a Sociologist* (Durham, N.C.: Duke University Press, 1979); Helen MacGill Hughes, "Robert Ezra Park: The Philosopher-Newspaperman-Sociologist," in *Sociological Traditions From Generation to Generation: Glimpses of the American Experience*, ed. by Robert K. Merton and Matilda White Riley (Norwood, N.J.: Ablex Publishing Corp., 1980), pp. 67–79. For a formal analysis of Park's sociological theory, see Barbara Klose Bowdery, "The Sociology of Robert E. Park," Ph.D. diss., Columbia University, 1951 (Ann Arbor: Xerox University Microfilms, Publication No. 2798, 1974).

7. "The Life Histories of W. I. Thomas and Robert E. Park," with an introduction by Paul Baker, *American Journal of Sociology* LXXIX (September 1973), p. 253.

8. Robert E. Park, "The Crowd and the Public," trans. by Charlotte Elsner, in *The Crowd and the Public and Other Essays*, ed. by Henry Elsner, Jr., (Chicago: University of Chicago Press, 1972), pp. 3–81.

9. Booker T. Washington, "Cruelty in the Congo Country,"*Outlook* LXXVIII (October 8, 1904), pp. 375–77. This article is reprinted in *The Booker T. Washington Papers,Vol. 8: 1904–1906*, ed. by Louis R. Harlan and Raymond W. Smock (Urbana: University of Illinois Press, 1979), pp. 85–90 where Park's authorship is acknowledged on p. 90.

10. For some representative discussions of two centuries of German social thought and its effect on American social and political science, see Horst Dippel, *Germany and the American Revolution, 1770–1800: A Sociohistorical Investigation of Late Eighteenth-Century Political Thinking*, trans. by Bernhard A. Huhlendorf (Chapel Hill: University of North Carolina Press, 1977); Carl Diehl, *Americans and German Scholarship, 1770–1870* (New Haven: Yale University Press, 1978); Jurgen Herbst, *The German Historical School in American Scholarship: A Study in the Transfer of Culture* (Port Washington, N.Y.: Kennikat Press, 1972), esp. pp. 129–60. See also Theodore Ziolkowski, *German Romanticism and Its Institutions* (Princeton: Princeton University Press, 1990).

11. See Arthur J. Vidich and Stanford M. Lyman, *American Sociology: Worldly Rejections of Religion and Their Directions* (New Haven: Yale University Press, 1985).

12. Cf. Noel Carroll, *The Philosophy of Horror or Paradoxes of the Heart* (New York: Routledge, 1990).

13. Cf. Roberta Garner, "Jacob Burckhardt as a Theorist of Modernity: Reading *The Civilization of the Renaissance in Italy*," *Sociological Theory* VIII:1 (Spring 1990), pp. 48–57 for a thesis comparable to that being presented in this book. For a different approach to the interpretation of Park's sociology—one with whose conclusions the present book does not agree—see Daniel Breslau, "The Mediations Between Sociology and Its Context in the Career of Robert Park: A Study in Pierre Bourdieu's Sociology of Science," paper presented at the 83d annual meeting of the American Sociological Association, Atlanta, Georgia, August 24–28, 1988.

14. Quoted in Raushenbush, op. cit., p. 43.

15. Booker T. Washington with the collaboration of Robert E. Park, *The Man Farthest Down: A Record of Observation and Study in Europe* (Garden City, N.Y.: Doubleday, Page and Co., 1913).

16. Booker T. Washington, *The Story of the Negro: The Rise of the Race From Slavery*, 2 vols. (Gloucester, Mass.: Peter Smith, 1969 [1909]).

17. For good examples of Booker T. Washington's outlook see *Negro Social and Political Thought, 1850–1920*, ed. by Howard Brotz (New York: Basic Books, Inc., 1966), pp. 351–463.

18. See Martin Bulmer, "Charles S. Johnson, Robert E. Park, and the Research Methods of the Chicago Commission on Race Relations, 1919–1922: An Early Experiment in Applied Social Research," *Ethnic and Racial Studies* IV:3 (July 1981), pp. 289–306.

19. For various perspectives on the "Chicago School" of Sociology see Robert E. L. Faris, *Chicago Sociology, 1920–1932* (San Francisco: Chandler Publishing Co., 1967; reprint, Chicago: University of Chicago Press, 1970); Martin Bulmer, *The Chicago School of Sociology: Institutionalization, Diversity, and the Rise of Sociological Research* (Chicago: University of Chicago Press, 1984); Dennis Smith, *The Chicago School: A Liberal Critique of Capitalism* (New York: St. Martin's Press, 1988); Edward Shils,

"Robert E. Park: 1864–1944," *The American Scholar* LX (Winter 1991), pp. 120–27; Vidich and Lyman, *American Sociology* . . . , op. cit., pp. 178–208. For the diffusion of Chicago's sociological perspective to Canada, see Marlene Shore, *The Science of Social Redemption: McGill, the Chicago School, and the Origins of Social Research in Canada* (Toronto: University of Toronto Press, 1987). See also "Robert E. Park's 'Notes on the Origins of the Society for Social Research,' with an introduction by Lester R. Kurtz," *Journal of the History of the Behavioral Sciences* XVIII (October 1982), pp. 332–40.

20. Robert E. Park, "Human Migration and the Marginal Man," in *Personality and the Social Group*, ed. by Ernest W. Burgess (Chicago: University of Chicago Press, 1929), pp. 64–65.

21. See Fred H. Matthews, "Robert Park, Congo Reform and Tuskegee: The Molding of a Race Relations Expert, 1905–1913," *Canadian Journal of History* VIII:1 (Spring 1973), pp. 60–61. In July 1913, Arthur A. Schomburg, secretary of the Negro Society for Historical Research in Yonkers, New York, read "Racial Integrity: A Plea for the Establishment of a Chair of Negro History in our Schools and Colleges, etc." before the Teachers' Summer class at Cheney Institute. Occasional Paper No. 3, Negro Society for Historical Research, 1913. For the story of the slow and painful development of a recognized discipline of Afro-American history see Elinor Des Verney Sinnette, *Arthur Alfonso Schomburg, Black Bibliophile and Collector: A Biography* (Detroit: New York Public Library and Wayne State University Press, 1989); August Meier and Elliott Rudwick, *Black History and the Historical Profession, 1915–1980* (Urbana: University of Illinois Press, 1986); Darlene Clark Hine, ed., *The State of Afro-American History: Past, Present, and Future* (Baton Rouge: Louisiana State University Press, 1986). For a critique of American sociological thought emphasizing its indifference to the record of African-American history, see Stanford M. Lyman, *The Black American in Sociological Thought: A Failure of Perspective* (New York: G. P. Putnam's Sons, 1972).

22. Raushenbush, op. cit., p. 177.

23. Robert E. Park, "Our Racial Frontier on the Pacific," *Survey Graphic* LVI (May 1, 1926), pp. 192–96.

24. Charles S. Johnson to Robert E. Park in 1935. Quoted in Raushenbush, op. cit., p. 152.

25. Ibid., p. 151. In 1988, the United States Information Service sponsored this author's lecture tour in Liberia, Ghana, and Nigeria. At the invitation of the faculty and administration of the University of Maiduguri in northern Nigeria, I presented a talk on the implications of Park's and, more especially, Frazier's theses on racial relations for the plural societies developing within the post-colonial states of contemporary Africa. Commenting on the talk was Dr. Princeton Nathan Lyman, at that time serving as United States Ambassador to Nigeria. Ambassador Lyman is the author's younger brother and a specialist in the political economy of development in Third World nations (See David C. Cole and Princeton N. Lyman, *Korean Development: The Interplay of Politics and Economics* [Cambridge: Harvard University Press, 1971]). He had met Samuel C. Adams, Jr. In his commentary, Ambassador Lyman emphasized the importance of institutionalizing the principles and praxes of justice in a racially plural society. See Stanford M. Lyman, "Ethnicity, Pluralism, and Their Implications for Africa and the World," University of Maiduguri Public Lecture Series No. 3, February 25, 1988, (Maiduguri, Nigeria: University of Maiduguri Press, 1988).

26. St. Clair Drake and Horace Cayton, *Black Metropolis: A Study of Negro Life in a Northern City*, rev. and enl. ed. (New York: Harper Torchbooks, 1962), 2 vols.

27. See two essays by St. Clair Drake, "The International Implications of Race and Race Relations," *The Journal of Negro Education* XX (Summer 1951), pp. 261–78;

and "The 'Colour Problem' in Britain: A Study in Social Definitions," *Sociological Review* n.s., III (December 1955), pp. 197–217.

28. Bill Workman, "Obituary: St. Clair Drake," *San Francisco Chronicle*, June 20, 1990, p. B6.

29. St. Clair Drake, *Black Folk Here and There: An Essay in History and Anthropology* (Los Angeles: University of California Center for Afro-American Studies, 1987, 1990), 2 vols. See also St. Clair Drake, "The Relations of the American and the African Negro in the Context of Pan-Africanism," Summary Report, Fourth Annual Meeting of the American Society of African Culture (New York: AMSAC, 1961), pp. 4–12.

30. St. Clair Drake, "The Tuskegee Connection: Booker T. Washington and Robert E. Park," *Society* XX:4 (May–June 1983), p. 92.

31. See the following works by E. Franklin Frazier: "Occupational Classes Among Negroes in Cities," *American Journal of Sociology* XXXV (March 1930), pp. 718–37; "Children in Black and Mulatto Families," *American Journal of Sociology* XXXIX (July 1933), pp. 12–29; "Negro Harlem: An Ecological Study," *American Journal of Sociology* XLIII (July 1937), pp. 72–88; "The Impact of Urban Civilization Upon Negro Family Life," *American Sociological Review* II (October 1937), pp. 609–18; "Ethnic and Minority Groups in Wartime, With Special Reference to the Negro," *American Journal of Sociology* XLVIII (November 1942), pp. 369–77; "Race Contacts and Social Structure," *American Sociological Review* XIV (February 1949), pp. 1–11; "Theoretical Structure of Sociology and Sociological Research," *British Journal of Sociology* IV (December 1953), pp. 292–311; "Racial Problems in World Society," in *Race Relations: Problems and Theory*, ed. by Jitsuichi Masuoka and Preston Valien (Chapel Hill: University of North Carolina Press, 1961), pp. 38–50; *Race and Culture Contacts in the Modern World* (New York: Alfred A. Knopf, 1957).

32. Werner Cahnman, "Robert E. Park at Fisk," *Journal of the History of the Behavioral Sciences* XIV (1978), p. 334.

33. See Helmuth James von Moltke, *Letters to Freya, 1939–1945*, ed. and trans. by Beate Ruhm von Oppen (New York: Alfred A. Knopf, 1990).

34. Luther Lee Bernard, *War and Its Causes* (New York: Henry Holt, 1944), pp. 153–54.

35. Robert E. Park, "Social Contributions of Physics," *The American Physics Teacher* VII:5 (October 1939), p. 328.

36. Robert E. Park, "Racial Ideologies," in *American Society in Wartime*, ed. by William Fielding Ogburn (Chicago: University of Chicago Press, 1943; reprint, New York: Da Capo Press, Inc., 1972), pp. 165–84.

37.Quoted from Mozell C. Hill, "Some Early Notes of Robert E. Park," *Phylon Quarterly* XIV:1 (First Quarter 1953), p. 86.

38. That the issues in the race problem that Park recognized are still matters of major debate can be illustrated by comparing an essay by the historian John Higham, "Integration vs. Pluralism: Another American Dilemma," *The Center Magazine* VII (July 1974), pp. 67–73, with Price M. Cobbs, M.D., "Valuing Diversity: The Myth and the Challenge," in *The State of Black America 1989*, ed. by Janet Dewart (New York: National Urban League, Inc., 1989), pp. 151–59.

Introduction

1. Robert E. Park, review of *Jews in a Gentile World, the Problem of Anti-Semitism*, by Isacque Graeber and Steuart Henderson Britt, in cooperation with Miriam Beard,

Jessie Bernard, Leonard Bloom, J. F. Brown, Joseph W. Cohen, Carleton Stevens Coon, Ellis Freeman, Carl J. Friedrich, J. O. Hertzler, Melville Jacobs, Raymond Kennedy, Samuel Koenig, Jacob Lestchinsky, Carl Mayer, Talcott Parsons, and Everett V. Stonequist, *American Sociological Review* IX (December 1944), pp. 710–11.

2. Mozell C. Hill, "Some Early Notes of R. E. Park," *Phylon: The Atlanta Review of Race and Culture* XIV:1 (1953), p. 86.

3. Park, review of *Jews in a Gentile World*, op. cit., p. 711.

4. Loc. cit.

5. Loc. cit.

6. Lester Ward, *Applied Sociology: A Treatise on the Conscious Improvement of Society By Society* (Boston: Ginn, 1906), pp. 213–15. For a discussion of Ward's thesis, see Arthur J. Vidich and Stanford M. Lyman, *American Sociology: Worldly Rejections of Religion and Their Directions* (New Haven: Yale University Press, 1985), pp. 27–30.

7. Stephen Toulmin, *Cosmopolis: The Hidden Agenda of Modernity* (New York: The Free Press, 1990), pp. 67–69, 86, 98, 107–17, 128, 132–33, 157, 160–61, 170, 191–92.

8. Max Weber, "Ethnic Groups," *Economy and Society: An Outline of Interpretive Sociology*, ed. by Guenther Roth and Claus Wittich (New York: Bedminster Press, 1968), I, pp. 385–98.

9. Robert E. Park, review of *World Order in Historical Perspective*, by Hans Kohn, *American Sociological Review* VII:4 (August 1942), p. 563.

10. Loc. cit.

11. Loc. cit.

12. Loc. cit.

13. Robert E. Park, "Racial Ideologies," in *American Society in Wartime*, ed. by William Fielding Ogburn (Chicago: University of Chicago Press, 1943; reprint, New York: Da Capo Press, 1972), pp. 165–84.

14. Horace R. Cayton, "Robert Park—A Great Man Died, But Leaves Keen Observation on our Democracy," *Pittsburgh Courier*, February 26, 1944; reprinted in Winifred Raushenbush, *Robert E. Park: Biography of a Sociologist* (Durham, N.C.: Duke University Press, 1979), pp. 176–77.

15. Park, review of *World Order in Historical Perspective*, op. cit., p. 563.

16. Henry Hughes, *Treatise on Sociology, Theoretical and Practical* (Philadelphia: Lippincott and Grambo, 1854; reprint, New York: Negro Universities Press, 1968).

17. See Stanford M. Lyman, "Henry Hughes and the Southern Foundations of American Sociology," in his edition of *Selected Writings of Henry Hughes: Antebellum Southerner, Slavocrat, Sociologist* (Jackson: University Press of Mississippi, 1985), pp. 1–72.

18. George Fitzhugh, "Sociology For the South," in *Ante-Bellum: Writings of George Fitzhugh and Hinton Rowan Helper on Slavery*, ed. by Harvey Wish (New York: Capricorn Books, 1960), pp. 41–96.

19. George Fitzhugh, *Cannibals All! or Slaves Without Masters*, ed. by C. Vann Woodward (Cambridge: The Belknap Press of Harvard University Press, 1960).

20. See Stanford M. Lyman, "System and Function in Ante-Bellum Southern Sociology," *International Journal of Politics, Culture, and Society* II:1 (Fall 1988), pp. 95–108.

21. See Harvey Wish, *George Fitzhugh: Propagandist of the Old South* (Gloucester, Mass.: Peter Smith, 1962).

22. George Frederick Holmes, *The Science of Society: Seventeen Lectures Delivered to his Class at the University of Virginia* (Richmond: Miller School Print, 1883).

23. See Leonidas Betts, "George Frederick Holmes: Nineteenth Century Virginia Educator," *Virginia Magazine of History and Biography* LXXVI (October 1968),

pp. 472–84; Frederick E. Salzillo, Jr., "The Development of Sociology at the University of Virginia: The First One-Hundred Years, 1873–1973," *Southeastern Review: A Journal of Sociology* III:1 (Winter 1976), pp. 11–25; Tipton R. Snavely, *The Department of Economics at the University of Virginia, 1825–1956* (Charlottesville: The University Press of Virginia, 1967), pp. 66–96; and Neal C. Gillespie, *The Collapse of Orthodoxy: The Intellectual Ordeal of George Frederick Holmes* (Charlottesville: The University Press of Virginia, 1972).

24. See Arthur J. Vidich and Stanford M. Lyman, "State Ethics and Public Morality in American Sociological Thought," in *Sociological Theory in Transition*, ed. by Mark L. Wardell and Stephen P. Turner (Boston: Allen and Unwin, 1986), pp. 44–58; and Stanford M. Lyman, "LeConte, Royce, Teggart, Blumer: A Berkeley Dialogue on Sociology, Social Change, and Symbolic Interaction," *Symbolic Interaction* XI:1 (Spring 1988), pp. 125–43.

25. See L. D. Stephens, *Joseph LeConte: Gentle Prophet of Evolution* (Baton Rouge: Louisiana State University Press, 1982).

26. James Alfred Aho, *German Realpolitik and American Sociology: An Inquiry into the Sources and Political Significance of the Sociology of Conflict* (Lewisburg: Bucknell University Press, 1971), pp. 14–15.

27. Ibid., pp. 25–111.

28. Quoted in Raushenbush, op. cit., p. 31.

29. Everett C. Hughes to James Aho, July 8, 1970, in Aho, op. cit., p. 316.

30. Robert E. Park, "The German Army: The Most Perfect Military Organization in the World," *Munsey's Magazine* XXIV:3 (December 1900), pp. 376–77.

31. Ward, op. cit., p. 215.

32. Everett C. Hughes and Helen M. Hughes, *Where Peoples Meet: Racial and Ethnic Frontiers* (Glencoe: The Free Press, 1952).

33. See the papers by Teggart reprinted in Grace Dangberg, *A Guide to the Life and Works of Frederick J. Teggart* (Reno: The Grace Dangberg Foundation, Inc., 1983), pp. 234–36, 250–51, 254–56, 258–59, 260–69, 274–95, 298–300, 312–15, 401–10, 525–34. Spykman's most prominent work is *America's Strategy in World Politics: The United States and the Balance of Power* (New York: Harcourt, Brace, 1942).

34. Perhaps the last vestige of the Teggartian approach to geopolitical studies at Berkeley is to be found in a master's thesis in political science that included among its supervisors Kenneth E. Bock, a disciple of Teggart. See Stanford M. Lyman, "The Impact of Germany on the North Atlantic Treaty Organization," unpublished master's thesis, University of California at Berkeley, 1957, esp. pp. 1–38.

35. Robert E. Park, "Culture and Civilization," in Everett C. Hughes, et al., *Race and Culture*, The Collected Papers of Robert Ezra Park, Vol. I (Glencoe: The Free Press, 1950), p. 19.

36. Robert E. Park, "Education and the Cultural Crisis," *American Journal of Sociology* XLVIII (May 1943), pp. 728–36. Reprinted in *Race and Culture*, op. cit., pp. 316–30.

37. Robert E. Park, "A King in Business: Leopold II of Belgium, Autocrat of the Congo and International Broker," *Everybody's Magazine* XV (November 1906), pp. 624–33; "The Terrible Story of the Congo," *Everybody's Magazine* XV (December 1906), pp. 763–72; "The Blood Money of the Congo," *Everybody's Magazine* XVI (January 1907), pp. 60–70.

38. Ironically, recent attempts to develop a historical sociology of the media either ignore Park's Congo essays in assessing his contributions to journalism (as does Daniel J. Czitrom, *Media and the American Mind: From Morse to McLuhan* [Chapel Hill: University of North Carolina Press, 1982], pp. 113–21), or fail to discuss him altogether (as in Hanns Hardt, *Social Theories of the Press: Early German and American*

Perspectives [Beverly Hills: Sage Publishers, 1979]). When Park's journalism is the topic of the investigation, his Congo essays go unmentioned (as in P. Jean Frazier and Cecilie Gaziano, "Robert Ezra Park's Theory of News, Public Opinion and Social Control," *Journalism Monographs* No. 64 [November 1979], pp. 1–47; and Lary S. Belman, "Robert Ezra Park: An Intellectual Portrait of a Journalist and Communication Scholar," *Journalism History* II [Winter 1975–1976], pp. 116–19, 122–24, 132).

39. Richard C. Helmes-Hayes, "'A Dualistic Vision': Robert Ezra Park and the Classical Ecological Theory of Social Inequality," *The Sociological Quarterly* XXVIII:3 (September 1987), p. 402.

40. Ibid., p. 400.

41. Jim Faught, "The Concept of Competition in Robert Park's Sociology," *Sociological Quarterly* XXVII:3 (September 1986), p. 370n. 7.

42. Ibid., p. 362.

43. Fred H. Matthews, *Quest For an American Sociology: Robert E. Park and the Chicago School* (Montreal: McGill-Queen's University Press, 1977), pp. 57–61.

44. Fred H. Matthews, "Robert Park, Congo Reform and Tuskegee: The Molding of a Race Relations Expert, 1905–1913," *Canadian Journal of History* VIII:1 (Spring 1973), pp. 38–39.

45. Ibid., p. 39.

46. Helen MacGill Hughes, "Robert Ezra Park: The Philosopher-Newspaperman-Sociologist," in Robert K. Merton and Matilda White Riley, eds., *Sociological Traditions From Generation to Generation* (Norwood, N.J.: Ablex Publishing Corp., 1980), p. 69.

47. Loc. cit.

48. William Graham Sumner, *Folkways: A Study of the Sociological Importance of Usages, Manners, Customs, Mores, and Morals* (Boston: Ginn and Co., 1940 [1906]), pp. 13–15.

49. James Elbert Cutler, *Lynch-Law: An Investigation into the History of Lynching in the United States*, with a foreword by W. G. Sumner (Montclair, N.J.: Patterson Smith, 1969 [1905]).

50. Sumner, foreword in Cutler, op. cit., p. v.

51. See, e.g., Henry Steele Commager, *The American Mind: An Interpretation of American Thought and Character Since the 1880's* (New Haven: Yale University Press, 1950), pp. 199–226.

52. Lester Frank Ward, *Pure Sociology: A Treatise on the Origin and Spontaneous Development of Society*, 2d ed. (New York: Macmillan, 1903, 1907; reprint, New York: Augustus M. Kelley, 1970), pp. 359–60. For a brief discussion of the differences between Ward's and Sumner's position on the race question, see Vidich and Lyman, *American Sociology*, op. cit., pp. 35n. 3 and 48n. 4.

53. N. S. Shaler, *The Neighbor: The Natural History of Human Contacts* (Boston: Houghton, Mifflin and Co., 1904), esp. pp. 51–191.

54. Nathaniel Southgate Shaler, *The Individual: A Study of Life and Death* (New York: D. Appleton and Co., 1905 [1900]).

55. For relevant examples of Park's use of Shaler's ideas see Robert Ezra Park, *Race and Culture,* The Collected Papers of Robert Ezra Park, Vol. I, ed. by Everett Cherrington Hughes, et al. (Glencoe: The Free Press, 1950), pp. 235–46.

56. Quoted in David N. Livingstone, *Nathaniel Southgate Shaler and the Culture of American Science* (Tuscaloosa: University of Alabama Press, 1987), pp. 138, 139, 142.

57. See Lyman, "System and Function in Ante-Bellum Southern Sociology," op. cit., pp. 96–102.

58. See Stephen Pearl Andrews, *The Science of Society: The True Constitution of*

Government in the Sovereignty of the Individual as the Final Development of Protestantism, Democracy and Socialism (Boston: Sarah E. Holmes, 1888; reprint, Weston, Mass.: M and S Press, 1970); *Love, Marriage, and Divorce, and the Sovereignty of the Individual: A Discussion Between Henry James, Horace Greeley, and Stephen Pearl Andrews, and a Hitherto Unpublished Manuscript, Love, Marriage, and the Condition of Woman by Stephen Pearl Andrews*, ed. by Charles Shively (Weston, Mass.: M and S Press, 1975); and Madeleine B. Stern, *The Pantarch: A Biography of Stephen Pearl Andrews* (Austin: University of Texas Press, 1968). For the relationship of this anarchistic sociology to the struggle for equal rights and the rise of Marxism see Vidich and Lyman, *American Sociology*, op. cit., pp. 165–66 n. 8 and the sources cited therein.

59. See the dedication page in Charlotte Perkins Gilman, *The Man-Made World or Our Androcentric Culture* (New York: Charlton Company, 1911).

60. In addition to the book cited *supra*, Gilman is noted for the following: *Women and Economics: A Study of the Economic Relation Between Men and Women as a Factor in Social Evolution* (Boston: Small, Maynard and Co., 1898; reprint ed. by Carl N. Degler, New York: Harper Torchbooks, 1966); *The Yellow Wallpaper* (Boston: Small, Maynard and Co., 1899; reprint with afterword by Elaine R. Hedges, Old Westbury, N.Y.: The Feminist Press, 1973); *Herland* (New York: Pantheon Books, 1979).

61. See Mary A. Hill, *Charlotte Perkins Gilman: The Making of a Radical Feminist, 1860–1896* (Philadelphia: Temple University Press, 1980), pp. 172–74, 279; Ann J. Lane, *To Herland and Beyond: The Life and Work of Charlotte Perkins Gilman* (New York: Pantheon Books, 1990), pp. 17–18, 255–56, 294, 337.

62. Charlotte Perkins Gilman, "A Suggestion on the Negro Problem," *American Journal of Sociology* XIV (July 1908), pp. 80–81.

63. Henry Hughes, *A Treatise on Sociology . . .* , op. cit., p. 291.

64. See Lyman, "Henry Hughes and the Southern Foundations of American Sociology," op. cit., pp. 19–28, 42–49.

65. Gilman, "A Suggestion on the Negro Problem," op. cit., p. 81.

66. Hughes, *Treatise on Sociology . . .* , op. cit., pp. 291–92.

67. Gilman, "A Suggestion on the Negro Problem," op. cit., p. 81.

68. Loc. cit.

69. Loc. cit.

70. Ibid., pp. 81–82.

71. Ibid., p. 82.

72. Ibid., p. 85.

73. It would seem that each generation of analysts of Park creates an image of him appropriate to the *Zeitgeist*. Thus, in the present era of a revitalized feminist consciousness, sociologist Mary Jo Deegan calls attention to Jane Addams' admiration of Gilman's book, *Women and Economics*, makes no mention of Gilman's antipathies toward blacks and Jews, eschews mention of Gilman's proposal for a state-controlled black work force, and designates Park as an antifeminist with a personality that was "[e]gocentric, brusque, cantankerous, and charismatic." As Deegan sees the matter, Park disdained and discouraged the researches of women social scientists; moreover, he "legitimized a conservative political role for sociologists and left a legacy to future sociologists who worked to maintain the status quo while mildly condemning it." Mary Jo Deegan, *Jane Addams and the Men of the Chicago School, 1892–1918* (New Brunswick, N.J.: Transaction Books, 1990), p. 158. My own interpretation varies profoundly from that of Professor Deegan.

74. John Cummings, "Ethnic Factors and the Movement of Population," *Quarterly Journal of Economics* XIV (February 1900), pp. 171–211.

75. See Marshall Hyatt, *Franz Boas, Social Activist: The Dynamics of Ethnicity* (New York: Greenwood Press, 1990), pp. 83–122.

76. W. E. B. DuBois, "Die Negerfrage in den Vereinigten Staaten," *Archiv für Sozialwissenschaft und Sozialpolitik* XXII (1906), pp. 31–79. Cited in Benjamin Nelson and Jerome Gittelman, introduction to Nelson, ed., "Max Weber, Dr. Alfred Ploetz, and W. E. B. DuBois (Max Weber on Race and Society II)," *Sociological Analysis* XXXIV:4 (Winter 1973), p. 308.

77. See Robert N. Proctor, *Racial Hygiene: Medicine Under the Nazis* (Cambridge: Harvard University Press, 1988), pp. 8, 14–21, 24–28, 95, 98, 292, 300, 345n. 61, 348n. 82; and Michael H. Kater, *Doctors Under Hitler* (Chapel Hill: University of North Carolina Press, 1989), pp. 91, 112–14, 230.

78. Nelson, ed., op. cit., p. 312.

79. Loc. cit.

80. "Max Weber on Race and Society," ed. by Benjamin Nelson, trans. by Jerome Gittelman, *Social Research* XXXVIII:1 (Spring 1971), p. 37.

81. In a recent discussion of the place of this school of thought in the sociology of race relations, Michael Banton has observed, "In the brief history of the anthropo-sociological school is seen a mixture of racist bias and ordinary bad luck. The features the anthropo-sociologists chose to measure were, in their day, the obvious ones, and they could not know in advance that their examination would prove so unrewarding." Michael Banton, *Race Relations* (New York: Basic Books, 1967), p. 39. However, despite Banton's citation of Smith College's Frank H. Hankins's critique of the anthropo-sociologists, it is to be noted that one of its leading advocates, William Z. Ripley, was appointed to Harvard University in 1901 to replace John Cummings, his principal critic, and was still on the faculty in the 1920s. See Robert L. Church, "The Economists Study Society: Sociology at Harvard, 1891–1902," in *Social Sciences at Harvard, 1860–1920: From Inculcation to the Open Mind*, cd. by Paul Buck (Cambridge: Harvard University Press, 1965), pp. 59, 61, 84. Moreover, Hankins held to the view that "the general backwardness of the negro . . . must be sought in differences of body and brain structure." Frank H. Hankins, *The Racial Basis of Civilization: A Critique of the Nordic Doctrine* (New York: Alfred A. Knopf, 1926), p. 307.

82. Carlos C. Closson, "The Hierarchy of European Races," *American Journal of Sociology* III:3 (November 1897), p. 327.

83. Georges Vacher de la Pouge, "Old and New Aspects of the Aryan Question," trans. by Carlos C. Closson, *American Journal of Sociology* V (November 1899), p. 338.

84. Ibid., pp. 339–41.

85. Ibid., pp. 341, 342.

86. Ibid., p. 343.

87. Ibid., p. 345.

88. Ibid., p. 346.

89. See Ernest Lee Tuveson, *Redeemer Nation: The Idea of America's Millennial Role* (Chicago: University of Chicago Press, 1968, 1974).

90. Vidich and Lyman, *American Sociology* . . . , op. cit., pp. 53–194.

91. See Forrest G. Wood, *The Arrogance of Faith: Christianity and Race in America from the Colonial Era to the Twentieth Century* (New York: Alfred A. Knopf, 1990), pp. 9, 365–81.

92. See, e.g., Arthur C. Holden, *The Settlement Idea: A Vision of Social Justice* (New York: Macmillan, 1922; reprint, New York: Arno Press, 1970), pp. 109–44.

93. Protestant missions to the Chinese in California antedated the Social Gospel movement, but all too often ran afoul of the labor-led, Irish, and Catholic anti-Chinese movement. See Rev. O. Gibson, *The Chinese in America* (Cincinnati: Hitchcock and Walden, 1877; reprint, New York: Arno Press, 1978; and Ira M. Condit, *The Chinaman As We See Him, and Fifty Years of Work for Him* (Chicago: Fleming H. Revell Co., 1900; reprint, New York: Arno Press, 1978). During the hey-

day of the Social Gospel, Donaldina Cameron (1869–1968) operated a Presbyterian rescue mission in San Francisco for Chinese girls and young women who were vulnerable to exploitation as prostitutes in the virtually womanless Chinatown. See Carol Green Wilson, *Chinatown Quest: The Life Adventures of Donaldina Cameron* rev. ed. (Stanford: Stanford University Press, 1950); and Mildred Crowl Martin, *Chinatown's Angry Angel: The Story of Donaldina Cameron* (Palo Alto, Calif.: Pacific Books, 1977).

94. See, e.g., Egal Feldman, *The Dreyfus Affair and the American Conscience, 1895–1906* (Detroit: Wayne State University Press, 1981), pp. 105–11.

95. See Robert A. Woods and Albert J. Kennedy, *The Settlement Horizon* (New Brunswick, N.J.: Transaction Publishers, 1990 [1922]), pp. 326–40; and Judith Ann Trolander, *Settlement Houses and the Great Depression* (Detroit: Wayne State University Press, 1975), pp. 134–47.

96. Cf. George Elliott Howard, "The Social Cost of Southern Race Prejudice," *American Journal of Sociology* XXII (March 1917), pp. 577–93.

97. For a sociological analysis of this issue, see Stanford M. Lyman and Arthur J. Vidich, *Social Order and the Public Philosophy: An Analysis and Interpretation of the Work of Herbert Blumer* (Fayetteville: University of Arkansas Press, 1988), pp. 66–91.

German Militarism, the Garrison State, and Total War

1. Robert E. Park, "The German Army: The Most Perfect Military Organization in the World," *Munsey's Magazine* XXIV:3 (December 1900), pp. 376–95.

2. Fred H. Matthews, *Quest For An American Sociology: Robert E. Park and the Chicago School* (Montreal: McGill-Queen's University Press, 1977), p. 34.

3. I shall not include Droysen in my discussion, despite James Alfred Aho's claim (in *German Realpolitik and American Sociology: An Inquiry into the Sources and Political Significance of the Sociology of Conflict* [Lewisburg, Pa.: Bucknell University Press, 1971], p. 34) that he espoused a realpolitik in the *Preussiche Jahrbücher*. Although he certainly espoused Prussian hegemony, Droysen (1838–1908) is primarily remembered as a methodologist whose opposition to positivism influenced Rickert, Dilthey, Simmel, and Windelband. See Werner J. Cahnman, "Max Weber and the Methodological Controversy in the Social Sciences," in Werner J. Cahnman and Alvin Boskoff, eds., *Sociology and History: Theory and Research* (London: The Free Press of Glencoe, 1964), pp. 106–08; and Ernst Breisach, *Historiography: Ancient, Medieval and Modern* (Chicago: University of Chicago Press, 1983), pp. 235–38, 278–81. Moreover, Droysen was among the seventy-three signers of the "Berlin Manifesto" that denounced the "shameful manner" in which "race hatred and the fanatacism of the middle ages" had been revived and directed against "our Jewish fellow citizens." See Oscar I. Janowsky and Melvin M. Fagen, *International Aspects of German Racial Policies* (New York: Oxford University Press, 1937), p. 41.

4. See Friedrich Meinecke, "Leopold von Ranke," in *idem, Historism: The Rise of a New Historical Outlook*, trans. by J. E. Anderson (London: Routledge and Kegan Paul, 1972), pp. 496–511.

5. Leopold von Ranke, "Preface to Universal History (1880)" in *idem, The Theory and Practice of History*, ed. by Georg G. Iggers and Konrad von Moltke (Indianapolis: Bobbs-Merrill, 1973), p. 163.

6. Park, "The German Army . . .," p. 395.

7. Leopold von Ranke, "A Dialogue on Politics (1836)," in Iggers and von Moltke, eds., op. cit., p. 118.

8. Ibid., p. 104.

9. Raymond James Sontag, *Germany and England: Background of Conflict, 1848–1894* (New York: W. W. Norton, 1969. Orig. pub. 1938), p. 49.

10. Quoted in Leonard Krieger, *Ranke: The Meaning of History* (Chicago: University of Chicago Press, 1977), p. 162.

11. Friedrich Meinecke, *The German Catastrophe: Reflections and Recollections*, trans. by Sidney B. Fay (Boston: Beacon Press, 1963. Orig. pub. 1950), pp. 9–10.

12. Friedrich Meinecke, *The Age of German Liberation, 1795–1815*, ed. by Peter Paret, trans. by Peter Paret and Helmuth Fischer (Berkeley: University of California Press, 1977), p. 128.

13. Quoted in Hans Kohn, "Introduction to the Harbinger Edition," Heinrich von Treitschke, *Politics*, abr. and ed. by Hans Kohn, trans. by Blanche Dugdale and Torbende Bille (New York: Harcourt, Brace and World, Inc., 1963), p. xii.

14. See Robert A. Pois, *Friedrich Meinecke and German Politics in the Twentieth Century* (Berkeley: University of California Press, 1972), p. 122.

15. Meinecke, *The German Catastrophe* . . . , p. 15. Meinecke's attitude toward the Jews is described by Pois (op. cit., p. 123) as that of a "social anti-Semite": "Meinecke might well have been very willing to have Jewish friends and students, presumably as long as each was possessed of a 'German heart'; however, his attitude toward the Jews as a group was decidedly prejudiced, and Nazi persecution of them never seems to have bothered him very much."

16. Heinrich von Treitschke, *Politics*, p. 132.

17. Ibid., pp. 126–27.

18. Ibid., p. 133.

19. Ibid., p. 129.

20. Ibid., p. 124. Treitschke, like so many others of his day—and, alas, of our own seems to have been unaware of the imposing civilizations that had flourished in Africa in pre-colonial times. For some representative correctives, see two works of Cheikh Anta Diop, *The African Origin of Civilization: Myth or Reality*, trans. by Mercer Cook (New York: Lawrence Hill, 1974); and *Precolonial Black Africa: A Comparative Study of the Political and Social Systems of Europe and Black Africa, from Antiquity to the Formation of Modern States*, trans. by Harold Salemson (Westport, Ct.: Lawrence Hill, 1987); J. C. de Graft-Johnson, *African Glory: The Story of Vanished Negro Civilizations* (New York: Walker and Co., 1954); and two works by Basil Davidson *The Lost Cities of Africa* (Boston: Little-Brown, 1959); and *The African Past: Chronicles from Antiquity* (New York: Grosset and Dunlap, 1964, 1967).

21. See Hajo Holborn, "The Prusso-German School: Moltke and the Rise of the General Staff"; and Gunther E. Rothenberg, "Moltke, Schlieffen, and the Doctrine of Strategic Envelopment," both in Peter Paret, with the collaboration of Gordon Craig and Felix Gilbert, eds., *Makers of Modern Strategy: From Machiavelli to the Nuclear Age* (Princeton: Princeton University Press, 1986), pp. 281–95, 296–325.

22. Park, "The German Army . . . ," p. 385.

23. Ibid., p. 386.

24. James Alfred Aho, *German Realpolitik and American Sociology*, op. cit., p. 213.

25. Robert E. Park, "The Crowd and the Public," trans. by Charlotte Elsner, in idem, *The Crowd and the Public and Other Essays*, ed. by Henry Elsner, Jr., (Chicago: University of Chicago Press, 1972), p. 53.

26. Quoted in Winifred Raushenbush, *Robert E. Park: Biography of a Sociologist* (Durham: Duke University Press, 1979), p. 80.

27. Robert E. Park, *The Immigrant Press and Its Control* (New York: Harper and Brothers, 1922; reprint, Montclair, N.J.: Patterson Smith, 1971), p. 412.

28. Park, "The German Army . . . ," p. 393.

29. Ibid., p. 382.

30. Meinecke, *The Age of German Liberation* . . . , p. 98.

31. Hans Kohn, "Notes," in Treitschke, *Politics*, p. 321n. 7.

32. Park, "The German Army . . . ," p. 382.

33. Ibid., p. 393.

34. Hans Speier, *German White Collar Workers and the Rise of Hitler* (New Haven: Yale University Press, 1986), p. 32.

35. Hans Speier, *Social Order and the Risks of War: Papers in Political Sociology* (New York: George W. Stewart, 1952), p. 293.

36. Park, "The German Army . . . ," p. 393.

37. Ibid., pp. 385–386.

38. Ibid., p. 393.

39. Ibid., p. 395.

40. Loc. cit.

41. Park, *The Immigrant Press and Its Control*, pp. 412–47.

42. Ibid., pp. 413–14.

43. Ibid., p. 417.

44. Loc. cit.

45. Ibid., p. 423.

46. Ibid., p. 421.

47. Ibid., pp. 421–33.

48. Ibid., p. 442.

49. Loc. cit.

50. Ibid., pp. 377–433.

51. See Matthew Hale, Jr., *Human Science and Social Order: Hugo Münsterberg and the Origins of Applied Psychology* (Philadelphia: Temple University Press, 1980), pp. 164–83; and Phyllis Keller, *States of Belonging: German-American Intellectuals and the First World War* (Cambridge: Harvard University Press, 1979), pp. 7–120.

52. Hugo Münsterberg, *The War and America* (New York: D. Appleton and Co., 1914, 1915).

53. Ibid., p. 210.

54. Ibid., pp. 68–78.

55. Ibid., p. 103.

56. Ibid., p. 174.

57. See Harry Liebersohn, *Fate and Utopia in German Sociology, 1870–1923* (Cambridge: The MIT Press, 1988), pp. 66–67.

58. Münsterberg, op. cit., pp. 201–02.

59. Ibid. pp. 176–82.

60. Ibid., p. 179.

61. See Edward Hagerman, *The American Civil War and the Origins of Modern Warfare: Ideas, Organization, and Field Command* (Bloomington: Indiana University Press, 1988), esp. pp. xiii–xvii, 207–09, 277–93.

62. See William Tecumseh Sherman, *Memoirs of General W. T. Sherman* (New York: Library of America, 1990 [1886]), p. 365.

63. Ibid., pp. 873–99.

64. Ibid., pp. 463–748.

65. Robert M. Utley, *The Indian Frontier of the American West, 1846–1890* (Albuquerque: University of New Mexico Press, 1984), pp. 11, 76–81, 93.

66. Ibid., p. 80.

67. Ibid., pp. 80–81.

68. Robert E. Bieder, *Science Encounters the Indian, 1820–1880: The Early Years of American Ethnology* (Norman: University of Oklahoma Press, 1986, 1989); Curtis M. Hinsley, *Savages and Scientists: The Smithsonian Institution and the Development of*

American Anthropology, 1846–1910 (Washington, D.C.: Smithsonian Institution, 1981); and Robert V. Bruce, *The Launching of Modern American Science, 1846–1876* (New York: Alfred A. Knopf, 1987), pp. 201–14, 269–362.

69. See Diane M. Pinderhughes, *Race and Ethnicity in Chicago Politics: A Reexamination of Pluralist Theory* (Urbana: University of Illinois Press, 1987); and Stow Persons, *Ethnic Studies at Chicago, 1905–45* (Urbana: University of Illinois Press, 1987).

70. See Michael C. Coleman, *Presbyterian Missionary Attitudes Toward American Indians, 1837–1893* (Jackson: University Press of Mississippi, 1985); Henry Warner Bowden, *American Indians and Christian Missions: Studies in Cultural Conflict* (Chicago: University of Chicago Press, 1981); and William T. Hagan, *The Indian Rights Association: The Herbert Welsh Years, 1882–1904* (Tucson: University of Arizona Press, 1985). For Africa see the second chapter of this book, *infra*.

71. Utley, op. cit., pp. 11–19, 213–16, 227–52, 263–66. For Africa see chapter 2.

72. Sherman, op. cit., pp. 900–55.

73. Utley, op. cit., pp. 123–26, 165, 169, 173, 183, 201, 224.

74. Ibid., p. 125.

75. Cf. Norman J. Bender, *"New Hope For the Indians": The Grant Peace Policy and the Navajos in the 1870s* (Albuquerque: University of New Mexico Press, 1989).

76. Utley, op. cit., pp. 99–202, 227–74. See also Frank McNitt, *Navajo Wars: Military Campaigns, Slave Raids, and Reprisals* (Albuquerque: University of New Mexico Press, 1990), pp. 298–430.

77. For the discussion of coercive assimilation, see Sarah E. Simons, "Social Assimilation," *American Journal of Sociology* VI:6 (May 1901), pp. 808–15. Subsequent essays in this series appeared in volumes VII:1 (July 1901), pp. 53–79; VII:2 (September 1901), pp. 234–48; VII:3 (November 1901), pp. 386–404; VII:4 (January 1902), pp. 539–56.

78. Simons, op. cit., VI:6, pp. 809–10.

79. For a critical reading, see Utley, op. cit., pp. 210–69.

80. Simons, op. cit., VII:4 (January 1902), p. 550.

81. Loc. cit. Emphasis supplied.

82. Robert E. Park and Ernest W. Burgess, *Introduction To the Science of Sociology*, 3d ed., rev. (Chicago: University of Chicago Press, 1969 [1921, 1924]), pp. 740–41.

83. Robert Allen Wooster, *The Military and United States Indian Policy, 1865–1903* (New Haven: Yale University Press, 1988), pp. 174–216.

84. See Stuart Creighton Miller, *"Benevolent Assimilation": The American Conquest of the Philippines, 1899–1903* (New Haven: Yale University Press, 1982), pp. 31–103, 129–252.

85. Wooster, op. cit., pp. 201–02.

86. See Stanley Karnow, *In Our Image: America's Empire in the Philippines* (New York: Random House, 1989).

87. Robert E. Park, "Our Racial Frontier on the Pacific," *Survey Graphic* LVI (May 1926), pp. 192–96.

88. Robert E. Park, "War and Politics," *American Journal of Sociology* XLVI (January 1941), pp. 551–70. Quotations that follow are paginated according to the reprint of this essay in Robert E. Park, *Society: Collective Behavior, News and Opinion, Sociology and Modern Society*, ed. by Everett Cherrington Hughes, et al. (Glencoe: The Free Press, 1955), pp. 50–68.

89. Ibid., p. 51.

90. Ibid., p. 52.

91. Ibid., pp. 52, 53.

92. Ibid., p. 53.

93. Ibid., p. 54.

94. Ibid., p. 55.

95. Park, "The Crowd and the Public," p. 14n. 21.

96. Ibid., p. 73.

97. Robert E. Park, "Modern Society," *Biological Symposia* VIII (Lancaster, Pa.: The Jacques Cattell Press, 1942), pp. 217–40. The quotations here and below are from the reprint in Park, *Society . . .* , p. 336.

98. Park, "Morale and the News," in Park, *Society . . .* , p. 137.

99. Ibid., p. 136.

100. Loc. cit.

101. Ibid., p. 138.

102. Park, "Symbiosis and Socialization . . . ," in Robert E. Park, *Human Communities: The City and Human Ecology*, The Collected Papers of Robert Ezra Park, Volume II, ed. by E. C. Hughes, et al. (Glencoe: The Free Press, 1952), p. 246.

103. Park, "War and Politics," p. 55.

104. Michael Geyer, "German Strategy in the Age of Machine Warfare, 1914–1945," in Paret, op. cit., pp. 537–38.

105. General Erich Ludendorff, *The Nation at War* (London: n.p.l., 1936), p. 54. Quoted in Park, "War and Politics," p. 55n. 8.

106. Park, "War and Politics," p. 55.

107. George Herbert Mead, "National-Mindedness and International Mindedness," *International Journal of Ethics* XXXIX (July 1929), pp. 400–04. Quoted in Park, "War and Politics," p. 55.

108. Park, "Morale and the News," p. 139.

109. Loc. cit.

110. Park, "War and Politics," p. 57.

111. Quoted from p. 158 in Michael Balfour and Julian Frisby, *Helmuth von Moltke: A Leader Against Hitler* (London: n.p.l., 1972), in Beate Ruhm von Oppen's introduction to her edition and translation of Helmuth James von Moltke, *Letters to Freya, 1939–1945* (New York: Alfred A. Knopf, 1990), p. 22.

112. Park, "War and Politics," p. 57.

113. Harold Lasswell, "The Garrison State," *American Journal of Sociology* XLVI (January 1941), pp. 455–68. Quotations here and *infra* are from the reprint in Dwaine Marvick, ed., *Harold D. Lasswell on Political Sociology* (Chicago: University of Chicago Press, 1977), pp. 165–78, at p. 165.

114. Harold Lasswell and Abraham Kaplan, *Power and Society: A Framework for Political Inquiry* (New Haven: Yale University Press, 1950, 1951), p. 175.

115. Lasswell, "The Garrison State," p. 168.

116. Park, "War and Politics," p. 53.

117. Park, *The Immigrant Press and Its Control*, op. cit., pp. 359–468.

118. See Jules Witcover, *Sabotage at Black Tom: Imperial Germany's Secret War in America, 1914–1917* (Chapel Hill: Algonquin Books, 1989).

119. Robert E. Park, "Racial Assimilation in Secondary Groups With Particular Reference to the Negro," *American Journal of Sociology* XIII (March 1914), pp. 606–19.

120. Richard Austin Thompson, *The Yellow Peril, 1890–1924* (New York: Arno Press, 1978), pp. 1–6.

121. Park, "Our Racial Frontier on the Pacific," p. 194.

122. Ibid., p. 192.

123. Ibid., p. 195.

124. Ibid., p. 196.

125. Loc. cit.

126. Robert E. Park, "Behind Our Masks," *Survey Graphic* LVI (May 1, 1926), p. 135.

127. Park, "Our Racial Frontier on the Pacific," p. 196.

128. Romanzo Adams, *Interracial Marriage in Hawaii: A Study of the Mutually Conditioned Processes of Acculturation and Amalgamation* (New York: Macmillan, 1937; reprint, Montclair, N.J.: Patterson Smith, 1969), p. 326.

129. Park, "Introduction," in Adams, op. cit., p. xiii.

130. See William Buxton, *Talcott Parsons and the Capitalist Nation-State: Political Sociology as a Strategic Vocation* (Toronto: University of Toronto Press, 1985), pp. 97–116.

131. Herbert Blumer, "Morale," in *American Society in Wartime*, ed. by William Fielding Ogburn (Chicago: University of Chicago Press, 1943; reprint, New York: Da Capo Press, 1972), pp. 207–32. See also the discussion in Stanford M. Lyman and Arthur J. Vidich, *Social Order and the Public Philosophy: An Analysis and Interpretation of the Work of Herbert Blumer* (Fayetteville: University of Arkansas Press, 1988), pp. 42–55.

132. *Final Report. Japanese Evacuation From the West Coast, 1942* (Washington, D.C.: United States Government Printing Office, 1943), p. 515 *et passim*; Roger Daniels, *Asian America: Chinese and Japanese in the United States Since 1850* (Seattle: University of Washington Press, 1988), pp. 227–28.

133. Robert Redfield, "The Japanese-Americans," in Ogburn, ed., op. cit., p. 145.

134. See Jacobus ten Broek, Edward N. Barnhart, and Floyd Matson, *Prejudice, War and the Constitution* (Berkeley: University of California Press, 1954), pp. 211–336; and *Personal Justice Denied: Report of the Commission on Wartime Relocation and Internment of Civilians* (Washington, D.C.: United States Government Printing Office, 1982).

135. Patrick S. Washburn, *A Question of Sedition: The Federal Government's Investigation of the Black Press During World War II* (New York: Oxford University Press, 1986).

136. See Carey McWilliams, *North From Mexico: The Spanish-Speaking People of the United States* (New York: Greenwood Press, 1968 [1948]), pp. 238–58, 264–65; and Mauricio Mazon, *The Zoot-Suit Riots: The Psychology of Symbolic Annihilation* (Austin: University of Texas Press, 1984, 1989).

137. See Erasmo Gamboa, *Mexican Labor and World War II: Braceros in the Pacific Northwest, 1942–1947* (Austin: University of Texas Press, 1990).

138. Michael G. Lacy, "The United States and American Indians: Political Relations," in *American Indian Policy in the Twentieth Century*, ed. by Vine Deloria, Jr., (Norman: University of Oklahoma Press, 1985), p. 92.

139. Fred B. Kniffen, Hiram F. Gregory, and George A. Stokes, *The Historic Indian Tribes of Louisiana From 1542 to the Present* (Baton Rouge: Louisiana State University Press, 1987), p. 296.

140. *Time*, October 23, 1950, p. 29. Quoted in *The Invisible Soldier: The Experience of the Black Soldier, World War II*, comp. and ed. by Mary Penick Motley (Detroit: Wayne State University Press, 1975), p. 258.

141. Charles E. Francis, *The Tuskegee Airmen: The Men Who Changed A Nation* (Boston: Branden Publishing Co., 1988).

142. See Marvin E. Fletcher, *America's First Black General: Benjamin O. Davis, Sr., 1880–1970* (Lawrence: University Press of Kansas, 1989), *passim*.

143. Orville C. Shirey, *Americans: The Story of the 442nd Combat Team* (Washington, D.C.: Infantry Journal Press, 1946), pp. 101–51. Motley, comp. and ed., op. cit., pp. 259–60; John Hersey, "'A Mistake of Terrifically Horrible Proportions,'" in John Armor and Peter Wright, *Manzanar: Photographs By Ansel Adams* (New York: Random House/Time Books, 1988), p. 35.

144. Tamotsu Shibutani, *The Derelicts of Company K: A Sociological Study of Demoralization* (Berkeley: University of California Press, 1978).

145. United States Department of the Interior, War Agency Liquidation Unit, *People in Motion: The Postwar Adjustment of the Evacuated Japanese Americans*

(Washington, D.C.: United States Government Printing Office, n.d.), p. 18; Audrie Girdner and Anne Loftis, *The Great Betrayal: The Evacuation of the Japanese-Americans During World War II* (London: Collier-Macmillan, 1969), pp. 332–35, 379.

146. George Johnston, "Heart Mountain's Fair Play Committee: So. Calif. JACLers Throw Spotlight on Nisei W.W. II Draft Resistance Movement," *Pacific Citizen* CIX (September 8, 1989), pp. 1, 10, 12.

147. Park, "Racial Ideologies," in Ogburn, ed., op. cit., p. 176.

148. Loc. cit.

149. See Arthur J. Vidich and Stanford M. Lyman, *American Sociology: Worldly Rejections of Religion and Their Directions* (New Haven: Yale University Press, 1985), pp. 94, 100n. 5, 192–93, 205–06, 238–42, 283–84.

150. Park, "Racial Assimilation in Secondary Groups . . . ," in *Race and Culture*, op. cit., pp. 204–09.

151. For a British "realist" analysis of these aims, see Peter Calvocoressi, Guy Wint, and John Pritchard, *Total War: Causes and Courses of the Second World War*, rev. 2d ed. (New York: Pantheon Books, 1989), pp. 298–99. For an ironic treatment of the "Four Freedoms" slogan and other patriotic pronouncements of the period, see Paul Fussell, *Wartime: Understanding and Behavior in the Second World War* (New York: Oxford University Press, 1989), pp. 143–80.

152. See John W. Dower, *War Without Mercy: Race and Power in the Pacific War* (New York: Pantheon Books, 1986).

153. See Jacobus ten Broek, Edward N. Barnhart, and Floyd Matson, *Prejudice, War and the Constitution*, 3d printing (Berkeley: University of California Press, 1968), p. vi; David J. Garrow, *The FBI and Martin Luther King, Jr.* (New York: Penguin Books, 1981); Kenneth O'Reilly, *"Racial Matters": The FBI's Secret File on Black America, 1960–1972* (New York: The Free Press, 1989); Ward Churchill and Jim Vander Wall, *Agents of Repression: The FBI's Secret Wars Against the Black Panther Party and the American Indian Movement* (Boston: South End Press, 1990).

154. Georg Simmel, "The Conflict in Modern Culture," in *idem, The Conflict in Modern Culture and Other Essays*, trans. and ed. by K. Peter Etzkorn (New York: Teachers College Press, 1968), p. 11.

155. Loc. cit.

156. Loc. cit.

157. Park, *The Crowd and the Public*, op. cit., p. 53.

158. Park, "The German Army . . .," op. cit., p. 395.

159. Park, *The Crowd and the Public*, op. cit., pp. 70–71.

160. Park, "The German Army . . . ," op. cit., p. 395. For the thesis that war has become fully autonomous in the twentieth century and even independent of the need for a reason to start, see Martin van Creveld, *The Transformation of War* (New York: The Free Press, 1991.)

161. Georg Simmel, *Schopenhauer and Nietzsche*, trans. by Helmut Loiskandl, Deena Weinstein, and Michael Weinstein (Amherst: University of Massachusetts Press, 1986), p. 5.

162. Raushenbush, op. cit., p. 168.

163. Loc. cit.

164. Park, "Symbiosis and Socialization: A Frame of Reference for the Study of Society," in Park, *Human Communities*, op. cit., p. 242.

165. Ibid., p. 253.

166. Loc. cit.

167. Ibid., p. 260.

168. Georg Simmel, "Conflict," in *idem, Conflict and the Web of Group-Affiliations*, trans. by Kurt H. Wolff (Glencoe: The Free Press, 1955), p. 26.

169. Harold Lasswell, "The World Revolution of Our Time," in *Harold Lasswell On Political Sociology*, op. cit., p. 211.

170. Park, "Modern Society," op. cit., p. 341.

Park's Congo Studies

1. See Derek Jarrett, *The Sleep of Reason: Fantasy and Reality from the Victorian Age to the First World War* (New York: Harper and Row, 1989).

2. Unless noted otherwise, the following is drawn from Max Nordau, *Degeneration*, popular edition; translated from the second edition of the German work; no translator designated, (London: William Heinemann, 1913). The first edition of this work appeared in German in 1892.

3. Ibid., pp. vii–viii.

4. Ibid., p. 2

5. For various appraisals of Nordau, see Jarrett, op. cit., pp. 159–76; Daniel Rick, *Faces of Degeneration: A European Disorder, c.1848–c.1918* (Cambridge: Cambridge University Press, 1989), pp. 20–26, 171–72; and two works by George L. Mosse, *Toward the Final Solution: A History of European Racism* (New York: Howard Fertig, 1987), pp. 84–87; *Nationalism and Sexuality: Middle Class Morality and Sexual Norms in Modern Europe* (Madison: University of Wisconsin Press, 1985), pp. 35–36, 42, 136, 140–41.

6. Nordau, op. cit., p. 537.

7. Ibid., p. 557.

8. Ibid., p. 560.

9. Loc. cit.

10. Josiah Royce, *The Problem of Christianity* (Chicago: University of Chicago Press, 1968 [1918]), pp. 93–94. For a discussion see Arthur J. Vidich and Stanford M. Lyman, "State, Ethics and Public Morality in American Sociological Thought," in *Sociological Theory in Transition*, ed. by Mark L. Wardell and Stephen P. Turner (Boston: Allen and Unwin, 1986), pp. 44–58, esp. pp. 44–47.

11. Nathaniel S. Shaler, *The Neighbor: The Natural History of Human Contacts* (Boston: Houghton, Mifflin and Co., 1904).

12. Nordau, op. cit., p. 560.

13. Loc. cit.

14. George E. Haggerty, *Gothic Fiction / Gothic Form* (University Park: The Pennsylvania State University Press, 1989), p. 17.

15. Ibid., pp. 16–17.

16. Booker T. Washington, "Cruelty in the Congo Country," *Outlook* LXXVIII (October 8, 1904), p. 377.

17. The following is taken from Karl Marx, *Early Texts*, trans. and ed. by David McLellan (Oxford: Basil Blackwell, 1972), pp. 178–83.

18. The following is taken from Max Weber, *The Protestant Ethic and the Spirit of Capitalism*, trans. by Talcott Parsons (New York: Charles Scribner's Sons, 1930), p. 17.

19. Mary Wollstonecraft Shelley, *Frankenstein, Or the Modern Prometheus: The 1818 Text*, ed. by James Rieger (Indianapolis: Bobbs-Merrill, 1974), p. 95.

20. The introduction is reprinted as Appendix A in ibid., pp. 222–29. The quotation is from p. 228.

21. Weber, op. cit., p. 181.

22. The first full-length fictionalization of the vampire was *Varney the Vampyre, or the Feast of Blood*, by James Malcolm Rymer or Thomas Pecket Prest. Originally published

in 1847, this two-volume work has been reissued with an introduction by E. F. Bleiler (New York: Dover Publications, 1972).

23. See Montague Summers, *The Vampire: His Kith and Kin* (New Hyde Park, N.Y.: University Books, 1960), pp. 273–74.

24. John Polidori, "The Vampyre," in E. F. Bleiler, ed., *Three Gothic Novels* (New York: Dover Publications, 1966), pp. 255–84.

25. Bram Stoker, *Dracula* (New York: Modern Library, n.d. [1897]).

26. John Hope Franklin, "George Washington Williams: The Massachusetts Years," *Proceedings of the American Antiquarian Society* XCII:2 (October 1982; reprint, Worcester, Mass.: American Antiquarian Society, 1983), pp. 243–63. Quotation from p. 243. See also John Hope Franklin, "George Washington Williams and Africa," in Lorraine A. Williams, ed., *Africa and the Afro-American Experience: Eight Essays* (Washington, D.C.: Howard University Press, 1981), pp. 59–76.

27. George Washington Williams, *History of the Negro Race in America From 1619 to 1880: Negroes As Slaves, As Soldiers, and As Citizens; Together With a Preliminary Consideration of the Human Family, An Historical Sketch of Africa, and An Account of the Negro Governments of Sierra Leone and Liberia* (New York: G. P. Putnam's Sons, 1883; reprint, New York: Bergman Publishers, 1968), 2 vols.

28. George Washington Williams, *A History of the Negro Troops in the War of the Rebellion, 1861–65, preceded by a Review of the Military Services of Negroes in Ancient and Modern Times* (New York: Harper and Brothers, 1887; reprint, New York: Bergman Publishers, 1968).

29. See Arthur J. Vidich and Stanford M. Lyman, *American Sociology: Worldly Rejections of Religion and Their Directions* (New Haven: Yale University Press, 1985).

30. The definitive biography of Williams is John Hope Franklin, *George Washington Williams: A Biography* (Chicago: University of Chicago Press, 1985).

31. Ibid., p. 113.

32. Williams, *History of the Negro Race in America*, op. cit., I, pp. 1–6.

33. See Winthrop Jordan, *White Over Black: American Attitudes Toward the Negro, 1550–1812* (Chapel Hill: University of North Carolina Press, 1968), pp. 17–20, 35–37, 41–43, 54–56, 60–62, 84, 111, 158, 200–01, 243–46, 308, 525.

34. Williams, *History of the Negro Race in America*, op. cit., I, pp. 9–10.

35. Ibid., I, p. 15.

36. Ibid., I, pp. 34–44.

37. Ibid., I, pp. 22–23. For the current status of the debate over African civilization's contribution to the classical cultures of antiquity, see Martin Bernal, *Black Athena: The Afroasiatic Roots of Classical Civilization, Vol. I: The Fabrication of Ancient Greece, 1785–1985* (New Brunswick: Rutgers University Press, 1987), esp. pp. 433–44.

38. Williams, op. cit., I, p. 22.

39. Ibid., I, pp. 24–25.

40. Ibid., II, p. 552.

41. Loc. cit.

42. Loc. cit.

43. Park, "An Autobiographical Note," in *Race and Culture: The Collected Papers of Robert E. Park, Vol. I,* ed. by Everett Cherrington Hughes, et al. (Glencoe: The Free Press, 1950), p. vii.

44. Quoted in Franklin, *George Washington Williams*, op. cit., pp. 10–11.

45. Ibid., pp. 180–242, 245.

46. "A Report upon the Congo-State and Country to the President of the Republic of the United States of America, by Colonel the Honorable Geo. W. Williams," dated at St. Paul de Loanda, Province of Angola (S. W. Africa), October 14, 1890. Reprinted in Franklin, *George Washington Williams*, op. cit., p. 279.

47. The following quotations come from "An Open Letter to His Serene Majesty Leopold II, King of the Belgians and Sovereign of the Independent State of Congo, by Colonel The Honorable Geo. W. Williams, of the United States of America," dated at Stanley Falls, Central Africa, July 18, 1890. Reprinted in Franklin, *George Washington Williams*, op. cit., pp. 243–54.

48. Ibid., p. 252.

49. On these people and their diaspora in Africa, see William J. Samarin, *The Black Man's Burden: African Colonial Labor on the Congo and Ubangi Rivers, 1880–1900* (Boulder, Colo.: Westview Press, 1989), pp. 30–34, 38, 41, 88, 127, 155, 167–68; and Akintola Wyse, *The Krio of Sierra Leone: An Interpretive History* (London: C. Hurst and Co., 1989).

50. "A Report on the Proposed Congo Railway, by Colonel the Honorable Geo. W. Williams, of the United States of America," dated at Stanley Falls, Central Africa, July 16, 1890. Reprinted in Franklin, *George Washington Williams*, op. cit., pp. 258–59, 262–63.

51. Quotations are from "A Report Upon the Congo-Free State and Country to the President of the . . . United States," in Franklin, *George Washington Williams*, op. cit., pp. 272–73.

52. Loc. cit.

53. H. N. Sherwood, "Early Negro Deportation Projects," *Mississippi Valley Historical Review* II (March 1916), pp. 484–508. For a thoroughgoing history and analysis of this movement in the nineteenth century, see R. J. M. Blackett, *Building an Antislavery Wall: Black Americans in the Abolitionist Movement, 1830–1860* (Ithaca: Cornell University Press, 1989), pp. 162–94, 209–16.

54. Paul Cuffe, "Letter to John James and Alexander Wilson," dated at Westport, Mass., on 6 mo 10th 1809, in *Apropos of Africa: Sentiments of American Negro Leaders on Africa from the 1800s to the 1950s*, ed. by Adelaide Cromwell Hill and Martin Kilson (London: Frank Cass, 1969), p. 11.

55. On Cuffe, see Sheldon H. Harris, *Paul Cuffe: Black America and the African Return* (New York: Simon and Schuster, 1972); and Lamont D. Thomas, *Paul Cuffe: Black Entrepreneur and Pan-Africanist* (Urbana: University of Illinois Press, 1986, 1988).

56. M. R. Delany, Chief Commissioner to Africa, "Official Report of the Niger Valley Exploring Party," in M. R. Delany and Robert Campbell, *Search For a Place: Black Separatism and Africa, 1860* (Ann Arbor: University of Michigan Press, 1969), p. 38.

57. Ibid., p. 110.

58. For Delany's own writings on how American blacks might be liberated, see his *The Condition, Elevation, Emigration, and Destiny of the Colored People of the United States, Politically Considered* (Philadelphia: Published by the Author, 1852; reprint, New York: Arno Press and the New York Times, 1968), esp. pp. 159–215. In his novel, *Blake, or the Huts of America*, serialized in *The Weekly Anglo-African* from November 26, 1861, to May 1862 and not published in book form until Beacon Press of Boston brought out an incomplete edition in 1970, Delany created a black West Indian slave-hero who advocates revolution in the United States and violent overthrow of the colonial slavocracy in Cuba. For various assessments of Delany, see Dorothy Sterling, *The Making of an African-American: Martin Robison Delany, 1812–1885* (Garden City: Doubleday, 1971); Victor Ullman, *Martin R. Delany: The Beginnings of Black Nationalism* (Boston: Beacon Press, 1971); and Cyril E. Griffith, *The African Dream: Martin R. Delany and the Emergence of Pan-African Thought* (University Park: Pennsylvania State University Press, 1975).

59. Earl Ofari, *"Let Your Motto Be Resistance": The Life and Thought of Henry Highland Garnet* (Boston: Beacon Press, 1972).

60. Wilson Jeremiah Moses, *Alexander Crummell: A Study of Civilization and Discontent* (New York: Oxford University Press, 1989), p. 132; Hill and Kilson, op. cit., pp. 44–67, 87–97, 109–21, 167–68, 172–215, 232–63, 304–36.

61. Alain Locke, "Apropos of Africa," *Opportunity* II (February 1924), p. 37. Reprinted in Hill and Kilson, op. cit., p. 350.

62. See George Shepperson and Thomas Price, *Independent African: John Chilembwe and the Origins, Setting and Significance of the Nyasaland Native Rising of 1915* (Edinburgh: Edinburgh University Press, 1958, 1963); and Georges Simeon Mwase, *Strike a Blow and Die: A Narrative of Race Relations in Colonial Africa*, ed. by Robert I. Rotberg (Cambridge: Harvard University Press, 1967).

63. Turner's role in the post–Civil War struggles for civil rights is briefly described in August Meier and Elliott Rudwick, "The Boycott Movement Against Jim Crow Streetcars in the South, 1900–1906," in *The Black Experience in America: Selected Essays*, ed. by James C. Curtis and Lewis L. Gould (Austin: University of Texas Press, 1970), pp. 106–07.

64. The definitive account of Turner's career is Edwin S. Redkey, *Black Exodus: Black Nationalist and Back-to-Africa Movements, 1890–1910* (New Haven: Yale University Press, 1969). See also August Meier, *Negro Thought in America, 1880–1915: Racial Ideologies in the Age of Booker T. Washington* (Ann Arbor: University of Michigan Press, 1964), pp. 28, 59–68, 71, 82, 185, 218, 272; and Wilson Jeremiah Moses, *The Golden Age of Black Nationalism, 1850–1925* (New York: Oxford University Press, 1978, 1988), pp. 23, 76, 90, 172, 177, 197–98, 200–01, 209, 268.

65. For the details of this matter—which are, necessarily, beyond the scope of the present study—see four essays by George Shepperson, "Ethiopianism and African Nationalism," *Phylon Quarterly* XIV (Winter 1953), pp. 9–18; "The Politics of African Church Separatist Movements in British Central Africa, 1892–1916," *Africa* XXIV (January 1954), pp. 233–45; "Notes on Negro American Influences on the Emergence of African Nationalism," *Journal of African History* I:2 (1960), pp. 299–312; "Pan-Africanism and 'Pan-Africanism': Some Historical Notes," *Phylon Quarterly* XXIII (Winter 1962), pp. 346–58. See also Robert I. Rotberg, *The Rise of Nationalism in Central Africa: The Making of Malawi and Zambia, 1873–1964* (Cambridge: Harvard University Press, 1967).

66. Hollis R. Lynch, "The Native Pastorate Controversy and Cultural Ethno-Centrism in Sierra Leone, 1871–1874," *Journal of African History* V:3 (1964), pp. 395–413. For Blyden's life and work, see Hollis R. Lynch, *Edward Wilmot Blyden: Pan-Negro Patriot, 1832–1912* (London: Oxford University Press, 1967).

67. See W. O. Brown, "Race Consciousness Among South African Natives," *American Journal of Sociology* XL (March 1935), pp. 569–81; and Charles W. Coulter, "Problems Arising From Industrialization of Native Life in Central Africa," *American Journal of Sociology* XL (March 1935), pp. 582–92.

68. See Leo Kuper and M. G. Smith, eds., *Pluralism in Africa* (Berkeley: University of California Press, 1969).

69. See G. Spiller, "Science and Race Prejudice," *Sociological Review* V (October 1912), pp. 331–48; Thomas Hodgkin, *Nationalism in Colonial Africa* (New York: New York University Press, 1957), pp. 48–54, 63–92 et passim.

70. See Henry McNeal Turner, "Emigration," *Voice of Missions*, April 1, 1900. Reprinted in *Black Nationalism in America*, ed. by John H. Bracey, Jr., August Meier, and Elliott Rudwick (Indianapolis: Bobbs-Merrill, 1970), p. 176.

71. William E. Bittle and Gilbert Geis, *The Longest Way Home: Chief Alfred C. Sam's Back-to-Africa Movement* (Detroit: Wayne State University Press, 1964).

72. DuBois's now famous statement, "The Problem of the twentieth century is the problem of the color line,—the relation of the darker to the lighter races of men

in Asia and Africa, in America and the islands of the sea," was first made in his address "To the Nations of the World" at the Pan African Congress in London, July 1900, where he served as chairman of the Committee on Address to the Nations. It opens chapter 2, "Of the Dawn of Freedom," of *The Souls of Black Folk: Essays and Sketches* (Greenwich: Fawcett Publications, 1961. Orig. pub. 1903), p. 23. According to P. Olisanwuche Esedebe, *Pan-Africanism: The Idea and the Movement, 1776–1963* (Washington, D.C.: Howard University Press, 1982), p. 45: "The Chicago Congress on Africa of 1893 may be taken as the beginning of Pan-Africanism as a movement."

73. See Louis R. Harlan, "Booker T. Washington and the White Man's Burden," *American Historical Review* LXXI (January 1966), pp. 441–67.

74. Booker T. Washington, *Up From Slavery: An Autobiography* (New York: Bantam Pathfinder Editions, 1963. Orig. pub. 1900), pp. 153–67.

75. DuBois, *The Souls of Black Folk*, op. cit., pp. 53–54.

76. See August Meier, *Negro Thought in America*, op. cit., pp. 110–14.

77. Ras Makonnen, *Pan-Africanism From Within*, recorded and ed. by Kenneth King (Nairobi, Kenya: Oxford University Press, 1973), p. 52.

78. Woodruff D. Smith, *The Ideological Origins of Nazi Imperialism* (New York: Oxford University Press, 1986), p. 34. Authorities differ as to the specific reasons that impelled Bismarck to reverse course on his original promise not to seek a colonial empire in Africa. In 1943, Hans Speier observed that "The military elite was not responsible for developing schemes of national aggrandizement and conquest. Social organizations like the German Navy League, the Pan-German League and the various societies interested in the acquisition and development of colonies were controlled and sponsored by the economic counter-elite and by intellectuals coming from the middle classes." "Ludendorff: The German Concept of Total War," in Hans Speier, *The Truth in Hell and Other Essays on Politics and Culture, 1935–1987* (New York: Oxford University Press, 1989), p. 102. Sebastian Haffner acknowledges the likelihood of the widespread explanation that Bismarck had adopted a policy of "social imperialism" for purposes of achieving greater domestic support but adds that, according to Hans-Ulrich Wehler, the colonial policy provided "a new national unifying factor in view of the waning enthusiasm over the creation of the by now ten-year-old Reich." *The Ailing Empire: Germany From Bismarck to Hitler*, trans. by Jean Steinberg (New York: Fromm International Publishing Corp., 1989), pp. 52–53. Paul M. Kennedy elaborates on the theses presented by Speier and Haffner, showing that both long- and short-term considerations went into Bismarck's reformulation of German foreign policy, including extending state intervention into German overseas enterprises; recognizing the new value of colonies that had arisen among the Powers since the 1860s; responding to the new national problems of industrial overproduction and a surplus population; seeking the support of the powerful pressure groups in Germany demanding an imperialist program; and, related to the latter point, winning over the right-wing National Liberals and separating them from the left-Liberal elements in their party. *The Rise of the Anglo-German Antagonism, 1860–1914* (London: The Ashfield Press, 1987), pp. 167–83.

79. Smith, op. cit., pp. 64–70.

80. Harlan, op. cit., p. 443.

81. Ibid., pp. 445–46. For Robinson's own account—written three years before his death—see his "Cotton-Growing in Africa," in Booker T. Washington, ed., *Tuskegee and Its People* (New York: D. Appleton and Co., 1906), pp. 184–99.

82. Harlan, op. cit., p. 446.

83. Smith, op. cit., p. 77.

84. Louis R. Harlan, *Booker T. Washington: The Wizard of Tuskegee, 1901–1915* (New York: Oxford University Press, 1983), p. 266.

85. Randall E. Stross, *The Stubborn Earth: American Agriculturalists on Chinese Soil, 1898–1937* (Berkeley: University of California Press, 1986), pp. 188–216. For a general account, see David Faure, *The Rural Economy of Pre-Liberation China: Trade Expansion and Peasant Livelihood in Jiangsu and Guangdong, 1870–1937* (Hong Kong: Oxford University Press, 1989).

86. Booker T. Washington, "Industrial Education in Africa," *Independent* LX (March 15, 1906), pp. 616–19. Reprinted in *The Booker T. Washington Papers Vol. 8: 1904–1906*, ed. by Louis R. Harlan and Raymond W. Smock (Urbana: University of Illinois Press, 1979), pp. 548–52. Quotation from pp. 551–52.

87. Harlan, "Booker T. Washington and the White Man's Burden," op. cit., pp. 446, 449.

88. Ibid., p. 450.

89. Robert E. Park, "Recent Atrocities in the Congo," *The World To-Day* VIII (October 1904), pp. 1328–31.

90. William Roger Louis and Jean Stengers, *E. D. Morel's History of the Congo Reform Movement* (Oxford: Clarendon Press, 1968), pp. ix–x.

91. Robert E. Park to E. D. Morel, January 15, 1905. Quoted in Louis and Stengers, op. cit., p. 184.

92. Louis R. Harlan, *Booker T. Washington: The Wizard of Tuskegee, 1901–1915*, op. cit., p. 270.

93. For details of the Protestant interest in the Congo—and its competition with Catholic missionaries said to be all too comfortable with Leopold's policies there—see Paul McStallworth, "The United States and the Congo Question, 1884–1914," Ph.D. diss., Ohio State University, 1954 (Ann Arbor: University Microfilms, 1988), pp. 209–47.

94. Ibid., p. 271.

95. Robert E. Park to Booker T. Washington, undated, about May 1905. Quoted in Harlan, "Booker T. Washington and the White Man's Burden," op. cit., p. 451.

96. Booker T. Washington, "Cruelty in the Congo Country," op. cit., pp. 375–77. Reprinted in *The Booker T. Washington Papers, Vol. 8: 1904–1906*, op. cit., pp. 85–90. On October 11, 1904, Washington sent Park the thirty dollars that *Outlook* had paid him for the article with a note: "I cannot feel I should accept this money since this article was so largely prepared by you." *Booker T. Washington Papers, Vol. 8: 1904–1906*, op. cit., p. 90n.

97. Quotations that follow are from the reprinted version in the *Booker T. Washington Papers, Vol. 8: 1904–1906*, op. cit., pp. 85–90.

98. Robert E. Park and Ernest W. Burgess, *Introduction to the Science of Sociology*, 3d ed., rev. (Chicago: University of Chicago Press, 1969. Orig. pub. 1921), p. 983.

99. Park and Burgess, op. cit., pp. 796–811, 816–46, 970–79.

100. Robert E. Park, "A King in Business: Leopold II of Belgium, Autocrat of the Congo and International Broker," *Everybody's Magazine* XV (November 1906), p. 624.

101. Park, "Recent Atrocities in the Congo," op. cit., p. 1328.

102. See E. F. Bleiler, "Horace Walpole and 'The Castle of Otranto,'" in *idem*, ed., *Three Gothic Novels*, op. cit., pp. xiv–xv.

103. Park, "A King in Business . . . ," op. cit., p. 625.

104. Loc. cit.

105. Ibid., p. 626.

106. See Hannah Arendt, *Eichmann in Jerusalem: A Report on the Banality of Evil* (New York: The Viking Press, 1963), esp. p. 253.

107. Robert E. Park, "The Terrible Story of the Congo," *Everybody's Magazine* XV (December 1906), pp. 763–72.

108. Park, "A King in Business . . .," op. cit., pp. 626–27.

109. Ibid., p. 627.

110. Ibid., p. 630.

111. Ibid., p. 632.

112. Ibid., pp. 631–32.

113. Loc. cit. Emphasis in original.

114. Ibid., p. 633.

115. Loc. cit.

116. Loc. cit.

117. Loc. cit.

118. Park, "The Terrible Story of the Congo," op. cit., pp. 763–64.

119. Joseph Conrad, *Heart of Darkness and the Secret Sharer* (New York: New American Library, 1950), pp. 66, 105–06.

120. See Chinua Achebe, "An Image of Africa: Racism in Conrad's *Heart of Darkness*," in *idem, Hopes and Impediments: Selected Essays* (New York: Doubleday, 1989), pp. 1–20.

121. Park, "The Terrible Story of the Congo," op. cit., p. 763.

122. Ibid., p. 765.

123. Ibid., p. 767.

124. Ibid., p. 769.

125. Ibid., p. 769.

126. Ibid., p. 771.

127. Ibid., p. 772.

128. Robert E. Park, "The Blood-Money of the Congo," *Everybody's Magazine* XVI (January 1907), pp. 60–70.

129. Ibid., pp. 60–61.

130. Ibid., p. 61.

131. Park, "The Terrible Story of the Congo," op. cit., p. 772.

132. For the details of this dispute, see Catherine Ann Cline, "The Church and the Movement For Congo Reform," *Church History* XXXII (March 1963), pp. 46–56.

133. Robert Park, "Autobiographical Fragment." Quoted in Fred H. Matthews, "Robert Park, Congo Reform and Tuskegee: The Molding of a Race Relations Expert, 1905–1913," *Canadian Journal of History* VIII (Spring 1973), p. 40.

134. Park, "The Terrible Story of the Congo," op. cit., p. 771.

135. Robert Park, "An Autobiographical Note," in *idem, Race and Culture, The Collected Papers of Robert Ezra Park, Volume I*, ed. by Everett Cherrington Hughes, et al. (Glencoe: The Free Press, 1950), p. vii.

136. Montague Summers, op. cit., p. 77.

137. Robert E. Park to E. D. Morel, January 15, 1905. Quoted in Louis and Stengers, eds., op. cit., p. 184.

138. McStallworth, op. cit., pp. 297–343.

139. See also the account in Ford Madox Ford, *A History of Our Own Times*, ed. by Solon Beinfeld and Sondra J. Stang (Bloomington, Ind.: Indiana University Press, 1988), pp. 122–32.

140. See Ruth Slade, "King Leopold II and the Attitude of English and American Catholics Towards the Anti-Congolese Campaign," *Zaire* XI (June 1957), pp. 593–612.

141. McStallworth, op. cit., p. 335.

142. *New York Times*, November 19, 1961. Quoted in Janet Smith, ed., *Mark Twain On the Damned Human Race* (New York: Hill and Wang, 1962), p. 181.

143. See Brian Tigre, *Imperialism's New Clothes: The Repartition of Tropical Africa, 1914–1919* (New York: Peter Lang, 1990).

144. E. D. Morel, *The Black Man's Burden: The White Man in Africa from the Fifteenth Century to World War I* (New York: Monthly Review Press, 1969 [1920]), p. 232. On the other hand, Morel's hands may not have been so clean in this matter. According to France's most distinguished critic of colonialism in Africa, Jean Suret-Canale (1921–): "In French Equatorial Africa and the Belgian Congo . . . it was the British trading houses which were ousted by the Franco-Belgian concessionaires. In those territories they did not have political authority behind them, and were thus reduced to revealing to the world the crimes of their competitors, in a not wholly disinterested spirit. E. D. Morel, the author of *Red Rubber*, which denounced the crimes of Leopold II and his agents in the Congo, represented the commercial interests of Liverpool." Jean Suret-Canale, *Essays on African History: From the Slave Trade to Neocolonialism*, trans. by Christopher Hurst (Trenton, N.J.: Africa World Press, Inc., 1988), p. 133n. 46.

145. Albion W. Small, "Christianity and Industry," *American Journal of Sociology* XXV (May 1920), p. 693.

146. See, e.g., four reviews by Robert E. Park: review of *The South Africans* by Sarah Gertrude Millin, *American Journal of Sociology* XXXIII (March 1928), pp. 834–35; review of *A Bibliography of the Negro in Africa and America* by Monroe N. Work, *American Journal of Sociology* XXXV (July 1929), pp. 126–27; review of *Caliban in Africa: An Impression of Colour Madness* by Leonard Barnes and of *Negro: National Asset or Liability?* by John Louis Hill, *American Journal of Sociology* XXXVII (March 1932), pp. 812–13; review of *European Colonial Expansion Since 1871* by Mary Evelyn Townsend, *American Journal of Sociology* XLVIII (January 1943), pp. 516–17.

147. Robert E. Park, review of *The Menace of Colour: A Study of the Difficulties Due to the Association of White and Colored Races, With an Account of Measures Proposed for Their Solution, and Special Reference to White Colonization in the Tropics* by J. W. Gregory, *American Journal of Sociology* XXXI (November 1925), p. 403.

148. Robert E. Park, review of *Enquiries into Religion and Culture* by Christopher Dawson, *American Journal of Sociology* XLI (July 1935), p. 110.

149. Georg Simmel, *Schopenhauer and Nietzsche*, trans. by Helmut Loiskandl, Deena Weinstein, and Michael Weinstein (Amherst: The University of Massachusetts Press, 1986), pp. 4–5.

150. Park, review of *Enquiries into Religion and Culture* . . . , op. cit., p. 110.

151. See, among many others, William J. Samarin, op. cit., pp. 5–28, 162–212, 223–38.

152. Park, review of *Enquiries into Religion and Culture* . . . , op. cit., pp. 110–11.

153. See Stanford M. Lyman, *The Seven Deadly Sins: Society and Evil*, rev. ed. (Dix Hills, N.Y.: General Hall, 1989), pp. 259–64.

154. Park, review of *Enquiries into Religion and Culture* . . . , op. cit., p. 111.

155. Loc. cit.

156. Robert E. Park, review of *Foundations of Christianity* by Karl Kautsky, *American Journal of Sociology* XXXI (March 1926), p. 686.

157. Robert E. Park, review of *Social and Cultural Dynamics, Vol. I: Fluctuation of Forms of Art; Vol. II: Fluctuation of Systems of Truth, Ethics, and Law; Vol. III: Fluctuation of Social Relationships, War, and Revolution* by Pitirim A. Sorokin, *American Journal of Sociology* XLIII (March 1938), p. 831.

158. Loc. cit.

159. Ibid., p. 827.

160. Robert E. Park, review of *Die Drei Nationalökonomien* by Werner Sombart, *American Journal of Sociology* XXXVI:6 (May 1931), pp. 1071–77.

161. See Martin Bulmer, *The Chicago School of Sociology: Institutionalization,*

Diversity, and the Rise of Sociological Research (Chicago: University of Chicago Press, 1984), pp. 151–89.

162. Robert E. Park, "Urbanization as Measured by Newspaper Circulation," *American Journal of Sociology* XXXV:1 (July 1929), pp. 60–79.

163. Park's brief commentary on a chess game adumbrates a later work by Erving Goffman. See Erving Goffman, "Fun in Games," in *Encounters: Two Studies in the Sociology of Interaction* (Indianapolis: Bobbs-Merrill, 1961), pp. 17–84.

164. Robert E. Park, "William Graham Sumner's Conception of Society: An Interpretation," *The Chinese Social and Political Science Review* XVII:3 (October 1933), p. 441.

Accomodations to Evil: The Conflict and Fusion of Race, Religion, and Culture in Park's America

1. See Stanford M. Lyman, *The Seven Deadly Sins: Society and Evil,* rev. ed. (Dix Hills, N.Y.: General Hall, 1989).

2. The foregoing has benefited from the discussion in Alan Macfarlane, "Evil," Chapter 5 of his monograph, *The Culture of Capitalism* (Cambridge: Basil Blackwell, 1987, 1989), pp. 98–122.

3. Hannah Arendt, *Eichmann in Jerusalem: A Report on the Banality of Evil* (New York: The Viking Press, 1963). For an extension of this argument that treats the Holocaust "as a rare, yet significant and reliable, test of the hidden possibilities of modern society," see Zygmunt Bauman, *Modernity and the Holocaust* (Ithaca: Cornell University Press, 1989). Quotation is from p. 12.

4. Dagmar Barnouw, *Visible Spaces: Hannah Arendt and the German-Jewish Experience* (Baltimore: Johns Hopkins University Press, 1990), p. 2.

5. See Robert E. Park, "Community Organization and Juvenile Delinquency," in *The City*, ed. by Robert E. Park, Ernest W. Burgess, and Roderick D. McKenzie (Chicago: University of Chicago Press, 1967 [1925]), p. 109.

6. Robert E. Park, "William Graham Sumner's Conception of Society: An Interpretation," *The Chinese Social and Political Science Review* XVII:3 (October 1933), pp. 430–41.

7. Robert E. Park, "Methods of Teaching: Impressions and a Verdict," *Social Forces* XX:1 (October 1941), p. 41.

8. It is now known that Washington carried on a secret campaign for the implementation of those very civil rights that his publicly espoused philosophy seemed to wish to postpone. See August Meier, *Negro Thought In America, 1880–1915: Racial Ideologies in the Age of Booker T. Washington* (Ann Arbor: University of Michigan Press, 1964), pp. 100–20; and Louis R. Harlan, "The Secret Life of Booker T. Washington," *Journal of Southern History* XXXVII (August 1971), pp. 393–416.

9. Robert E. Park, "A City of Racial Peace," *World To-Day* IX (August 1905), pp. 897–99. Quotation from p. 898.

10. Robert E. Park, "Negro Home Life and Standards of Living," *Annals of the American Academy of Political and Social Science* XLIX (September 1913), pp. 147–63.

11. Park, "A City of Racial Peace," op. cit., p. 898.

12. See Joan Campbell, *Joy in Work, German Work: The National Debate, 1800–1945* (Princeton: Princeton University Press, 1989), pp. 7–130, 178–275 *et passim*.

13. Park, "A City of Racial Peace," op. cit., p. 898.

14. See R. H. Tawney, *Religion and the Rise of Capitalism: A Historical Study*

(Holland Memorial Lectures, 1922) (New York: Mentor, 1958 [1926]); Karl Lowith, *Max Weber and Karl Marx*, trans. by Hans Fantel, ed. by Tom Bottomore and William Outhwaite (London: George Allen and Unwin, 1982), pp. 28–67, 100–07; H. M. Robertson, *Aspects of the Rise of Economic Individualism: A Criticism of Max Weber and His School* (Clifton, N.J.: Augustus M. Kelley, 1973 [1933]); Werner Sombart, *The Jews and Modern Capitalism*, trans. by M. Epstein (New Brunswick, N.J.: Transaction Books, 1982); Jacob Viner, *Religious Thought and Economic Society: Four Chapters of an Unfinished Work*, ed. by Jacques Melitz and Donald Winch (Durham: Duke University Press, 1978), pp. 151–92; Kurt Samuelsson, *Religion and Economic Action: A Critique of Max Weber*, trans. by E. Geoffrey French, ed. by D. C. Coleman (New York: Harper Torchbooks, 1964); and Robert W. Green, ed., *Protestantism and Capitalism: The Weber Thesis and Its Critics* (Boston: D. C. Heath and Co., 1959).

15. Max Weber, *The Protestant Ethic and the Spirit of Capitalism*, trans. by Talcott Parsons (New York: Charles Scribner's Sons, 1930).

16. See the discussion in Campbell, op. cit., p. 219.

17. Georg Simmel, *Schopenhauer and Nietzsche*, trans. by Helmut Loiskandl, Deena Weinstein, and Michael Weinstein (Amherst: University of Massachusetts Press, 1986), p. 5.

18. Quoted in Margaret Connell Szasz, *Indian Education in the American Colonies, 1607–1783* (Albuquerque: University of New Mexico Press, 1988), p. 153.

19. Park, "A City of Racial Peace," op. cit., p. 898.

20. Weber, *The Protestant Ethic . . .* , op. cit., p. 95.

21. Ibid., p. 132.

22. Ibid., pp. 134–35.

23. Ibid., p. 136.

24. Loc. cit.

25. Loc. cit.

26. Ibid., p. 248n. 138.

27. Ibid., p. 264n. 24.

28. See, e.g., Roger L. Ransom, *Conflict and Compromise: The Political Economy of Slavery, Emancipation, and the American Civil War* (Cambridge: Cambridge University Press, 1989), pp. 225–34.

29. See Winthrop Jordan, *White Over Black: American Attitudes Toward the Negro, 1550–1812* (Chapel Hill: University of North Carolina Press, 1968), pp. 35–37, 54, 56, 60, 62n., 84, 111, 200–01, 307–08.

30. Daniel B. Thorp, *The Moravian Community in Colonial North Carolina: Pluralism on the Southern Frontier* (Knoxville: University of Tennessee Press, 1989), pp. 52–57.

31. Henry Hughes, *Treatise on Sociology, Theoretical and Practical* (Philadelphia: Lippincott, Grambo and Co., 1854; reprint, New York: Negro Universities Press, 1968), p. 95. See also Stanford M. Lyman, ed., *Selected Writings of Henry Hughes: Antebellum Southerner, Slavocrat, Sociologist* (Jackson: University Press of Mississippi, 1985).

32. See Stanford M. Lyman, "System and Function in Antebellum Southern Sociology," *The International Journal of Politics, Culture, and Society* II:1 (Fall 1988), pp. 95–108; reprinted in Lyman, *Civilization: Contents, Discontents, Malcontents, and Other Essays in Social Theory* (Fayetteville: University of Arkansas Press, 1990), pp. 191–201.

33. George Frederick Holmes, *The Science of Society: Seventeen Lectures Delivered to His Class at the University of Virginia, Session 1882–3* (Richmond: Miller School Print, 1883), Lecture XVII, p. 8.

34. Joseph LeConte, *The Race Problem in the South* (New York: D. Appleton and Co., 1892; reprint, Miami: Mnemosyne Publishing Co., 1969), pp. 359–82.

35. Quoted in Roberta Sue Alexander, *North Carolina Faces the Freedmen: Race Relations During Presidential Reconstruction, 1865–1867* (Durham: Duke University Press, 1985), p. 33.

36. Joe M. Richardson, *Christian Reconstruction: The American Missionary Association and Southern Blacks, 1861–1890* (Athens: The University of Georgia Press, 1986), pp. 121–40, 257–62.

37. Cf. Benjamin E. Mays, *The Negro's God as Reflected In His Literature* (New York: Atheneum, 1968), pp. 139–46.

38. Booker T. Washington, *Up From Slavery: An Autobiography* (New York: Bantam Books, 1963 [1901]), p. 155.

39. Booker T. Washington, ed., *Tuskegee and Its People* (New York: D. Appleton and Co., 1906).

40. Roscoe Conkling Bruce, "The Academic Aims," in Washington, ed., *Tuskegee and Its People*, op. cit., p. 56. Emphasis supplied.

41. Park, "A City of Racial Peace," op. cit., pp. 897–98.

42. Robert E. Park, "Methods of Teaching: Impressions and a Verdict," op. cit., p. 41.

43. Park, "A City of Racial Peace," op. cit., p. 899.

44. The following draws on Szasz, op. cit., pp. 149–71.

45. Winthrop S. Hudson, *Religion in America: An Historical Account of the Development of American Religious Life*, 2d ed. (New York: Charles Scribner's Sons, 1973), p. 54. As part of his edition of letters he and Booker T. Washington had collected during the course of their joint and separate activities in the South, Park included a letter from Augustus G. Spangenberg's *Journal of Travels in North Carolina, 1752.* The letter describes without comment the situation affecting black-white-Indian relations in the colony and includes materials on the use of tax revenues and fines to discourage intermarriage, the criminal process invoked to prosecute slaves who buy or sell their masters' property without permission, and the punishment of servitude employed against anyone who assists a slave in escaping from bondage. See "Letters Collected by R. E. Park and Booker T. Washington," *The Journal of Negro History* VII:2 (April 1922), pp. 206–07.

46. Lewis W. Spitz, *The Protestant Reformation, 1517–1559* (New York: Harper and Row, 1985), pp. 126–27.

47. Ernst Troeltsch, *The Social Teachings of the Christian Churches*, trans. by Olive Wyon (New York: Harper Torchbooks, 1960 [1911]), II, p. 720.

48. Ibid., pp. 720–21.

49. Weber, *The Protestant Ethic . . .* , op. cit., pp. 64–65.

50. Sidney E. Ahlstrom, *A Religious History of the American People* (New Haven: Yale University Press, 1972), pp. 242–43.

51. Robert Henry Billigmeier, *Americans From Germany: A Study in Cultural Diversity* (Belmont, Calif.: Wadsworth Publishing Co., 1974), p. 23.

52. Robert E. Park, "The German Army: The Most Perfect Military Organization in the World," *Munsey's Magazine* XXIV:3 (December 1900), pp. 376–95.

53. Quoted in William Buxton, *Talcott Parsons and the Capitalist Nation-State: Political Sociology as a Strategic Vocation* (Toronto: University of Toronto Press, 1985), p. 100.

54. Robert E. Park, foreword to Maurice T. Price, *Christian Missions and Oriental Civilizations: A Study in Culture-Contact* (Shanghai: Privately printed, 1924), p. v.

55. Booker T. Washington, *The Story of the Negro: The Rise of the Race from Slavery* (Gloucester, Mass.: Peter Smith, 1969 [1909]), II, p. 253.

56. Albert Bernhardt Faust, *The German Element in the United States—With Special*

Reference to Its Political, Moral, Social, and Educational Influence (New York: The Steuben Society of America, 1927), I, p. 232.

57. Szasz, op. cit., pp. 204–05.

58. Leonard Dinnerstein, Roger L. Nichols, and David M. Reimers, *Natives and Strangers: Blacks, Indians and Immigrants in America,* 2d ed. (New York: Oxford University Press, 1990), pp. 21–22.

59. Faust, op. cit., I, p. 233; Hudson, op. cit., p. 116.

60. Thorp, op. cit., pp. 168–204.

61. John R. Woodard, "North Carolina," in *Religion in the Southern States: A Historical Study,* ed. by Samuel S. Hill (Macon, Ga.: Mercer University Press, 1983), p. 230.

62. Thorp, op. cit., p. 206.

63. Gilbert Tennent, "The Necessity of Holding Fast the Truth," (1743), in *The Great Awakening: Documents Illustrating the Crisis and Its Consequences,* ed. by Alan Heimert and Perry Miller (Indianapolis: Bobbs-Merrill Co., Inc., 1967), pp. 490–500.

64. Ahlstrom, op. cit., p. 243.

65. Szasz, op. cit., pp. 200–03; Dinnerstein, Nichols, and Reimers, op. cit., pp. 36–43; Wilbur R. Jacobs, *Dispossessing the American Indian: Indians and Whites on the Colonial Frontier* (Norman: University of Oklahoma Press, 1985 [1972]), p. 60.

66. See William G. McLoughlin, *Champions of the Cherokees: Evan and John B. Jones* (Princeton: Princeton University Press, 1990), pp. 18, 23, 36–37, 65, 84, 86, 93, 131, 147, 154, 206, 208, 211, 397, 399.

67. Klaus Wust, *The Virginia Germans* (Charlottesville: The University Press of Virginia, 1969), pp. 136–38.

68. Thorp, op. cit., pp. 107–77, 199–206.

69. Billigmeier, op. cit., pp. 26–27.

70. Robert M. Calhoun, "Ethnic Protestantism," in *Encyclopedia of Southern Culture,* ed. by Charles Reagan Wilson and William Ferris (Chapel Hill: University of North Carolina Press, 1989), p. 1284.

71. Park, "A City of Racial Peace," op. cit., p. 898.

72. Ibid., pp. 898–99.

73. Washington, *The Story of the Negro,* op. cit., II, p. 119.

74. Park, "A City of Racial Peace," op. cit., p. 899.

75. Billigmeier, op. cit., p. 116.

76. Park, "A City of Racial Peace," op. cit., p. 899.

77. Thorp, op. cit., pp. 52–57.

78. McLoughlin, op. cit., pp. 390–92. See also W. Craig Gaines, *The Confederate Cherokees: John Drew's Regiment of Mounted Rifles* (Baton Rouge: Louisiana State University Press, 1989), pp. 12–13, 21–22, 40, 45–47, 97.

79. Washington, *The Story of the Negro,* op. cit., II, p. 252.

80. Loc. cit.

81. Park, "A City of Racial Peace," op. cit., pp. 898–99.

82. Ibid., p. 898.

83. Robert E. Park, "An Autobiographical Note," in *Race and Culture: The Collected Papers of Robert Ezra Park,* Vol. I, ed. by Everett Cherrington Hughes, Charles S. Johnson, Jitsuichi Masuoka, Robert Redfield, and Louis Wirth (Glencoe: The Free Press, 1950), p. viii.

84. Robert E. Park, "Our Racial Frontier on the Pacific," *Survey Graphic* LVI:3 (May 1, 1926), pp. 192–96.

85. See Stanford M. Lyman, "The Race Relations Cycle of Robert E. Park," *Pacific Sociological Review* XI:1 (Spring 1968), pp. 16–22. This essay has been reprinted

in Lyman, *Civilization: Contents, Discontents, Malcontents, and Other Essays in Social Theory*, op. cit., pp. 127–35.

86. Robert E. Park, "The Problem of Cultural Differences," in *Race and Culture*, op. cit., p. 12.

87. Ibid., p. 14.

88. The following draws on Robert E. Park, "Racial Assimilation in Secondary Groups With Particular Reference to the Negro," *American Journal of Sociology* XIII:5 (March 1914), pp. 606–19.

89. Ibid., p. 612.

90. Ibid., p. 613.

91. Loc. cit.

92. Loc. cit.

93. Ibid., pp. 615–17. In the year that Park was born, one of the most intriguing of the schemes to export the freedmen—their proposed colonization in Ecuador—had failed to materialize. See Robert L. Gold, "Negro Colonization Schemes in Ecuador, 1861–1864," *Phylon: The Atlanta University Review of Race and Culture* XXX (Fall 1969), pp. 306–16.

94. Robert E. Park, "Politics and 'The Man Farthest Down,'" in Park, *Race and Culture*, op. cit., p. 172.

95. Rayford W. Logan, *The Negro in American Life and Thought: The Nadir, 1877–1901* (New York: The Dial Press, 1954).

96. Park, "Negro Home Life and Standards of Living," op. cit., pp. 147–63.

97. Robert E. Park, "The Bases of Race Prejudice," *The Annals of the American Academy of Political and Social Science* CXXXX (November 1928), p. 20.

98. Park, "Negro Home Life and Standards of Living," op. cit., p. 147.

99. Ibid., pp. 147–48.

100. Ibid., p. 155.

101. Park, "The Bases of Race Prejudice," op. cit., p. 20.

102. See Loren Schweninger, *Black Property Owners in the South, 1790–1915* (Urbana: University of Illinois Press, 1990), p. 216.

103. Robert E. Park, "The City: Suggestions for the Investigation of Human Behavior in the Urban Environment," in Robert E. Park, Ernest W. Burgess, and Roderick D. McKenzie, eds., *The City*, op. cit., p. 2.

104. Robert E. Park, "The Conflict and Fusion of Cultures With Special Reference to the Negro," *The Journal of Negro History* IV:2 (April 1919), p. 116.

105. Park, "Negro Home Life and Standards of Living," op. cit., p. 156.

106. Ibid., pp. 159–60.

107. Ibid., p. 149.

108. Park, "Foreword" to Price, op. cit., pp. v–vi.

109. Park, "Negro Home Life and Standards of Living," op. cit., pp. 61–153.

110. Loc. cit.

111. Robert E. Park, "Agricultural Extension Among Negroes," *World To-Day* XV (August 1908), p. 820.

112. See Standish Meacham, *Toynbee Hall and Social Reform, 1880–1914: The Search for Community* (New Haven: Yale University Press, 1987).

113. Charles Howard Hopkins, *The Rise of the Social Gospel in American Protestantism, 1865–1915* (New Haven: Yale University Press, 1940); Ronald C. White, Jr., and C. Howard Hopkins, *The Social Gospel: Religion and Reform in Changing America* (Philadelphia: Temple University Press, 1976), pp. 3–50.

114. Cecil Greek, "The Social Gospel Movement and Early American Sociology, 1870–1915," *The Graduate Faculty Journal of Sociology*, New York: New School for Social Research, III:1 (Fall 1978), pp. 30–42.

115. Hopkins, op. cit., pp. 156–57, 178.

116. Arthur C. Holden, *The Settlement Idea: A Vision of Social Justice* (New York: Macmillan, 1922; reprint, New York: Arno Press and the New York Times, 1970), pp. 15–17.

117. Residents of Hull House, *Hull House Maps and Papers: A Presentation of Nationalities and Wages in a Congested District of Chicago, Together With Comments and Essays on Problems Growing Out of the Social Conditions* (New York: Thomas Y. Crowell, 1895; reprint, New York: Arno Press and the New York Times, 1970).

118. White and Hopkins, op. cit., pp. 51–70; Holden, op. cit., pp. 109–30. The fears about Catholic and Jewish immigrants and their potential for sullying the Protestant programs of relief and uplift propelled some elements of the movement to adopt an attitude of xenophobia and to demand restrictions on immigration. See Nathan Irvin Huggins, *Protestants Against Poverty: Boston's Charities, 1870–1900* (Westport, Ct.: Greenwood Publishing Co., 1971), pp. 69, 155–56.

119. Robert A. Woods and Albert J. Kennedy, *The Settlement Horizon* (New Brunswick, N.J.: Transaction Publishers, 1990 [1922]), pp. 337–38.

120. Ibid., p. 336.

121. Washington, *Up From Slavery*, op. cit., p. 155.

122. Loc. cit.

123. Booker T. Washington, "The Economic Development of the Negro Race Since Its Emancipation," in *The Negro in the South: His Economic Progress in Relation to His Moral and Religious Development*, The William Levi Bull Lectures for the year 1907 (New York: The Citadel Press, 1970), pp. 45–75; W. E. B. DuBois, *The Black North in 1901: A Social Study* (New York: Arno Press and the New York Times, 1969). A series of articles originally appearing in the *New York Times*, November-December, 1901.

124. John Patrick McDowell, *The Social Gospel in the South: The Woman's Home Mission Movement in the Methodist Episcopal Church, South, 1886–1939* (Baton Rouge: Louisiana State University Press, 1982), pp. 84–115.

125. Washington Gladden, "Some Impressions Gained During a Visit to the Southern United States," baccalaureate sermon, Atlanta University, 1903. Excerpted in White and Hopkins, op. cit., pp. 104–07.

126. Quoted in Jacob H. Dorn, *Washington Gladden: Prophet of the Social Gospel* (Columbus: Ohio State University Press, 1967), p. 294.

127. Washington, "The Economic Development of the Negro Race Since Its Emancipation," op. cit., p. 74.

128. Park, "Agricultural Extension Among the Negroes," op. cit., p. 820.

129. Marianne Weber, *Max Weber: A Biography*, trans. and ed. by Harry Zohn (New York: John Wiley and Sons, 1975), p. 296.

130. Talcott Parsons, "Full Citizenship for the Negro American? A Sociological Problem," *Daedalus: Journal of the American Academy of Arts and Sciences* XCIV:4 (Fall 1965), pp. 1009–54.

131. Quoted in Mays, op. cit., p. 142.

132. "Letters Collected by R. E. Park and Booker T. Washington," op. cit., pp. 215–19.

133. See Arnold Cooper, *Between Struggle and Hope: Four Black Educators in the South, 1894–1915* (Ames: Iowa State University Press, 1989), pp. 15–16, 43–44.

134. See Kenneth M. Stampp, *The Era of Reconstruction, 1865–1877* (New York: Alfred A. Knopf, 1965), pp. 125–34; and Michael L. Lanza, *Agrarianism and Reconstruction Politics: The Southern Homestead Act* (Baton Rouge: Louisiana State University Press, 1990).

135. See Otto H. Olsen, ed., *Reconstruction and Redemption in the South* (Baton Rouge: Louisiana State University Press, 1980), pp. 80, 93–96, 135–38, 215–17; Pete

Daniel, *The Shadow of Slavery: Peonage in the South, 1901–1969* (Urbana: University of Illinois Press, 1972), pp. 19–42; and Dwight B. Billings, Jr., *Planters and the Making of the New South: Class, Politics, and Development in North Carolina, 1865–1900* (Chapel Hill: University of North Carolina Press, 1979), pp. 145–87.

136. Gunnar Myrdal with the assistance of Richard Sterner and Arnold Rose, *An American Dilemma: The Negro Problem and Modern Democracy* (New York: Harper and Brothers, 1944).

137. Gunnar Myrdal, "The Worldwide Emancipation of Underdeveloped Nations," in Arnold Rose, ed., *Assuring Freedom to the Free: A Century of Emancipation in the U.S.A.* (Detroit: Wayne State University Press, 1964), p. 100.

138. Lawrence Goodwyn, *The Populist Movement: A Short History of the Agrarian Revolt in America* (New York: Oxford University Press, 1978), p. 123.

139. Park, "Agricultural Extension Among the Negroes," op. cit., p. 821.

140. Daniel, op. cit., pp. 65–81.

141. Ray Stannard Baker, *Following the Color Line: American Negro Citizenship In the Progressive Era* (New York: Harper Torchbooks, 1964 [1908]).

142. Ray Stannard Baker, "A Pawn in the Struggle for Freedom," *American Magazine* LXXII (September 1911), p. 610. Quoted in Daniel, op. cit., p. 81.

143. Park, "Agricultural Extension Among the Negroes," op. cit., p. 821.

144. Ibid., p. 822.

145. Ibid., p. 823.

146. Loc. cit.

147. Ibid., pp. 823–25.

148. Ibid., p. 825.

149. Loc. cit.

150. Ibid., p. 826.

151. Park, "Racial Assimilation in Secondary Groups . . . ," op. cit., pp. 606–07.

152. Park, "Agricultural Extension Among the Negroes," op. cit., p. 826.

153. See the following works by Herbert Blumer, "The Study of Urbanization and Industrialization: Methodological Deficiencies," *Boletim de Centro Latino-Americano de Pesquisas em Ciencias Sociais* II (May 1959), pp. 17–34; "Early Industrialization and the Laboring Class," *The Sociological Quarterly* I (January 1960), pp. 5–14; "Industrialization and the Traditional Order," *Sociology and Social Research* XLVIII (January 1964), pp. 129–38; "The Future of the Color Line," in *The South in Continuity and Change*, ed. by John C. McKinney and Edgar T. Thompson (Durham: Duke University Press, 1965), pp. 322–36; "Industrialisation and Race Relations," in *Industrialisation and Race Relations*, ed. by Guy Hunter (New York: Oxford University Press, 1965), pp. 220–53; "Industrialization and the Problem of Social Disorder," in *Studies in Comparative International Development* V: 1969–1970 No. 3 (New Brunswick: Rutgers University-Sage Publications, 1971), pp. 47–58; *Industrialization as an Agent of Social Change: A Critical Analysis*, ed. by David R. Maines and Thomas J. Morrione (New York: Aldine de Gruyter, 1990). See also Stanford M. Lyman and Arthur J. Vidich, *Social Order and the Public Philosophy: An Analysis and Interpretation of the Work of Herbert Blumer* (Fayetteville: University of Arkansas Press, 1988), pp. 55–105.

154. Robert E. Park, "The Conflict and Fusion of Cultures With Special Reference to the Negro," op. cit.

155. Ralph Ellison, "An American Dilemma: *A Review*," in *idem*, *Shadow and Act* (New York: Random House, 1964), p. 308.

156. Morris Janowitz, review of *Shadow and Act*, *American Journal of Sociology* LXX (May 1965), p. 733.

157. César Graña, *Meaning and Authenticity: Further Essays on the Sociology of Art* (New Brunswick, N.J.: Transaction Publishers, 1989), pp. 42–43.

158. Barbara Ballis Lal, *The Romance of Culture in an Urban Civilization: Robert E. Park on Race and Ethnic Relations in Cities* (London: Routledge, 1990), pp. 155, 154.

159. James A. Geschwender, *Racial Stratification in America* (Dubuque, Ia.: Wm. C. Brown Publishers, 1978), p. 246.

160. Park, "Racial Assimilation in Secondary Groups," op. cit., p. 611.

161. Park, "The Conflict and Fusion of Cultures . . . ," op. cit., p. 113.

162. Ibid., p. 115.

163. Park, "Racial Assimilation in Secondary Groups . . . ," op. cit., p. 611.

164. See Andrew D. Weinberger, "A Reappraisal of the Constitutionality of 'Miscegenation' Statutes," Appendix G in Ashley Montagu, *Man's Most Dangerous Myth: The Fallacy of Race*, 4th ed., (Cleveland: World Publishing Co.-Meridian Books, 1965), pp. 402–26.

165. Robert E. Park, "Mentality of Racial Hybrids," *American Journal of Sociology* XXXVI (January 1931), pp. 534–51. Reprinted in Park, *Race and Culture*, op. cit., pp. 377–92. Quotation from p. 392.

166. Ibid., p. 377.

167. Park, "Racial Assimilation in Secondary Groups . . . ," op. cit., p. 611.

168. Park, "The Conflict and Fusion of Cultures . . . ," op. cit., pp. 115–29.

169. Ibid., p. 116.

170. Ibid., p. 129.

171. Ibid., p. 118.

172. Ibid., p. 129.

173. Ibid., pp. 129–30.

174. Ibid., p. 130.

175. Loc. cit.

176. Ibid., p. 118.

177. Ibid., p. 120.

178. Ibid., p. 121.

179. Ibid., pp. 121–22.

180. Ibid., p. 122.

181. Ibid., p. 123.

182. Ibid., p. 125.

183. Loc. cit.

184. Ibid., p. 126.

185. Ibid., p. 128.

186. Loc. cit.

187. Loc. cit.

188. Ibid., pp. 128–29.

189. Ibid., p. 131.

190. Ibid., p. 133.

191. Robert E. Park, "Negro Race Consciousness as Reflected in Race Literature," *American Review* I (September-October 1923), pp. 505–16.

192. Park, "The Conflict and Fusion of Cultures . . .," op. cit., p. 133.

193. Loc. cit.

194. See Emmett J. Scott, *Negro Migration During the War*. Preliminary Economic Studies of the War, No. 16. Carnegie Endowment for International Peace (New York: Oxford University Press, 1920; reprint, New York: Arno Press and the New York Times, 1969), pp. 81–82.

195. See Linda O. McMurry, *Recorder of the Black Experience: A Biography of Monroe Nathan Work* (Baton Rouge: Louisiana State University Press, 1985), pp. 81–82.

196. See Judith Ann Trolander, "Introduction to the Transaction Edition," of Woods and Kennedy, op. cit., pp. xvii–xix.

197. Sheldon Avery, *Up From Washington: William Pickens and the Negro Struggle for Equality, 1900–1954* (Newark, Del.: University of Delaware Press, 1989), pp. 15–111.

198. Paul A. Carter, *The Decline and Revival of the Social Gospel: Social and Political Liberalism in American Protestant Churches, 1920–1940* (Hamden, Ct.: Archon Books, 1971), pp. 130–33.

199. Robert E. Park, review of *Race Orthodoxy in the South and Other Aspects of the Negro Problem*, by Thomas Pearce Bailey, *Journal of Negro History* I:4 (October 1916), p. 449.

200. Loc. cit.

201. See Robert E. Park, "Negro Race Consciousness as Reflected in Race Literature," op. cit.

202. Robert E. Park, review of ten books on black American songs, folklore, drama, and poetry in *American Journal of Sociology* XXXIII:6 (May 1928), p. 990.

203. Robert E. Park, in an untitled review essay of six literary, musical, and cultural books in *American Journal of Sociology* XXXI (May 1926), p. 822.

204. Robert E. Park, review of *The Negro in our History*, by Carter G. Woodson and *Social History of the American Negro*, by Benjamin Brawley, *American Journal of Sociology* XXVIII:5 (March 1923), p. 614.

205. Park, review essay on ten books on black American songs, folklore, drama, and poetry, op. cit., p. 990.

206. Booker T. Washington with the collaboration of Robert E. Park, *The Man Farthest Down: A Record of Observation and Study in Europe* (Garden City, N.Y.: Doubleday, Page and Co., 1913).

207. Robert E. Park, review of *The Negro from Africa to America*, by W. D. Weatherford, *American Journal of Sociology* XXXI:2 (September 1925), p. 259.

208. W. D. Weatherford, *The Negro from Africa to America* (New York: George H. Doran and Co., 1924).

209. Horace Kallen, *Culture and Democracy in the United States: Studies in the Group Psychology of the American Peoples* (New York: Boni and Liveright, 1924; reprint, New York: Arno Press and the New York Times, 1970).

210. Park, review of *The Negro from Africa to America*, op. cit., p. 260.

211. Robert E. Park, untitled review essay of seven books on slavery and race relations in the United States, in *American Journal of Sociology* XXXII:4 (January 1927), p. 642.

212. Robert E. Park, "Culture and Civilization," in *idem, Race and Culture*, op. cit., p. 16.

213. Loc. cit.

214. See Marcel Mauss, "A Category of the Human Mind: The Notion of Person, the Notion of 'Self'," *Sociology and Psychology: Essays*, trans. by Ben Brewster (London: Routledge and Kegan Paul, 1979), pp. 57–94; Emile Durkheim and Marcel Mauss, *Primitive Classification*, trans. and ed. by Rodney Needham (Chicago: University of Chicago Press-Phoenix Books, 1967 [1903]); Emile Durkheim, "Note on Social Morphology," *On Institutional Analysis*, trans. and ed. by Mark Traugott (Chicago: University of Chicago Press, 1978), pp. 88–92.

215. Robert E. Park, review of *The Menace of Colour . . .* , by J. W. Gregory, in *American Journal of Sociology* XXXI:3 (November 1925), p. 403.

216. Robert E. Park, "Our Racial Frontier on the Pacific," *Survey Graphic* IX (May 1926), p. 196.

217. Ibid., pp. 192–95.

218. Robert E. Park, review of *Harvard Studies. I. Varia Africana*, ed. by Oric Bates, in *Journal of Negro History*, III:2 (April 1918), p. 199.

219. Robert E. Park, review of *A History of Barbados, 1625–1685*, by Vincent T. Harlow, in *American Journal of Sociology* XXXIII:4 (January 1928), p. 670.For an update of the issue, see Hilary Beckles, *A History of Barbados: From American Indian Settlement to Nation-state* (Cambridge: Cambridge University Press, 1990).

220. Benjamin Brawley, *Social History of the American Negro* (New York: Macmillan, 1922).

221. Robert E. Park, review of *The Negro in our History*, by Carter Godwin Woodson and *Social History of the American Negro*, by Benjamin Brawley, op. cit., p. 615.

222. See August Meier and Elliott Rudwick, *Black History and the Historical Profession, 1915–1980* (Urbana: University of Illinois Press, 1986), pp. 14–15, 20, 32–33, 37, 136n., 307.

223. Robert E. Park, review of *Mobilität der Bevölkerung in den Vereinigten Staaten*, by Rudolph Heberle, in *American Journal of Sociology* XXXVI:4 (January 1931), p. 657.

224. Robert E. Park, review of *Christian Mass Movements in India . . .*, by J. Waskom Pickett and *Christian and New World Culture*, by Archibald Baker, in *American Journal of Sociology* XLI:2 (September 1935), pp. 248–49.

225. Park, "Racial Assimilation in Secondary Groups . . . ," op. cit., p. 622.

226. Park, review of *Harvard Studies. I. Varia Africana*, op. cit., p. 199.

227. Robert E. Park, review of *Les Daïmons du Culte Voudo*, by Arthur Holly in *Journal of Negro History* VII:2 (April 1922), p. 226.

228. Robert E. Park, review of *Life in a Haitian Valley*, by Melville J. Herskovitz in *American Journal of Sociology* XLIII:2 (September 1937), pp. 346–48.

229. Lal, op. cit., pp. 150–51, 154–55.

230. Werner Cahnman, "Robert E. Park at Fisk," *Journal of the History of the Behavioral Sciences* XIV (1978), pp. 333–34.

231. Robert E. Park, review of ten books on black American songs, folklore, drama, and poetry, op. cit., p. 989. See also two reviews by Park, review of six books on black American songs, spirituals, poetry, and the New Negro in *American Journal of Sociology* XXXI:6 (May 1926), pp. 821–24; and review of *Negro Americans, What Now?* and *Along This Way*, both by James Weldon Johnson, in *American Journal of Sociology* XL (May 1935), pp. 837–40.

232. Alain Locke, ed., *The New Negro* (New York: Atheneum, 1968 [1925]).

233. Nathan Irvin Huggins, ed., *Voices From the Harlem Renaissance* (New York: Oxford University Press, 1976).

234. Alain Locke, "The Negro and His Music" in idem, *The Negro and His Music and Negro Art: Past and Present* (New York: Arno Press and the New York Times, 1969 [1936]), pp. 70–117.

235. Jean Toomer, *Cane* (New York: Harper and Row, 1969 [1923]).

236. Countee Cullen, "Heritage," in *The Poetry of the Negro, 1746–1949*, ed. by Langston Hughes and Arna Bontemps (Garden City, N.Y.: Doubleday and Co., 1949), pp. 121–25.

237. *Harlem Renaissance: Art of Black America*, introduction by Mary Schmidt Campbell (New York: Harry N. Abrams, Inc., 1987), pp. 105–54.

238. Park, review of *Life in a Haitian Valley*, op. cit., p. 348.

239. Hortense Powdermaker, *After Freedom: The Portrait of a Community in the Deep South* (New York: Viking Press, 1939).

240. Robert E. Park, review of *After Freedom: The Portrait of a Community in the Deep South*, by Hortense Powdermaker, *American Journal of Sociology* XLV:4 (January 1940), p. 612.

241. Ibid., p. 613.

242. Robert E. Park, review of *The Populist Movement in Georgia*, by Alex Matthews Arnett and *The Fascist Movement in Italian Life*, by Dr. Pietro Gorgolini, *American Journal of Sociology* XXX:3 (November 1924), pp. 360–61.

243. Robert E. Park, review of *European Colonial Expansion Since 1871*, by Mary Evelyn Townsend, *American Journal of Sociology* XLVIII:4 (January 1943), p. 516.

244. Robert E. Park, review of *The Anti–Slavery Movement in England: A Study of British Humanitarianism*, by Frank J. Klingberg and *British Slavery and Its Abolition, 1823–38*, by William Low Mathieson, *American Journal of Sociology* XXXIII:2 (September 1927), p. 291.

245. Robert E. Park, review of *Races, Nations, and Classes: The Psychology of Domination and Freedom*, by Herbert Adolphus Miller, *American Journal of Sociology* XXXI:4 (January 1926), p. 536.

246. Loc. cit.

247. Park, review of *European Colonial Expansion Since 1871*, op. cit., p. 517.

248. Park, review of *Mobilität der Bevölkerung . . .* , op. cit., p. 658.

249. Robert E. Park, review of six books on China, *American Journal of Sociology* XXXIII:3 (November 1927), p. 474.

250. Robert E. Park, review of *The Development of Extraterritoriality in China*, by G. W. Keeton, *American Journal of Sociology* XXXVII:5 (March 1932), p. 809.

251. Loc. cit.

252. Ibid., p. 807.

253. Robert E. Park, review of four books on India, *American Journal of Sociology* XXXII:2 (September 1926), p. 303.

254. Ibid., p. 304.

255. Loc. cit.

256. Loc. cit.

257. Loc. cit.

258. Loc. cit.

259. Robert E. Park, review of five books on immigration, race, and intelligence, *American Journal of Sociology* XXXII:2 (September 1926), p. 303.

260. Robert E. Park, introduction to *Interracial Marriage in Hawaii: A Study of the Mutually Conditioned Processes of Acculturation and Amalgamation*, by Romanzo Adams (New York: Macmillan, 1937; reprint, Montclair, N.J.: Patterson Smith, 1969), pp. vii–xiv.

261. Ibid., pp. xiii–xiv.

262. Ibid., p. xiii.

263. Robert E. Park, "Racial Ideologies," in *American Society in Wartime*, ed. by William Fielding Ogburn (Chicago: University of Chicago Press, 1943; reprint, New York: Da Capo Press, 1972), p. 183.

264. Loc. cit.

265. Loc. cit.

266. E. Franklin Frazier, "Ethnic and Minority Groups in Wartime, With Special Reference To the Negro," *American Journal of Sociology* XLVIII (November 1942), pp. 369–77.

267. Samuel C. Adams, Jr., "The Acculturation of the Delta Negro," *Social Forces* XXVI (December 1947), p. 205.

268. Loc. cit.

269. Robert Park to Horace Cayton. Quoted in Horace R. Cayton, "Robert Park: A Great Man Died but Leaves Keen Observation on Our Democracy," *Pittsburgh Courier* February 26, 1944. Before his death, Mr. Cayton kindly presented me with a typed copy of the obituary he had written to Park.

270. Robert E. Park, "The Nature of Race Relations," in *Race Relations and the*

Race Problem: A Symposium on a Growing National and International Problem with Special Reference to the South, ed. by Edgar T. Thompson (Durham, N.C.: Duke University Press, 1939), p. 45.

271. Park, "Racial Ideologies," op. cit., p. 183.

Concluding Remarks

1. Stanford M. Lyman, "The Rise and Decline of the Functionalist-Positivist Paradigm: A Chapter in the History of American Sociology," *Hyoron Shakaikagaku* (Doshisha University Social Science Review) No. 20 (March 1982), pp. 4–19.

2. See George Ritzer, ed., *Frontiers of Social Theory: The New Syntheses* (New York: Columbia University Press, 1990).

3. Lewis Coser, "American Trends," in *A History of Sociological Analysis*, ed. by Tom Bottomore and Robert Nisbet (New York: Basic Books, 1978), p. 318.

4. Alvin W. Gouldner, *The Coming Crisis of Western Sociology* (New York: Basic Books, 1970).

5. Stephen Park Turner and Jonathan H. Turner, *The Impossible Science: An Institutional Analysis of American Sociology* (Newbury Park, Calif.: Sage Publications, 1990).

6. Pierre L. van den Berghe, "From the Popocatepetl to the Limpopo," in Bennett M. Berger, ed., *Authors of Their Own Lives: Intellectual Autobiographies By Twenty American Sociologists* (Berkeley: University of California Press, 1990), p. 431.

7. Alan Sica, "Social Theory's 'Constituency,'" *The American Sociologist* XX:3 (Fall, 1989), p. 240.

8. Quoted from an epigraph in Robert K. Merton, *Social Theory and Social Structure*, rev. and enl. ed. (Glencoe, Ill.: The Free Press, 1957), p. 3.

9. See Stanford M. Lyman, *Civilization: Contents, Discontents, Malcontents, and Other Essays in Social Theory* (Fayetteville: University of Arkansas Press, 1990).

10. Benjamin Nelson, "On the Origins of Modernity: The Author's Point of View," in *On the Roads to Modernity: Conscience, Science and Civilizations—Selected Writings by Benjamin Nelson*, ed. by Toby E. Huff (Totowa, N.J.: Rowman and Littlefield, 1981), p. 3. Emphasis in original.

11. Robert E. Park, "Methods of Teaching: Impressions and a Verdict," *Social Forces* XX:1 (October 1941), p. 40n. 2.

12. *Loc. cit.*

13. John Milton Cooper, Jr., *Pivotal Decades: The United States, 1900–1920* (New York: W. W. Norton, 1990).

14. Rayford W. Logan, *The Negro in American Life and Thought: The Nadir, 1877–1901* (New York: The Dial Press, 1954).

15. See, e.g., Herman Schwendinger and Julia R. Schwendinger, *The Sociologists of the Chair: A Radical Analysis of the Formative Years of North American Sociology, 1883–1922* (New York: Basic Books, Inc., 1974), pp. 383–409. For a critique of the Schwendingers' thesis, see Dennis Smith, *The Chicago School: A Liberal Critique of Capitalism* (New York: St. Martin's Press, 1988), pp. 111–33.

16. Fred H. Matthews, *Quest for an American Sociology: Robert E. Park and the Chicago School* (Montreal: McGill-Queens University Press, 1977), p. 3.

17. See Herbert Hill, "Anti-Oriental Agitation and the Rise of Working-Class Racism," *Society* X:2 (January–February, 1982), pp. 43–54.

18. See Stanford Morris Lyman, *Chinatown and Little Tokyo: Power, Conflict, and*

Community Among Chinese and Japanese Immigrants in America (Millwood, N.Y.: Associated Faculty Press, Inc., 1986), pp. 233–53.

19. See Earl M. Maltz, *Civil Rights, the Constitution, and Congress, 1863–1869* (Lawrence, Kansas: University Press of Kansas, 1990).

20. See Loren Miller, *The Petitioners: The Story of the Supreme Court of the United States and the Negro* (New York: Pantheon Books, 1966), pp. 102–17; and Benjamin B. Ringer, *"We the People" and Others: Duality and America's Treatment of Its Racial Minorities* (New York: Tavistock Publications, 1983), pp. 157–285.

21. For documentation and analysis of Washington's clandestine struggles to effect the civil rights of blacks, see Louis R. Harlan, "The Secret Life of Booker T. Washington," *Journal of Southern History* XXXVII (August, 1971), pp. 393–416.

22. Cooper, Jr., op. cit., p. 76.

23. Theodore Roosevelt, *African Game Trails: An Account of the African Wanderings of an American Hunter-Naturalist* (New York: Scribner, 1910; reprint, New York: St. Martin's Press, 1988), p. 120.

24. See W. E. B. DuBois, "Declaration of Principles of the Niagara Movement, (1905)" and "Resolutions of the Niagara Movement, (August 15, 1906)," in *Negro Social and Political Thought, 1850–1920: Representative Texts*, ed. by Howard Brotz (New York: Basic Books, Inc., 1966), pp. 533–39; Stephen R. Fox, *The Guardian of Boston: William Monroe Trotter* (New York: Atheneum, 1970), pp. 31–144; Charles Flint Kellogg, *NAACP: A History of the National Association for the Advancement of Colored People, Vol. I, 1909–1920* (Baltimore: The Johns Hopkins Press, 1967), pp. 31–88, 139–54, 183–208.

25. Kellogg, op. cit., pp. 209–46; Linda O. McMurry, *Recorder of the Black Experience: A Biography of Monroe Nathan Work* (Baton Rouge: Louisiana State University Press, 1985), pp. 118–44 *et passim.*

26. Fox, op. cit., pp. 168–185; Kellogg, op. cit., pp. 155–82.

27. See Andrew D. Weinberger, "A Reappraisal of the Constitutionality of 'Miscegenation' Statutes," in Ashley Montagu, *Man's Most Dangerous Myth: The Fallacy of Race*, 4th ed. (Cleveland: Meridian Books, 1965), pp. 402–26; Robert J. Sickels, *Race, Marriage and the Law* (Albuquerque: University of New Mexico Press, 1972), pp. 10–31, 64–110; Paul R. Spickard, *Mixed Blood: Intermarriage and Ethnic Identity in Twentieth-Century America* (Madison: University of Wisconsin Press, 1989), pp. 233–342.

28. Matthews, op. cit., p. 114.

29. Robert E. Park and Ernest W. Burgess, *Introduction to the Science of Sociology* (Chicago: University of Chicago Press, 1921; 2d ed., 1924), p. 665.

30. Emile Durkheim and Marcel Mauss, "Note on the Notion of Civilization," trans. by Benjamin Nelson, *Social Research* XXXVIII (Winter 1971), pp. 808–13.

31. See David Hackett Fischer, *Albion's Seed: Four British Folkways in America* (New York: Oxford University Press, 1989). For the Celtic origins of white Southern culture, see Grady McWhiney, *Cracker Culture: Celtic Ways in the Old South* (Tuscaloosa: The University of Alabama Press, 1988).

32. For further elaboration of this point, see Stanford M. Lyman, "The Significance of Asians in American Society," in *idem, Civilization* . . . , op. cit., pp. 149–59.

33. See Arthur J. Vidich and Stanford M. Lyman, *American Sociology: Worldly Rejections of Religion and Their Directions* (New Haven: Yale University Press, 1985).

34. Forrest G. Wood, *The Arrogance of Faith: Christianity and Race in America from the Colonial Era to the Twentieth Century* (New York: Alfred A. Knopf, 1990), pp. 365–84.

35. Robert E. Park, "Walt Whitman," in Florence R. Freeman, "A Sociologist Views a Poet: Robert Ezra Park on Walt Whitman," *Walt Whitman Review* XVI (December 1970), p. 103.

36. See Stanford M. Lyman, "The Race Relations Cycle of Robert E. Park," in *idem, Civilization* . . . , op. cit., pp. 127–35.

37. For a memoir of Park's last years at Fisk University in 1942—one that emphasizes his ambivalence on the race   question—see Werner J. Cahnman, "Robert E. Park at Fisk," *Journal of the History of the Behavioral Sciences* XIV (1978), pp. 328–36.

38. See Florence R. Freeman, op. cit., pp. 99–104.

39. See George Cotkin, *William James: Public Philosopher* (Baltimore: Johns Hopkins University Press, 1990).

40. For a thoughtful discussion of this issue by a Japanese sociologist who, like Park, was influenced by Simmel and lived in the same era as Park, see Yasuma Takata, *Principles of Sociology*, ed. by Shin'ichi Ichimura (Tokyo: University of Tokyo Press, 1989), esp. pp. 205–12, 273–96.

41. William Graham Sumner, "The Influence of Commercial Crises On Opinions About Economic Doctrines," An address before The Free Trade Club, New York City, May 15, 1879, in *Essays of William Graham Sumner*, ed. by Albert Galloway Keller and Maurice R. Davie (Hamden, Ct.: Archon Books, 1969), II, pp. 62–63.

42. Helmuth James, Graf von Moltke (1907–1945), the great-grand nephew of Bismarck's chief-of-staff, became an ardent anti-Nazi and paid with his life for his principles. In a wartime letter to his correspondent in England, he discounted the possibility of a revolution against Hitler but favored a program for decentralizing Germany and thought that this could be facilitated by and through the churches. See Helmuth James von Moltke, *Letters to Freya, 1939–1945*, trans. and ed. by Beate Ruhm von Oppen (New York: Alfred A. Knopf, 1990), pp. 281–90.

43. See Kenneth M. Stampp, *The Imperiled Union: Essays on the Background of the Civil War* (New York: Oxford University Press, 1980), pp. 3–71, 191–270.

44. Woodrow Wilson, "The Reconstruction of the Southern States," *The Atlantic Monthly* LXXXVII:519 (January 1901), pp. 1–15.

45. See five books by Ulrich Bonnell Phillips: *Georgia and State Rights* (Macon, Ga.: Mercer University Press, 1984 [1902]); *American Negro Slavery: A Survey of the Supply, Employment and Control of Negro Labor as Determined by the Plantation Regime* (Gloucester, Mass.: Peter Smith, 1959 [1918]); *Life and Labor in the Old South* (Boston: Little, Brown and Co., 1963 [1929]); *The Course of the South to Secession: An Interpretation*, ed. by E. Merton Coulter   (New York: Hill and Wang, 1964 [1939]); *The Slave Economy of the Old South: Selected Essays in Economic and Social History*, ed. by Eugene D. Genovese (Baton Rouge: Louisiana State University Press, 1968). See also John Herbert Roper, *U. B. Phillips: A Southern Mind* (Macon, Ga.: Mercer University Press, 1984); John David Smith and John C. Inscoe, eds., *Ulrich Bonnell Phillips: A Southern Historian and His Critics* (New York: Greenwood Press, 1990).

46. See Kenneth M. Stampp, ed., *The Causes of the Civil War* (New York: Simon and Schuster—Touchstone, 1974); and Thomas J. Pressly, *Americans Interpret Their Civil War* (New York: The Free Press, 1962).

47. See six books by Kenneth M. Stampp: *Indiana Politics During the Civil War* (Bloomington: Indiana University Press, 1978 [1949]); *And the War Came: The North and the Secession Crisis, 1860–61* (Chicago: University of Chicago Press, 1950); *The Peculiar Institution: Slavery in the Ante-Bellum South* (New York: Alfred A. Knopf, 1956); *The Era of Reconstruction, 1865–1877* (New York: Alfred A. Knopf, 1965); *The Imperiled Union: Essays on the Background of the Civil War*, op. cit; *America in 1857: A Nation on the Brink* (New York: Oxford University Press, 1990). See also Kenneth M.

Stampp and Leon F. Litwack, ed., *Reconstruction: An Anthology of Revisionist Writings* (Baton Rouge: Louisiana State University Press, 1969). For a neo-Marxist revisionism, see five works by Eugene D. Genovese: *The Political Economy of Slavery: Studies in the Economy and Society of the Slave South* (New York: Pantheon, 1965); *The World the Slaveholders Made: Two Essays in Interpretation* (New York: Pantheon, 1969); *In Red and Black: Marxian Explorations in Southern and Afro-American History* (New York: Pantheon, 1971); *Roll, Jordan, Roll: The World the Slaves Made* (New York: Pantheon, 1974); *From Rebellion to Revolution: Afro-American Slave Revolts in the Making of the Modern World* (Baton Rouge: Louisiana State University Press, 1979). See also Elizabeth Fox-Genovese and Eugene D. Genovese, *Fruits of Merchant Capital: Slavery and Bourgeois Property in the Rise and Expansion of Capitalism* (Oxford: Oxford University Press, 1983). Among the many other revisionist writings sociologists would benefit from careful readings of Larry E. Tise, *Proslavery: A History of the Defense of Slavery in America, 1701–1840* (Athens: University of Georgia Press, 1987); Robert William Fogel, *Without Consent or Contract: The Rise and Fall of American Slavery* (New York: W. W. Norton, 1989); Eric Foner, *Reconstruction: America's Unfinished Revolution, 1863–1877* (New York: Harper and Row, 1988); and Peter J. Parish, *Slavery: History and Historians* (New York: Harper and Row, 1989).

48. Stanley M. Elkins, *Slavery: A Problem in American Institutional and Intellectual Life*, 3d ed., (Chicago: University of Chicago Press, 1976), pp. 81–139. See also Ann J. Lane, ed., *The Debate Over Slavery: Stanley Elkins and His Critics*, (Urbana: University of Illinois Press, 1971).

49. See two books by Pierre van den Berghe, *Man in Society: A Biosocial View* (New York: Elsevier, 1975); and *The Ethnic Phenomenon* (New York: Elsevier, 1981), pp. 1–57, 237–62.

50. Tamotsu Shibutani, *Society and Personality: An Interactionist Approach to Social Psychology* (Englewood Cliffs, N.J.: Prentice-Hall, 1961), pp. 544–48.

51. Robert E. Park, "Introduction," in Everett V. Stonequist, *The Marginal Man: A Study in Personality and Culture Conflict* (New York: Charles Scribner's Sons, 1937; reprint, New York: Russell and Russell, Inc., 1961), pp. xiii–xviii.

52. Kenneth E. Bock, *Human Nature and History: A Response to Sociobiology* (New York: Columbia University Press, 1980), p. 138.

53. Georg Simmel, "The Stranger," in *The Sociology of Georg Simmel*, trans. and ed. by Kurt H. Wolff (Glencoe: The Free Press, 1950), pp. 402–08; Robert E. Park and Ernest W. Burgess, op. cit., pp. 317–27.

54. Georg Simmel, "The Metropolis and Mental Life," in Wolff, ed., op. cit., pp. 409–24.

55. Frederick J. Teggart, *Theory and Processes of History* (Berkeley: University of California Press, 1941), pp. 149–50, 196–97, 272–96, 307–12. See Robert E. Park, "Human Migration and the Marginal Man," *American Journal of Sociology* XXXIII (May 1928), pp. 881–93.

56. Bock, op. cit., p. 139.

57. Loc. cit.

58. See James R. Grossman, *Land of Hope: Chicago, Black Southerners, and the Great Migration* (Chicago: University of Chicago Press, 1989).

59. E. Franklin Frazier, *The Negro Family in the United States*, rev. and abr. ed. (Chicago: University of Chicago Press—Phoenix Books, 1966); *E. Franklin Frazier on Race Relations*, ed. by G. Franklin Edwards (Chicago: University of Chicago Press, 1968), pp. 119–238.

60. E. Franklin Frazier, *The Negro Church in America* (New York: Schocken Books, 1963).

61. E. Franklin Frazier, *Negro Youth at the Crossways: Their Personality Development in the Middle States* (New York: Schocken Books, 1967 [1940]).

62. E. Franklin Frazier, "Durham: Capital of the Black Middle Class," in *The New Negro*, ed. by Alain Locke (New York: Atheneum, 1968 [1925]), pp. 333–40; and *Black Bourgeoisie: The Rise of a New Middle Class in the United States* (Glencoe: The Free Press and Falcon's Wing Press, 1957).

63. St. Clair Drake and Horace R. Cayton, *Black Metropolis: A Study of Negro Life in a Northern City*, rev. ed. (New York: Harper Torchbooks, 1962 [1945]), 2 vols.

64. See Stanford M. Lyman and Arthur J. Vidich, *Social Order and the Public Philosophy: An Analysis and Interpretation of the Work of Herbert Blumer* (Fayetteville: University of Arkansas Press, 1988), pp. 55–94.

65. Bart Landry, *The New Black Middle Class* (Berkeley: University of California Press, 1987), pp. 232–33.

66. Robert D. Bullard, "Conclusion: Problems and Prospects," in *idem*, ed. *In Search of the New South: The Black Urban Experience in the 1970s and 1980s* (Tuscaloosa: University of Alabama Press, 1989), p. 173.

67. William J. Wilson, ed., "The Ghetto Underclass: Social Science Perspectives," *Annals of the American Academy of Political and Social Science* DI (January 1989), pp. 8–192.

68. William J. Wilson, *The Truly Disadvantaged: The Inner City, the Underclass, and Public Policy* (Chicago: University of Chicago Press, 1987). For evidence that the black migration out of the South did not prove to be an unmixed economic blessing, see Nicholas Lemann, *The Promised Land: The Great Black Migration and How It Changed America* (New York: Alfred A. Knopf, 1991).

69. Jack D. Douglas, *The Myth of the Welfare State* (New Brunswick, N.J.: Transaction Publishers, 1989), p. 119.

70. Ibid., p. 413.

71. K. Sue Jewell, *Survival of the Black Family: The Institutional Impact of U.S. Social Policy* (New York: Praeger, 1988), p. 133.

72. See E. Franklin Frazier, "The Negro Family in Bahia, Brazil," *American Sociological Review* VII (August 1942), pp. 465–78; Melville J. Herskovitz, "The Negro in Bahia, Brazil: A Problem in Method," *American Sociological Review* VIII (1943), pp. 394–402; E. Franklin Frazier, "Rejoinder: The Negro in Bahia, Brazil," *American Sociological Review* VIII (1943), pp. 402–04. The three essays are reprinted in *Intergroup Relations: Sociological Perspectives*, ed. by Pierre van den Berghe (New York: Basic Books, 1972), pp. 103–38. See also Melville J. Herskovitz, *The Myth of the Negro Past* (New York: Harper and Brothers, 1941); and E. Franklin Frazier, *The Negro in the United States*, rev. ed. (New York: Macmillan, 1957, 1963), pp. 3–21.

73. There are at least three separate but interrelated positions on this question. First is the thesis that African culture had penetrated that of Classical Antiquity and exerted profound effects on the latter. See Martin Bernal, *Black Athena: The Afro-Asiatic Roots of Classical Civilization, Vol. I: The Fabrication of Ancient Greece, 1785–1985* (New Brunswick, N.J.: Rutgers University Press, 1987). Second is the thesis that fundamental features of African spiritual, material, and praxiological cultures not only survived the rigors of the African diaspora, but also affected the ways of life of generations of African Americans. See Roger Bastide, *African Civilisations in the New World*, trans. by Peter Green (New York: Harper and Row, 1971); Robert Farris Thompson, *Flash of the Spirit: African and Afro-American Art and Philosophy* (New York: Vintage, 1984); Molefi Kete Asante, *The Afrocentric Idea* (Philadelphia: Temple University Press, 1987); Joseph E. Holloway, ed., *Africanisms in American Culture* (Bloomington: Indiana University Press, 1990); Norman E. Whitten, Jr., and John F. Szwed, eds., *Afro-American*

Anthropology: Contemporary Perspectives (New York: The Free Press, 1970), pp. 63–230; Patricia Jones-Jackson, *When Roots Die: Endangered Traditions on the Sea Islands* (Athens: University of Georgia Press, 1987). Third is the thesis that there has emerged a distinctive Afro-American culture that blends Africanisms with the black American experience in a unique way. See Roger D. Abrahams, *Deep Down in the Jungle: Negro Narrative Folklore from the Streets of Philadelphia* (Hatboro, Pa.: Folklore Associates, 1964); Katrina Hazzard-Gordon, *Jookin': The Rise of Social Dance Formations in African-American Culture* (Philadelphia: Temple University Press, 1990); Charles P. Henry, *Culture and African American Politics* (Bloomington: Indiana University Press, 1990).

74. See two works by Mechal Sobel, *Trabelin' On: The Slave Journey to an Afro-Baptist Faith* (Princeton: Princeton University Press, 1988); and *The World They Made Together: Black and White Values in Eighteenth-Century Virginia* (Princeton: Princeton University Press, 1987).

75. Robert E. Park, review of *Sumner Today: Selected Essays by William Graham Sumner*, ed. by Maurice R. Davie, *American Sociological Review* VI:3 (June 1941), p. 406.

from
"The German Army:
The Most Perfect Military Organization in the World"

The Kaiser and King Albert of Saxony at a review. King Albert is a field marshal and inspector general of the German Army, and commanded a corps in the war with France.

Field Marshal Count Von Moltke, chief of the Prussian and German general staff from 1858 to 1888.

William I, King of Prussia from 1861 to 1888, and the first emperor of reunited Germany.

At the German Army maneuvers—a field battery opening fire.

A military
steeplechase—German
dragoons displaying
their skill as cross
country riders.

"Auf Dem Fechtboden"—a course in fencing is part of the regular
training of the German officer.

Grenadier Guards drawn up in front of the Schloss in Berlin, with the Kaiser, General Von Bock, and three of the imperial princes.

At the German Army maneuvers—an infantry skirmish line.

At the German Army maneuvers—infantry awaiting attack. In heavy marching order, the German infantryman carries more weight than any other soldier in Europe, but he is trained to march exceedingly well.

A German cavalry band on the march.

Officers of the Grenadier Guards, wearing the Blechmutze, the old Prussian helmet which is a relic of the days of Frederick the Great.

Troops drawn up in Unter den Linden on the occasion of the Austrian emperor's visit to Berlin, on May 4, 1900. The German and Austrian emperors are in the carriage in the center of the engraving. (From a photograph by Kühn, Berlin.)

from
"Recent Atrocities in the Congo State"

A lad with both hands destroyed.

A Belgian official of the Congo
Free State with a native corporal.

A boy maimed by Congo soldiers.

Congo soldiers. Such men as these are charged with wantonly shooting down women and children with the approval of their white officers.

Leopold inspecting the motor boats at the Monte Carlo exposition.

Leopold II, King of Belgium.
(Photograph by Russell & Sons,
London, England.)

The Royal Palace at Brussels.

The Archduchess Stephanie,
Leopold's daughter.

The late Queen of the Belgians.
(Copyright by The London
Stereoscopic Company, London,
England.)

from
"The Terrible Story of the Congo"

Cannibal sentries set over native villages by the king's agents. These men are
known to have committed hundreds of murders of unarmed and helpless blacks.

The State Camp at Bikoro. Showing stores and workmen, and a squad of the king's lawless black soldiery.

A palaver with the natives. Types of the rubber gatherers who are being decimated by the methods of the State.

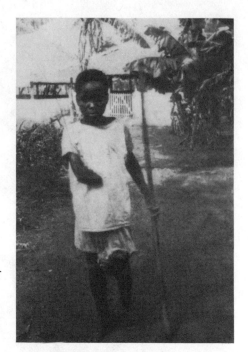

An example of the work of
Leopold's promised civilization.
A boy of Illinga, mutilated by
State soldiers during a rubber raid.

Nsala, of Wala, and the remains of his five-year-old daughter. Both wife and child
were eaten at a cannibal feast by the king's soldiers.

from
"The Blood-Money of the Congo"

The Royal Villa at Ostend.

A cannibal guard, paid soldier of
Leopold in the Congo.

Cleo de Merode, one of the
king's Parisian favorites.
(Courtesy of the Theatre
Magazine, New York.)

E. D. Morel, secretary of the
British Congo Reform
Association.
(Photograph by Russell & Sons,
London, England.)

A salon in the king's Palace at Laeken. The most luxurious royal residence
on the continent.

from

"Agricultural Extension Among the Negroes"

The Negro Conference at lunch. At these conferences the farmers compare experiences, and the success of one stimulates the others.

A mothers' meeting at the Tuskegee Institute.

Members of the Farmers' Institute on the Experiment Farm.

A model Negro village near Tuskegee Institute.

One of the offshoots of the Tuskegee Institute. During the past two years twenty-eight such schools have been erected in Macon County.

Selected Works of
Robert E. Park

Militarism and Nationalism

The German Army

The Most Perfect Military Organization in the World

HOW THE GEOGRAPHICAL POSITION OF THE GERMAN EMPIRE
MAKES NECESSARY A GREAT ARMED FORCE READY FOR INSTANT
ACTION—HOW THE ARMY IS ORGANIZED, AND HOW IT HAS
REACHED ITS PRESENT HIGH DEGREE OF EFFICIENCY.

The night of July 15, 1870, is memorable in the history of Berlin. For two
days the city had been filled with the rumors of war. At eleven o'clock that
night, General von Moltke, chief of the general staff, left his quarters in the
Königsplatz and drove rapidly in the direction of Schloss. Crowds of excited
burghers cheered him as he passed through the monumental Brandenburg
Gate and entered the historical thoroughfare Unter den Linden.

As by a sudden intuition, all the world seemed to have guessed that the
summoning of the highest officer of the Prussian army to the palace at this
critical moment could mean but one thing. The order for the mobilization of
the army of the North German Federation was, in fact, issued that night.
Two days later, France formally declared war upon Germany.

On August 3, just nineteen days from the date of the beginning of the
mobilization, Germany had concentrated on the French border, at Trèves,
Mayence, and Landau, three completely equipped armies, numbering five
hundred and fifteen thousand men. France, whose plan had been to surprise
her opponent by a sudden and impetuous invasion, was able to oppose the
German host with but two hundred and thirty thousand widely scattered and
immobile troops.

The German force pushed forward with the vast and irresistible precision
of some gigantic machine. The French, under the shock of its advance, rolled
back in headless confusion to the shelter of their fortresses—first Strasburg,
then Metz—and were cornered at Sedan. Victor Hugo, in describing the

Robert E. Park, "The German Army: The Most Perfect Military Organization in the
World," *Munsey's Magazine*, XXIV:3 (December 1900), pp. 376–95.

great battle fought around the last named town, said: "Sedan was the mortar, the German army was the pestle; between them the French army was ground to powder."

The battle of Sedan, which virtually decided the Franco Prussian war, was fought September 1, six weeks after war was first declared. The results of these six weeks, from July 15 to September 1, revealed to a somewhat startled Europe that a new power had made its appearance in the world; and this new power was the German army.

GERMANY'S MILITARY PROBLEM

At the opening of the Franco Prussian war the German army was undoubtedly the most effective fighting machine in existence. For thirteen years General von Moltke had been chief of the general staff. During this time he had brought the organization to a stage of perfection that it has never since surpassed, if, indeed, it has equaled it.

It is not difficult to estimate in general terms the sources of this superiority. Partly it was the genius of the leader, partly it was the character of the German people, but finally it was the organization of the army itself as a military machine.

The old Prussian army, with which Frederick the Great had hewn an empire out of central Europe, went to pieces under the blows of the French battalions at Jena. The organization of the present German army, modeled upon that of Prussia, dates from this Prussian defeat. The catastrophe of 1806 impressed upon the minds of the men of that day one important fact, namely, that Prussia, from the very nature of her geographical position, was likely to be called upon from time to time to fight for her very existence as a nation.

This fact of geographical position is important.

General von Moltke, speaking in the Reichstag in 1880, said: "As far as concerns our geographical positions, our neighbors have what I shall call the liberty of their back doors. They have behind them either the Pyrenees or the Alps, or a half civilized population from whom one has nothing to fear. We are in the center of all the great powers, the very center. Our neighbors upon the east and upon the west face only one way. We must face in all directions. Our neighbors have even in time of peace posted large forces on our frontier, while our troops must remain equally distributed over the whole country."

This defines the military necessity of Germany, out of which the German army sprang. It is this fact of geographical position that has steadily set the problem of German military strategy, and determined finally the character of the army itself. For this army was, primarily and before all, created for defense.

THE GERMAN NATION IN ARMS

The problem that presented itself to Scharnhorst, Hardenberg, and Stein, the men who gave its first form to the existing organization, was this: "What is necessary in order that the state, in the emergencies that arise, may defend itself with all the force and with all the resources that it possesses?"

The first and immediate answer to this question seemed to be that every able bodied citizen should enter the army. This was the origin of the law, since adopted by France, which declares that every citizen shall also be a soldier, and for a certain term bear arms in defense of the country. Henceforth, the army was to be nothing less than the nation in arms.

The subsequent division of this army into what we call in America the regulars, and then into the reserve, the *landwehr*, or militia, and the *landsturm*, which latter consists of all persons from seventeen to fifty capable of bearing arms, not included in the previous division, followed afterwards as details for giving effect to the general principle.

The regulations as to the term which every citizen was to serve in each of these divisions have varied. The rule at present is two years in the regular army, seven years in the reserve, ten years in the *landwehr*, and after that, service in the *landsturm*, which is called into existence only in time of great necessity. These measures at once converted the army into the great national school it ever since has been.

A second regulation of importance was that which set aside the rule that made noble blood a condition of becoming an officer, and declared, instead, that not prestige, but education and natural talent, should fix rank and determine advancement in the army. This left the position of highest command open equally to the son of the *bauer* and the son of the prince.

The two regulations supplemented each other. As the first declared that every citizen should have his place in the army, the second provided a means for determining what that position should be. Henceforth, position and rank were to be left to the decision of a merciless and impartial competition that spared no man.

This second regulation became, naturally enough, the guiding principle in all subsequent inspection and tests to which officers and men were from time to time subjected, particularly in those grand military examinations, the spring and fall maneuvers, which were part of the elaborate system of education and training in the art of war established in Prussia and other states of Germany.

Gradually, as the science of war has extended to the more minute details of military activity, the necessity of this training and education has given birth to a number of special schools. In addition to the numerous cadet schools, there have been established in recent years a large number of technical academies, devoted entirely to the training of soldiers in some particular branch of the service. For instance, there is the shooting school for infantry at Spandau, the fencing school for officers in Berlin, and, in various parts of Germany, the several artillery schools where soldiers are taught to handle the larger weapons of war. In short, there are schools for everything from field surgery to military horseshoeing. Finally, there is the Kriegs Akademie, a sort of war college, such as it is now proposed to establish in the United States, where officers are trained in the policy and strategy of high command.

The ground lines for the organization of the German army had been established, first, in the *allgemeine wehrpflicht*, the law which prescribed that every citizen capable of bearing arms should serve in the army; second, in the law that made advancement dependent on education or service. In the new organization which General Scharnhorst gave the army after 1806, these two rules were rigidly enforced. All were to serve, and all were to have the same opportunities to advance. They have ever since remained cardinal principles in the German army. The princes of the royal house of Prussia must each serve his time in the army, just the same as the humblest peasant's son. When Bismarck accompanied the king to the front in the war of 1870, the chancellor's sons, Herbert and William, were fighting as privates in the ranks. It is related that, during the war, Bismarck once remarked rather complainingly, yet with a certain touch of pride, when his son had not advanced as rapidly as he had hoped: "You see how little nepotism there is with us. My son has been serving for twelve months, and has not been promoted, whilst others who have not served more than a month are ensigns already."

THE GERMAN GENERAL STAFF

The rule which treated all alike had an inspiring effect upon the rank and file of the soldiers, and the patient, never ending drill and instruction then instituted have given in the course of years a machine-like perfection to the movements of the army. One thing, however, was lacking to the earlier organization, and that was a proper and adequate directive, such as was later developed in the general staff, the brain of the army.

Every organization—and the German army is a striking illustration of the principle—presents a double aspect. On the one side it is a machine, a tool, and on the other it is what I may call an organized experience, a will. The superiority of the German army over a crowd of German peasants or a Berlin mob is just the superiority of a highly organized group of persons over a mass that has almost no organization at all.

The mob has nerves, but it has no brain. It has neither the machine-like automatism that one finds in a well drilled army, nor has it the self control to act with foresight and as a unit. The two things, automatism and self control, go together. The centering of control in one part of an organization requires a corresponding automatism elsewhere; and the one cannot exist without the other.

Now, the army organization, as Scharnhorst left it, lacked that perfect self control and foresight which was necessary to bring it to the highest state of perfection. For this purpose a new organization was created within the larger one, and this new organization was called the general staff.

It is not precisely correct, however, to say that the general staff was a thing wholly new to the German army. It was, indeed, one of the institutions that Frederick the Great brought into existence, and it did good service as early as the war against Napoleon in 1813. But it was not until 1821, under General Müffing, that it began to acquire anything like the importance that it now possesses.

It is to General Müffing that the Prussian army owes the institution of those extended topographical researches and those voyages of reconnaissance and observation that were to play so important a rôle in the future development of the art of war. But more important still for the future of the army was an order of the general cabinet issued in January, 1821, according to which the chief of the general staff, who had previously been subject to a civil officer, the minister of war, received a position immediately under the king. The same order contains this important detail: "The chief of the army in peace shall henceforth be the commander in chief in time of war."

This meant that the preparation of the army in time of peace was to extend beyond the instruction of general tactics and drill. Henceforth the educational work was to include the ultimate necessities of warfare. In this order, no doubt, was the origin of those long campaigns of preparation which were henceforth to be fought out through so many years in the quiet of the general staff building in the Königsplatz. Here also was the origin of that inquisitive interest which Prussian army officers began to manifest in the topography of Prussia's neighbors, their military equipment, and their political necessities—matters that theretofore had been left rather to the diplomats and the civil members of the government than to the army.

THE NEW CONDITIONS OF MODERN WAR

General von Moltke took his place as chief of the general staff on October 29, 1857. He found the position suitable to his disposition and his talents. To a less active mind than his, it might have seemed that there was little to do beyond living up to the traditions of his predecessors, among whom, by the way, was General von Krauseneck, called the creator of the grand maneuvers.

Moltke's service to the Prussian army did not, indeed, consist in adding anything fundamentally new to the army organization. Rather, it consisted in carrying out and completing with unparalleled resolution and energy the intentions of the organization as it already existed.

It happened, however, that since the War of Liberation, from 1813 to 1815, Prussia had had no important campaign. Great changes had taken place in the world, however, since Napoleon could overrun Europe with a hundred thousand men.

The locomotive was invented by Robert Stephenson before 1820, and first came into practical use in Germany about 1830. Six years later, Morse, having perfected the telegraph instrument, made it possible to use the electric wire for communication between distant points. The two things were typical of those peaceful forces that had slowly and insensibly changed the whole character of Europe.

These same forces had altered the military problem. The improved means of transport made it possible to concentrate at any point of the kingdom, within a fortnight, an army almost as great as that with which Napoleon invaded Russia in 1812. The new means of communication vastly widened the field of operation, and made it possible to wage war on a grand scale. In all his battles, Frederick the Great never commanded an army of more than sixty thousand men, and most of his victories were gained with fewer than thirty thousand. When the Germans invaded France in 1870, Von Moltke had under his direct command three armies numbering together more than half a million soldiers.

To take advantage of the new conditions, a new science and a new art of war were required; a new order of military genius, also—one who could compass a vast number of details, and focus upon a plan of action all the new forces that modern science had brought into existence. Such a genius was Moltke, the student of battles, a man who planned campaigns in the quiet of his study with the calm deliberation of a scholar.

MOLTKE'S WORK FOR THE GENERAL STAFF

It was Moltke's intuition that modern wars were to be waged with the railway and telegraph. He it was who first perceived that modern science had given to a capable leader the means of concentrating and putting in action an army larger than had ever before been dreamed of, an army that was nothing less than a nation in arms.

To this perception he added the knowledge which is expressed in the simple military maxim, that to wage war is to attack.

"In a war begun," he said once in the Reichstag, "the greatest benefit is to end it quickly. To that end, it should be established that all means, without exception, are good, no matter how odious. I do not agree with the declaration made at St. Petersburg, that the weakening of the enemy's forces constitutes the only proper method of warfare. No; we should direct our attack against all the means and resources that the enemy possesses—against his finances, his railways, his food supply, even his prestige."

Under the influence of a mind so deliberate and profound, inspired also by a conception of war so formidable and audacious, the work of the Prussian general staff assumed a much wider scope, while at the same time its investigations became more searching and practical. In 1857, when Moltke became chief, the personnel of his bureau was composed of sixty four officers, a number which could be increased, however, to eighty three in time of war. In 1867 his subordinates numbered one hundred and nine. The necessities of the mobilization of 1870 increased them to one hundred and sixty one. At the present day there are two hundred and seven officers in the general staff.

As it exists today, it is as Moltke left it. It is divided into the "greater general staff," with headquarters in Berlin, which in time of peace devotes itself to the study and preparation for war, and the general staff in command of troops.

THE DUTIES OF THE GENERAL STAFF

The greater general staff has a special organization of its own. The chief has supreme charge over its work and studies, and employs a free hand in its control, recruiting it from among the officers of the whole army. It is divided into six sections, to which are assigned the duty of following all military events beyond or within the borders of the country. It is their duty to study to the foundation all questions concerning recruiting, organization, armament, geography, fortifications, not neglecting the political stability of the countries to which they are assigned.

To the first section are assigned Sweden, Russia, Turkey, and Austria; to the second, Germany, Denmark, Italy, and Switzerland; to the third, France, England, Belgium, Holland, Spain, Portugal, and America. A fourth section is charged with the study of transportation. Its work is not confined merely to the railways and transport facilities of Germany, but it must know the systems used by other countries.

Finally, there is a section devoted to military history, and another to geography and statistics. These two latter are formed entirely from that portion of the general staff called, in contradistinction to the *haupt etat*, the *neben etat*. The *neben etat* concerns itself with the purely scientific studies of the general staff. Of the two hundred and seven officers of the general staff, at present fifty eight belong to the *neben etat*.

The members of the general staff who are in command of troops have assigned to them, in time of peace, the care of the fortifications and the arrangements for the mobilization of the army. Their duty consists in putting into practice the plans which have been worked out in the greater general staff.

An important part of the work of the general staff is that of instruction in the Kriegs Akademie, an institution that dates also from the time of General Scharnhorst and the reorganization of 1806. It is a school for the higher instruction of officers. No student is admitted until he has served from three to five years in command of troops, and then only after he has passed a searching examination as to mental and moral qualifications. The course of study lasts three years, and graduates either go back to active service or may at once be received as members of the general staff.

The general staff and the war college, which is so intimately connected with it, did not originate with Moltke, but it was under him that they gained the efficiency which has made the German army a model for all the world. It is Moltke's merit that he perceived the overwhelming importance in war of careful preparation in time of peace.

"The next war," he once said at a gathering of officers in Berlin, "will be a war in which strategy and command will play a leading part. Our campaigns and our victories have instructed our enemies, who are equal to ourselves in numbers, armament, and courage. Our strength will be in the command, in the directive—in a word, in the general staff, to which I have consecrated the last days of my life. That strength will excite the envy of our enemies, but they will not possess it."

THE FIGURES OF GERMANY'S ARMED STRENGTH

The present peace strength of the German army is somewhere in the neighborhood of six hundred thousand men. In October, 1899, the precise figure was 472,292, exclusive of 23,088 higher officers, 2,107 surgeons, and 78,217 under officers. By a law of 1896, this strength is to be gradually increased until March 31, 1904, when it is intended that it shall reach 502,506, not including the officers mentioned, nor the one year volunteers.

In time of peace, the army is divided into eighteen corps, exclusive of the corps of the imperial guards, and of the two that make up the Bavarian army. Every corps is composed of two divisions, to which is added a battalion of sharpshooters, one of field and one of foot artillery, and one battalion of pioneers. The guards have two divisions of infantry and one of cavalry. The eleventh corps has three divisions.

Every division is composed of two brigades of infantry and two of cavalry. An exception is the first division, which consists of three brigades of infantry and two of cavalry. Every brigade is composed of two or three regiments, each of which is divided into three, or sometimes two, battalions. The battalion, which is the smallest tactical unit in the German infantry, is composed at its lowest strength of eighteen officers and 501 men; at its highest strength, of twenty two officers and 639 men. Every brigade of cavalry consists of two regiments, each of which is divided into three squadrons. The squadron, which is the smallest tactical unit in the cavalry, is composed at its lowest strength of four officers and 138 men, with 137 horses; and at its highest, of four officers and 146 men, with 140 horses.

These troops are distributed over a territory of 208,738 square miles—about five times the size of the State of Ohio. The location of the corps headquarters will indicate how this distribution is made. In northwest Germany there is one corps at Cassel, in the province of Hesse; another at Munster, in Westphalia; a third at Hanover; a fourth at Altona, and others at Magdeburg, Dresden, and Berlin. In east Germany the headquarters are at Stettin, Dantzic, and Königsberg, on or near the Baltic, and at Posen and Breslau, fronting the Russian and Austrian frontiers.

Naturally, the greatest concentration is on the French border in Alsace and Lorraine, the chief battle ground of the Franco Prussian war. There is a corps at Strasburg, another at Coblenz, and a third at Metz—Metz which Moltke said was worth an army of a hundred and fifty thousand men. The troops stationed at these points are reinforced by the corps at Stuttgart and Karlsruhe. Finally, there are the two Bavarian corps, one at Würzburg and the other at Munich.

THE EMPIRE'S GIRDLES OF DEFENSE

But in addition to the troops stationed at the strategic points of the frontiers and at important railway centers within the empire, there are the fortifications, which constitute an important part of the great military machine.

Here again it appears how large a part of Germany's military necessity is founded in her geographical position. Neither on the west nor on the east are her boundaries favorable to the defense of the country. The natural divisions of Germany, so far as they exist, seem to be made by the great rivers which flow from south to north. It is along these rivers that the German fortifications are distributed.

In accordance with this method of division, the defenses of the empire appear as four distinct girdles. The first, the western, centers along the line of the Rhine. Within this district lie the fortifications of Metz and Diedenhofen, close on the French border, with Bitsch behind them in the forests of the Vosges. Then, on the Rhine are New Breisach, Strasburg, Germersheim, Mainz, Coblenz and Ehrenbreitstein, Cologne, and Wesel, the latter an important railway center. All these fortresses are concentrated in and about what has always proven the most vulnerable point in the empire, the point at which the hereditary foes of Germany have struck again and again. Here the generals of Louis XIV marched in to ravage and destroy; here the great Napoleon repeatedly hurled in his irresistible legions; and here again France aimed her attack in 1870. To the south, the chain of fortresses is prolonged by Ulm and Ingolstadt, commanding the valley of the Danube.

The eastern girdle embraces the district from the Pregel, close on the Russian border, to the Vistula and the upper and middle Oder. In this district the fortress of Königsberg, with Pillau, marks the central point in the extensive province of East Prussia. Upon the Vistula lie Dantzic, Graudenz, and Thorn; on the Warthe, Posen; and at the middle part of the Oder, Glogau. In this district are included also the fortifications at Glatz and Neisse.

In the third or inner zone, Magedeburg, Küstrin, and Spandau serve as military and supply depots. The kingdom of Saxony still retains the fortress of Königstein on the upper Elbe, close to the Austrian frontier, at the point where that stream rushes through the mountains.

Lastly, there is the coast district, which is guarded by the fortresses of Pillau, at the entrance of the Frische Haff; Dantzic, at the mouth of the Vistula; Swinemünde, at the mouth of the Oder; Friedrichsort, at Kiel; Cuxhaven, at the mouth of the Elbe; Geestemünde, at the mouth of the Weser; and Wilhelmshaven, at the Jade. Heligoland forms an outpost in the North Sea, and the western entrance of the Kaiser Wilhelm canal is protected by the works at Brunsbüttel.

GERMANY'S READINESS FOR WAR

This is the German army as it stands today upon its own soil, silent, observant, calm, in an attitude of formidable defense. Upon its own soil, and in such an attitude, this vast, silent army is one of the most impressive things in the world.

In the political and geographical position in which Germany finds itself, the strategy of first importance consists in the evolution of a method by which this great machine can be moved—moved swiftly and with precision. The reserves are to be called in, the fortresses armed, and the troops concentrated. This is the work of mobilization.

In order to facilitate both mobilization and recruiting, the empire is divided into nineteen army districts, each of which has a commander. Upon this commander, in time of war, falls the important duty of mobilizing, equipping, and despatching the regiments, sending out first, at the appointed time, the regular troops, then the reserve, then, if so directed, the *landwehr*, and finally the *landsturm*.

Naturally, the details of the mobilization are not made public. Not since 1870 has the army had occasion to execute the maneuver on a grand scale; but it is certain that Germany is no less prepared today than it was then. In that remarkable memorial addressed to the King of Prussia in 1868, in which Moltke outlined the plan of campaign against France, even to the details, as it was fought out two years later, he said:

> Our plans for mobilization are complete, even to the minute points. Six railways are at our disposal for the purpose of transporting the troops to the region between the Rhine and the Moselle. The charts, which fix to the fraction the day and hour of embarkation and disembarkation, are ready.
>
> On the tenth day the first divisions will be able to disembark not far from the French frontier; on the thirteenth day the troops of two army corps will be assembled there, and on the eighteenth day the number of our forces will amount to three hundred thousand men, who on the twentieth day will be joined by their supply trains.

With what precision this prediction was fulfilled two years later is already a familiar tradition. Yet something more than method and organization was necessary to accomplish that great task. The mobilization of 1870, which was little short of the migration of a nation in arms towards the threatened frontier, was successful because it had behind it the will of the nation.

But this will of the nation, whence came it? It was founded in a bitter experience extending over many years of warfare, founded in an ancient conviction inherent in the Teutonic race, the conviction that the man or the nation that is not willing to fight for its own does not deserve to live.

It is just this Teutonic faith in the trial by battle, modified but in essence the same, to which Moltke gave utterance in one of those rare speeches of his in the Reichstag, always in defense of the army, and this time in defense of war itself.

"Eternal peace," said he, "is only a dream, and not even a happy dream. War is an institution of God, a principle of order in the world. In it the most noble virtues of men find their expression—courage as well as abnegation, fidelity to duty, and even love and self sacrifice. The soldier offers his life.

"Without war the world would fall into decay, and lose itself in materialism."

[Sombart on Sociology]

Political economy, as a scientific discipline, and particularly in its theoretic aspects, is not what it should be, at least according to the author of this volume. Far from it. It is uncertain as to its subject matter; it is confused as to its methods; it is unable to define its place among the sciences; it has failed to find a name that is at once descriptive and unambiguous. Political economy or, as the author calls it, national economy is, as a matter of fact, neither economy nor national. Its subject matter is rather "those human activities that are directed to the production and distribution of commodities." However, in view of the fact that national economy is, of all other expressions in use, the most familiar to students and the one least burdened with antecedent assumption, the author has adopted it as his own.

In view of the disagreement among different writers as to subject matter and method, Sombart proposes to achieve order and understanding where there is now only confusion and chaos, by examining the logical foundations upon which the different schools have erected their different theoretic structures.

There are, he says, three and only three fundamental points of view from which economic and social institutions generally have been or can be considered and investigated. There are, of course, many "systems" and schools, so that the three fundamental types rarely present themselves pure and unmodified in any single system. The original and *urforms* miscegenate, so to

Robert E. Park, an untitled review essay of *Die Drei Nationalökonomien,* by Werner Sombart (München und Leipzig: Verlag van Duncker & Humblot, 1930), *American Journal of Sociology* XXXVI:6 (May 1931), pp. 1071–77.

speak, and produce mixed types of economic theory. However, all systems tend to fall into one of the three general categories, which Sombart describes as (1) *die richtende*, that is the judging, assessing, evaluating; (2) *die ordnende*, that is, the natural-scientific and before all statistical; (3) *die verstehende*, i.e., interpretive or "understanding." There are three fundamental types of political economy because there are three and only three fundamental questions to which science seeks an answer. They are: (1) what ought to be, (2) what is, (3) why.

The first and most obvious problem of every social science is the practical one: What, under the circumstances, ought to be done? This has, in fact, been the point of departure for most social sciences that sought to deal with practical problems. A social science, however, which conceived its problem in this fashion, inevitably formulates its conclusions in the imperative rather than in the indicative mood. It assumes, as soon as it attempts to formulate conclusions intended to have general application, the form and character of a normative rather than an empirical science. It terminates in a metaphysical conception of the cosmos rather than a mathematical formula describing events. The representatives of the normative (*richtende*) economy "imagined," he says, that they were creating a science; what they produced was a metaphysics.

One may, however, approach the subject matter of economics from a different view. One may ask not what should be but what is and how did it come about. This involves description and explanation, and if this description is to achieve the exactness of the physical sciences, and if this explanation is to have the validity of a natural science formula, essentially the same procedure is required in dealing with events in the social as in the physical world. That is, what is perceived concretely must be described abstractly, conceptually, and eventually in quantitative terms.

" 'Exact' implies description in mathematical formulae. Such description is designed to fulfil the supreme demand of natural science; it makes possible knowledge having universal validity. He who seeks universal validity seeks before everything else mathematical precision."

Most of the laws of economics—at least those that can be expressed in the form of a mathematical equation—seem to be founded on the simple mathematical insight that a part is less than the sum.

Sombart does not say that the part is less than the whole, because there is nothing that corresponds to the conception of a whole in mathematics. Mathematical "wholes" are conceived as a mere constellation of units with no necessary connection between the parts. Sombart cites as an example of these mathematical laws the statement that when the fund from which wages are to be paid is fixed, wages cannot exceed the total amount of that fund. It follows, therefore, that if wages rise at one point they must decline at another. This is the so-called wage-fund law. Not all quantitative laws in economics are so obvious as this, to be sure, but they all turn out to be applications of the same elementary mathematical insight. There are, to be sure, other kinds of laws in political economy, but they do not always have this exactness of the mathematical formula.

One may approach the subject matter of political economy from a fundamentally different point of view. One may ask not merely what is, but why. One may seek to discover not merely how things came to be, but wherefore, and for what purpose, and to what end. One fundamental difference between natural phenomena and cultural phenomena consists in the fact that culture exhibits just this evidence of design and purpose for which one seeks in vain in nature, that is, physical nature. The difference between a limb on a tree, for example, and a club in the hand of a savage, to use Goldenweiser's illustration, is not any difference in the physical characteristics of either but simply in the fact that the club has a use. The club is not merely a limb or a stick; it is a tool or a weapon. In short, a cultural artefact is a symbol which may have different meaning for different people in different cultures. To know it means to understand it. It requires, in other words, a kind of knowledge which Sombart and other German writers have described as a "*verstehende Wissenschaft*," i.e., *die verstehende Ökonomie* and *die verstehende Soziologie*.[1]

To understand a thing in this sense is to take account of the reason, the purpose, and, in general, the function which it performs in a given cultural complex. We understand a tool as we understand a language, not by description of the parts of speech of which it is composed, nor of the rules of syntax which describe how words are put together, but by interpreting these formal symbols in terms of the sentiments and ideas they are intended to express.

It is generally regarded as a defect and a limitation of the social sciences that the knowledge which they seek is based on interpretation rather than description and explanation. Sombart, on the other hand, regards it as a defect of the physical sciences that they are limited to description and explanation and are not able to penetrate to the significance and meaning of the events and objects which they seek to describe. His argument rests on his definition of the concept of *Wesen*, for which there seems to be no precise definition in English. Cultural science is fundamentally *Wesenswissenschaft*. *Wesen* may be perhaps translated as "essence" in the sense in which Santayana uses that term.[2] In this sense the essence is an ideal object; one that can be completely defined and therefore like the platonic idea an object that is never completely realized empirically.

In the physical sciences *Wesen* or essence seems to have been identified with the notion of substance, which has been rejected by the physical scientists as something metaphysical and therefore beyond the ken of an empirical science. The abstract concept, which has taken the place and plays the rôle in

---

[1] See Max Weber, *Gesammelte Aufsätze zur Wissenschaftslehre,* particularly "Die Objektivität sozialwissenschaftlicher and sozialpolitischer Erkenntnis," pp. 146–214.

[2] See George Santayana, *Realm of Essence* (New York: Chas. Scribner's Sons, 1927).

the physical sciences formerly occupied by substance, is now regarded as a mere tool of thought. We treat the thing "as if" it conformed to the concept, and we are justified in so treating it as long as this procedure serves the purposes of knowledge.

Wesen, however, as Sombart conceives it, is not a mere nominalistic and instrumental thing. The connection between the parts which constitute the whole is real and necessary. What constitutes an object in the sense of natural science, on the other hand, is merely the constellation of constant factors or indexes by which it is identified. But as these constant factors have no visible connection it is not assumed that such connections exist. Just the opposite is the case in the social science. There the constituent elements of the thing and their connections can be known. *Sociale Wissenschaft* is *Wesenswissenschaft.*

Sombart's *Modern Capitalism* we may use to illustrate this point. What holds the parts together and makes a whole of the physical and moral structures which constitute modern capitalism is the purpose for which each one of these parts exists. Having discovered what the sense, meaning, and function of these different parts of the whole are, we are able to define its *Wesen,* and to distinguish, therefore, what is fundamental and necessary from what is incidental and accidental. We are able to understand every unique manifestation of the capitalistic system by referring and relating it to this more fundamental and ideal object Sombart describes as *Wesen.* One may, perhaps, make the distinction between a natural science conception of an object and its *Wesen,* as Sombart conceives it, a little more precise by the use of an illustration—a game of chess, for example.

Looking at a chess game in operation, observing it objectively as a natural phenomenon, one may discover how, in general, the different pieces may be expected to move. If one is ingenious and patient enough he may be able to calculate, within limits, what the result of a certain line of play may be. But he will never be able to find out as long as he merely seeks to describe objectively, that is, in mathematical and statistical terms, the changes taking place upon the chess board, just what the game is about or what the different players are trying to accomplish. The *Wesen* of a chess game, as Sombart would describe it, is identical with the general rules and purposes of the game—rules which at once guide and limit the player in his playing. This *Wesen* can be understood quite apart from the specific purposes which any player at any point in the game may happen to have. The moves and tactics of every individual player as well as the general plan and purpose of the game become intelligible only when one understands what each player is trying to achieve. The general purpose is common to both players though each has his own individual notion of how to play to win.

Sombart conceives modern capitalism as a phenomenon occurring within the limits of a definite historical tradition. It is this tradition which corresponds to the rules of the game. If one is to live and succeed in the modern world he can do so in the long run only as he conforms to the rules of the game in which his fortunes are involved. These rules are not, of course, defined in legislation. Rather, the laws are themselves based on more fundamental conceptions like those of private property, free labor, and exchange for profit. These conceptions are implicit in the system and in the mores which support it. Meanwhile the rules of the game are in process of change. Capitalism, as we know it today, may come, Sombart says has come, to an end. A new and different game with different rules is coming into existence.

It is impossible within the limits of a few pages to convey an adequate notion of the wealth of ideas and of historic reference and illustrations with which Sombart has sought to expound and to justify his own peculiar conception of political economy. This conception is based on methods of procedure and assumptions the direct oppposite of those made familiar to us by the natural scientists. It is, in a sense, an assault not only upon the methods but upon the aims of natural science, so far as these have been imposed upon the social sciences.

What he conceives in the way of a social science, however, is something that is neither history nor natural science but a *mittelding;* something between but different from both. One may, perhaps, describe it as a form of natural history, that is to say a history in which an individual is described not in all his uniqueness but with reference to what is characteristic, what is typical of him as an individual. It is, however, the historic individual rather than the ideal type as defined by Max Weber[3] with which Sombart is concerned.

What the exact sciences have sought to do has been to describe their methods of procedure with such precision and exactness that by repeating them one can accumulate, transmit, and test knowledge without the insight that is necessary to discover it. History and the social sciences have never been able to devise a method of procedure so precise and so exact. The historian, on the other hand, has sources of knowledge which are denied the student of physical knowledge. The historian has a chance to go behind the appearances and inquire into the sources of the actions he records, the intentions and purposes of the behavior that he observes. Historical knowledge is based on, and limited by, experience and insight; the insight of the man who writes, but also the insight of the man who reads. Therefore, as has been frequently pointed out, history has to be constantly rewritten to make it intelligible to each new generation.

The social sciences are more or less in the same situation as history. On the other hand, to the extent that they describe events and objects that are comparable and therefore not unique they can and do assume the characteristics of an exact science. Sombart, in his zeal to defend an opposite procedure, might not admit this. Certain writers, however, like Teggart, have conceived of a "comparative history." Comparative history inevitably leads to generalizations,

---

[3] Op. cit., pp. 200ff.

generalizations that are valid within limits and under conditions that can be defined with more or less precision. Under such circumstances history inevitably assumes the characteristics of sociology. Sombart, by the way, is quite clear that economic science is not something which should be set off as different from sociology; rather, economics, as he conceives it, is sociology.

Sombart has undertaken in *Die Drei Nationalökonomien* to set forth and justify the point of view, the concepts, and, in general, the frame of reference in which his studies of capitalism have been conceived and carried out. This monumental work of, which the first chapters were published in 1902 and the last in 1927, constitutes his life's task. No doubt the best, in the long run, the only, justification for the tools that a man uses is the work that he produces with them, and this is eminently true in the present instance. It is, nevertheless, interesting and instructing to have from the author himself an account of the nature of his task as he conceives it, particularly when that involves, as it does in this case, a critical review of the history and present tendencies of theoretic interest in a field in which there are so many divergent schools of thought.

The difficulty with Sombart's exposition of his own system and of his criticism of others seems to be his determination to achieve a formulation of general political-economic theory that will conform in all its minute details with a work already completed. This has, apparently, led him to pile up distinctions and definitions and give them an importance which they would not otherwise have had; to assume that every detail of his work must be justified on principle; and that every divergence from the logical construction he has erected is heretical and to be condemned.

Sombart has cited something like 350 authors in the course of this brilliant and scholarly work. Some of them he damns utterly. With most of them he disagrees. In view of the unique character of his own life work it seems that the world might have understood his purpose, point of view, and method somewhat better if he had written his personal confessions rather than a treatise on the logic of the social sciences.

William Graham Sumner's Conception of Society

*An Interpretation**

William Graham Sumner was born in Paterson, New Jersey, October 30, 1840. His father, Thomas Sumner, came from Lancashire, England, in 1836. He migrated to America because his father, who was a weaver, had been ruined when power driven machinery replaced the hand loom in the textile industry.

Sumner, after graduation from college, went abroad for further study. He was at Göttingen in 1864, where he studied history, and at Oxford in 1866, where he studied Theology. In 1872 he was elected professor of political and social science in Yale College. He had previously been rector of Calvary Church, New York City. He wrote extensively and on a variety of subjects, and since his death these scattered writings have been edited and published by his former colleague, Albert Galloway Keller, Professor of the Science of Society at Yale University.

In 1899 Sumner began to write a textbook on Sociology from materials which he used in his lectures. But at a certain point, as he says, he found that he wanted to introduce his own statement of the mores, and thereupon he turned aside to write a treatise on the "Folkways." This volume, which the author referred to as "my last book", is probably the most original contribution of any American writer thus far to the subject of Sociology.

Robert E. Park, "William Graham Sumner's Conception of Society," The Chinese Social and Political Science Review XVII:3 (October 1933), pp. 430–41.

[* An address delivered before the Chinese Social and Political Science Association in December, 1932.]

Folkways is not a systematic treatise and nowhere in this volume has the author attempted a final and fundamental description of society, as he conceived it. There is, nevertheless, implicit in this and other writings of Sumner a conception of society which is unique and, in the present state of the social sciences, useful as well. It is useful because it is comprehensive; brings together so many divergent points of view—biological, economical, political, historical—and because it is based on so wide a range of knowledge of the ways in which men have been observed to act, when they act collectively.

Society, according to Sumner, is in its most obvious aspect, a territorial organization and hence, primarily a geographical phenomenon. The conception of "primitive society that we ought to form," he says, "is that of small groups scattered over a territory. The size of the groups is determined by the conditions of the struggle for existence." [1] Within each one of these scattered groups there is peace and order. But between those different groups the normal relations are those of mutual hostility. Having its origin under these circumstances society has grown by the expansion of the area in which it was possible to maintain peace.

Peace within and war without constitute the conditions under which human nature and society come into existence and the conditions under which they continue to exist. The significant thing is that the peace within is invariably a function of the war without.

"Society," says Sumner, is a form of "antagonistic coöperation" and this phrase is intended to cover all the relations into which men enter and live, in society.

Sumner is not concerned in his study of the Folkways with the individual. He takes the individual as something given, a biological unit which, when associated and bound together through custom and interest with other such units, constitutes society. It has not occurred to him, perhaps—or at any rate he is not concerned at the moment with the fact—that the biological individual assumes only in society the character of a person, and that these individual personalities are very largely a product of their associations. This aspect of society was later developed by Cooley in his Human Nature and the Social Order, and more particularly by Thomas and Znanieski in their monumental work, The Polish Peasant. [2]

The reason Sumner is so little concerned with the individual is because he is, or was at the time Folkways was written, so little concerned with processes. The individual is invariably an innovating factor in social change, while the function of customs and institutions, and ultimately of every form of social control is to conserve, adapt and transmit these institutions and all other forms

[1] Sumner, W. G., Folkways, Boston, Ginn, 1906. p. 12.

[2] Cooley, C. H., Human Nature and the Social Order, New York, C. Scribner's Sons, 1902. Thomas, Wiliam I., and Znanieski, [F.], The Polish Peasant, New York, A. A. Knopf, 1927.

of coöperation and collective action in which are ordinarily carried on that form of life we call social.

In *Folkways* the volume upon which this paper is mainly based, Sumner sought, on the whole, to analyze and describe the different forms and types of relationship into which men have become involved in their efforts to cooperate and act collectively.[3] He was not at the moment greatly concerned with processes by which these customs and institutions came into existence; although he does refer to them, in his account of the classes and masses.[4]

It is with these relationships—*Beziehungen,* to use von Weise's [*sic*] term—with which this paper is concerned.[5] Not all of these relationships, it must be confessed, are explicitly set forth in Sumner's text. They are, however, implicit in his general conception of society and it is the intention of what follows not only to formulate these notions but to set them forth in some sort of systematic order. In doing this it is not my purpose to expound Sumner's philosophy but rather to exhibit the logical structure of his thought.

Looked at abstractly, and from the point of view of statistical enumeration, society presents itself as a mere numerical aggregate, the units of which are distributed in space. This special distribution exhibits, however, certain characteristic patterns and certain recurring constellations of people and of habitations,—i.e., villages, towns, cities, etc.—which suggest the influence of tendencies and the play of forces not reckoned with so long as societies arc regarded as mere sums and aggregates of isolated and independent units. It is not that this isolation and independence does not exist. It does, but not in the degree and to the extent which this conception of society would seem to suggest.[6]

As a matter of fact any existing distribution of population is probably due to what Sumner has described as "the competition of life". Man is everywhere involved in a struggle with other men,—and with the living organisms by which he is surrounded,—for a place and a position within the limits of the habitable world, what the Greeks called the *aekonomiae* [*sic*]. This struggle is itself a societal force since it leads man to enter into associations and alliances with other men in order not merely to live, but to live more abundantly. The distribution of the population, in all its characteristic forms, turns out thus to be an evidence of, and an index to, the existence within the population group of a form of competitive cooperation, which is one of the characteristic aspects

---

[3] *Folkways,* pp. 39–54.

[4] For a statement of Sumner's conception of the historical and evolutionary process, see Sumner, W. G., and Keller, A. G. *Science of Society,* 4 vols. New Haven, Yale University Press, 1927.

[5] Leopold von Wiese and Becker, H., *Systematic Sociology,* New York, Wiley, 1932, pp. 43–44.

[6] Gras, N. S. B. *An Introduction to Economic History,* New York, Harper, 1922.

of every society. The distribution of population which results from the competition of life is what may be called the ecological organization of society. A
society that is organized ecologically, that is on a territorial basis, is not merely
a society, it is a community.

The tendencies or forces which have effected the existing distribution of
world population are mainly, but not wholly, economic. People come
together, much as do the different plant species that constitute a plant community, because they are useful to one another. If they succeed in establishing
relatively stable relations among themselves it is because there are some
advantages in a division of labor and in an exchange of goods and services.
Primarily the territorial is an aspect of the economic organization, and every
community, whatever other more intimate relations it implies, rests upon a
communal economy. Thus, in the course of his economic history, man has
developed in historical succession, as Gras has pointed out, a village, town,
city and metropolitan economy, and in the present world economy all of
these different historical types persist, considerably modified to be sure by
their interrelations as parts of one vast complex and world community.

The competition of life, as Sumner has conceived it, is a broader and more
inclusive affair than economic competition, since economic competition
invariably takes place within the limits of some established moral and political
order—within the limits, at least, of some sort of consensus and understanding—in which the free play of competition is measurably restricted and controlled. On the other hand competition goes on, even within the limits of
civil society, in manifold ways of which we who are most concerned are only
dimly conscious or wholly unaware. The "competition of life" is what
Darwin called "the struggle for existence". Economic competition on the
other hand, is the struggle for a livelihood and for a vocation, i.e., for a place
in the traditional and accepted economic order.

Commerce and industry, the economic division of labor, and all the institutions which exist to effect an exchange of goods and services are directly
and indirectly the consequences of economic competition. Economic competition, however, is but one aspect of the competition of life.

The effects of competition, particularly in those conscious forms we call
rivalry and conflict, are reflected back upon and modify the individual personalities involved. Trade and barter, for example, as they are conducted in a
primitive market, intensify in the individual his self-consciousness and his
egoism. Personal conflict of any sort seems to enhance the individual's sense
of personal freedom and of personal responsibility. It is one of the ways in
which individuation takes place, i.e., the process by which each of us, sooner
or later, and then only more or less, comes into possession of his personal
freedom, i.e., his moral independence of the custom and tradition in which
he has grown up.

On the other hand cooperation and collective action lessen the personal
tension in the individual and increase the solidarity of the group. Thus

competition, when it becomes conscious, manifests itself subjectively by modifying the individual's conception of himself; and objectively, by determining his status in the group, since the status which any person achieves in any society is due, finally, to his success in the rôle he is assigned, or assumes, to play there.

Thus the individual ego, which may [be] said to expand with personal success, correspondingly shrinks under the humiliation of personal defeat, and this is due in part at least to the fact that the individual's conception of himself, which is so important a function in individual conduct, is very largely the reflection he sees of himself in the eyes of his fellows.

It has been said, and not without some truth that, of all the animals, man is the one of whom we know the least. Even what we know with anything like certainty about mankind we seem to have learned from the study of creatures whose behavior is far less elaborate than our own. We know, however, that man does not carry on in the competition of life, nor even in the struggle for a livelihood, in the free, independent and self-determined fashion of the economic man, as the classic economists conceived him. Always he is bound by custom, convention, tradition and conscience. Most of the traits of mankind that are characteristically human,—his vocation, politics and religion—are acquired not merely in competition, but in cooperation with other men, and in general through participation in the common conscious life of the race.

Sumner seems to have conceived society in general somewhat as he described primitive society, as "a group of groups." Each of these groups, like the individuals of which it is composed, is a more or less morally isolated [entity]; an independent center of life, of interest and of action. It is what Sumner calls a "we-group".

In the isolation and intimacies of these so-called "we-groups", the individuals who composed them are often so completely submerged, and so completely subordinated, that sometimes they do not seem to exist as independent personalities. Sumner called these smaller collective units we-groups because the use of that term, with reference to itself, was a recognition by each group of its individual identity, solidarity, and unique position with reference to every other.

This is the significance of the term *ethnocentrism* which Sumner seems to have coined to describe a relationship between groups, similar to that which exists between individual persons. Ethnocentrism describes a point of view from which one's own group is the center of everything, and all others are scaled down and rated with reference to it. On the whole one must admit that this naïve view of things is more or less inevitable and founded in human nature since, from the point of view of action, distances and values are necessarily reckoned from the point of view of the actor, and the relative importance of things is naturally estimated, not merely from the point of their abstract desirability, but from their accessibility to control and ultimate consumption.

Ethnocentrism was apparently coined on the analogy of ego-centrism and, as Sumner uses it, seems to apply more to those small and scattered ethnic groups of which primitive society is composed. But it seems to apply to any "we-group":—that is any group which, because of its moral isolation and of the pressing necessity for concerted and collective action, has developed an *esprit de corps* which enables it to act effectively, in a hostile environment. The primitive tribe is, perhaps, the typical instance of such a we-group, but a religious sect, a boy's gang, a nationality or a nation that feels itself in a perilous position, or even a minority party in a hostile public are, characteristic examples of the we-group and of the situation in which the characteristic traits of we-groups manifest themselves. Fundamentally, I suppose, a we-group is any group that acts collectively.

The significant thing with reference to these "inter" and "intro" relationships,—i.e., the relationship between groups and the relationship between the individuals that compose them,—is that they are, as Sumner says, "correlative to each other". "The relation of comradeship and peace in the we-group, and of hostility and war toward others-groups, are correlative to each other." The rule that hostility without tends to mobilize and raise the morale of the forces within applies with equal validity to individuals and to groups. From the fact that loyalty, discipline and peace in the in-group seem to be the normal response to hostility and warfare in the inter-group, there emerges the conception of two correlative systems of relationships, moral and political. In the ingroup the relations of individuals, based as they are on intimate and personal associations, once they are fixed in customs and sanctioned by religion, assume the character of a moral order.

On the other hand inter-group relationships, based largely on accom[m]odation between otherwise hostile units, may be described in contrast to intra-group relations, as political, or something approaching it. They are political in the sense that they represent a *modus vivendi,* however arrived at, between parties of divergent and conflicting interests.

Such an accom[m]odation may involve nothing more than a temporary alliance. It may involve the permanent subordination of one group by the other. It is Oppenheimer's contention that historically the state is such an accom[m]odation: that in fact the state has arisen in every instance as the result of a conquest of a sedentary and agricultural, by [a] nomadic people, with the result that the agricultural people constituted the laboring, and and [*sic*] the nomads the ruling caste.[7] In any case [t]he subordination and superordination of peoples, however they arise, once they are accepted and sanctioned by religion as well as law, tend to lose their character as political *modus vivendi* and assume the form and function of a sacred institution.

Thus Negro slavery in the United States, which arose historically in

[7] Oppenheimer, F., *The State,* New York, Vanguard Press, 1922, Ch. II.

Virginia and elsewhere as a successor and a substitute for white servitude, gradually gained legal definition and recognition and, finally came to have, in the Southern States at least, the sanction of the church. The origin of the system of caste in India is more obscure but it seems to have been, in the first instance, a *modus vivendi* between peoples of different racial stocks.

People who live together are not always incorporated into the same moral and political order. The Jews, in the long course of their raical [sic] and tribal history, have lived among many peoples in relations that Israel Zangwell [sic] once described as symbiotic i.e. they participated in the economic life, but chose to maintain their moral independence and their ancient tribal religion and culture. Though they did not intermarry with the peoples among whom they resided, they did not, as might have been expected, constitute a caste.

Society thus resolves itself, upon analysis, into a hierarchy of relationships—ecological, economic, political and moral—ranging from associations that are purely symbiotic and biological,—such as exist between plants and animals in a plant or animal community—to those more intimate, personal, even mystical associations, such as one ordinarily meets in the family, in primitive society and in religious sects.

Social relationships are manifestly, complex and difficult to classify. However the systems of relationships here sketched arc typical, at least of societies territorially organized, and represent, as a matter of fact, just those obvious aspects of society upon which, historically, most concepts of society have been based. Furthermore, concepts of society, like concepts in other fields of observation and investigation, are ordinarily nothing more than descriptions, a little more general and a little more precise, of objects viewed from some special and restricted point of view. It is obvious, therefore, that almost any society, depending upon the point of view from which one looks at it, may be regarded as 1) a statistical unit, or "mere geographical expression", to use Metternich's famous phrase, 2) an ecological organization, or 3) an economic, 4) a political or 5) cultural entity.

From these different points of view any society, territorially organized, may become the subject of at least four distinct social sciences: 1) human geography and human ecology, 2) economics, 3) political science and 4) social anthropology and sociology, not to mention history which, although it has formulated no concept of society of its own, is probably more important for the understanding of society and human relations generally than any or all the others.

If now we attempt to examine a little more closely these different systems of relationships in which individuals in society are inevitably involved, viz. the ecological, economic, political and moral, we find ourselves in difficulty because of the fact that, although these different forms of association exist in greater or less independence of one another, they rarely occur in isolation. Thus there is no question that man lives with other men, as he does with the plants, animals and other living things, in relations that are often parasitic or symbiotic, at any rate biological rather than social.

Consider, for example, the gypsies, the criminals, outlaws and professional beggars,—pariah peoples, who, in our great cities, live in a region we call the "under world". The relation of these people to ourselves is not exactly social. They do not cooperate in the common tasks and they do not live according to the accepted codes. Simmel refers to them as the "inner enemies"—but they are actually neither enemies, nor rebels. They are, perhaps, more properly described, parasites, alien organisms, performing no function in the communal economy. But after all, they are not quite that either, for we hold ourselves, somehow and to some extent, morally responsible for them.

On the other hand, in the larger world community, we are in relations that are rather more symbiotic than social with vast numbers of people who, without knowledge of us or we of them, are toiling silently, in remote places, to maintain this vast structure of international exchange and division of labor in which we live. But even in the small local communities, where we are in some sort of personal contact with one another, the competition of life goes on, below the level of economic competition, in ways of which we are not wholly conscious and over which we have little control. The vital nexus by which man is bound up with other men is manifest in the manner in which disease is communicated. As Carlyle put it, the essential brotherhood of man is disclosed in places we least expected to find it,—by plague and pestilence.

Fundamentally the human, like the plant or animal, community, is an agglomeration of individuals living together in just this vital independence. There is, however, this difference: in the plant community there is no consensus. Plants are not inhibited by the knowledge of what other plants expect of them. They are not controlled by custom, fashion, convention, etiquette, public opinion and public policy, nor inhibited by any sort of taboo or fear of the immediate or ultimate consequences of their acts. In short the plant community is a geographical and ecological phenomenon, but it is not—in the sense in which that is true of the human community—a society.

This does not mean that the forms of competition and cooperation which are responsible for the plant associations do not exist among human beings. It means, simply, that in the human community the forces or tendencies which bring men together in some sort of symbiosis are modified by other forces, notably political and moral, so that the resulting distribution and ecological organization is [sic] not what it would be if these more or less conscious forms of association—economic, political and moral—were not superimposed upon it.

The plant community is one in which—if I am permitted to employ a political term in a biological sense,—the individuals of which it is composed, live in harmonious anarchy, a condition akin to that natural harmony as conceived by Adam Smith and the physiocrats, in which the individual man, by pursuing exclusively his individual profit, contributed the most possible to the general welfare.

In human society this harmony is complicated by communication, since communication, as John Dewey has pointed out, always involves some degree of participation, by those who communicate, each in the life of the other. Men are so constituted that, as they become aware of other men,—that is aware of them as persons,—they are disposed, just in the degree that this acquaintance becomes intimate and personal, to act toward them—as Kant's fundamental law of ethics, prescribes—as if they were follow [sic] creatures like themselves. The fundamental ethical law, as Kant stated it, is this: men should always and everywhere treat men as persons rather than things.

As a matter of fact this is, measurably and on the whole, the way men do deal with one another in so far as the distances,—social as well as physical—which separate them are reduced and eventually dissolved. The moral order imposes itself upon the geographical and natural, just in so far as communication becomes not merely less difficult but more intimate and complete.

Imperialism

Recent Atrocities in the Congo State

For years vague and distorted rumors of outrages perpetrated in the wild interior of Africa have drifted down the Congo to the settlements and mission posts of the lower river. Now and then these whispered horrors coming down the river thus have been transmitted in letters home, or have been brought back in the tales of the returned missionaries.

But the mission stations in the interior are very wide apart; means of communication are rare. Crimes of the kind here referred to are not usually committed within sight or sound of a mission post. So it is that the tales that have reached us from there have usually been listened to and dismissed with a shudder as one of the incidents of that terrible process of civilization whose results, as we see them under our very eyes, are often melancholy enough.

In recent years the volume of missionary tales has grown ever larger and larger; the accounts of the outrages of the native soldiery more terribly specific, until certain minds have reached the firm conviction that not only are the tales of travelers and missionaries literally true, but that they are the legitimate and inevitable fruits of the system of dealing with native peoples which is now in operation in the Congo State—a system more ruthless than any the world has known since the Spanish conquest of America.

Meanwhile, the voice of protest that reaches us from the dark continent is no longer an occasional and anonymous whisper. Men have come forward who speak openly and with knowledge. These men are no longer attacking individuals, but are now making war upon the system. This attack upon the system, rather than upon the individuals who are working in it, has already

Robert E. Park, "Recent Atrocities in the Congo State," *The World To-Day* VIII (October 1904), pp. 1328–31.

had consequences. There is no mistaking the nature of the threat which is contained in the latest bulletin of Governor-General Fuchs. Certain influences, he says, are at work in the Congo which are undermining the authority of the state, and these influences emanate from the Protestant mission posts.

"I have already called the attention of the government to this grave situation," he says, "and the measures that it will entail if it continues. Already the local officers have found it necessary to act on their own initiative to safeguard the authority of the state, and if necessary the governor-general will consider the advisability of putting into operation the powers that the decree of September 15, 1889, puts at his disposal in the case of strangers who use their influence with the natives against the state."

THE CRIMES OF TWO MONTHS

Meanwhile the testimony in regard to the atrocities continues to accumulate. The following is an extract from a letter of John H. Harris, of the Congo Balolo Mission, at Beringa, date May 1, 1904:

> During the last two months the following outrages against others have been committed in the immediate vicinity of this station:
>
> At the village of Bolumboloko the sentry shot Bokama.
>
> At the village Lotoko the sentry Jangi shot the chief Iiumbu and two others.
>
> At Ekorongo the sentry Bomolo shot Isekalasumba.
>
> At Ekorongo the sentry Ikombi shot Bosasa.
>
> At Bolima Ilangala and others shot six men and two women.
>
> The cases have been investigated by the judges—the first I have ever seen on the Congo—and whose district is larger than France and Germany put together. All these cases are proved beyond doubt to have been mere acts of bullying. Even the required rubber was completed! Hardly was his investigation complete before I had to call attention to some more dark deeds close at hand.
>
> A month or six weeks ago my boy, Bomolo, was allowed to visit his friends on the opposite bank of the river. When he came back he told me of the usual stealing and blackmailing by these armed bullies, but as these things are normal I said nothing to the officials. Three days ago I sent him to buy some nets that I required, but the poor lad arrived at his friend's house only to find that his brother-in-law had been shot by Ilanga.
>
> Another sentry, Befoja, had shot the woman Boali. Ekofa, another sentry, had shot the man Nsala. Another brute of a sentry, named Ifutu, had demanded fish of a woman named Bongwalanga. She gave him all she had

got, but because it was not sufficient, he cut off her head and that of her daughter, a young girl named Lofinda.

Besides other witnesses, I have the sworn testimony of Ifeko, who picked up the headless corpses of his relatives and helped to bury them.

I need not tell you the state of the people or the sorrow of the relatives.

IN THE CAMP OF THE REFUGEES

A. E. Scrivener, who was the first white man, other than a government official, to enter the Domain Privé and describe conditions there, has recently made another expedition to a district where a number of refugees of the Basengele and Bakutu tribes are now living. As it is dangerous for white men to know too much, and still more for natives to make statements against the government, Mr. Scrivener has not mentioned names or places in his accounts:

Here are some specimens of the stories I have heard from some of the Basengele and Bakutu:

—— went with others to the white man's station with their rubber. They were one basket short. For this basket the white man demanded that a man should be given him, and took from among them ——, made him stand at some little distance from the others and then shot him with a gun he brought from his house. Another day he was at the same place and saw —— shot in the same way by the white man. This was because the man had killed a goat (his own), but they were told that nothing they had was their own, but belonged to the State. Another day he was at the same place and saw a party of people come in with their rubber. It was short of the proper amount. The white man received it and sent them home, and soon afterward sent six soldiers with rifles to shoot them in their own village. Two men and two women were killed.

—— said he went to the same post mentioned above with other people, taking rubber with them. One of their number was of very light complexion for a native. A soldier called the white man's attention to this, when he called out angrily that one like himself should not live on the station with him, and took his gun and shot the man as he stood a little apart from his friends.

—— was going with a soldier in the direction of the rubber forest. They met a man coming from the forest. "Why have you no rubber?" said the soldier. "It is coming behind with my boy." But the soldier shot and killed the man as he stood in the road. Another day he was with the same soldier and went with him to the gardens. They saw a man working in the cassava. "Why are you not away cutting rubber?" "Look at my cassava, it is all being eaten by the buffaloes, and I want to save a little of it to eat." Then the soldier shot him.

EXAMPLES OF CONGO JUSTICE

The crimes here charged were committed in the remotest region of the Congo State, from which no information is obtainable except from the natives themselves. A letter dated May 17, 1904, from John H. Weeks, a missionary at Monsembe Station, in Haut Congo, cites the following examples of the arbitrary methods of dealing with the natives which have come under his observation recently:

> Libulula, on the south bank of the river, was formerly a large town stretching for a considerable distance along the bank. The chief, with his family, lived at the upper end of it. During the last eight or nine years the town has gradually decreased, until at last at the lower end of the town was a collection of nineteen miserable huts. At the other end Ngwa, the chief, lived with his wives and family, and for hundreds of yards in between, where formerly people had lived, there was nothing but grass. Last year the commissaire of the district ordered Ngwa to remove his houses to the lower end, and live with the people. Ngwa did not wish to leave the place where his fathers had lived before him; he paid his share of the taxes and could not see any reason for the order to move lower down the river. As the commissaire insisted, Ngwa had to comply, but being undesirous to leave, he was naturally slow to obey, so he was taken a prisoner, put in chains, and made to carry bricks. He treatment was such that before his time had expired he died, on August 16, 1903.
>
> The crime: Slowness to obey a whimsical and unreasonable order of the commissaire. Punishment: Chains and treatment resulting in death. Ngwa's share of the taxes was divided among the rest of the people, so the State lost nothing by his death, but the burden of the people was increased. When I was visiting that part a few weeks ago, I asked an intelligent native where all the people were. He said: "Some have died of sleep-sickness, some have run away, but plenty have died from worry and grief of heart, because of oppression."
>
> Mangumbe, a headman of Monsembe, was appointed a chief by the State, and given a medal certificate to that effect. He received no remuneration, but was made responsible for the fortnightly tax due from this section of the district. Mangumbe was appointed a medal chief in the early part of 1902, and things went along fairly well until June and July of last year. Sometimes he went up with the tax, at other times he sent a responsible headman with it. During the above months, the State officials began to worry him to go up with every fortnightly tax himself, a most unreasonable demand to make of a headman who had affairs of his own to occasionally attend to; but then, of course, he should have no affairs of his own. It is two days' hard paddling to Bangala—one day to deliver the tax, and one day paddling down, leaving ten days to procure his share of the next tax and gather the rest from the people.
>
> Last July, Mangumbe sent the tax up by a headman, and he himself went twenty to thirty-five miles down river to buy a goat ready for the

next tax. Down came a messenger, calling him to Bangala (Nouvelle Anvers), but not finding him there, the messenger had to go down to Malele, where Mangumbe was bargaining for a goat. Mangumbe returned at once, collected the next tax, and went with it to Bangala. No fault was found with the tax, but because he did not take up the previous tax himself he was sentenced by the commandant in charge (the commissaire was up the Mongala River) to eight days carrying bricks in the chains. Mangumbe said, "I did not come with the tax because I went to buy a goat for the next tax." That made no difference; soldiers were called, and he was taken away to the chains.

Just before his eight days were up the commissaire (who in the meantime had received my letter of June 13) returned, and increased the sentence to twenty-two days. We can not help putting the increase of sentence down to the commissaire's irritation at receiving our communication from the same town to which Mangumbe belonged. Did he suspect that Mangumbe had given me the information about Mabata's irregular fine of 57,000 rods, and to punish him for it increased his sentence to twenty-two days?

Mangumbe was chained next to Ngwa, and between them they had to carry a heavy box of bricks. A soldier always accompanied them, and there are witnesses to prove that the butt end of the gun was used often on Mangumbe's back and side. Their treatment of him was such that he died within twenty-four hours of Ngwa, and his corpse was brought here on August 18. Mangumbe's share of the tax was divided among the people, so their burden became heavier, but the State lost nothing.

The crime: Not going up personally every fortnight with the tax. Punishment: Chains and ill-treatment resulting in death.

No report has as yet been received in America as to the results of recent measures that the government has taken to bring pressure upon American and English missionaries to prevent "the undermining of state authority," and it is doubtful, in view of the international origin of the Congo State and of the existing treaties, if the government will have the courage to enforce the threats that it is now making against the missionaries.

A King In Business

Leopold II of Belgium, Autocrat of the Congo and International Broker

I

A new figure looms large on the horizon of Europe! A figure strange, fantastic, and ominous—the king who is capitalist, *le roi d'affaires*; the man who unites in himself the political and social prestige of a reigning monarch with the vast material power of a multimillionaire.

Assume, by way of illustration, that John D. Rockefeller had, by an act of Providence or a freak of fortune, in his young manhood been made perpetual President of the United States, and that he had retained as perpetual President all that thrift and cautious daring which enabled him to create the Standard Oil Company.

Suppose that he had then chosen to use his position as perpetual President to further his private interests as a money-getter. Consider the advantages of his position, at home and abroad, from the point of view of high finance: he would be able to control legislation at home, in the interest of his own private enterprises, and would have at his command all the machinery of the foreign diplomatic service to aid him in his intrigues abroad.

No doubt he would find himself hampered in his operations by constitutional formulas, the nagging criticism of legislators and the inquisition of the press. But the art of controlling public opinion has, in recent years, reached a high state of perfection. Through the elaborate machinery of the modern press bureau a man of this president's wealth could reach and influence the entire world.

Suppose, now, that with all this vast power at his command, he had got the colonies of the United States, Porto Rico, the Philippines, and the rest,

Robert E. Park, "A King in Business: Leopold II of Belgium, Autocrat of the Congo and International Broker," *Everybody's Magazine* XV (November 1906), pp. 624–33.

including Santo Domingo and Cuba, absolutely under his control, so that he could treat them as his personal possession and the inhabitants as something between tenants and serfs.

With the tremendous power he had acquired abroad he would then increase his power at home, aiming to make it as absolute there as it was in the colonies.

Conceive all this, not as the mere furniture of some fairy-land, but as an actual situation, and you will have a working knowledge of the conditions that exist in the thrifty little country of Belgium, of which Leopold II is king, business manager, and general superintendent.

II

The seat of the Belgian Court is the king's palace, which stands in the left lobe of the heart-shaped figure that three boulevards have cut out of the heart of the Belgian capital. This palace is the official headquarters of His Majesty, in his dual capacity of Belgian ruler and sovereign of the Congo State.

Facing the royal palace is the *Palais de la Nation*, where the two chambers of the Belgian Parliament, the Senate and the Chamber of Deputies, hold their sessions. Between the two is a park. Here a few years ago one might often see a tall man, in a sack coat and derby hat, striding along, with his shoulders well back, as if he were walking for a wager. He had invariably a cane in his hand, and his trousers rolled up, although the path might be perfectly dry and the sun shining. One would have said, at the first glance, that this was a man of business, or perhaps a gentleman farmer, with just a touch of the sport about him.

But a second glance would have convinced even the stranger that the tall figure, six feet five inches, with large, impassive features, eyes "glittering with intelligence and with malice," bearing aloft that imposing and inimitable beard, could be none other than Leopold, King of Belgium, the most unique figure, and the most enterprising monarch in Europe; and, in all probability, the richest man in the world.

The popular conception of Leopold II is a typical creation of the daily press. Newspapers have produced an endless series of little cinematographic portraits of the king in which all that is superficially characteristic of him has been exaggerated, while the large and simple outlines, which might have revealed the essential traits of his personality, have been neglected. He has been by turns revealed in the rôle of the jaded pleasure-seeker, pursuing a new sensation in the purlieus of the Parisian boulevards; the royal sport, lending a vogue to the gaming-tables at Ostend, in which he was, it is charged, a secret partner; the domestic tyrant, driving his wife into retirement by the brutalities of his scandalous life, imprisoning his daughter in an asylum because she rebelled against a marriage without love or respect; the miserly libertine, who after squandering money lavishly on his mistresses, robbed his wife of her fortune while she was living, and cheated his daughters out of their heritage after she was dead.

But the daily press, which writes history by flash-light, gives us in the end only caricatures.

In all these little scenes, which have been more or less dramatized to suit the popular taste, it is the actor rather than the real personage that we see. Leopold is less the avaricious adventurer, philanthropist, and satyr than a cynical man of the world, who sees through, even while he enjoys, the pretty, visible, trivial world of sport, fashion, and affairs. His real life is with the great game of high finance, where he seeks not merely money and the power money gives, but the reestablishment, behind the forms of a constitutional government, of something corresponding to the old feudal absolutism. The story goes that the king's physician once asked him how he would like to be president of a Belgian Republic instead of king. The king smiled cynically and asked: "How would you like to be a veterinary surgeon?"

The truer picture of the king is that which represents him, in his château just outside Brussels—living in the midst of luxury, in the "most commodious palace in Europe," with almost austere simplicity. At Laeken the daily order of his life is somewhat as follows:

The king rises punctually at five, calls his *valet de chambre,* and proceeds rapidly with his toilet. As soon as he is dressed, he drinks a pint of water, and, if the weather permits, takes a short brisk walk in the garden, alone. The chamber in which he has passed the night shows none of the refinements of an effeminate luxury. The furniture is simple and not for show. The bed is that of a soldier rather than that of a king and a millionaire. Indeed, the whole atmosphere of the room, reflecting, as it does, the dominant note in the king's character, is quite middle-class.

At six o'clock the first post arrives from the city. The king disposes of it in the course of his morning exercise, classifying it, and making notes as he walks. Upon his return he responds briefly to all pressing correspondence, reserving that which requires a more extended reply or a more careful examination.

At half past seven the second mail arrives from the city. This is always large. Varied and multitudinous as these letters are, each one is the subject of the king's personal care and attention. He dictates replies to his secretary, plans the duties of the day, and fixes the list of those whom he will receive or summon. While he goes to breakfast an orderly delivers his commands to the persons concerned.

After breakfast the king takes a second walk, during which he discusses with an official who accompanies him the day's program, and formulates his decisions in regard to each item. At eleven o'clock he returns, and swallows, before seating himself again at his desk, two large glasses of pure water. He repeats this draft at numerous times during the day, believing that this regimen has contributed much to the preservation of his remarkably good health.

In the meantime a third post has arrived, and after disposing of this he takes a third walk, at the end of which he is ready for luncheon. This is a comparatively formal function, at which he meets the Princess Clementine, the maids of honor, and other members of the household, but the king, who has adopted the American maxim, "Time is money," disposes of it in the briefest time possible. There is little said, and the meal, which begins at precisely 12.30, is usually finished twenty minutes later.

After luncheon the king, accompanied as usual by his orderly, drives directly to Brussels, where at one o'clock he gives audience to those who have arranged to see him. When the weather is fair, and business does not compel him to go to Brussels, Leopold usually takes another long walk. Frequently he choses the Meysse Avenue, which leads from his palace at Laeken to that of Bouchout, where his unfortunate mad sister, the "tragic widow" of the ill-fated Maximilian of Mexico, has been for many years a prisoner.

Toward three or four o'clock he returns from that mournful visit, and takes again his "bowl of water," or a cup of tea. In the meantime a fourth and a fifth mail have arrived, and the king disposes of these immediately before dinner, which is served at six.

Thus his day is taken up with a mingling of physical and mental activities which enables him to accomplish a prodigious amount of real labor and still preserve to a remarkable degree, in spite of his seventy-one years, the mental and physical vigor of youth.

He works with unusual rapidity, but with an extraordinary sense for details, never signing a paper before he has examined critically every word and phrase. He has the trait of all great executives, of wishing to be understood and seconded on the instant, and with a word. It is this which has given rise to the report that he is abrupt with his employees, dry with his orderlies, and inflexible with his ministers.

Though King Leopold has been, as he promised at his coronation, "a Belgian, heart and soul," there are few men more cosmopolitan. He employs men of all nationalities in the Congo State. Of Americans, some of whom he has found useful in his business enterprises, he is supposed to be especially fond. It was chiefly with the aid of two Americans, Henry M. Stanley and General Henry Sanford, that he first succeeded in establishing himself in Africa. For some years, Thomas F. Walsh, "the Cripple Creek mining man," was said to be partner in his American mining ventures. He recruits his officers in the Congo State largely from the Swedish and Italian governments. He employed Englishmen in the work of the exploration in the Congo. But his ideal clerk the king finds among the Belgians, in whom the bureaucratic spirit is strongly marked. Wherever Leopold has found a foothold in China,

Persia, or Africa, it is to Belgians alone that he has entrusted the task of administration.

Although Leopold, true to the traditions of his father, has maintained the rigor of the court ceremonial, and has done much to increase, among a people who have little genius for parliamentary government, the power and prerogatives of the crown, personally he is the most democratic of monarchs. He travels much, and almost always incognito. He has been more than once known to arrive in Paris with no other luggage than that which he carried in a single hand-satchel.

In 1902 the Chinese Prince Tsai-Chen visited the king, who was then at Ostend. Leopold received him in the most ceremonious way, in the morning. That afternoon some mandarins, of the prince's suite, were seen looking in wonder and astonishment at the king, in careless civilian attire, mounting a slot-machine, and after weighing himself, announcing to the admiring crowd that he weighed just eighty-five kilograms, one kilogram more than when he arrived.

Such is the strange old man who has succeeded in gaining a domination over his own country unequaled by that of any other monarch in Europe, and who holds in his inflexible hands a vast commercial empire, which extends to the uttermost limits of the earth.

When an ex-minister was asked, in the lobby of the Belgian chamber last spring, what he considered the dominating purposes in Leopold's life, he replied: "The king has but two dreams. To die a milliardaire" (the possessor of one thousand million francs), "and to disinherit his daughters."

The statement contains about as much truth as one can ordinarily condense into an epigram. Leopold undoubtedly hates his daughters, Louise and Stephanie. He has tried, in an endless number of ways, to set aside, to their detriment, the provisions of the civil code in the matter of parental succession. But at seventy-one, even the most worldly man must needs think of something other than money and the satisfaction of his personal malice.

The king has yet to consolidate his power and to perpetuate the situation he has created.

III

Other monarchs have had more or less illicit relations with the stock-market. Gossip says that half the thrones of Europe are indirectly allied with the Standard Oil Company. But Leopold has gone openly into the money markets; he has put himself at the head of the Belgian group of financiers and led the crusade for foreign concessions.

At the present time Belgium has no less than fifty concessions in China.

They are established in Siam, in Persia, and Morocco. A French and Belgian syndicate owns more than half the debts of Santo Domingo. It is safe to say that there is not a spot on the globe where the weakness or rottenness of local government has cast the scent of concessions on the air that Belgians are not already settled, or hovering about expectantly.

In the scramble for foreign concessions, Leopold, the financier, has been greatly aided by Leopold, the king. Not only has he used all the diplomatic machinery of the Belgian Government to secure for his own companies the concessions he desired, but actually he has spent the government's funds to exploit them. He borrowed thirty-one million francs from the Belgian Government to carry on his Congo enterprise, and then took the money from the sinking fund created to pay back this loan and put it in the Pekin-Hankow Railway scheme in China. In all these operations he has acted with the untrammeled freedom and singleness of purpose of a captain of high finance, giving about as much consideration to the interests of Belgium as a railway president does to the interests of the stockholders.

In this disposition to look upon the state rather as a business concern than a political organization, and to exercise, in the struggle "to get results," the arbitrary powers of a general manager, one may see the temper and the type of the business monarch.

Leopold II became King of Belgium December 17, 1865, when he was thirty years of age. He had hardly been installed upon the throne when he presented to the chambers a law fixing his income from the state at 3,300,000 francs. This was 700,000 francs more than his father had received, but, in the enthusiasm of the moment, the law passed, and there has been no complaint since that the king does not earn his salary.

He came to the throne prepared for the task he has since undertaken to perform. He had traveled widely in Africa, Asia Minor, and the Far East. Perceiving that Belgium, with the densest population in Europe, was in sore need of markets for her manufactures, he had already formulated the policy that has been the one great thought of his reign—the idea of a colonial empire.

Belgium, however, was a little country, with an insignificant army. Her few feeble attempts at colonization, one in Guatemala, South America, and the other in the Island of Formosa, had failed. Besides, being a neutral state, called into existence for the convenience of the powers, and having aside from this no good excuse for being, it was doubtful if Belgium was entitled to have colonies at all.

It is a testimony to the political genius of King Leopold that he has turned every one of these weaknesses to his own and Belgium's advantage. Because Belgium was feeble and neutral and, to all appearances, a mere international convenience, the country offered an ideal situation for an international broker and business man. Leopold made of himself the middleman for the Powers, engineering projects and conducting negotiations for them which, because of international jealousies, they did not think it advisable to carry on in their own names. There is more than a suspicion that in China, and also in Persia, Leopold has been at once the partner and the agent of Russia, and probably, at different times and places, of Germany and of France. The story of the Pekin-Hankow Railway is a case in point:

When, in 1896, the Chinese Government determined to build a railway from Pekin to Hankow, it was expected that Chinese capital would be used. After it appeared that the imperial treasury would be unable to bear the expense, American capitalists were invited to assist in the construction; that failing, the government turned to Belgium.

The preliminary contract was made with a Belgian syndicate in 1897. Before it was ratified, Lord Salisbury telegraphed, June 9, 1898, to Sir Claude MacDonald, British Minister at Pekin: "Her Majesty's government entertained objections to the Pekin-Hankow line when it originally heard the concessions were granted to the Belgian syndicate; when there is likelihood of the Russo-Chinese bank, which is tantamount to Russia's government, financing the southern section of that railway, that objection is greatly increased. A concession of this nature is no longer a commercial or industrial enterprise, and becomes a political movement against British interests in the Yangtse."

Surely a curious situation in which a railway, owned by the King of Belgium, becomes an instrument of political aggression in the hands of Russia.

In the same year in which the king got the concession for the northern branch of the railway from Hankow to Pekin, the American China Development Company, of which the late Senator Brice was first president, obtained the concession for the extension of that line from Hankow to Canton. By the terms of this concession, it was agreed that the Americans "could not confer the rights of these agreements on other nations or people of other nationality."

In spite of this provision, toward the close of 1899 General Whittier, who, after the death of Senator Brice, had become the head of the American company, was, it is said, employed under instructions from Brussels to purchase a controlling number of shares in the American company. The effect of this was to put Leopold in control of the whole railway form Pekin to Canton.

If you will look at the map of China, and follow with your eye the line of the railway from Pekin to Canton, you will see that it cuts that vast and populous empire through the middle. Recall that at this time Russia had already inaugurated in Manchuria the method of "conquest by railway and bank," and you will perceive the vast proportions of the political movement that Russia had projected, and but for the intervention of Japan, would perhaps have carried to completion, with the aid of Belgium's business monarch.

Russia aimed at the dismemberment or gradual absorption of China. But what was the ultimate goal of Leopold's ambition? Knowing that possession of a railway meant in China political control, did he intend, finally, to turn this road over to Russia, giving her a single line of railway from St. Petersburg across Siberia, through Manchuria and China, to Canton? Or did he dream that, after using the influence of China and France to obtain the concession and to build the road, he might depend upon the jealousy of England and China to hold the road permanently for himself? That would have permitted him to apply in Central China the process of absorption, which Russia was at that time employing in Manchuria.

Any such dream of "peaceful conquest" was dispelled in the smoke of the Russo-Japanese war. China has since bought back, at considerable profit to Belgian as well as American investors, the concessions that she granted to Americans alone. As a result of the slow transaction, American prestige in China has been severely shaken, and the American tradesman is the sufferer.

IV

The Pekin-Hankow-Canton Railway, although financially profitable, was, considering the vast result at which it aimed, a failure. But the Congo State has been a success, and the proportions of that achievement reveal the vast perspective of the king's schemes.

It is not possible within the limits of one brief article even to sketch the story of the wide-extended intrigue, the ruthless waste of life, and the financial hocus-pocus that have enabled the King of Belgium not only to set up in the interior of Africa a political absolutism, but to create a commercial monopoly, the most gigantic the world has ever known. For it comprises not only 800,000 square miles of the richest soil in the world, but includes also the forced labor of the 20,000,000 serfs who inhabit it.

The facts in the story are these: September 12, 1877, there took place in the palace in Brussels one of the most momentous of those "little conferences" that in the last forty years have so often been held in this same palace. As a result of this meeting, the "International Association for the Exploration and Civilization of Central Africa" was formed.

This was a mere preliminary. Four years later when Stanley crossed Africa and by one bold stroke tore aside the veil of mystery that had up to that time concealed the interior of the dark continent, Leopold saw the goal of his ambitions clear before him. He summoned the returned explorer to Brussels. As a result of that visit a new organization was formed. It was called "The Society for Studies in the Upper Congo."

The name had a harmless and academic sound. It was, however, but a mask for the real enterprise, which was commercial and political. The king hired Stanley and hurried him off to Africa. He was to establish stations along the Congo River, make treaties with the native chiefs, and, in short, do what he could to establish the sovereignty of the association in that region.

The enterprise was pushed with haste and secrecy, but the scramble for the possession of Africa had already begun, and one of the secondary results of this venture was the Berlin Conference. This met in 1884, and declared the Congo Basin neutral territory. It was to be a sort of international common, to which the commerce and the missions of all nations should have free entry. Leopold was appointed international guardian of this political orphan. For five years he kept the doors of the Congo State wide open, encouraging missionaries of all denominations to enter, and inviting the trade of the world. Then, in 1890, he took advantage of the Brussels Anti-Slavery Conference to wring from the Powers the right to levy import duties.

There was a grand change of scene. The king himself, in the name of the state, now entered actively into trade. In the sixteen years since that time he has crowded out or absorbed all private trade in 800,000 of the 900,000 square miles of territory in the state. Trade has been supplanted by taxation. The territory of the state has been parceled out among stock companies, who pay fifty per cent of the profit to the state for the privilege of assessing and collecting these taxes. The men employed to collect the taxes are mostly armed savages.

Leopold says that the results are civilization. The missionaries say they are hell. *But everybody admits that they are profitable.*

At the close of the Berlin Conference in 1885 the world looked upon the Congo State as a sort of international colony of which King Leopold had been appointed trustee. By the time he had begun to capitalize its wealth and the labor of its people, and to sell the stocks on the Brussels Exchange, the Congo had come to be regarded as a Belgian colony.

It seems inconceivable that a single man should claim as his personal property a territory so vast. But there is no mistaking the meaning of his recent proclamation. No one can put it more plainly than this:

> "This situation is without precedent and unique, I admit, as was the creation of the state. All the responsibilities, as all the liabilities of the foundation of a regular government by private initiative, *without any link with the metropolis*, the midst of an atmosphere where the creation of a state was looked upon as unrealizable, have fallen upon me. Belgium was good enough to help me to a certain extent with her moneys. But *the task of constituting the new state was mine exclusively. The Congo then could only be, and has been, a personal enterprise.* Now there is no more legitimate or respectable right than the right of the author to his own work, fruit of his labor. *The Powers surrounded the birth of the new state with their good-will, but none of them were [sic] called upon to participate in our efforts; none possess [sic] any right of intervention, which nothing could justify.* There is no special international law for the Congo. The Act of Berlin adopted a few general principles relating to the conventional Basin of the Congo. These principles apply in equal manner to all the states having possessions on the conventional Basin, and curtail, in so

far as such were specified, some of their sovereign rights. . . *These rights must be energetically proclaimed,* because *Belgium possesses none in the Congo apart from those which will come to her from me."*

The Congo State is the most unique government on earth, a commercial monopoly farmed by an autocrat.

It was reported some years ago that, up to 1892, the period at which the state began to pay, Leopold had invested something like 30,000,000 francs in the Congo. What he has since taken out of the state from direct and indirect sources no one knows. This is the one fact of his private and public life that the king has most zealously guarded. Four years ago the minister of one of the great Powers representing his government at Brussels said that the king's enterprises in the Congo brought him an income of about $5,000,000 per annum. E. D. Morel, the editor of the *West African Mail,* who knows more than most people about the Congo and Leopold, believes that the king's revenue from this source is "at least £1,000,000 and probably more."

Viewed merely as a business enterprise the Congo State has been an immense success. But the Congo is more to Leopold than an investment. It is the bulwark of his enormous personal influence and power in Belgium. The inheritance of this royal Captain of Industry was a little kingdom, made up of heterogeneous elements, Catholic and Protestant, Germanic and Gallic, patched together and presented to his father by the Powers in 1830. The Constitution, founded on the model of England, provided for a king who should reign, rather than rule; whose function seemed to be limited to providing a sort of ornamental façade, behind which the parliament, representing the people, was to conduct the affairs of the state. While the king has shared none of the German emperor's medieval aspirations, he has, perhaps, done more than any other monarch to reestablish the principle of personal government and to show how it is possible, in modern Europe, to rule even though you are king.

When the king capitalized the Congo situation, put the stocks on the Antwerp market and made them pay enormous dividends, he went far toward converting the Belgian public to the notion of his personal and absolute government in the Congo. When again, with the capital he had taken out of the Congo, he put himself at the head of the Belgian financiers and led the campaign for foreign concessions, he gathered about him the strongest influences in the Belgian state. And, later, when the possession of foreign concessions opened new markets for Belgian manufactures and Belgium began to grow rich under the impetus the king had given to foreign trade, Belgian manufacturers discovered that there were sound reasons for letting the king run Belgium.

The fact of the matter is that it is easier to sit tight and not murmur under a General Manager than it is under a king or any other form of government. The reason is that we expect personal dignity, intelligent consideration, justice, and the like from a king. We ask only one thing of a General Manager—dividends. The crucial question is: "Has he the goods?"

If the Belgian public and the Belgian Government have shown in recent years an otherwise incredible subserviency to a king whose private life has been a public scandal, and whose public career a shameless and unscrupulous clutching after gold, it is because they recognize in him the General Manager. Those who have not bowed to the prerogative of the king have yielded to the imperious necessities of business.

A few weeks ago, at an exciting meeting of the Wells-Fargo Company, the attorney for E. H. Harriman, the railway magnate, being hard pressed to defend his client, gave the first utterance to the "new thought" in high finance. Speaking to the stockholders he said: "He (Mr Harriman) cannot be replaced, for he moves in a higher world, into which we may not enter." It is to this doctrine of "the higher world," applied here to the relation between magnate and stockholder, that Leopold has given in Belgium the later application.

Stated simply, this doctrine means that the men who are supreme in the world of finance are endowed, by the very necessities of the great interests that they represent, with an arbitrary power, like the authority imposed by military necessity, which supersedes the ordinary political rights of ordinary human beings. It means that the "divine right" has been transferred from the king to the financier.

The fact is, that while other countries have shown an increasing disposition to take from capital its control of the industries, in Belgium we may see a country where capital, represented by the king, has taken possession of the government. Of the results of this policy the Congo Free State is, however, the capital illustration.

As the king says, the situation is unique and unprecedented. But the Socialists are right when they point to King Leopold as the crowned incarnation of the aspirations and tendencies of a business people and a business age.

The Terrible Story of the Congo

"If the administration of the Congo Free State is civilization, what then is barbarism?"—From Speech by Herbert Samuel, British M.P.

Ask any missionary who has been to Africa, any traveler who has sailed up the brown, sullen flood of the great Congo River, any agent, even, who has perhaps returned to God's country for a brief breathing-space, what they have severally found in the Congo Free State, and they will look at one another, and at you, and give you one word, gravely, in answer:

"Hell."

Perhaps you will be properly shocked, maybe you will protest; and if so, this will be the best thing that could happen to you, for you will then receive enlightenment, and your eyes will perforce be opened to what is going on at this very day, in this very hour, in the name of Civilization.

Who is the owner of the vastest private estate in the world—900,000 square miles of it? Who is the promoter of the most stupendous scheme of loot and robbery that modern times can show? Who, single-handed, has laid waste a country, drenched a land in blood, offered up tens of thousands of human lives on the altars of his greed and his lust for gold, and hoodwinked the powers of the earth into believing that he did it in the interest of philanthropy and civilization? Who but Leopold, King of the Belgians?—the astute, the wily, the conscienceless, and the philanthropist—always the philanthropist!—who played a game of chess with the nations, with twenty million black men as his helpless pawns, and gold beyond all counting as the reward of his winning.

Robert E. Park, "The Terrible Story of the Congo," *Everybody's Magazine* XV (December 1906), pp. 763–72.

This estate, this checker-board upon which he plays his game, lies in the black heart of Africa; an estate—five times as large as the combined areas of Cuba, Hawaii, Porto Rico, and the Philippines, and more than half the size of the Roman Empire—considered by him so absolutely his own possession that he bequeaths it away in his will, as he does his personal property. How does it come to be so wholly his? How has he reached such a pinnacle of despotic power, in a day when personal government is a thing of the past, and a sovereign is more or less a figurehead?

Prior to 1876 the civilized world was shocked and startled into protest by tales of the atrocities of the Portuguese slave-trade along the Congo and in the adjacent territories—a protest that crystallized and took form in the African International Association, which met in Brussels in 1876, summoned by Leopold of Belgium, to discuss measures for stamping out slavery and its concomitant horrors in the Congo, for ameliorating conditions there, and for opening up the country to trade and to civilization. The scheme was broadly philanthropic and entirely legitimate, and as such was entered into by the powers.

No sooner was the Association organized than, with Machiavellian wiliness, Leopold set about obtaining for it the status of an independent government. Still in his character of philanthropist, he sent for Henry M. Stanley, who had crossed Africa, and who knew the country and the people as perhaps no other white man has ever known them. Because he dreamed of opening a new continent, rich in virgin wealth, to the trade and civilization of the world, Stanley entered with enthusiasm into the plans of the Association. There followed discussions and expeditions that resulted in his obtaining those treaties with the natives on which the Association based its claim to sovereignty in the Congo Basin. In all the history of exploration and discovery there is nothing more grand than his work; the tragedy and the pathos of it lie in the fact that it was intended for and should have effected nothing but good; it has so far led to nothing but evil.

Nine years of expensive experiment and exploration in Africa, and much agitation and wire-pulling in Europe, were required to gain Leopold's object. Then, in 1884, when the public had been educated to see in the enterprise a labor of humanity and mercy, the Association was replaced by the Congo Free State. The powers, led by the United States, sanctioned its creation; but at a conference held in Berlin in 1885, in which fifteen powers were represented, they laid down strict regulations as to its government, clearly defined its mission as one of philanthropy and civilization, and pronounced the "entire territory neutral and open to the trade of all nations."

And Leopold, the philanthropist, seeing that the game was going all his way, agreed to all they said, and bided his time to make his next move. This was openly to proclaim himself monarch of the Congo Free State, with the same expressed policy of liberality.

From this proceeding—effected almost noiselessly for all its momentous-ness, and the more readily that the officers of the Association were for the most part Leopold's personal agents—dates all the misery and the tragedy that were to come.

It suited the policy of the king for the next five years to keep the Congo open to trade with the natives, and to encourage private enterprises. Then began the tightening of the grip of the iron hand in the velvet glove.

Import duties had been expressly prohibited by the Berlin Conference. In 1890, however, the king took advantage of the Anti-Slavery Conference at Brussels to wring from the powers a reluctant consent to the levying of import duties of ten per cent. ad valorem, on the reasonable ground that the principal burden of putting down the slave-trade must fall upon the state within whose dominions it was principally carried on. For this purpose, the State, up to that time dependent on the king's generosity—Leopold had regu-larly contributed over one million francs annually toward its support—must find new sources of revenue. Again the powers hesitated to set Leopold more firmly in his self-appointed place; but again the philanthropist persuaded them. The internal slave-trade should be suppressed, root and branch; more, the indiscriminate sale of liquor in the territory of the Congo should be regu-lated. What more was needed to win public sympathies? The United States Congress, petitioned by the Woman's Christian Temperance Union and the Christian Endeavor Society—which rose at once to the bait—gave way; the other signatory powers did likewise.

At once the vast Congo property, which, so far as the king was concerned, had formerly possessed merely speculative value, became a negotiable asset. On the strength of it, the very next day Leopold borrowed twenty-five mil-lion francs from Belgium. In return for this, the king made his will, bequeath-ing what was now in effect his personal property, the Congo Free State, to Belgium, agreeing to surrender the territory to the latter at the end of ten years.

He kept his word as to the suppression of the internal slave-trade. But, as in all other things, there are degrees in slavery. In the eastern districts the Arab slave-raiders had converted the provinces of which they held control—notably Manyema and Malela—into the most prosperous regions of Central Africa, and had established a civilization relatively well advanced. For if the Arab destroyed, he also rebuilt; his policy was to be tolerated in that it was constructive as well as destructive. But Leopold's forces, in 1893, attacked and routed the Arabs east of Tanganyika—incidentally annexing immense quanti-ties of ivory, grain, rice, and coffee—forcing vast hordes of Congolese who were now, ironically enough, called Freedmen, into a veritable slavery worse than their former serfdom. What was bad, they made worse; and where they found a thriving country, they left a ruined desert.

II

See for yourself the picture as it was:

A brown, oily river, rolling its swollen length through the rank luxuriance of tropical forests, through tangled jungle lands, through vast and silent seas of bush, dark, secretive, and impenetrable. Here and there are the mangy scars of clearing, where native villages lie sprawled, where plantations of bananas, patches of maize and yams, spring to mushroom-like growth beneath the African sun. Teeming black life lurks in that jungle, asking nothing of the world, following out its own scheme of existence to its own appointed end, absorbed in its own businesses, its own loves and fears and hates. A fertile land, ripe for the conqueror, a land of untapped wealth in rubber, ivory, iron, copper, gold, and grain, needing only proper exploitation to yield up its abundance and to prosper gloriously.

This is the Congo Free State as the agents of Leopold found it—and no grimmer irony than that name holds can be conceived—a Free State which, body and soul, was to be enslaved to one man's despotic will. This is the Congo Free State of which, in October, 1884, the manifesto of the International Association declared:

"Thanks to trade, all this produce will enter into circulation; the counterpart of its value will return to Africa, for which it will be a source of prosperity."

And this is the Congo Free State of which M. de Smet de Naeyer, during the course of the famous three days' Congo debate in the Belgian House, July, 1903, affirmed:

"They [the natives] are not entitled to anything; what is given them is a veritable gratuity."

There you have it—Promise and Performance! Between the lines of these two sentences one may read the whole dark tragedy of wreck and ruin.

What this tragedy was to be, none could have foretold from its beginnings. Upon a day, white men appeared on the banks of the brown, oily river, amid the sprawling, contented villages, and held palaver with the chiefs.

"There was rubber in the forests; bring much rubber, basketfuls of rubber, and it would be paid for."

This was something new—the idea that rubber might be bartered for objects of price. It looked like an easy way of obtaining red cloth, blue beads, bright rods of brass. Rubber poured into the stations; cloth and beads and brass were given in exchange; fair and honest trade was established along the Congo. And this was not so many years ago.

But before long the white men demanded more rubber—for the same amount of beads and cloth and brass. The natives demurred. Fewer and fewer rods were forthcoming; more and more rubber was required. The natives grew sullen; the State sent out soldiers to uphold the demands of the white men.

The soldiers discovered that the quickest and cheapest method, when the full tale of the ivory or rubber was not complete, was to raid the villages, seize men and women as "hostages," and hold them until the measures were brought in pressed down and running over. And of this system, and what grew out of its enforcement, more hereafter.

As has been said, Leopold had encouraged general trade throughout the Congo territories, and the establishment of private enterprises—until the passing of the Brussels Anti-Slavery Act in 1890, by virtue of which he was established in what, in effect, was supreme authority, and was left in position to do as he chose. To appreciate at its full value what occurred, and the methods by which he crushed out the competition of these smaller companies, the question of property, which is the root and meaning of the whole situation that has upbuilt itself in the Congo, must be understood.

Article 2 of the Ordinance of July 1, 1885, runs as follows:

"No one has the right to occupy without title the vacant lands, nor dispossess the natives of the land which they occupy; the vacant lands are to be regarded as belonging to the State."

This is no more than any state has the right to claim; but it is admitted that the law of the Free state has never defined what should be understood as "land occupied by the natives." Therefore, for want of this legal definition, the State has calmly assumed that such land comprises "only those parts of the territory that are included within their villages or under their cultivation." This limitation is significant, for since the greater part of the vast area of the Congo country has never been cultivated, this interpretation gives the State absolute and exclusive proprietary rights to nearly all the land. This State territory is called the *Domaine Privé*. It is divided into those sections controlled by the concessionaire companies, the areas in which the "free" black subjects of the king are taxed to provide the revenues necessary to maintain the administration, and the *Domaine de la Couronne*. Theoretically, therefore, it covers the entire area of the Congo territories above Leopoldville, with the exception of a few tracts of land, along certain rivers nominally open to trade, which are held by traders, such as the Lulonga Company, who have the right to exact a *titre d'im pôl*; with the exception also of a small portion of the lower Congo, where a meager business—not an Afro-European transaction, but a retail trade for local European consumption—is done to the tune of perhaps $1,000,000 per annum. This is worthy of remark, however, for the fact that it is the only trade, in the sense of value received for goods delivered, that is carried on in the Congo State. What passes as the Congo "trade" is extortion and plunder.

Formerly the State had allowed the natives living on this so-called "vacant land" to gather rubber and produce for sale to European merchants. But about 1890 the State evidently saw the folly of giving to others what it might keep for itself, and issued stringent regulations forbidding the natives to collect and sell, and the merchants to buy. In this it put forth the claim, just enough in the letter if not the spirit of the law, that it was merely exerting its rights as a landowner. This move had the effect of at once cramping the smaller traders beyond the point of discomfort. The next step put them out of business as independent concerns.

After the anti-slavery crusades of 1893, in which the whole world had applauded the king's self-sacrifice and benevolent intentions, and had complacently abandoned the reins to his humane hands, the custom was established of converting the king's native soldiery into State police, for the purpose of patrolling each new territory as it was subdued. The State's military officers thus became, by an entirely logical process, the State's commercial agents; and the State, through them, was brought into still closer competition with these private companies. Naturally, under the circumstances, this competition could end in but one way. For the king and the State were one, and it is not good business to compete with kings who let it be understood that their right is might. The natives who had supplied these private traders with ivory and rubber were forced to supply the State's agents instead. Some of the larger companies at first protested that this freezing-out process was contrary to the decree of the Act of Berlin, but their protests were useless. They were frozen out, or they were driven out by force; they were arrested, and at least one of them, Charles Henry Stokes, who had been guilty of the offense of selling weapons to the natives, was hanged. Finally, if they were strong enough to do so, they compromised, and entered into alliance with the State. The State assigned these companies certain sections of the *Domaine Privé,* granting them the right to work the land with forced native labor. In return the companies handed over fifty per cent. of their profits to the State. Thus was established the concessionaire system, which at once had the effect of letting loose the full tide of brutality and outrage from both State and companies' agents upon the helpless blacks.

That the companies made full use of their opportunities is proved by their profits. The most successful of these trusts, known as the A. B. I. R., made profits amounting to 18,004,172 francs, during the five years from 1898 to 1903, and paid dividends equal to 8,375 francs upon shares of which the nominal value was 500 francs. Thus, in five years, the profits of this one company have been more than eighteen times as large as the capital stock. In 1900 the profits amounted to 5,896,025 francs, or nearly six times the value of the capital stock. At that time the market value of the shares—of which Leopold owned one-half in the name of the Congo State—was 54,000,000 francs, or fifty-four times the original par value.

Of the *Domaine de la Couronne*—the lands of the Crown—which is included in the *Domaine Privé,* separate mention must be made.

Imagine a kingdom within a kingdom; the inmost heart of the richest and most fertile region of the rich and fertile Africa, hidden deep in inaccessible forests and trackless swamps; a land whose secrets are so jealously guarded, in order that its owner may enjoy its spoils undisturbed, that until the debate of

July, 1903, in the Belgian House, the world was unaware of its very existence; a land shrouded darkly in mystery, of which the tale will never be fully told. Somewhere in the back country it lies, another El Dorado, but only one white man who is not an agent either of the State or of the favored companies has ever been known to pass its boundaries. And it is here, in his hidden treasure-house, that the king coins blood and sweat into his private hoard of gold.

How much treasure he has torn from it in the ten years since he marked it for his own, is his secret, and his only. But one may guess at the amount, from the fact that it is the richest rubber-yielding district in the State, and that the reports of its depopulation show that it is being worked for all it is worth.

Professor Félicien Cattier, of the University of Brussels, after an exhaustive study of all the conditions involved, estimates the king's income at from seventy to eighty million francs. E. D. Morel goes further, and calls it one hundred million. He notes in this connection the fact that for the past ten years the estimated revenue from the *Domaine Privé*, amounted to only 114,356,630 francs, which are the proceeds of taxation in kind, viz., rubber, ivory, and copal; whereas, in that same period, rubber alone, amounting in value to a strict minimum of 360,107,200 francs, has been exported from the country.

The *Domaine de la Couronne* is apparently so organized that it reaps for its owner all the benefits and bears none of the burdens of the other portions of the territory. Such an administrative division of the State has been effected that the section previously mentioned as taxed for the support of the administration is forced to bear almost the entire burden of this support, while the revenue from the other sections, representing the profits of the enterprise, go directly into the pockets of the king. The finances have been so manipulated that while the concessionaire companies, which collect the revenues of the State, are making fabulous profits, and while the king is secretly drawing millions from the Congo for his private enterprises in Belgium, China, and the Riviera, *the State budget invariably shows a deficit.*

And Leopold has known how to make the Congo profitable in still other ways. Professor Cattier estimates that the king has obtained something like 161,000,000 francs from the various Congo loans contracted in recent years. The face value of these loans, which the Congo State or its successors will one day have to pay in full, amounts to 300,000,000 francs, or $60,000,000. Emil Vandervelde, referring to this matter in the parliamentary debate of February, 1906, says:

"What is particularly deplorable is that it seems that the money borrowed by the Congo State has not been utilized in its development. So far as any value can be attached to the yearly financial statements of the colony, the total deficit of the Congo has amounted to 27,000,000 francs only. Now 130,000,000 francs have been borrowed, in addition to the 31,000,000 loaned by Belgium. If we subtract this deficit of 27,000,000 from the 130,000,000 francs, there remain over 103,000,000 francs which seem to have been expended otherwise than in the Congo."

The "Trade" statistics of the State, recently published, show that in the last six years, from 1900 to 1905 inclusive, merchandise—eighty per cent. rubber—to the value of 307,455,927 francs has been exported, against imports to the value of 130,223,015 francs. The exports, therefore, exceeded the imports by 177,232,912 francs, showing that, if the trade figures of other West Coast colonies—where the imports are almost invariably in excess of the exports— are any criterion, Leopold, according to its own figures, is looting the country to the extent of about $6,000,000 a year. These figures gain added significance from the fact that of this merchandise imported, more than three-quarters consisted, not of goods for the benefit of the native producer, but of government material, stores, etc.

In effect, the king, since he has had a free hand in the Congo, has practically put the State in pawn. One curious result of his policy is that in capitalizing the Congo enterprise, and putting the stock of his concessionaire companies on the market, he has turned the present system into a vested interest, and has sold to presumably innocent investors the forced labor of the natives—has, in other words, used the machinery of commerce to create in Europe a property in slaves.

III

Look once again at the brown, oily river, rolling swollen and sullen between its banks; at the ragged clearings where the villages and plantations stood. But this time the picture has changed. There are steamers on the river; there are factories on the banks; there are towns and stations. And there is the civilization of the Philanthropist.

Jungle encroaching foot by foot upon the clearings, obliterating the plantations, closing over the crops; villages deserted, with empty houses and blackened fires; in place of teeming life, the silence of desolation. A whole fertile land violated and despoiled; a doomed land, crushed under conquest, overhung by the black cloud of despotic oppression, of misery unparalleled in the world's history today; a land from which blood and gold have been drained without mercy; a land of dying peoples.

This is the Congo Free State as Leopold, the Philanthropist, has made it.

One who has visited the Congo regions cannot fail to be impressed with the atmosphere of gloom and mystery that overhangs the dark land like the shadow of a pall—an atmosphere from which arise two widely differing effects. The first is subtle, intangible, yet indisputable—the almost inevitable influences of climate and environment upon the white man's temperament and character. Loneliness, homesickness, the overwhelming sense of exile; a gradual alteration of standards and ideals, often a loosening of moral fiber (which in the circumstances is not at all to be wondered at); physical debilitation—these go to make a factor which must be reckoned with. How much this factor has to do with the condition in the Congo is a problem; that it has to do with it, is very sure. The second effect is by intention. It is not to the interest of the State that its internal economy should be exposed to the white light of criticism. With admirable skill, therefore, the officials have turned to account this atmosphere of sinister mystery; have made of it a cloak of secrecy which conceals its commonest dealings with the outside world. Furtiveness and secrecy are in the air; a man entering the service of the State never knows what is before him until he has been initiated and pledged to the preservation of the "trade secrets." Many a young fellow of good instinct, reaching his post, and only then appreciating the full horrors of his duties, has begged piteously to be allowed to return—and has been refused.

In accordance with this policy of secrecy, the State has never explained why it is necessary to maintain a native standing army of 20,000 men, armed with repeating rifles; why the companies should have their own troops, at least 10,000 more—an armed force, this, larger than is maintained in the whole of their West African dominions by France, England, and Germany combined. Is it for the protection of the whites? Scarcely, since the total number of white men in the territories is barely 2,500. Yet there is a reason, and what it is the State itself betrays.

To understand the true significance of this, a glimpse at the system of government under which the State is run must be given.

In power supreme, of course, is the King-Sovereign, and the affairs of the State are directed from Brussels. The local government, in the hands of a governor general, is administered at Boma, the State capital, with territorial courts, a lower court, a court martial, and a court of appeals. Besides the judges of the bench there are a large number of officers of the judicial police, under the supervision of the State Attorney, with well-defined limitations of territory and authority. But the system, which looks well enough theoretically, fails in the practise for several reasons, chief among which are the facts that the number of the courts is far too limited for the vast extent of territory under their jurisdiction; that throughout the country at large administrative powers are vested, as a rule, in the District Commissioners, who usually have little knowledge of the law; and that the above-mentioned limitations of authority are more often honored in the breach than in the observance.

What, then, is the excuse and the occasion for such an army? It is there to force the collection of rubber by the natives. Formerly used to conquer the country, it is now used to coerce "trade."

A native army, thinly veneered with discipline and training, is at best an edged tool to handle. In this case, unlimited authority, the fact of never being called to account for his actions, the natural tendency of the savage to bully those weaker than himself, and the advantage of weapons, made of the black an ideal instrument of an inhuman policy of which, as E. D. Morel aptly says, "his officers, himself, and his fellow-natives are the victims in different degrees of suffering."

What are the methods of coercion that such an army would be likely to use? And what are the results of these methods? To these two questions the answer is a tale so horrible in some of its instances as to be unprintable. What may be told is this:

A certain amount of rubber, or copal, is demanded from a village within a certain time. It is brought by the blacks into the station, weighed, and, if found up to measure, paid for after this fashion:

PRODUCTION.
Per basket of pure rubber, worth $5.25.

PAYMENT.
1 Knife, worth 12 cents.

Six and one-half tons of gum copal, worth £364, or about $1,750, is levied yearly from a single village. In payment for his full year's work, each adult householder receives 31 cents. Again, another village, with a total population—including children—of 240 persons, is compelled to provide for the government one ton of carefully prepared foodstuffs *per week,* receiving in return a total sum of $3.80. More commonly, payment consists of a certain measure of salt and a yard or two of calico. And these are but isolated instances. Multiply them by ten thousand and you will still fall short of a realization of actual existing conditions.

Now, suppose the tale of rubber or copal is not complete. The offending village is raided by the soldiers. Men, women, and little children are either dragged away as "hostages," to be held until their fellow villagers have contrived to make up the deficiency, or are shot down like dogs, and their right hands cut off and turned over to the State as evidence of duty done. Cartridges cost money; and for every cartridge gone from a soldier's belt a hand must be produced.

(A framework of sticks under which a slow fire is burning; on this framework fourscore human hands—eighty severed hands, thin black hands with stiffened fingers, small, chubby, dimpled hands, slowly mummifying in the smoke—it makes a pleasing picture of civilization, does it not?)

The State claims that only dead bodies are mutilated by the cutting off of hands and by other methods more barbarous than this—and that it is a native custom, for the securing of trophies of warfare. But missionaries will tell of living people, maimed in ways beyond all healing; and missionaries and students alike bear witness that no study of native life has shown the slightest trace of any such "custom," which is solely one of the evidences of philanthropy and civilization.

The Rev. E. D. Sjöblom, of the American Baptist Missionary Union, who was one of the first to report these matters to Europe, tells of the finding of a

dead mother with her two children two or three days after one of these rubber raids, "The mother was shot and the right hand was taken off. On one
side was the elder child, also shot, and the right hand also taken off. On the
other side was the younger child, with its right hand cut off, but the child, still
living, was resting against the mother's breast."

E. J. Glave, who went to Africa first in 1883, as a member of the International Association, and again, independently, in 1894, has a horrible tale to tell
of the chaingangs of women, tied by the neck or ankles, held as hostages at
the stations at the mercy of native sentries until the village from which they
had been taken should bring their ransom in rubber or ivory; of the little,
homeless, fatherless, motherless children, most of them naked and covered
with ulcers and sores, many of them with a half-healed stump where the right
hand had been hacked away, herded together on the river-boat for transport
to the school colony near Leopoldville; of the flogging of men, women, and
children with *chicotte,* an instrument so terrible that "that a man who receives
one hundred blows is often nearly killed and has his spirit broken for life"; of
the degradation of village chiefs before their people in ways of devilish inge-
nuity and bestiality; of the lawless lust and violence of the black sentries.

But even these horrors pall—and the world has heard these tales before.
The more atrocious crimes, which cannot even be told in print, usually occur
in the back country where missionaries and travelers rarely penetrate, and are
made known only through accident.

Cannibalism exists, in spite of the dictum of the report of the Inquiry
Commission. Dr. Hinde has told that after one particularly murderous battle,
in which the fierce Botetela tribe of Congolese negroes had been used against
the Arabs, every member of these cannibal allies had at least one body to eat.

"All the meat was cooked and smoke-dried, and formed provisions for the
whole of the force and for all of the camp-followers, for many days afterward. . . ." Dr. Hinde presents a somewhat novel point of view: "During the
war in which we were now engaged for two years, we reaped, perhaps, the
only advantage that could be claimed for this disgusting custom. In the night
following a battle, or the storming of a town, these human wolves disposed of
all of the dead, leaving nothing even for the jackals, and thus saved us, no
doubt, from many an epidemic."

IV

To all the charges brought against it, the government answers that it is doing its best to eliminate the evils which are sapping the life of its colony. Are not, it asks, these evils to some extent inseparable from the early stages of any great colonizing enterprise? Was Rome built in a day? Would the world have the Congo run on the lines of a pink tea? Coercion is absolutely necessary, since, through the effects of climate and environment, the country is wholly dependent on native labor; if this labor is not voluntary, it must be forced.

If Leopold has hoodwinked the other nations, he has not deceived his own, which regards him with neither respect nor affection.

In his speech of July, 1903, in the Belgian House, Emil Vandervelde said:

"There is no doubt that the economic results of this régime have been very brilliant for the sovereign of the Congo State and for the companies of the *Domaine Privé,* but not for Belgium. Belgian trade in the Congo does not amount to even one per cent. of the general trade of Belgium."

Earlier criticism of the gross mismanagement and oppression in the State was met by flat denials; then by promises of inquiry—which came to nothing until the report of the Inquiry Commission in 1905. This latter, although in certain significant instances a marvel of diplomatic evasion of facts, of clever juggling with truth, does recognize and deplore the gravest abuses. But Leopold prepared himself well to hoodwink public opinion and offset criticism, by the establishment of a Press Bureau, on which he has spent millions for the purpose of showing to the world, through its medium, conditions as they should be, and not as they are.

To sum up, here are a few concrete facts which are worth remembering when the Congo State is named:

There is no trade in the Congo. There is, instead, forced production, extortion, and an organized system of plunder.

There has never been freedom; there is, and always has been under Leopold's rule, virtual and absolute slavery.

The supply of ivory is practically exhausted; in certain districts the yield of rubber has nearly ceased.

The land is being depopulated at the rate of 15,000,000 in twenty years; vast stretches of country are devastated; from these districts the natives who have escaped slaughter have fled into the depths of the forests, miserable, outcast, and hopeless.

Mutilaton, outrage, and degradations unspeakable, death by shooting, by starvation, by the lash, and by the halter, are visited by armed black soldiers, at the instigation of a handful of whites, upon unarmed and helpless natives, whose only crime is their inability to gratify promptly enough the lust and the rapacity of their masters.

And all this with the knowledge and the sanction of one man, the King-Sovereign, the Philanthropist!

How long will the nations permit this state of things to endure? Already there are faint stirrings of conscience, of a realization of responsibility. The growl of national disapproval rises; there are resolutions, and discussions, and cries of pity and shame.

Meanwhile, making the most of his opportunity, the Vampire sits sucking the lifeblood of the victim that has slowly ceased to struggle. By the time the powers have bestirred themselves to action, he, full-gorged, will fling the carcass at their feet and say:

"Take it—what is left is yours."

The Blood-Money of the Congo

You have looked into the inmost secret treasure-house of Leopold the King—Leopold, the Philanthropist of the Congo and of Belgium!—you have learned the methods whereby he has coined into gold the sweat and blood of a dying people; you have watched mutilated men and women staggering under baskets of rubber beneath the lash of his armed and brutal sentries; you have seen fourscore severed hands, the mummied hands of his living victims, impaled on stakes before a smoking fire as evidence from his agents of duty well performed. And now, inevitably, you ask:

"What does it all mean? What becomes of this vast wealth, wrung from a nation's agony? Who benefits by its outpouring? It comes to him, millions of dollars of it, every year; where does it go, and what does its owner do with it?"

Where does it go, this blood-stained Congo gold? Into the fairy palaces, the wonderful gardens of enchantment in which this grim old, gray old king delights. Into the collections of rare and priceless trees and shrubs and flowers that have made his conservatories at Laeken famous throughout Europe. Into the white hands of the women who, each for her brief hour, have ruled the Congo's lord—the Queens of the Congo, whose jewels are bought with human lives. Into all the far-reaching schemes of aggrandizement which a most marvelous combination of wiliness, political sagacity, and selfish ambition can devise, and limitless wealth and a diabolic ability in choosing the proper tools can execute. And, lastly, into the huge machine—his gigantic Press Bureau—which is all that maintains Leopold's good name before the

Robert E. Park, "The Blood-Money of the Congo," *Everybody's Magazine* XVI (January 1907), pp. 60–70.

world; a machine grinding tirelessly, night and day, that its owner may pose as the Philanthropist, and not be exposed as the Vampire.

Nothing reveals him as the modern business King so plainly as does this mechanism, which involves the most highly perfected business methods of the twentieth century. Consider this aged monarch's position: very well he knows how fragile is his hold on the Congo Free State, and that as the Powers entrusted it to him, so they can take it away. Very well indeed he knows what danger threatens; for, carefully guarded as are the dark secrets of the Congo, little by little they leak out in the stories of missionaries and travelers. But between Leopold and this danger is the intangible but mighty protection of his realization of the great force of public opinion and his mastery of the art of swaying it through the press, founded, as that art must always be, on a deep knowledge of human nature. He knows—no psychologist better—how judgment is suspended when a missionary's story of atrocities is balanced with a contradictory one. He knows what stories allay suspicion, what carry strongest conviction; knows what to suppress, what to emphasize.

See for yourself his great machine in operation:

When Professor Cattier's book, which was the first to reveal to Belgians the actual situation in the Congo State, was published in Brussels, the Press Bureau learned that several reviews of it were about to appear in French newspapers. At this time the recent Morocco Conference was taking place at Algeciras; the situation was critical, and France was anxious for the assistance of even so small a power as Belgium. Leopold, who, it is said, was at Beaulieu with his latest inamorata, Baroness Vaughn, sent instructions to the Belgian representative at Algeciras. Shortly afterward, so the story goes, the latter met the French plenipotentiary, and in the course of conversation stated that he had just come from the German minister, Baron Radowitz, who had expressed surprise at the unfriendly attitude toward the Congo State maintained by some French papers, and had added: "We in Germany judge you less severely." Mention was made of Mr. Cattier's book, and the evil consequences which might result in France from his criticisms; and it was hinted, gently, that if Belgium were compelled to choose, she might, in the end, feel it necessary to favor Germany against France. M. Revoil immediately cabled the gist of this conversation to the French Premier, M. Rouvier. The effect was instantaneous. M. Rouvier summoned the editors of certain newspapers and pointed out how matters stood. The reviews of Mr. Cattier's book were suppressed.

This story indicates but one phase of Leopold's scheme for misleading the public as to the true condition of affairs in the Congo Free State—the most stupendous system of advertising and hypocritical double-dealing that history can show, maintained at an enormous cost for the sole purpose of concealing the Crime of the Congo. This scheme was organized shortly before 1903, at the instigation of the King, by M. Dufourney and General Baron Wahis, Governor-General of the Congo Free State, as the "Federation for the

Defense of Belgian Interests Abroad." The undertaking would have been entirely legitimate, save for the fact that Belgium has no "interests abroad," since she owns not a foot of foreign soil. It was simply and solely the King's monopolization of the Congo that was to be defended. Belgium, as a nation, has no interest in the Congo, and does not care two straws about it.

The Federation prospered from its inception. A circular was sent to all Belgian Chambers of Commerce, to business, military, and professional men, urging them to uphold the King in the efforts to protect Belgium—and incidentally the Congo—from foreign interference. A few prominent men were quietly informed that they would be pleasing the King personally by allowing their names to appear on the circular. With this clear intimation that the King was behind it, therefore, countless industrial and business organizations— some of which have profited largely by the King's enterprise—enrolled themselves under the banner of the Federation.

At once, from the Central Offices of the latter, was issued a publication, in English, French, German, and Italian, entitled "The Truth About the Congo." This was sent, and is still sent, to every member of the French, English, Belgian, German, and Italian parliaments. The following extract from the first published circular of the Federation, in the light of subsequent events, is worth notice:

> Our sole weapon shall be truth. . . . Neither attacks upon foreign nations, nor mere idle polemics shall flow from our pen . . . It is to the reason of our readers that we shall appeal, and not to political passion. Our task will be performed, and we shall disappear, when the general mind of the public shall have become enlightened.

But the distribution of circulars was not enough. It was necessary to get in direct touch with the people themselves, as well as with their representatives. An ingenious system of press subsidies and press-cutting operations was therefore organized; a Press Bureau on a mammoth scale, doing business all over the world—a vast machine, created by and run for the benefit of one man, deliberately and cold-bloodedly planned to deceive those whom it professed to enlighten.

The Bureau is directed from its Central Office, Rue Pepiniere, No. 41, Brussels, and is supported by the revenues obtained from the Domaine de la Couronne. Its *modus operandi* is somewhat as follows, varying according to circumstances:

An article, perhaps descriptive of the Congo State, its railways, or its advance toward "civilization," is drafted in the Central Office, and submitted to the King's principal Congo secretaries, M. de Cuvelier or M. le Capitaine Liebrechts. Copies of it are then sent broadcast to all the newspapers that are subsidized or otherwise influenced by the Bureau, to the numerous European papers which deal with Colonial affairs, and to the American Sunday papers. Each copy is first translated into the language of the paper for which it is intended. In due time all this matter comes back to the Central Office in Brussels through the medium of the press-clipping bureaus. It is said that every such bureau in Europe and America is employed by Leopold. The clippings thus obtained are then used in the Federation's Bulletin as a genuine expression of the editorial opinion, and from them a periodical is made up, printed in three languages, in three parallel columns. Here the matter contained in the clippings is so rehashed as to show the virtue and benevolence of the King and the ignorant perversity of those who oppose him. This periodical is then sent out to libraries, to institutions of learning, to influential persons everywhere, and especially to members of parliament in the different countries where the Congo is likely to come up for discussion.

Books dealing with the Congo question are sent out through the medium of the Press Bureau. A notable instance is "The Story of the Congo State," by Wellington Wack, which has been especially prepared for the United States and is gradually finding its way into most of the negro mission-schools of the South, and from which the negroes are being taught that Leopold is a benefactor of their race. Copies of the works of this agent of the King are to be found not only in all large libraries, but in most of the smaller ones as well. Consequently, when interest is aroused in regard to the Congo, and a reader goes to a library to consult an authority, he will always find a representative of the Press Bureau, so to speak, on guard. These books, and others like them, are splendidly advertised by the Press Bureau, and translations of them are sent all over the world.

Another book published and for a time widely circulated is a translation of the famous Report of the Commission of Inquiry of 1905. In the translation, this report has been softened and in certain parts deliberately falsified, but even as it stands is a terrrible indictment of the Congo State. An account of what the Press Bureau did with this report in England is interesting—and highly suggestive.

A copy of the *Bulletin Officiel* of the Congo State was sent to the English papers by the "West African Missionary Association." It contained, in the vernacular, this Report of the Commission of Inquiry, and with it was what professed to be an epitome of the contents in English—"an accurate summarized version." Subsequent examination showed that this epitome had been first drawn up in French and then translated from French into English. It was most carefully compiled, and was even more mild than the very mild indictment of the Commission. Thus emasculated, the report had been given by the Brussels Press Bureau to a Roman Catholic priest, the head of a religious order to which King Leopold has been particularly generous; had been brought by him to England and distributed to the press as coming through the "West African Missionary Association." No such associaton is in existence. The majority of the papers published the convenient "translation"; but the London *Daily Chronicle,* instead of using the latter, translated the original document for itself, and thereby exposed the whole plot. The mischief, however, had been done; and English readers in general were left with a very inadequate idea of the Commission's report.

But the efforts of the Brussels Bureau to make use of the English press have not, in most cases, met with marked success. Nearly all the London and provincial editors have been approached, directly or indirectly; their offices have been flooded not only with the matter issued by the Federation and with articles sent out by the Press Bureau, but also with libelous communications directed against the reformers, and especially against Mr. Morel, who by his exposures of the true situation in the Congo has brought upon himself the implacable hatred of the "Congo crowd." The attitude of the *Times* alone has given rise to unfavorable comment. The fact that its Brussels correspondent is on friendly terms with King Leopold, together, possibly, with political reasons, may account to some extent for the benevolent neutrality observed by the *Times* toward Leopold and his works.

Leopold's right-hand man in England is Sir Alfred Jones, the president of the Liverpool Chamber of Commerce, consul of the Congo Free State at Liverpool, and partner of the King in the Cie Belgie Maritime du Congo, which is the ocean carrier for the Congo State. He has served the King well—but then his contract with the Congo State at the present time nets him annually, it is said, between $200,000 and $250,000. When Consul Casement's startling report of conditions in the Congo was received by the English Government, Sir Alfred was instructed to bring pressure to bear upon Lord Lansdowne to prevent its publication. Leopold added a warning in the shape of a scarcely veiled hint that public opinion in Belgium would be so incensed at the report that it would be impossible to continue the carrying contract with a British steamship company. But Lord Lansdowne was immovable and the report was published. Thereupon Leopold started off on his famous pilgrimage to the Courts of Europe, seeking to counteract the impression which the report could not fail to make.

Chief among Leopold's enemies are the missionaries. The various schemes by which he has sought to render their stories ineffective, and has made them serve his purposes, evidence of almost incredible wiliness. For instance, by clever juggling he made it appear at one time that the English agitation for Congo reform was an anti-Catholic movement; hence Roman Catholicism was invited to attack it. An arrangement made with the Vatican twenty years ago that the Congo field should be reserved chiefly for the Belgian orders, was proof sufficient of his farsightedness, for it made control of these orders, as Belgian subjects, comparatively easy. The wisdom of this precaution was proved when the atrocities perpetrated in the Congo were openly denounced by the Protestant missionaries, and the Roman Catholic press came promptly to Leopold's support. Since that time, however, the Catholic world has come to understand Leopold's nefarious schemes and has turned against him.

Another instance shows the English Baptist Missionary Society victimized. In January, 1903, after the world had commenced to concern itself with

Congo abuses, Leopold succeeded in persuading representatives of this society to cross the channel and read an address thanking him for the protection he had given their work in the lower section of the Free State. He received them with all the formality and ceremony befitting an embassy from a foreign Power. Of course the Press Bureau heralded this event to the ends of the earth, and the English Baptist Missionary Society found itself in the position of having given public indorsement to that it has since learned to regard as an intolerable iniquity.

Early in his campaign of defense, Leopold realized the necessity of operations in the United States, where official action is easily controlled by public opinion. Accordingly, in 1902 came one James Gustavus Whiteley, an American and the present Consul-General of the Congo at Baltimore, to be Leopold's first press agent in America. When in 1904 it was proposed to discuss at the peace Congress at Boston the international status of the Congo State, Mr. Whiteley was given the official title of the Congo Consul. It was said that he was appointed "to promote good relations between the United States and the Congo," there being absolutely no trade between the two countries to serve as excuse for his official being.

To resist the effort to have the subject of the Congo presented to the Peace Congress, Leopold sent a personal embassy. It was on this occasion that August Belmont, who, with the Rothschilds, had given the King's Press Bureau a somewhat perfunctory support, wrote a personal letter to certain New York newspapers, asking them to suspend judgment until the King's representatives arrived with "The Truth About the Congo," which they were bringing by freight.

The personal embassy consisted of Mr. George Head, Dr. Sarolea, and Professor Nerincx. Mr. Head, who worked through lectures on the Congo, secured a room in Tremont Temple, where the Peace Congress was held, on the day when the Congo was discussed, and, with a cleverness worthy of his employer, he contrived to make his lectures appear merely a continuation of the sesssions of the Peace Congress. Both he and Professor Nerincx remained here, endeavoring by lectures and other means to convince the American public that no matter what might be the actual conditions in the Congo, none of the Powers, and least of all the United States, has the right to interfere.

In addition to these means of protecting his interests, and to his manipulation of the press, Leopold has for two years made the Belgian embassy in Washington little less than his Congo lobby; and the Belgian minister, Baron Moncheur, has, in public and in private, devoted himself unremittingly to the King's personal enterprise in Africa.

To the credit of the American press and people, it may be said that all these efforts have not met with much more of success here than in England, though an amazing amount of confusion has been created in the public mind of both countries—and confusion serves Leopold's interests only second to corruption. In addition, now that American interest in the Congo has risen to a point that might well cause its autocrat fresh alarm, he has fortified himself by conceding 8,400,000 acres of the richest rubber country in the world to a French-American-English company whose American head is that astute financier, Thomas F. Ryan. Upon this powerful ally Leopold depends to prevent the consideration of the Congo situation in the coming Congress.

In 1898 Leopold secured the adoption of his own colonial policy in the neighboring French possession, a territory some 600,000 square miles in extent, known as the *Congo français*. His object in this was clear enough. It has been explained that in the Congo controversy the main issue has been the claim of Leopold and his personal friends to the absolute ownership of the soil, the produce of the soil, and the labor of the peoples of Central Africa. If one of the great Powers also having possessions in the Congo could be induced to put forward the same claims of ownership, it was obvious that Leopold would find himself in a much stronger position at the final day of reckoning, since he could say: "You also are being attacked—we must make common cause against our common critics."

Thanks to the influence of the Chief of the French Colonial Party, M. Eugène Etienne, the Minister for War in the present French cabinet, Leopold gained his ends. The territory of the *Congo français* was parcelled out, into forty-four concessionaire companies, which were given absolute ownership of the land and the natives. Although floated as French concerns, these companies, with very few exceptions, were financed and controlled from Belgium. The combined results of the wiliness of Leopold and the shortsightedness of the French have been extraordinary. The French Congo has been handed over to the mercy of the King's adherents, who have secured for thirty years the right to pillage the enormous areas conceded to them. In thirty years' time the French Congo will be ruined for generations. France is getting absolutely nothing for her share of the bargain save a slight increase of revenue from the export duty on the increased quantities of rubber which are going out of the country—and this revenue, for the most part, is absorbed in the military expenditure required to suppress the perpetually recurrent native outbreaks. The rubber exported from the country does not even pass through French hands or give employment to French artisans. Ninety-nine per cent. of it is shipped to Antwerp, and is disposed of in that port. The shares of these Concessions are not even quoted on the Paris Bourse and are never mentioned in the French financial papers. On the other hand, the Antwerp Bourse and the financial organs of Brussels and Antwerp deal in them largely.

The French press has maintained silence not only in regard to the atrocities in the Congo State, but also in regard to those which followed the adoption of the concessionaire system in the French Congo. Reports of an appalling nature poured in to successive colonial ministers, and were suppressed. Several Paris papers got hold of them, and were either ordered to keep silence or were bribed to do so. At length the truth could no longer be kept back. The result last year, as all the world knows, was a series of frightful disclosures.

But through corruption, peculation, and bribery, the evils have been permitted to go on unchecked.

In Italy the situation is somewhat different. Here, in addition to subsidizing the press, Leopold has made use of the Italian army as a tool for his own interests. By inducing Italy to lend him enough of her officers to command his African army, he has been enabled to say, when the exploits of that army were denounced in England: "Observe these outrageous attacks upon the honor of your officers. My cause, through them, is your cause; we must stand together."

All this has been changed, however, within the last few months. The reports of Italian officers as to the duties assigned them in the Congo State, their resignations, and their protests, have led to fierce debates in the House, and to the revolt of the more reputable organs of public opinion against Leopold and his gold. The charges of attempts to poison him, brought by Captain Baccari, envoy from the King of Italy to the Congo, have also contributed to arouse public sentiment. Yielding therefore to pressure, Italy has determined that no more of her officers shall be permitted to go to the Congo. Within the coming year the last of the Italian officers will have left their Congo stations, and Italy will have washed her hands of the King of the Congo and his works.

This is the machine, huge, and grinding tirelessly night and day, of which the wheels are oiled by blood and the motive power is that endless stream of Congo gold. What it costs him—surely an appalling sum—is the King's secret, and his alone. He must have many secrets, the Philanthropist!

And the rest of the Congo blood-money?

Into the palaces, the chateaux, the gardens which Leopold is forever constructing or laying out, goes a steady stream of his Congo gold. At Brussels, Ostend, Villefranche, Cape Ferrat—wherever he has made his residence, he has been constantly engaged in remodeling and changing. He has spent 30,000,000 francs in rebuilding and embellishing his palace at Laeken, which in 1890 was burned almost to the ground. This palace is the most luxurious royal residence on the Continent, and the plans of its present form were drawn up by the king himself. Some of the priceless treasures which were destroyed during the fire can never, of course, be replaced—for instance, the Gobelin tapestries, worth several million francs, which were sent by Marie Antoinette of France to her sister, the Archduchess Marie Christian. Its collections of porcelains, statuary, miniatures, and portraits are famous throughout Europe. Here is kept the gold and silver plate which, it is said, not even the collection at Windsor can surpass in beauty and costliness. At state banquets the courses are served alternately upon gold and silver.

In order that the king may come and go quietly, as he wills, there has been constructed a tunnel, connecting the railway with the palace, by means of which his Majesty is enabled to step from the house into his private car. It was built at a cost of 3,000,000 francs by the Belgian State, which owns the railways, as a personal favor to the king. In return, when the Belgian House refused to vote the necessary sum for the erection of an arch to commemorate the independence of Belgium, Leopold subscribed 5,000,000 francs.

These silent flittings of the king, to which he is greatly given, have at times been found inconvenient by his ministers, who have supposed their sovereign hard at work in his study until his whereabouts were reported in some remote corner of the world. It is told that once, when his ministers had found themselves unable to gain access to him, they were suddenly astounded by reading a press account of the arrival in the Mediterranean of the royal yacht, with the king and his three daughters on board. Glowing descriptions followed of their public reception at the various ports at which they touched. As the three princesses were at home in the palace at the time, the affair, in the light of the king's well-known proclivities for unconventional amusements, took on a sufficiently lurid hue. To prevent scandal more than usually flagrant, the princesses shut themselves up in the palace, where they remained until their father saw fit to appear again, as quietly and unexpectedly as he had vanished. The "daughters" in the case were three actresses whose names were bywords on the boulevards of Paris.

One of the more innocent extravagances of the king is a hobby for collecting rare plants and flowers from all parts of the world. The glass houses at Laeken are famous all over Europe. In the midst of these conservatories stands one of the most unique churches in existence. It is circular in form, topped by a dome of glass which is supported by twenty granite columns. In the spaces between these columns stand statues of the twelve apostles. Strange flowers bloom here, making splashes of vivid color amid the gleaming of gold and silver candlesticks and sacred vessels; growing palms embower the plain stone altar, and from the heart of the greenery above it flames a great electric cross. Vines festoon the carven gallery of the choir; mingled with the breath of incense is the heavy perfume of exotics. Birds fly from branch to branch above the heads of worshipers, flitting in and out among the shrines of painted saints.

Where the king got his fondness for collecting Japanese pagodas no one seems to know. But collect them he does, in all materials, bronze, porcelain, gold, ebony, ivory, and silver, in all sizes, from miniature creations of the beautiful Japanese art to the great structure which stands in the park at Laeken. This is the celebrated Japanese tower, pagoda-shaped, and hung with electric globes, which cost the king two million francs. Rumor has it that this fantastic structure is an extravagance of luxury, filled with rare and precious things, curios, and objects of art from the four corners of the earth, from which no one derives the smallest benefit save the king himself. For no one enters here without Leopold's express permission—and this mandate applies, brusquely and specifically, to "women, photographers, and newspaper men."

Other estates and extravagances has Leopold, to absorb still more of the gold which comes to him so easily—his villa at Ville-franche, overlooking the

Mediterranean with its wonderful landscape gardens and also—in illustration of the practical temper of its owner—a vast kitchen garden, laid out under the personal superintendence of the king, where he raises his own vegetables to supply his table. Until recently he was principal owner of the great gambling establishments at Ostend and Spa. It was said that he intended the former to outrival in magnificence even Monte Carlo. Five million dollars have lately been spent in Ostend, on improvements of the grounds and buildings.

At Cape Ferrat Leopold is building a sanitarium for those of his Congo employees who become invalided in the service. At the Park of Tervueren, just outside Brussels, he has also under way a vast Congo museum, which, when completed, will cost 30,000,000 francs.

Ever on the alert for new sensations, Leopold has taken up with avidity each new fad as it has come into fashion. He rides; he used to bicycle; he motors; and among his machines he has an immense touring automobile, containing a bedroom and a kitchen, exquisitely appointed.

One must admit that the maintenance of a private press bureau and the passion for building palaces, museums, and gambling hells on a grandiose scale are expensive tastes. Yet Leopold by no means confines himself to these. Yearly he spends untold thousands upon the women of the half-world who chance to please his fancy—the Queens of the Congo, whose jewels are bought with human lives.

There was an obscure little Parisienne, a ballet-dancer, slender, dark-eyed, with the face of a Madonna—called Cléo de Merode. Upon a night Leopold saw her from his box—and made her the talk of two continents. She was only a little white rat of the theatre, demure, with dark hair drawn low over her ears, and a pale beauty of which she was fully aware; but he made her the queen of the glittering tinsel world of Paris. He paved the way for more magnificent gifts by a trifle in the shape of a pearl necklace worth $100,000. Such jewels, such furs, such flowers, such equipages, were lavished upon the little danseuse, with her Perugino eyes and her Botticelli hair, that even Paris, the *mondaine,* was forced to sit up and gasp.

There was Madame d'Esteffe, on whom a caustic-tipped French pen first fastened the title of Queen of the Congo. For this reason:

Madame had set her heart upon a particularly valuable diamond necklace, but at that time the Congo was not the paying venture it has since become. One day she mentioned to the king a suggestion made to her by certain Congo adventurers. This was that the king should capitalize his rights to collect tribute from the natives, and in this way obtain the money necessary for carrying on the exploitation of the Congo on a grand scale. It is to be hoped that she had no notion to what her suggestion might lead, for this was the origin of that Concessionaire system which has wrought such havoc in the heart of Africa. Thus, it is added, Madame got her diamonds, and Leopold, his idea.

Lastly, there is the reigning favorite, "Baroness Vaughn"—daughter of a janitor at Budapest, sister of a fruit-seller of Paris—clear-eyed, fair-faced, with masses of chestnut hair. She is known as the king's "morganatic wife."

Royalty is badly handicapped in its amours, as well as in its *affaires du cœur,* since it is ever under the magnifying glass of public opinion. But making all allowance possible, the fact remains that the scandals attached to Leopold's name have added nothing to his popularity. Even among his royal confrères this holds good. Queen Victoria especially detested him, and never received him save when she could not help it, and then only officially.

Were it not for his treatment of his family, one might feel a vagrant pity for him, restless, selfish, and cynical as he is, for it is written that he shall possess nothing but what his gold may buy him. With all his palaces, he has no home; with all his adventures, he has never had a romance.

The Queen of Belgium died deserted and alone, so far as husband and children were concerned. Once she left him, unable to endure longer his insults and neglect, and returned to him unwillingly, only after long persuasion by friends and ministers, who pleaded for "the good of the state." Once she attempted suicide. Of his daughters, two are notorious—Louise, wife of Prince Leopold of Saxe-Coburg, and Stephanie, who married Crown Prince Rudolph of Austria-Hungary—the third and youngest, Clémentine, is a victim of moping melancholia, whose chief longing in life is to take the veil and escape from what she cannot remedy.

There is not a public man in Europe who has shown himself more indifferent to his personal reputation than has Leopold. In his relations with his wife and children as well as with his mistresses he has evidenced the same callous and contemptuous disregard of public opinion. He made away with every florin of his wife's dowry. He refused to be reconciled to his daughters at the time of their mother's death, and even refused them permission to visit her dead body at Spa, or to take part with him in the funeral ceremonies.

Few people know that this hard-headed man of many businesses is troubled by a superstition. He and his daughters have a superstitious dread of the last two weeks in January. During that period nearly all the misfortunes of his life, by an odd coincidence, have overtaken him. While still Duke of Brabant, before his accession to Belgium's throne, he lost his only son, who died after a mysteriously sudden illness. Crown Prince Rudolph of Austria, the king's son-in-law, met his violent and mysterious death in the hunting lodge at Meyerling, in the latter part of the king's month of fate. In January, 1890, the palace at Laeken burned, and Princess Clémentine, who barely escaped with her life, was so overwrought by the sight of her governess perishing in the flames that for many months it was feared she would lose her reason in precisely the same manner in which Leopold's only sister, the ex-Empress Carlotta, lost hers. The latter's definite insanity also, curiously enough, dates from January.

This, then, is Leopold, financier, and roué, but never philanthropist, not as he would show himself to the world, but as the world is beginning to see him. What has he done for Belgium? Given her a few public buildings, for which she pays, since they are the property of the state, and of which he receives the use and benefit, minus the expense; promised her future gifts when he himself shall have finished with them.

What part is Belgium getting in the king's Congo wealth? No part at all. It goes, as we have seen, into the press bureau which proclaims his virtue to a credulous world; into his private enterprises, into the hands of courtesans and favorites. That is all. The power he has built up is the power of Leopold, not the power of Belgium. He has not scrupled to hoodwink and blind her as shamelessly as he has deceived the world.

Not in the interests of the state nor of civilization has he pushed his gigantic schemes, for these mean nothing to him. What will happen to them when he is through he neither knows nor cares. He has played his game well, the Hypocrite. But the cloak is being stripped from him; he stands forth a king without honor, despised, sneered at. What will the world do with him, now that it sees him as he is? That is a question which the world alone can answer. But, if the Congo's blood is not to stain still another page of history, the question must be answered soon.

The Yellow Press

There is a popular notion that a newspaper is something that is printed merely; that, once off the press the newspaper, like a brick, is a completed and marketable product. This, as newspapermen well know, is a mistake. It is not enough to edit a paper and print it. It is equally important that it should be circulated and read. A paper that is printed but does not circulate is, in fact, not a newspaper at all. It must have revenue to make it independent; and must have readers to make it influential. Circulation is a measure of both. The necessity of getting and keeping a circulation has very largely determined the character of the newspaper as it exists in America today. The struggle for existence has been a struggle for circulation.

The type of newspaper that exists is the type that has survived. The men who may be said to have made the modern newspaper—James Gordon Bennett, Charles A. Dana, Joseph Pulitzer, and William Randolph Hearst— are the men who, after they had discovered the kind of paper that men and women would read, had the courage to publish it.

The daily newspaper is an urban institution. Reading, which was a luxury in the country, has become a necessity in the city. This is true, in part, because city people—who live in tenements or in apartment houses or in hotels—have, generally speaking, no neighbors. In such a world it is almost as necessary to be able to read a newspaper as it is to speak the language. How else can one know what is going on in this vastly complicated life of the city? Newspapers and newspaper circulation have inevitably grown with the growth of cities. For that reason newspapers circulate more widely in cities,

Robert E. Park, "The Yellow Press," *Sociology and Social Research* XII: 1 (September 1927), pp. 3–11.

and particularly in great cities than they do in small towns and in rural communities. In Chicago, for example, there are 91 papers, published and circulated every day for every one hundred of the population. Outside of the city, the proportion is 19 newspapers circulated for every one hundred of the population.

One other thing that explains the extraordinarily wide circulation of the American newspaper is the extraordinary success of American editors and reporters in writing the news. American newspapers are notoriously easy to read. If there are more newspapers read in America, in proportion to the population, than in any other country in the world, it is because newspaper men in America have been more able and willing, than newspaper men elsewhere, to address themselves to the average man, rather than to the intelligentzia [sic].

The ordinary man, we are told, thinks in concrete images. He gets his ideas in the form of anecdotes and pictures and parables. he finds it difficult and tiresome to read a long article, unless it is dramatized, and takes the form men call a "story." Everything in the American newspaper is a story. "News story" and "fiction story" are two forms of modern literature that are now so much alike that it is sometimes difficult to distinguish them.

The *Saturday Evening Post*, for example, writes news in the form of fiction, while the daily press writes fiction in the form of news. When it is not possible to present ideas in the dramatic form of a story, the ordinary reader likes them stated in a short paragraph.

It is said that James E. Scripps founded the *Detroit News*, one of the most successful afternoon papers in the United States, on the very simple psychological principle that the ordinary man will read a newspaper item in the inverse ratio to its length. Mr. Scripps' method of measuring the efficiency of his newspapers, therefore, was to count the number of items that they contained. The paper that had the largest number of items was the best paper. This is just the reverse of Mr. Hearst's methods. His papers have fewer items but they have more pictures. The fundamental principle upon which both types of paper are conducted is the same. Both have succeeded by making the newspaper easy to read.

In their efforts to make the newspaper readable to the least-instructed reader, to find in the daily news material that would thrill the crudest intelligence, publishers have made one important discovery. They have found that the difference between the highbrow and the lowbrow, which once seemed so profound, is largely a difference in vocabularies. I can illustrate the point by a story. My friend Alexander Johnson is a particularly successful public speaker. He talks to all sorts of people and enjoys it. He had made a particularly successful speech one day to the congregation of an immigrant church. The priest asked how it was that he was able to speak so readily and intelligibly to an audience that was strange to him and more or less strange to the language that he used. "Well, I'll tell you," he said. "I used to be the head of an institution for the feeble-minded. It was part of my duty every Sunday to speak to them. I have found that if you can speak to the feeble-minded, you can speak to any one."

This is just the discovery that the American newspaper has made. The writers for the newspaper found that if they could make themselves intelligible to the common man, it was even less difficult to make themselves understood by the intellectuals. The character of the present-day newspaper in America has been profoundly influenced by this fact.

Now the newspapers that have done the most to increase the number of newspaper readers in this country have been undoubtedly the so-called yellow press. Long before the yellow press had arrived upon the scene, the newspaper men had begun to experiment and make discoveries concerning the idiosyncracies of the popular mind. They discovered, for one big thing, that the average man is a good deal more interested in news than in opinion, that he would a good deal rather read about a dog fight in Podunk than an earthquake in Peru. Horace Greeley had a keen sense of what the public wanted, in the way of news. This is evident from a letter he once write [*sic*] to a young man who was about to start a country newspaper. This is what he wrote:

> Begin with a clear conception that the subject of deepest interest to an average human being is himself; next to that, he is most concerned about his neighbors. Asia and the Tongo Islands stand a long way after these in his regard. It does seem to me that most country journals are oblivious as to these vital truths. If you will, so soon as may be, secure a wide-awake, judicious correspondent in each village and township of your country, some young lawyer, doctor, clerk in a store, or assistant in a post office will probably send you whatever of moment occurs in his vicinity, and will make up at least half of your journal of local matter thus collected, nobody in the county can long do without it. Do not let a new church be organized, or new members be added to one already existing, a farm be sold, a new house be raised, a mill be set in motion, a store be opened, nor anything of interest to a dozen families occur, without having the fact duly though briefly chronicled in your columns. If a farmer cuts a big tree, or grows a mammoth beet, or harvests a bounteous yield of wheat or corn, set forth the fact as concisely and unexceptionally as possible.

Horace Greeley knew what news was. But he belonged to an older and different tradition than that represented by the modern newspapers. He published a journal of opinion, and he was one of the last of the great editors whose opinions counted. The modern newspaper which finally blossomed into the yellow journal had a different and a humbler origin. In 1833, Benjamin Day, with a few associates, started a paper as he put it, "for mechanics and the masses generally." The price of this paper was one cent. But the publisher expected to make up by larger circulation, and by advertising, the loss sustained by the lower price.

At that time the other New York papers were selling for six cents each.

Their circulations were limited, but they were respectable. The new penny paper, the *New York Sun*, was less respectable, but it soon gained a much wider circulation, "among the mechanics and the masses generally." Of course it succeeded, not merely because of its cheaper price, but because it printed more police news and less politics, than any of its rivals.

The old time journalists were inclined to have a contempt for news, unless it was political news. In any case, news was regarded by them simply as material upon which to base editorials. I think it was Charles A. Dana who once said that he was willing to print in his paper "anything that God would let happen." But the old time journalists felt a responsibility to their readers that the later newspapers have not shared. If God let things happen that were not in accordance with the conceptions of the fitness of things, they simply suppressed them. They refused to take the responsibility of letting their readers learn about things that they knew ought not to have happened.

The old time journalist, so far from addressing himself to the average man, was distinctly distrustful of the masses. Manton Marble, who was editor of the *New York World* before Joseph Pulitzer took it over, used to say that there were not 18,000 people in New York City to whom a well-conducted newspaper could afford to address itself. If the circulation of his paper went above that figure, he was sure there must be something wrong with it. Before Mr. Pulitzer took it over, the circulation had actually sunk to 15,000. The old *New York World* conserved the type of the old, conservative paper down to the 80's. By that time, in all the larger cities, the independent newspapers, the papers which emphasized news rather than politics, had completely supplanted the older journals of opinion. This change was largely due to the enterprise of James Gordon Bennett, founder of the *New York Herald*. Bennett, following the example of Day, of the *Sun*, set the pace for the new form of journalism.

In fact, as Will Irwin says in the only adequate account that has ever been written of the American newspaper, "James Gordon Bennett invented news as we know it." Bennett, like some others who have contributed most to modern journalism, was a disillusioned man, and for that very reason, perhaps, a ruthless and cynical one. "I renounce all so-called principles," he said in his announcement of the new enterprise. By principles he meant, perhaps, editorial policies. His salutatory was at the same time a valedictory. In announcing the purposes of the new journalism he bade adieu to the aims and aspirations of the old. Henceforth the editors were to be news gatherers and the newspaper staked its future on its ability to gather, print, and circulate news.

Up to the last quarter of the nineteenth century, that is to say, up to about 1880, most newspapers, even in our large cities, were conducted on the theory that the best news a paper could print was a death notice or a marriage announcement.

Up to that time the newspapers had not yet begun to break into the tenements, and most people who supported a newspaper lived in homes rather than in apartments. The telephone had not yet come into popular use; the automobile was unheard of; the city was still a mosaic of little neighborhoods, like our foreign-language communities of the present; neighborhoods, in which the city dweller still maintained something of the provincialism of the small town.

Great changes, however, were impending. The independent press was already driving the old-time newspaper to the wall. There were more newspapers than either the public or the advertisers were willing to support. It was at this time and under these circumstances that newspaper men discovered that circulation could be greatly increased by making literature out of the news. Charles A. Dana had already done this in the *Sun,* but there still was a large section of the population for whom the clever writing of Mr. Dana's young man was caviar.

The Yellow Press grew up in an attempt to capture for the newspaper a public whose only literature was the family story paper or the cheap novel. The problem was to write the news in such a way that it would appeal to the fundamental passions. The formula was: "love and romance for the women; sport and politics for the men."

The effect of the application of this formula was to increase enormously the circulation of the newspapers, not only in the great cities, but all over the country. These changes were brought about mainly under the leadership of two men, Joseph Pulitzer and William Randolph Hearst.

Pulitzer had discovered, while he was editor of the *St. Louis Post Dispatch,* that the way to fight popular causes was not to advocate them on the editorial page but to advertise them in the news columns. It was Pulitzer who invented muck-raking. It was this kind of journalism which enabled Pulitzer, within a period of six years, to convert the old *New York World,* which was dying of inanition when he took it, into the most talked about, if not the most widely circulated paper in New York City.

Meanwhile, out in San Francisco, Mr. Hearst had succeeded in galvanizing the old moribund *Examiner* into new life, making it the most widely read newspaper on the Pacific Coast.

It was under Mr. Hearst that the "sob sister" came into vogue. This is her story, as Will Irwin told it in Collier's, February 18, 1911:

> Chamberlain (managing editor of the *Examiner*) conceived the idea that the city hospital was badly managed. He picked a little slip of a girl from among his cub reporters and assigned her to the investigation. She invented her own method; she "fainted" on the street, and was carried to the hospital for treatment. She turned out a story "with a sob for the unfortunate in every line." That was the professional beginning of "Annie Laurie" or Winifred Black, and of a departure in newspaper writing. For she came to have many imitators, but none other could ever so well stir up the primitive emotions of sympathy and pity; she was a "sob squad" all by herself. Indeed, in the discovery of this sympathetic "woman writing," Hearst broke through the crust into the thing he was after.

With the experience he had gained on the *Examiner* in San Francisco, and with a large fortune that he had inherited from his father, Hearst invaded New York in 1896. It was not until he reached New York and started out to make the *New York Journal* the most widely read paper in the United States that yellow journalism reached the limit.

Pulitzer's principal contribution to yellow journalism was muck-raking, Hearst's was mainly "jazz." The newspaper had been conducted up to this time upon the theory that its business was to instruct. Hearst rejected that conception. His appeal was frankly not to the intellect but to the heart. The newspaper was for him first and last a form of entertainment.

It was in the Sunday newspaper that the methods of yellow journalism were first completely worked out. The men chiefly responsible for them were Morrill Goddard and Arthur Brisbane. It was Goddard's ambition to make a paper that a man would buy even if he could not read it. He went in for pictures, first in black and white, and then in colors. It was in the *Sunday World* that the first seven-column cut was printed. Then followed the comic section and all the other devices with which we are familiar, for compelling a dull-minded and reluctant public to read.

After these methods had been worked out in the Sunday paper, they were introduced into the daily. The final triumph of the yellow journal was Brisbane's so-called "Heart-to-Heart Editorials." The art of the thing consisted in telling in the simplest language possible—and with the aid of diagrams and pictures—what everyone had always known. Nowhere has Herbert Spencer's maxim, that the art of writing is economy of attention, been so completely realized.

The yellow press, in the sense that the term was used in the early 90's, no longer exists. It has passed into history. Not that the press has not retained all, or most all of the characteristics which it acquired in that dazzling period of newspaper enterprise and innovation, but these innovations no longer dazzle nor bewilder us.

Looking back upon it now, we can see that whatever else it was responsible for, the yellow press did make reading easy and popular. It did bring within the circle of a single public a larger number of people and a wider range of interests and intelligence than any other type of newspaper has ever done before. The circulation of newspapers between 1880 and 1890, when the yellow press was in its first bloom, increased 135.2 per cent. In the period from 1880 to 1921 the total circulation of newspapers in the United States increased from 3,566,395 to 33,741,742.

That, in brief, is the story of the Yellow Press. All that I need to add is this: The yellow press, as a form of literature, was at least democratic.

The Black American—
Fifty Years after Emancipation

A City of Racial Peace

Situated a little off the steel highway that connects Washington and Atlanta, Winston-Salem is a bustling little town of perhaps fifteen thousand or twenty thousand inhabitants and one of the most prosperous manufacturing towns in the South. Fourteen years ago a young colored man, who had been a teacher in Livingston College, North Carolina, and was at the time principal of the graded school of Winston, determined to move out of the city and establish himself on a piece of ground outside its limits. He chose a position on a hill, divided from the city by a broad and deep ravine across which a railway has flung a high embankment, where land was cheap and the view unobstructed. Here he built himself a house and invited other colored men who wanted homes of their own and appreciated the view to join him. Later he founded, with what means he had at hand, an industrial school, still tramping twice daily across the ravine to his school in the city and back.

The industrial school added a new attraction to the settlement on the hill, and soon "Columbia Heights," as it was called, presented the appearance of a respectable negro village. Meanwhile the school had grown so large that its founder was able to give up his position in Winston and devote all his time to it. That was the origin of the Slater Industrial and State Normal School, which has gone steadily forward since that time, making friends first in Winston-Salem, then in the state at large, and in the North, until it is now so fully on its feet that its founder, Professor S. G. Atkins, though still nominally its president, has felt justified in taking up a larger work that was offered to him as secretary of the educational department of the A.M.E. Zion Church.

Robert E. Park, "A City of Racial Peace," *The World To-Day* IX (August 1905), pp. 897–99.

Meanwhile the settlement has grown to a village of forty houses, mostly owned by the men who live in them. A hospital, fully equipped, has been erected in the neighborhood of the school. The school itself has outgrown its old buildings and has increased the number of its students to about three hundred. A handsome brick building on the crest of the hill marks the center of its activities which extend themselves to the fields, the shops and the neighboring common school, in which the pupils in the normal school get practical training in schoolroom work. The hospital, too, serves as a training school for nurses, while providing a place where the sick and injured of the city and the surrounding country can, in cases of dire necessity that often arise, be properly cared for.

The task of administering the various enterprises which the school and settlement that surrounds it have called into existence is not an easy one and could perhaps scarcely have been carried out as wisely as it has without the counsel and assistance which Winston business men have given. It is of especial interest that this success has been possible by the coöperation of the white people, North and South, with the black people themselves.

"I have had one definite aim in all that I have undertaken to do here," said Mr. Atkins, in speaking of his work, "and that has been to induce the white people to coöperate with the colored people in the support of this school, and what it stands for."

That Mr. Atkins has been successful in his attempt to promote an understanding between the races is shown not only by the respectful and sympathetic manner in which ministers, lawyers and business men refer to him and his work, but in the progress that has been made under these favorable circumstances by colored people. They are represented in the professions by men who seem to have earned the entire respect of their white neighbors. There is a first-class drug store run by a colored man, a number of prosperous grocers, one of whom, after five years, is erecting a three-story brick building at an expense of $10,000. There are several well-to-do liverymen and a large number of petty shopkeepers.

Special circumstances have, perhaps, contributed to put the two races in Winston-Salem on terms of mutual good will. Some of these are to be found in the history of the city itself. Salem, founded in 1752, is an old Moravian settlement. It is one of those many communities that the missionary enterprise of Count Zinzindorf [sic] and his followers have scattered over the earth, in which thrift and industry have united with pure religion to give the world a true example of the "Simple Life." One of the motives which led to its establishment was the desire to carry Christianity to the Indians and negroes. In fact, the first person baptized in Salem as Bishop Rondthaler informed me when I visited there recently, was a slave. Though comparatively few negroes have been taken into the church a large number of negro children, who have subsequently joined other denominations, have been educated in the Moravian Sunday schools. It is natural that this kindly people should be well-disposed to efforts of the colored people to better their conditions. They have, in fact, given Professor Atkins from the outset, not only material aid, but what is even more important, their counsel and continued moral support. Mr. H. E. Fries, president of the board of trustees, is from one of the old Moravian families.

Meanwhile Winston has learned to take an interest in this negro school and settlement at Columbia Heights, looking at it from a somewhat different point of view. Its tobacco factories employ negro labor. The R. J. Reynolds Tobacco Company has grown to be a vast concern employing no less than thirty-two hundred hands, mostly negroes. In this factory one sees whole families at work with, perhaps, a baby under the bench asleep or playing about on the floor. One sees also, what is more interesting still, whites and blacks, male and female, working side by side, performing the same tasks and receiving the same wages. The colored laboring population are regarded as a valuable asset by the people in Winston. This is shown by the fact that they have imposed a prohibitive tax of $700 upon the employment agents who come there to stir up discontent and incite the negroes to go elsewhere.

The manufacturers in Winston have also begun to learn that it pays to look after their employees. Mr. R. J. Reynolds, of the R. J. Reynolds Tobacco Company, finding that his works were embarrassed by the sickness of his employees, which was often prolonged for want of nursing, proposed to give $5,000 to erect a hospital for the colored people, on a condition that a like sum was given by others. The offer was accepted and the other $5,000 was made up largely among the colored people of the city and the surrounding country. Thus was established the hospital connected with the Slater Industrial School.

Recently Mr. Booker T. Washington visited Winston-Salem and made an address to whites and blacks on the subject of their mutual relations to the negro problem. He was received enthusiastically by the best members of both races. To him it was a profound gratification to visit a city where, to a greater degree, perhaps, than in any other city in the South, that solution of the negro problem has been taken to heart, that Mr. Washington first publicly urged upon a southern audience of whites and blacks ten years ago at the Atlanta Exposition.

Agricultural Extension Among the Negroes

Among other cares the nations, those weary Titans whose work we call civilization, have always had their missions, home and foreign. Among the latter I count that most modern expression of the missionary spirit, the University Settlement. The greatest mission station in the world, however, construing the term in this broad sense, is situated in a little country village in the "black belt" of Alabama—Tuskegee.

The name Tuskegee—accent on the penult thus, Tuskegée—is historic. Once upon a time, before the white man came, and in fact long after, there was a tribe of Indians who bore the name and possessed the country. In that day the name was spelled as it is pronounced, Tuskigi. After the Indians were driven into exile in 1836, rich planters built their mansions here and owned and ruled, in baronial style, the whole surrounding country, which was rich in cotton, corn and slaves. Once there was a noted military academy here, where the aristocracy sent its sons to get the polish and discipline of gentlemen. To-day the name of this quaint and quiet little country village, over whose vine-clad and moss-grown mansions the memory of the ancient days still throws a sort of melancholy charm, is known around the whole world, but the village owes its fame to the location near it of a Negro school. The distance from Tuskegee of the Indian wigwams to the Tuskegee of this Negro school, with its worldwide reputation, is not wide, but it covers a deal of history and is suggestive of possibilities.

Tuskegee Institute is generally known as a school, merely, and Booker T. Washington, who founded and conducts it, is regarded, perhaps, simply as a

Robert E. Park, "Agricultural Extension Among the Negroes," *The World To-Day* XV (August 1908), pp. 820–26.

heroic type of the Negro schoolmaster. But Tuskegee is a school with a special mission and an extraordinarily far-reaching and practical method of enforcing it. During the years that I have had an opportunity to study its work, I have traced its influence, through many devious channels, to connections with persons and organizations all over the South and North, and everywhere I have found it a helpful, hopeful, stimulating force in the lives of the individuals and of the masses that it touched. It is one detail of this mission work of the Institute, the work in its own county of Macon, Alabama, that is described in the article that follows.

At the outset, be it noted that Tuskegee is the center of a farming district where blacks already outnumber the whites five to one and Negro immigration is steadily increasing that ratio. The land is frequently poor, but it is for that reason easy to buy. The Negro farmers have found Macon County in other ways, also, a good place in which to live. For instance, there are schools here, and, quite as important, racial peace.

Looking out from the sandy ridge on which the village stands, you seem to see on every hand a vast unbroken forest, green and waving, touched here with a bit of sunlight and there with a bit of shadow until, in the blue distance, it melts into the horizon. Distributed about, at irregular intervals in this seemingly boundless, waving ocean of green, are the farms and the farmers, twenty thousand people in an area of 650 square miles. These farms are merely ragged spaces hacked out of the forest, interspersed with noiseless little streams that trickle out across your path from the deep woods, and connected with wandering lines of country roads that crawl painfully over crests of sandy hills and plunge headlong into yawning wayside crevices.

Here, as elsewhere in the South, the evil condition of the roads is one of the elements of the problem. Making travel difficult, it emphasizes the farmer's isolation, deprives him of the stimulating agitations of communal life and makes concerted action difficult, besides adding one tug more to the lure of the city.

Shortly after the war the Negroes began to build their own churches. These in the surrounding country bear such cheerful names as Mt. Zion; Magnolia, Sweet Gum, Rising Star and Liberty Hill, and they have in turn given their names to the little, vague and hopeful Negro communities of which they are the centers. It was in these buildings that many of the schools were first started. It was here, in the debates of which the country people used to be so fond, that such important questions as: "Which is the greater, the pen or the pencil?" or "Which is the more useful, the mule or the horse," were ardently discussed, sometimes for months at a time. In short, these little churches were the intellectual and social centers of the communities.

But in all practical matters the people on the plantations continued after the war as before, under the domination of the white men in the towns, for whom they worked and from whom they obtained their supplies. When it came to a dispute about money they still trusted the white man better than they did themselves and usually went to him to arbitrate their difficulties. Emancipation, except for the possibilities that it opened, seemed to make but little practical change in the actual condition of the people. As one old Negro farmer said to me: "We was so ig'nant we didn't know no dif'rence, 'cept den we's workin' fo' de white folks and now we's wo'kin fo' oursel's."

The old farmer who made that remark is still unable to read or write, but he owns one thousand one hundred acres of land. Feeble as were the ties that bound the freedmen together, there was always some individual in each of these communities whose word went farther than the words of others. Sometimes it was an enterprising and successful farmer; sometimes a preacher who had settled on the soil; now and then it was a schoolteacher. In the spring of 1892 Mr. Washington sent out special invitations to these men, so far as he knew them or was able to learn of them, to visit him at Tuskegee and talk over matters of common interest. He was particular to insist that there were to be no set speeches. He invited about seventy-five people, but over four hundred came, and this was the origin of the first Tuskegee Negro Conference, which now draws many hundreds of people to Tuskegee every year from all parts of the South.

The first purpose was to arouse a public sentiment among the farmers and create among them a real interest in the common, mundane and practical affairs of life. In order to stimulate progress in these directions Mr. Washington got the men who had succeeded to tell how they had done it. The stories that were brought out in this way were unexpectedly interesting. They showed the difficulties and the human nature in the situation; revealed the heroism in the struggles of these obscure and narrow lives. These stories, heard at the conferences, were carried home by the members present and repeated in all the dark corners of the county and state. They became a sort of oral literature, since there was no written one, and eventually traveled far and wide, over the whole black South.

Since then there has been established in Macon County a Negro farmers' paper which seeks to stimulate the progress of the county by reporting it from week to week. It is also the medium for bringing the people in the different parts of the county in touch with each other and the Institute. Readers are invited to address questions of all sorts to the editor, which are then answered by the teachers in the Institute. They are mostly questions concerning the farm. It is used also to some extent as a reading book in the country schools and it has the value of interesting the children and giving them the notion that reading has some connection with real things, an impression it is hard for them to get from ordinary reading books.

The Negro conferences serve to arouse enthusiasm for and direct attention to the real and practical interests, but they do not give the people instruction in the ordinary sense of the term. The first attempt to instruct the farmers was undertaken in 1897 when the agricultural faculty started what was called the Farmers' Institute, a sort of monthly school day for Negro farmers.

In the early days of the Institute metaphysical theories of farming were popular. The changes of the moon played a great part in the calculations and the theories of the old Negro farmer, and it was some years before it was possible to get him down to early plowing and terrestrial notions about crops. That time has long passed, and yet these monthly farmers' meetings have not become so dry and matter-of-fact as to be tiresome. At a recent meeting the subject of discussion was the sweet potato. One member was telling about some experiments he tried with the Georgia yam and the Dooley sweet potato.

"Des seems to me," he said, "I know dem potatoes and dey knows me, jus' same as if we grow'd up in de same fambly." He was trying to impress upon the members of the Institute how deeply he had got into the secrets of that type of potato's disposition and behavior, and his genial fancy made of the tuber at once a friend and a brother.

All sorts of practical matters come up for consideration at the Farmers's Institute. They do not disdain to discuss there such simple and practical matters as the importance of soap and water and the value of daily baths. At one of the meetings the Conference Agent, that is the man who attends the local conferences which have been formed to supplement the work of the annual conference, had been "lamming onto"—to use one of his own picturesque expressions—the patent medicines and the folly of people who purchased them, when one old farmer, in a burst of contrition, confessed that he had paid $9 to a traveling agent and mortgaged a pig to pay for a medicine that promised to cure almost everything, and after all his wife had to go to a doctor.

Now that the Negro is free, every one calling himself a merchant is at liberty to search out and exploit his weaknesses and the average black man on the farm who is good-natured and disposed to trust the white man has a great many things to learn that are not taught in books.

Between Christmas and St. Valentine's day there is a period when the necessity of the revolving seasons seems to impose no definite task upon the southern farmer. The cotton has been picked and sold, the spring plowing has not been started. During this time the thrifty farmer is fixing up his fences and the "hands" are busily spending their year's wages or making contracts for the coming season. In any case, there is more or less idleness at home and considerable mischief abroad.

It was in order to fill this vacancy in the farmer's calendar with some useful occupation, and one that had, at the same time the interest of change and a recreation, that the Agricultural Department of the Institute established in 1904 what is known as the "Short Course." During the first fifteen days of January the school farm is practically turned over to the farmers and their sons and daughters. Many of them ride, every day, long distances to attend the lectures that are given in this course; others come directly to the school and live, making of the time a sort of vacation. Lecturers from the Agricultural Department at Washington and from the neighboring agricultural school for whites at Auburn attend these meetings and assist in the instruction. It is for them part of the general effort they are making to extend to the masses of the population on the soil a knowledge of better methods of farming. For the farmers themselves, the "Short Course" is a sort of winter Chautauqua.

Two years after the "Short Course" was started, the late Morris K. Jesup gave the Institute the funds with which to build and equip what is known as an "Agricultural Wagon" for the purpose of going directly to the farmers with the instruction which the school had to offer them. The wagon was fitted out with specimens of the best modern machinery, including a revolving churn, butter molds, diverse cultivators, cotton choppers, and various sorts of fertilizers, milk testers, cream separators and a number of charts and other demonstration material. The novelty of the plan aroused widespread interest and paved the way for the introduction, the next year, of the "demonstration farms," which are carried on under the direction of a graduate of the school acting as field agent of the Agricultural Department at Washington. The funds for the work, however, are furnished by the General Education Board of New York. The plan of this work is to establish throughout the country "demonstration plots" on the lands of a few selected farmers who agree to cultivate the land under the direction and with the seed of the Agricultural Department.

The effect of these demonstrations, conducted by farmers on their own soil, has been that of moral tonic. Its value lies not merely in the fact that it has shown them how to do, but it has convinced them at the same time that the thing could be done.

There is an old farmer who is something of a local celebrity, living a few miles north of the Institute on a tract which a company, known as the Southern Improvement Company, purchased some years ago for the purpose of selling it out in small tracts to Negro farmers. At a farmers' meeting recently the old man gave voice to some weighty sentiments.

"When I fus' came down here three years ago, I had nuth'n but my wife. Now I own forty acres of land; I own my own mule and wagon and plenty corn in my crib." The old fellow braced himself up. "Yes sah! Dese meet'n shu' done help me. I'se much improved. My old gray mule is learn'n too. She drives better. And you know," he continued, "'fore I came here dey use ter call me 'Old Giles,' but since I own's my own home, and has a plenty of eberyting, dey call me Mr. Hill."

There is a good deal of philosophy in the old man's remarks. They serve to illustrate to what extent character is bound up with success, and in the final analysis it is character, character in the individuals and character in the communities, that industrial education and industrial missions are seeking to build up.

I had an opportunity recently to attend one of these farmers' "demonstration" meetings. It was held at Mt. Zion, that is to say at a point ten miles north of Tuskegee, where there is a schoolhouse, a church, a half-dozen scattered Negro land-owners, and some score or more of tenant farmers, a typical Negro farming community, such as are to be found in this region.

The school was one of the twenty-eight erected during the past two years by colored communities of the county, aided by a fund administered by the Institute for the improvement of Negro rural schools. With the assistance of this fund and under the direction of its agent, the colored have been able to rebuild their schoolhouses, double the length of their school terms and practically set up a school system of their own throughout the county. In this way the rural schools have been brought into intimate working relations with the Institute and have become a sort of missionary outposts for all the work the Institute is seeking to do among the masses of the people. It was at one of these missionary outposts of the school that the meeting was held.

The agricultural wagon was drawn up under the convenient shade of a giant oak. The mules that brought it thither were turned adrift to browse in the fragrant grass by the roadside. The school-bell sounded and presently there drifted up the road one little group of habitants and then another. Slowly and uncertainly, and with that curious shyness that country folks seem to catch from the wild creatures of the wood, they approached and stood gossiping in low tones, eying the wagon with its contents curiously out of the corners of their eyes.

Presently there came from the opposite direction, in which the white settlement was situated, a sturdier and more determined group. The white people had heard about the wagon and had come up to see what there was to learn.

Presently—the listeners lounging about or sitting on the ground under the tree, the "lecture," as they called it, began. I remember among other things the "demonstrator" told us about a new and marvelous kind of grass of which the people about Zion had never heard—alfalfa. He recommended it among other plants as a kind of "green fertilizer," which would restore nitrogen to the soil and furnish, at the same time, an excellent fodder for the cattle. Soon we were all, white or black, engaged in a lively discussion of the merits and the possibilities of the new legume which was to take the place of the familiar cow-pea in the economy of the farmer.

It was a curious and interesting picture. I could not but notice the contrast in the races. The white men were short, incisive and energetic in their movements and their speech. The Negroes were softer and more flowing. But there we were, white folks and black folks, out under the tree, listening to a Negro schoolmaster. And for the moment, because we had found a common interest, the race problem was solved. We were discussing how we could improve the farming methods of the people and enrich the country. The race distinctions were there, to be sure, but they presented for the instant at least, no problem.

We who have studied social institutions, know that they are not manufactured out of hand by legislatures or created by proclamations. They grow slowly, and like the coral islands, by the silent and unseen labors of innumerable individual creatures. All the same I came away with the feeling that I had assisted at one of those silent, unnoticed processes. Here was construction going on. A new institution was growing up.

What I had seen, however, was merely one detail of an experiment in social upbuilding, "community-building" they call it sometimes down here, more elaborate and on a larger scale, perhaps, than was ever before attempted. Also it was an experiment!

Negro Home Life and Standards of Living

Before the Civil War there were, generally speaking, two classes of Negroes in the United States, namely free Negroes and slaves. After the Civil War and the abolition of slavery, the plantation Negroes remained, for the most part, upon the soil and formed a class of peasant farmers. This class, which represented 80 per cent of the race, constituted the base of the social structure, so far as such a thing may be said to have existed at that time, among the members of the race. Above this there was a small class composed in part of free Negroes, in part of a class of favored slaves, all those in fact whom education, opportunity or natural ability had given material advantages and a superior social position. It was this class which took the leadership directly after the war.

In recent years the number of occupations in which Negroes are engaged has multiplied and the area of the Negro's activities, except perhaps in the realm of politics, has greatly extended. The descendants of the free Negroes and of those slaves who started with superior advantages directly after the war have gone very largely into the professions. They are lawyers, physicians, teachers, musicians, playwrights and actors. One of the highest paid performers on the vaudeville stage today is a colored man. Several of the most successful composers of popular songs are colored. Others are engaged in various kinds of social service. They are missionaries to Africa, secretaries of Young Men's Christian Associations, social settlement workers, and so forth. In almost every instance it will be found that the men and women who have gained distinction in any of the professions mentioned were the descendants either of free Negroes or of a class which I have called favored slaves.

Robert E. Park, "Negro Home Life and Standards of Living," *Annals of the American Academy of Political and Social Science* XLIX (September 1913), pp. 147–63.

In the meantime there has grown up in recent years a vigorous and push-ing middle class, composed of small contractors, business men of various sorts, bankers, real estate and insurance men. The two largest fortunes left by Negroes of which we have any record were made in real estate speculations. Thomy Lafon, who died at his house in New Orleans in 1892, left a fortune which was appraised at $413,000 and Colonel John Mackey, who died in Philadelphia in 1902, left property which was valued at $432,000 and was probably worth very much more, since a large part of it was coal and mineral land in Kentucky.

At the same time, from among the peasant farmers, there has grown a small class of plantation owners. These men farm but a small portion of the land they own, and rent the remaining to tenants, to whom they stand in the position of capitalists. Usually they will run a small store from which they make advances to their tenants. Although there were, among the free Negroes of the South before the War, a certain number who owned large plantations, and some who owned slaves, the Negro plantation owners in the South today have been recruited almost wholly from the ranks of the planta-tion Negroes. They represent, in other words, men who have come up.

The growth of a Negro middle class, composed of merchants, plantation owners and small capitalists, has served to fill the distance which formerly existed between the masses of the race at the bottom and the small class of educated Negroes at the top, and in this way has contributed to the general diffusion of culture, as well as to the solidarity of the race.

Although the distinction between the upper and lower strata of Negro social life is not so clearly marked now as formerly, the descendants of the dif-ferent types of antebellum Negroes have preserved, to a very large extent, the traditions, sentiments and habits of their ancestors, and it will contribute something to understanding the social standards, the degree of culture and comfort which the Negro peasant, the Negro artisan, business and profes-sional man enjoy today to take some account of those earlier, ante-bellum conditions out of which they sprang.

The great majority of the slaves were employed in only the crudest form of unskilled labor. They were field hands, working under the direction of an overseer and reckoned, along with the stock and tools, as part of the equip-ment of the plantation. Under these circumstances the amount of general cul-ture and knowledge of the world which they obtained depended upon the extent and character of their contact with the white man and with the outside world. This differed greatly in various parts of the country. There was per-haps, no part of the South where the plantation Negro grew up on such easy and familiar terms with his master as in southwestern Virginia. Here the farms were small; the crops were varied; servant and master worked side by side in the field and lived upon an equality rarely if ever seen in the states farther South. The effects of these ante-bellum conditions may be clearly seen today. There is no part of the South, perhaps no part of the United States where the small Negro farmers are more independent and prosperous, or where the two races get on better together, than, for example, in the region around Christianburg, Va.

The homes of the Negro farmers in this region would be regarded as comfortable for a small farmer in any part of the country. They are frequently two-story frame buildings, surrounded by a garden and numerous outbuildings. The interior of these homes is neat and well kept. They contain a few books, some pictures and the usual assortment of women's handiwork. A general air of comfort and contentment pervades the homes and the community. Nearby there is a little six months country school. You learn, also, that one or two of the children have completed the course in the public school and have been sent away to a neighboring academy to complete their course.

The contrast between one of the homes in this part of Virginia and a similar home in a region like the sea islands, off the coast of South Carolina is striking, particularly if you have come, as was true in my case, almost directly from one to the other. In the sea islands the slaves were more isolated than in almost any other part of the South. The result is apparent in the condition and lives of the Negro people today. Outside of the towns they live, for the most part, on little farms of ten and twenty acres which were sold to them by the federal government directly after the war. These homes are quaint little nests, often curiously improvised to meet the individual necessities of the household. The people are on the whole densely ignorant, but possess a shrewd and homely wit that makes conversation with them an interesting exercise. Among themselves they speak a dialect that is scarcely intelligible to an outsider and they have many quaint and curious customs, some of which may have their source in Africa. Among other things peculiar to the people of these islands are there [sic] "prayer houses." These prayer houses are a local institution, older and different from the churches which were introduced after the Civil War. Connected with these prayer houses, also, there are religious forms and exercises, older and cruder than those practised in the churches. What is recognized elsewhere as a weakness of the Negro race, and perhaps of all isolated and primitive peoples, namely a disposition to cherish personal enmities, and to split and splinter into factitious little groups, finds abundant illustration here. There are probably more little churches, more little societies, and, if I can judge, more time and energy wasted in religious excitements and factional disputes among the people of the sea islands than in any similar group of colored people anywhere in the South. As is, perhaps, to be expected, where so much time and energy are expended in litigious and ceremonial excitements there is not much left for the ordinary business of daily life. In spite of this fact I am disposed to believe that the home life of the sea island people is more comfortable and quite as wholesome as that of the peasants in many parts of southern Europe which I have visited.

It was notorious, even in slavery times, that the up-country Negroes were superior to the coast Negroes, and this seems to be true today, even of those remote parts of the black belt where the Negroes are still living very much as they did in slavery times. I visited not long ago, one of these isolated little communities, situated on the rich bottom lands along the upper reaches of the Alabama River. The settlement consisted of, perhaps, a hundred families, who are employed during the year on one or two of the plantations in the neighborhood. Ordinarily, on the old fashioned plantations such as these, the tenants would live in the "quarters," as they did in slavery days, or in little huts scattered about on the land they tilled. In this case, however, owing to the fact that the cultivated land was so frequently inundated by spring floods, the tenants of each plantation were located on a little stretch of sandy soil which the spring flood never reached, although it often covered all the surrounding country. This stretch of sand is dotted, at convenient distances, with giant live oak trees, which afford a welcome shade and give the effect of a natural park. On this little sandy oasis are scattered at irregular intervals the homes of the people of the settlement. They are, for the most part, little rude huts with two or three rooms and a few outbuildings. Sometimes there are fruit trees in the garden in front of the houses, with a barn, pig stys, hen yards, in the rear and on the other sides, the number of these buildings depending upon the thrift of the farmer.

Most of the people who live here have grown up in the settlement or have married into it. At one of the neatest of these little cottages I met a little withered old man, who proved to be the patriarch of the community. His memory went back, I found, to the time when the region was a wilderness. He knew the history of every family in the settlement. A large portion of them were, in fact, his children and grandchildren and he told me, in response to my questions, the whole story of the pioneers in this region and of the manner in which the land was cleared and settled. He himself had never been away from the plantation except for a few months during the war, when he ran away to Mobile. The little house in which he lived was the typical two-room cabin, with a wide open hallway, or rather porch, between the two sections of the house. The interior was rather bare, but everything about the house was clean and neat. A vine grew over the porch, a gourd hung from the beams, and a few trees were in blossom in front of the house.

The other houses in the community are much like this one, some of them even smaller. One of the more enterprising citizens, however, who was, as I remember, the only land owner, has erected a new four-room house. In this house there was a rug on the floor, a few pictures, most of them family portraits, some books, generally what are known as "race books," which contain uplifting accounts of the progress of the race. Besides these, there were several copies of a weekly farm paper, a few government agricultural bulletins and a large framed lithograph portrait of Booker T. Washington. Another thing which distinguished this house from the others was the possession of a screen door, a further evidence that the owner of the house was an exceptional person in this community.

The principal diet here, as elsewhere among the Negro farmers in the South, consists of fat pork, corn bread with syrup, and greens. In addition to this, there are on occasions eggs and chicken and perhaps tea and coffee. A really thrifty housewife, however, knows how to brew tea from herbs gathered in the woods, and at certain seasons of the year there are fish and game in abundance.

The budget of an average Negro tenant farmer as accurately as I was able to obtain it, worked out about as follows:

Rent, two bales of cotton and seed	$150.00
Clothing for a family of six	76.75
Groceries	125.00
Physician and medicines	9.00
"Christmas money"	15.00
Church and school	5.00
Average cost of fertilizer and farm equipment, feed for mule, etc	162.75
Total expense	543.50
Cash	56.50
Total	$600.00

There is always room for a wide margin in these accounts. In a bad season or when cotton is cheap the value of the tenant's portion of the crop may fall far below the estimated income of $600. With a good season it will amount to considerably more.

The average tenant farmer will spend as much money during the cropping season as the grocer or the banker who is advancing him will permit. An actual month's rations for a farmer of this class is as follows:

Chops, four bushels }	
Oats, five bushels } for mule and other stock	7.50
Flour, 50 pounds	1.95
Meal, one bushel	1.00
Meat	1.50
Lard	.50
Sugar	.60
Groceries	.95
Total	$14.00

To this must be added $4 in cash which will make the total cash of the monthly ration for a family of six, $18. This ration will of course be supplemented by the products of the garden and of the farm. A thrifty farmer, however, can reduce the amount of his purchases at the store to almost nothing. He can raise his own cane and make his own syrup; he can raise his own fodder, and supply himself with pork and corn meal from his own farm. This is what he usually does as soon as he sets out to buy a farm of his own.

There has been great improvement in recent years in the living condition of the Negro farmers in most parts of what is known as the Black Belt. This is particularly true of those sections of the country where the Negroes have begun to buy land or where they have come in contact, through schools or through agents of the farm demonstration movement, with the influences that are changing and improving the method and technique of farming throughout the South.

Wherever one meets a little colony of Negro land owners and wherever one meets a Negro who has risen to the position of farm manager, one invariably finds improvement in the character and condition of the Negro home. Whenever a good school is established it is usually the center of a group of thrifty Negro farmers. Not infrequently a Negro farmer, who has acquired a little land or a little money, will sell his property and move to another state or another county in order to obtain good country school accommodations for his children. Macon County, Alabama, for example, in which the Tuskegee Institute is located is said to have more Negro landowners than any other county in the South, and very many of these have come into the county during the past five or six years since an effort was made by the Tuskegee Institute to build up and improve the country schools in that county. A large proportion of colored farmers in Macon County live at present in near four- and five-room cottages. The standard of living has been appreciably raised in this and neighboring counties.

Census statistics show that the number of Negro landowners is increasing throughout the South about 50 per cent more rapidly than the white. Ownership of land invariably brings with it an improvement in the stability and the comfort of the home. The number of large landowners and farm managers is likewise increasing. Recently I visited the house of a Negro "renter" in Georgia. He was, in fact, not the ordinary tenant farmer but rather a farm manager. He himself farmed but a small portion of the land he rented, subletting it to tenants over whom he exercised a careful supervision. He was a man who had never been to school, but he had taught himself to read. He was living in a large comfortable house, formerly occupied by the owner of the plantation. This man was not only a good farmer but, in his way, he was something of a student. Among his books I noticed several that had to do with the local history of the country during slavery times, which showed that he had an amount of intellectual curiosity that is rare in men of his class. This was further shown by his eagerness to talk about matters of which he had read in the newspapers in regard to which he wanted more information. He had, as I remember, about $5,000 in the bank and was looking forward to purchasing very soon the plantation upon which he was living.

I have frequently met Negro farmers, old men who had come up from slavery, who owned and conducted large plantations, although they could neither read nor write. One man in Texas, who owned 1,800 acres of land told me that, until recent years, he had carried all his accounts with his tenants in his head. Finding however, that, as he grew older, he was losing his ability to remember he had hired a school teacher to keep his accounts for him. Sometimes these men who have struggled from the position of peasant to that of a planter live in much the same way as their tenants. But the next generation is usually educated and learns to spend, even if it has not learned to make.

In the North, as might be expected, Negroes farm better and live better than they do in the South. One of the most successful farmers in the state of Kansas is Junius G. Groves of Edwardsville, Kans. Groves was born a slave in Green County, Ky. He went over to Kansas with the exodus in 1879. He started in 1882 to raise potatoes on a rented farm of 6 acres. He now owns 503 acres in the Kaw Valley upon which he raised last year a crop of 55,000 bushels of potatoes. With the aid of his sons, who were educated in the Kansas Agricultural College, Groves has applied scientific methods to his farming operations. By this means he has been able to raise his maximum yield on a single acre to 395 bushels. He has recently erected a handsome modern house which a writer in *The Country Gentleman* describes as "a twenty-two room palace overlooking a 503 acre farm." A farmer like Groves, however, belongs to what I have described as the middle class, composed of men who operate on a relatively large scale and with their own capital.

Although the great majority of the slaves were employed at work in the fields there were, on every large plantation in the South before the Civil War those who were employed as carpenters, stonemasons, and blacksmiths. In all the larger cities also, there were a certain number of Negro mechanics who hired their own time and were given a good many of the privileges of the free Negroes. Negro slaves were also employed as sailors, as locomotive firemen, as well as in other positions requiring skill and a certain amount of responsibility. Slaves of this class were better treated than the ordinary field hand. They were better housed, better clothed and better fed, and, with the exception of the house servants, were allowed more privileges than the other people on the plantation. At the close of the War, therefore, there were a considerable number of trained workmen among the former slaves. Of all the people who came out of slavery these were, perhaps, as a class, the most competent self-respecting, and best fitted for freedom.

In spite of this fact Negroes have probably made less advance in the skilled trades than in other occupations. The reason is not far to seek. With the growth of cities and manufacturing industries since emancipation, great changes have taken place in the character and condition of skilled labor in the South. The cities have drawn more heavily upon the white than the colored portion of the populations and, whenever there has been a change or reorganization in an industry, the poor white man has profited by it more than the Negro. The cotton mills, the majority of which have been built since the war, employ almost exclusively white labor and it is only recently that Negroes have anywhere been employed as operatives in any of the spinning industries. In certain occupations, like that of barber and waiter, the Negro has been very largely crowded out by foreign competition.

Labor unions have almost invariably sought to keep Negroes out of the skilled trades. In those occupations, however, in which the Negro has shown his ability to compete and has managed to gain a sufficient foothold to compel recognition, as for example in the coal and iron industries, the timber and turpentine industries and, to a less extent, in the building trades, labor unions have made earnest effort to bring Negroes into the unions and have thus insured for them the same wages and ultimately the same standards of living as prevail among white artisans of the same class.

As a rule the Negro has made less progress in occupations in which he formerly had a monopoly, like that of barbering and waiting, than in new occupations into which he has entered since emancipation. Wherever Negroes have had to win their way by competition with the white man they are, as a rule, not only more efficient laborers, but they have invariably adopted the white man's standards of living.

There are, particularly in every large city as well as in every small town in the South, multitudes of Negroes who live meanly and miserably. They make their homes in some neglected or abandoned quarters of the city and maintain a slovenly, irregular and unhealthy sort of existence, performing odd jobs of one kind or another. Very few colored people of the artisan class, however, live in these so-called "Negro quarters." There are always other quarters of the city, frequently in the neighborhood of some Negro school, where there will be another sort of community and in this community a large proportion of the people will be composed of Negro artisans and small tradesmen. They will live, for the most part, in little three- or four-room houses and, if they happen to own their homes, there will be a vine training over the porch, curtains in the windows, a rug or carpet on the floor. The children who go to school will be neatly and tidily dressed. There will be a few books in the front bedroom, a little garden in the rear of the house and a general air of thrift and comfort about the place.

In the course of time, if the family continue to prosper, the children will be sent to a secondary or high school. The eldest will go away to a normal school or college of some kind, and the eldest boy will go, perhaps, to Tuskegee or some other industrial school. When these children return home they will sometimes go to work to earn money enough to help other younger members of the family to enter the school which they have attended and thus, in time, the whole family will manage to get a moderate amount of education.

When all the members of the family work together in this way there are the best possible relations in the home. It is in those homes, of which there are unfortunately too many in every town and city, where the father works irregularly and the mother is compelled to do day labor, that one meets idle and neglected children, a large proportion of whom grow up to recruit the shiftless, loafing and criminal class.

As a rule the Negro artisan is thrifty. The following budget is that of a journeyman printer.

Living expenses	$240
Clothing	60
Church and school	12
Medicine and medical attendance	16
Insurance, taxes and interest	84
Incidentals	48
Savings	150
Total	$610

This man lives in a neat five-room cottage which he owns. His wife conducts a little store and in addition to his work as journeyman printer he conducts a little Sunday School paper. He is district superintendent of Sunday schools in the neighboring county, and employs his Sundays in visiting the Sunday schools under his charge and in circulating, incidentally, the paper he publishes, so that, at the present time, his annual revenue is considerably larger than his earnings at his trade.

Negroes who are employed in industries in which the laborers are organized, as for example the building trades and the coal and iron industries, earn more, but, perhaps save less. Negro miners earn frequently as much as from $100 to $150 per month. These men live well, according to their light, but they are notoriously wasteful and improvident and, except in those cases where their employers have taken an interest in their welfare, they have made little if any advance in their standards of living over the farm laborers or tenant farmers from which they, in most instances, are recruited.

Among the free Negroes in the South there were, in slavery times, a certain number of planters and slave owners. Some of the Negro planters of Louisiana were wealthy, for four or five of them were said in 1853 to be worth between four and five hundred thousand dollars each. Others were small traders, peddlers, blacksmiths, shoemakers and so forth. In some of the older cities of the South, like Charleston, S.C., there was a little aristocracy of free Negroes, who counted several generations of free ancestors and because of their industry, thrift and good reputation among their white neighbors, enjoyed privileges and immunities that were not granted to other free Negroes in the South.

Not only in Charleston but in Baltimore, Washington, D.C., Philadelphia, New York and New Orleans there were similar groups of free colored people, who were well to do and had obtained a degree of culture that raised them above the mass of the Negro people, free or slave, by whom they were surrounded. Associated with the free Negroes were a certain number of privileged slaves who were frequently the illegitimate sons of their masters.

It was from this class of free Negroes and privileged slaves that, a little later on, the professional class among the Negroes, the lawyers, the physicians and to a very large extent the teachers, were recruited. It was not until after politics as a profession for Negroes began to decline in the South, that a number of men who had entered politics directly after the Civil War began to go into business. As they had, in many instances, either by inheritance or as a result of their savings while they were serving the government, succeeded in accumulating a certain amount of capital, they frequently went into some sort of real estate or banking business.

About 1890 the first successful bank was started by Negroes. There are now more than sixty such banks in the United States. Either in connection with these banks or independently there have been organized small investment companies for the purchase or sale of real estate and, as the demand for homes by Negroes of all classes has grown rapidly in recent years, the number of these institutions has multiplied.

As business opportunities have increased, the number of Negro business men has been recruited from the professional classes. Very frequently Negro physicians have started drug stores in connection with the practice of their profession, and from that they have gone into real estate or banking.

As the opportunities for Negro lawyers have been small, particularly in the South, most of them have connected themselves with some sort of business in which their legal knowledge was of value—real estate, insurance, saving and investment associations, and so forth.

One of the wealthiest Negroes in the South today started as a physician, made his money in the drug business and in real estate, and has since become a banker. The president of the largest Negro bank in the South, the Alabama Penny Savings Bank, was formerly a minister.

It is in this way that the ranks of the Negro business men have been recruited from the members of the educated classes.

However, the first Negro business men were, not as a rule educated. In the North, before the war, the most successful Negro business men were barbers and caterers. In the South, directly after the war several Negroes who had made small fortunes started in the saloon business. They had been employed, perhaps, as porters and bartenders and eventually went into business for themselves. There were special opportunities in the whisky business, because in the bar rooms whites and blacks met upon something like equality. It was not until recently that the regulators of the liquor traffic in certain cities required separate bars for the different races. Even now there is usually a back door for Negroes. Sometimes, where the bulk of the trade is supplied by Negroes, they have the front door and the whites the back.

In certain other business-like undertakings, in which Negroes have found that they could get better service from black men than from white, Negroes early found a business opportunity which they have since largely exploited. The wealthiest Negro in New York today is an undertaker.

A number of Negroes, who began as journeymen in the building trades, rose to the position of contractors and then became large landlords, living upon their rents. In one comparatively large city in the South the most successful baker and in another, the most successful fish dealer, are Negroes. These men have been successful, not because of any special opportunity opened to them, as in the case of the Negro physician and the Negro undertaker, but because they were enterprising, and knew how to handle the trade. Both these men do the larger part of their business with the white rather than with the colored people.

The president of the largest and most successful Negro insurance company in the South, the North Carolina Mutual and Provident Association, was formerly a barber. In most instances the successful business men have been men with very meagre education and very few opportunities. These pioneers, however, have made opportunities for others and they have accumulated an amount of capital and experience which has laid the foundation for an enterprising middle class, now rapidly advancing in wealth and in culture.

As soon as a Negro has succeeded in accumulating a little money, his first ambition is to build himself a comfortable home. At first the Negro's attempts at home building are, as might be expected, a little crude. For example, if he plans his own house, he usually puts the bathroom off the kitchen. After he gets a bathroom he will probably want to have some pictures on the walls. The thing that strikes his fancy is usually something in a large gilt frame such as one can buy cheap in an auction store. Then he acquires a gilt lamp, an onyx table, perhaps, and a certain amount of other furniture of the same sort.

If, in addition to a comfortable home, he has gained a moderate amount of education, he wants to travel, and see something of the world. This disposition on the part of the Negro, whenever he can find excuse for it, serves, however, to correct his first crude attempts at home decoration and to widen his views about the value and convenience of a well-planned house. The numerous conventions which every year bring together large numbers of Negroes from all over the country provide an excuse for travel. The fact that it is difficult for Negroes to get hotel accommodations in many parts of the country put upon every colored man who has a comfortable house, the obligation of opening his house to every member of his race who comes well recommended. Some times Negroes who have been a little extravagant in building and furnishing a house are very glad to rent rooms to a select class of travelers. In any case, Negroes are naturally hospitable. They take a very proper pride in their houses, when they happen to have good ones, and are always glad to entertain visitors.

As a result of this custom of keeping open house Negroes are doubtless more disposed than they otherwise would be to take pride in the care and decoration of their homes. There may be something, also, in the explanation which one colored man made for building and equipping a home in a style which seemed a little beyond his means. He said: "We may have been, wife and I, a little extravagant in building and furnishing our house, but the house in which we were born had none of these things, and we are trying to make up to our children what we missed when we were little." The result of this is that for the Negro travel is often an education in home building. In every home he enters he notices closely and when he returns home he profits by what he learns.

Negroes of the better class not only travel a great deal in this country but a considerable number of educated Negroes go abroad every year and from these journeys they bring back not only many new and happy impressions but also a considerable amount of information in the art of living that they do not have the opportunity to get at home. In the course of time all this experience and information filter down and are used by the well-to-do class of Negroes everywhere.

The number of really cultured Negro homes is, as might be expected, small. One reason is that thoroughly educated Negroes are as yet few in number. The handsomest home I visited was that of a physician in Wilmington, Del. This man was living in a fine old ante-bellum mansion with extensive grounds, which has recently sold, I have been informed, for something like $50,000. This house not only had the charm of individuality, but it was furnished, so far as I am capable of judging, in perfect good taste. It contained one of the best general libraries I have seen in a private house. The mistress of this house was a graduate of Wellesley College. There are perhaps a dozen other houses owned by Negroes in the United States that could compare with this.

The entertainment in a Negro house is likely to be lavish. No matter how frugal the family may live at other times, there must be no stinting of the entertainment of guests. Not infrequently it will happen that a young colored man who has pinched and struggled to save money while he was getting an education, or while he was struggling to get himself established in business, will spend all his income as soon as he reaches a point where he is admitted into the upper grades of colored society.

One man, a physician in a northern city, with an income which averages between $5,000 and $6,000 a year, showed me his bank book covering a period of eighteen years during which time he had spent $103,000. And yet this same man, during the time that he was working, sometimes as a school teacher and at other times as a house servant on a salary of $25 or $30 a month, had saved $3,000 to put himself through college. Another young man told me that he had saved enough money as a porter in a Negro barber shop, while he was learning the trade, to buy a shop of his own but had lost it, when, after becoming the proprietor of the shop, he was admitted to what he called "society."

It is difficult to determine accurately the income of the well-to-do Negroes in this country. There are two and perhaps three physicians whose incomes from their practice alone amounts to $10,000 a year. There are several lawyers who make as much. A considerable number of men in business or in other professions make considerably more. As a rule, the business men save their money but men in the professions usually spend it.

The average income of a Negro physician in the South is not over $1,500 but very frequently enterprising physicians will add to their regular earnings by maintaining a sanitarium or private hospital.

The most popular profession among the Negroes is, perhaps, that of teaching, one reason being that, in the past comparatively little preparation was required to enter it. Neither teaching nor the ministry is as popular as it used to be. One reason is the demand for men and women with better preparation; another is the poor pay. The better schools are, however, increasing salaries, particularly those of principals and of a higher grade of teachers. The following budgets indicate the standard of living among the better paid teachers:

Budget Estimate for Year.

Insurance, taxes, etc	$168
Living expenses	384
Medicine and medical services	96
Clothing	144
Miscellaneous and incidental	66
Literature	42
Savings and investment	300
Total	$1,200

Living expense does not include vegetables from garden or house rent, which is paid by institution.

2

Allowance to mother		$120
Charity, benevolence and religious		150
Property		300
Groceries		300
Life	86	
Insurance} Household goods	6	92
Upkeep of house		100
Education of sister		90
Clothing		275
Books, magazines and papers		25
Total		$1,452

Fuel, light, house rent furnished by state. Total income between $1,800 and $2,000.

The first of these budgets is that of one of the better paid teachers of one of the best of the larger industrial schools. The second is that of the principal of another of these institutions.

Negroes of all classes are willing to make and do make great sacrifices to secure the education of their children, but in the upper classes, where the children are few, they are usually spoiled; while on the plantation, where they are many, the family discipline is likely to be severe.

Home life among the educated and well-to-do Negroes appears as a rule, to be happy and wholesome; but nowhere is this more true than in those families where the parents, though educated, the income is so small that all members of the family are impelled to work together to maintain the standards of living and secure for the children an education, equal, if not superior, to that which the parents have enjoyed.

The Negro has made great progress in many directions during the past half century, but nowhere more so than in his home, and nowhere, it may be added, do the fruits of education show to better advantage than in the home of the educated Negro.

Letters Collected by R. E. Park and Booker T. Washington

This is an extract from the publications of the Southern History Association, Spangenberg's Journal of Travels in North Carolina, 1752.[1]

Whoever comes to North Carolina must prepare to pay a poll tax. Poll tax is required from all white men, master or servant, from 16 years of age and on; all Negroes and Negresses pay poll tax from their twelfth year. Whoever marries a Negro, or Indian, a mixed blood—his children are liable to the fourth degree from the twelfth year on, and the female Indian or Negro is also taxable. Should this tax not be paid to the sheriff—by whom it is demanded, he is empowered to sell anything belonging to the delinquent party, he can seize at public vendue, and after keeping enough to pay his own fees and satisfy the tax he returns the remainder to the party.

When anyone wishes to marry he must go to the clerk of his county and deposit a Bond for fifty pounds, as assurance that there is no obstacle or impediment to his marrying.

He then receives a certificate which he presents to the Justice, who gives him his license: he may then get married. The fees are 20 shillings for the clerk—five shillings for the Justice; 10 shillings for the Minister. Should the "Banns be published," however the license fee is not required. Should the marriage not be performed by the Minister, his fee must, nevertheless, be offered to him. Whoever marries a Negress, Indian, Mulatto or anything of mixed blood, must pay a fine of fifty pounds. Whoever marries such a couple must also pay a fine of fifty pounds.

Robert E. Park and Booker T. Washington, "Letters Collected by R. E. Park and Booker T. Washington," *The Journal of Negro History* VII:2 (April 1922), pp. 206–22.

[1] This extract and the documents which follow were collected by Dr. R.E. Park.

If a slave or servant buys or sells anything without his master's knowledge and consent, the parties dealing with him shall not only lose three times the amount bargained for, but also pay a penalty of six pounds.

Whoever assists a slave to escape from his master, be it much or little, shall serve the master 5 years, as punishment.

The following is a letter from an investigator seeking in Ohio information concerning the Randolph slaves:

November 18, '08

Dr Park:—

The following is what I found in answer to your questions concerning the Randolph slaves in Ohio:

In Virginia, they lived in Charlotte and Prince Edward Counties on the Roanoke River.

They traveled overland, in wagons and carts from there to Cincinnati and from Cincinnati, to Mercer Co., in Ohio by flat boats. The land which is said to have been bought for them was in Mercer Co.

The settlers of the Community were mainly Germans who would not allow the landing of the Negroes where [sic] they arrived there.

The Colony then moved down the Miami River, settled in camp in Miami County not far from the towns of Piqua and Troy.

They never got possession of any of the land supposed to have been purchased for them.

The citizens of Piqua held a mass meeting to discuss the condition of the Negroes in Camp, to decide upon some course of action in regard to them.

The decision was to find employment for them wherever they could and distribute them accordingly. Some were sent to Shelby County-Sidney, about 12 miles N. E. of Piqua—being the county seat. Several descendants live in this community yet.

Many remained in & about Piqua & Troy where there are still few of the old ones & many descendents [sic]. Some were sent into Indiana and other parts of Ohio. There were 385 of them.

The most noted of them is Mr. Goodrich Giles. His father was a member of the Colony. His mother belonged to another planter in Virginia & did not get to go.

Mr. Giles is without any question a Negro. He farms & has succeeded at it. He owns 425 acres of land just out from Piqua not an acre of which is said to be worth less than one hundred dollars. He lives in a good roomy brick house, has good farm buildings, is supplied with farming implements and though old is still active—leading in his work.

His crop this year consists of about,

4500 bus. Corn

500 bus. Oats

1400 bus. Wheat

100 tons Hay with potatoes & other crops in smaller quantity but enough to do him.

He raises most of his meat. Has twelve horses & fifteen cows.

He is a good churchman, attends, counsels and pays. Believes in lodges & helps them too. His city property is said to be worth from $15,000 to $20,000. His obligations he says are very slight, well within his ability to handle. The best citizens of the community are loud in praise of him.

Mr. Fountain Randolph went up with the colony a boy. He is not very active now & has not prospered as Giles has, but lives in his own house of brick with four rooms I think, and is still respected by the community. He & Giles lead in trying to keep the descendents [sic] of the colony together & in the effort to get the land which it is claimed was bought for them.

Randolph still lives in Piqua, A son of his, John S. Randolph was born there, educated in the city schools, and was called to Macon, Ga. several years ago to teach in the schools there, is reported to have done well, established a school at Montezuma, Ga. known as Bennett University. I have not had chance to look him up or his work.

A Miss Anna Jones born at Troy, O. is a descendent [sic] who has been prominent as teacher I was told. Mr. Fountain Randolph said she now lives & teaches at Wilberforce as Mrs. Coleman. I wrote Prof. Scarborough about her but have not heard from him.

Mr. Robert Gordon living at Troy is prospering in business and is greatly helped— says Mr. Randolph, by his wife who is one of the descendants.

Mr. Samuel White at Troy is a prosperous farmer owning his farm & is a successful Tobacco grower. He is a descendent [sic].

Mr. Cash Evans is a prosperous barber in Piqua. He is one of the descendants & is said to own several houses there.

In the summer of 1901 Messrs Goodrich Giles & Fountain Randolph started what became known as "The Randolph Slave Society."

It grew out of a custom in Ohio of holding what they call "Family Reunions" one day in each year. This is a day of feasting and special amusement of some kind when all the members and relatives of a family from far and near are brought together and rejoice among themselves.

The day chosen is usually the anniversary of the birth of some member of the family when all others make special effort to cheer that one, bringing presents & greetings of various sorts.

Giles & Randolph being impressed with this, arranged for a picnic and invited all the members of the Randolph colony that could be reached and their descendents [sic]. A number came and spent the day pleasantly together. A permanent organization was effected. Mr. Fountain Randolph was made President & still holds that position.

That meeting and later ones attracted attention. The Newspapers got interested and began to write them up. The story of their going into Ohio, of the land which was said to have been bought for them in Mercer Co., and of the refusal of the settlers to permit them to occupy the land and more was set forth in the papers. Then lawyers began to talk with them about the lands. A colored lawyer named Henderson from Indianapolis was among the first to call upon them advising that the land could be secured. He was employed to look it up. He advised & secured the employment of a white lawyer, Mr. Johnson at Salina, O. in Mercer Co. to assist him in working out the matter. Mr. Johnson is said to have a certified copy of the Randolph will providing for the liberation of the slaves—their transportation into Ohio, the purchase of land for them, its distribution among them etc. How much money has been raised for the lawyers I could not find but some money has been raised & more probably will be.

Speaking of John Randolph the Master, old Mr. Fountain said "my father said he had lots of peculiarities about him. He never sold a slave & never allowed them to be abused. He never sold any produce as corn, meat and stuffs used by the slaves without first enquiring of the slaves if they could spare it. He would say to the person wanting to buy "You must ask my slaves." "and my mother said:" continued Mr. Randolph "He would often go among his slaves, parents & children & pat them on the head saying 'all these are my children.' His chief body guard was a faithful slave called John White for whom some special mention & provision was made in the will."

This man went with the colony to Ohio, was respected by the others & treated by them just as if he had not been favored by the Master, says Mr. Randolph.

The master gave as his reason for not marrying that should he die—his heirs would want to hold the slaves or sell them and he wanted neither of the things to happen.

He often called the slaves together and asked which they preferred: "Freedom while he lived or after his death and they always said after his death."

Mr. Fountain Randolph has in his possession an old copy of "Life of Randolph of Roanoke" written by Hugh A. Garland, & Published in New York in 1850 by D. Appleton & Co. It is in two volumes. Mr. Randolph had both Vols. but loaned Volume I to the Indianapolis lawyer & has not been able to get it back.

The Randolph will is set forth in Vol. II from which I made the following notes:

Will 1st written in 1819 & left with Dr. Brockenbrough saying:

"I give my slaves their freedom to which my conscience tells me they are justly entitled. It has long been a matter of deepest regret to me that the circumstances under which I inherited them and the obstacles thrown in the way by the laws of the land have prevented my emancipating them in my life time which it is my full intention to do in case I can accomplish it. All the rest & residue of my estate (with exceptions herein after made) whether real or personal, I bequeath to Wm. Leigh, Esq., of Halifax, Atty at Law, to the Rev. Wm. Meade of Frederic and Francis Scott Key Esq., of Georgetown, D.C. in trust for the following uses and purposes viz:

1st To provide one or more tracts of land in any of the States or Territories not exceeding in the whole 4000 acres nor less than 2000 acres, to be partitioned & apportioned by them in such manner as to them shall seem best, among the said slaves.

2nd To pay the expense of their removal & of furnishing them with necessary cabins, clothes & utensils.

In 1821 another Will was written saying: 1st I give and bequeath to all my slaves their freedom—heartily regretting that I have ever been the owner of one.

2nd I give to my executor a sum not exceeding $8,000 or so much thereof as may be necessary to transport & settle said slaves to & in some other state or Territory of the United States, giving to all above the age of 40 not less than ten acres of land each.

Then special annuities to his "old faithful servants Essex & his wife, Hetty, same to woman servant Nancy to John (alias Jupiter) to Queen and to Johnny his body servant." In 1826 a codicil was writen confirming previous wills. In 1828 a codicil to will in possession to Wm. Leigh Esq., confirming it as his last will and testament revoking any and all other wills or codicil at variance that may be found.

In 1831 on starting home from London another codicil adding to former provision as follows:

Upwards of 2000 £ were left in the hands of Baring Bros, & Co of London & upwards of 1000 £ in the hands of Gowan & Marx to be used by Leigh as fund for executing the will regarding the slaves.

Respectfully yours,

The following account and the clipping attached thereto give an interesting story of the success and the philanthropy of a Negro:

I was born in Milledgeville, Ga. about the year 1867. My mother belonged to a white man by the name of Dr. Garner Edwards. My father belonged to a different family. About two weeks after I was born my mother died. She was still working for the same people who once owned her. She was much liked by them so they decided to keep her child and try and raise it. They taught me at home so when I went to school I knew how to read and write. They sent me to school four or five years. Dr. Edwards had a son by the name of Miller or (Buck) Edwards. It was through him that I received my schooling as Dr. was old and Miller was the support of the house. After years Miller died and I had to stop school and go to work. I worked in a number of stores in Milledgeville and was always trusted.

My earnings I always carried them home and gave them to the white people. They never asked me for anything. They gave me all I made but I thought they needed it more than I, so that went on for a number of years. At this time I was about twenty years old so I told them I was going to Macon, Ga. to work. I secured work at the Central R. R. Shop. I worked on the yard a number of months. During that time I was called off the yard at different times to work in the office when some one wanted to get off.

Finally I was given one office to clean up. My work was so satisfactory until I was moved from the shop to the car shed and was given a job of delivering R. R. Mail. I was promoted three times in two years. It was then where I became acquainted with a route agent. He boarded at the same house. We were often in conversation. He was telling me of a daughter he had in school. I told him I wanted to go but was not able. He ask me did I know Booker Washington. I said no. He said well he runs a school where you can work your way through school. I told him I would like to go so he gave me the address. I wrote and received a little pamphlet. I was looking for a catalogue so I was much disappointed in getting this little book and said it was not much. But I decided to go and try. I did not have much money. I had been living high in Macon and spending all I made. I did not stay to make more but left in about four weeks after I received the first letter. I asked for a pass to Montgomery. It was given me. I arrived in Montgomery with 10 or 12 dollars. I said well I am going to school so I will have a good time before going so I got broke did not know any one, thought my trip was up. I walked up the street one morning. In passing a drug store I saw a young man inside. I step back a few steps to look again. I recognized it to be some one I knew some years ago so the first thing came in mind was to borrow enough money from him to take me to Tuskegee. After a long talk he asked me where I was going and what I was doing there, so now was my chance. I told him I was on my way to Tuskegee. He said it was a fine that he had worked up there. I told him I had spent all the money I had and wanted to borrow enough to get there which he very liberally responded. But before I saw him I begged a stamp and some paper and wrote to Mr. Washington that if he would send me the money to come from there I would pay him in work when I came. I received an answer from Mr. Logan stating that if I would go to work there it would not be long before I would get enough money to come on so I borrowed some money from that man and landed there with $3.40. The food was very poor so I soon ate that up. I was not satisfied at first and wanted to leave but I did not have any money and did not want to write home because I did not want my white people to know where I was until I accomplished something so I made up my mind that if all these boys and girls I see can stay here, I can too. So I was never bothered any more. I went to work at the brick mason's trade under Mr. Carter. They did not have any teacher at that time. Soon after Mr. J. M. Green came and I learned fast and was soon a corner man. I was a student two years and nine months. After that time I secured an excuse and left for home. I was very proud of my trade and all seemed to be surprised as no one knew where I was but my white people. I wrote to them once a month and they always answered and would send me money, clothes something to eat. They were very glad I had gone there and tried to help me in many ways when I got home. They had spoken to a contractor and I had no trouble in getting work. I worked at home about two years. Meantime I received a letter from Mr. Washington stating he would like for me to return and work on the chapel, which I did. At this time I was a hired man and not a student. I worked for the school five or six years. Within that time I had helped build two houses in Milledgeville Ga. and paid for them and bought me thirty acres of land in Tuskegee, Ala. I felt very grateful to the school for she has help me in a great many ways. I have always had a great desire to farm but I said I never would farm until I owned my own land and stock.

So three years ago I bought some land and I am at the present time farming. I like it and I expect I will continue at farming instead of my trade. My white people are as good to me now as they were when I was a boy. I made it a rule not to ask them for anything unless I was compelled to but when I do they always send more that I ask for. I will say that I did not know the real value of a dollar until I had spent 2 years and nine months at Tuskegee. The teachings from the various teachers and the Sunday evening talks of Mr. Washington made an indellible impression upon my heart. I remember the first Sunday evening talk that I ever heard him. He spoke of things that were in line with my thoughts and I have tried to put them in practice ever since I have been connected with the school. There is one word I heard Mr. W. Speak 13 years ago that has followed me because I was taught the same words by my white people and they were not to do anything that will bring disgrace upon the school you attend. I was taught not to do anything that will bring disgrace upon the people that raised you. There are a number of other thoughts that I will not take time to mention for I have thanked him a thousand times for those Sunday evenings talks.

Garner J. Edwards

The Republican— Springfield, Mass.—Dec. 6, 1902.

The Milledgeville (Ga.) *News* of November tells the following interesting story of one of the young colored men connected with Booker T. Washington's school at Tuskegee, in regard to the work of which Mr. Washington is to speak in the high school hall in this city the 10th:-

> A case has come to the News which deserves more than a mere passing mention. The story deals with the prettiest case of loyal Negro's devotion and gratitude to his white benefactors that we ever knew of. When we refer to the incident as a story we mean that there is in it a good subject for a real story with a genuine hero. And every word of it is true; in fact, there is more truth in it than we feel at liberty to tell.
>
> About 30 years ago Buck Edwards of this city picked up a very small and dark-colored boy and undertook, in his language, "to raise him and make something of him." Mr. Edwards clothed and fed the boy, and in a general way taught him many things. In return the boy was bright and quick, and rendered such return as a boy of his years could. His name was Garner, and in time he came to be known as Garner Edwards, which name I think he yet clings to.
>
> In the course of human events, Mr. Edwards passed from the stage of life and went to reap the reward of those who rescue the perishing and support the orphans. After his death, Mr. Edward's sisters, Misses Fanny and Laura, continued to care for the boy, and raised him to manhood. Garner

was proud of his family, "and was as faithful as a watchdog, honest at all times, and a great protection["] to the good ladies who were befriending him, and who were now also alone in the world without parents or brothers. When Garner grew into manhood he did not forsake the home that had sheltered him, but insisted that it was his home—the only home he knew—and that it was his duty and pleasure to aid in supporting it; and he did come to bear a considerable part of its expenses.

Garner learned to be a brickmason, and finally moved to Alabama. He became acquainted with Booker Washington, the great Negro Educator, and the acquaintance ripened into friendship. Washington aided Garner in getting work that would enable him to take a course in the school at Tuskegee and at the same time be self-sustaining. Here as in all other of his positions, Garner made a good record and won many honors. In the meantime he did not forget the folks at home, and his remittances to them were always punctual. After finishing school he married, but continued in the employ of the school and Booker Washington and is there yet.

Sometime ago Miss Laura had a fall and sustained a painful injury which confined her to her room. As soon as Garner heard of it he telephoned to Warren Edwards here to provide the best medical attendance possible, and to supply every want at his expense. Following the telegraph came his wife, a trained nurse, "to take care of his white folks," and she is here yet performing every duty with a devotion seldom witnessed. Garner wanted to come too, very much, but he sacrificed the pleasure to keep his salary doing, "because they might need something."

Garner paid the taxes on the old home for years, but in the meantime he has saved enough to buy him another home in Alabama. No one of any color could have been more faithful and appreciative, and such gratitude and devotion as this humble Negro has shown for his white benefactors is a lovely thing to behold in this selfish day. It is said that he never once presumed anything or forgot his place and the respect due those around him.[2]

The following letter and list accompanying it explain themselves:

BELOIT, WIS. Dec. 28, 1906

Dear Mr. Washington

In answer to your telegram for names of graduates and former students engaged in farming in Ala I send the following. I know there are others especially former students but I cannot now recall names. I will try to add to the list if possible.

I would say in regard to the Bowen sisters they have about 600 acres of land and look after the cultivation of it and some parts Cornelia and Katie care for directly actually raising a crop. McRae farmed last year at Louisville, Ala. the year just closing. Mr. W. A. Menafee has 200 acres of land at Alexander City. This he superintendents by two visits each year.

[2] The Springfield Republican, Dec. 6, 1902.

Those marked with a cross farm on their own land. Edwards and Barnes own land at Snow Hill which they farm by the labor of others. Whether they and Mr. Chambliss come under the head of farmers according to your idea you can decide.

I leave January 3 for Denmark, S.C. You can write me there till further notice.

Yours
(Signed) R. C. Benford

GRADUATES AND FORMER STUDENTS ENGAGED IN FARMING IN ALA. WHOLLY OR IN PART

*Cornelia Bowen '85 also teaches	Waugh, Ala.
J. T. Hollis '85 also teaches	Armstrong, Ala.
*Berry Brown Campbell '84 also nurses	Waugh, Ala.
W. D. Floyd, teaches also	Hawkinsville, Ala.
Watt Buchanan 1889 farming wholly	Montgomery, Ala.
*Enoch Houser 1889 also teaches	Antangville, Ala.
William Chambliss 1890	Tuskegee, Ala.
*Davis Henry 1890	Bells Landing, Ala.
*Abner Jackson 1890	Newville, Ala.
John W. Perry 1890	Myrtle, Ala.
Abner Edwards 1890	Salem, Ala.
*J. H. Michael 1890	Mt. Meigs, Ala.
Robert B. Sherman 1890	Sprague Jc., Ala.
*H. A. Barnes 1893	Snow Hill, Ala.
*W. J. Edwards 1893	Snow Hill, Ala.
*N. E. Henry 1893	China, Ala.
Sophia Momen 1894	Notasulga, Ala.
*C. A. Barrows 1894	Snow Hill, Ala.
*S. F. Bizzell, has a store 1894	Hammac, Ala.
E. W. McRae 1894 also teaches	Louisville, Ala.
*Moses Purifoy 1894 also teaches	Evergreen, Ala.
*J. C. Calloway 1896 also teaches	Dawkins, Ala.
Geo. W. Henderson, preacher 1899	Hannon, Ala.
*Martin A. Menafee, Treasurer 1900	Alexander City, Ala.
George K. Gordon, Dairying 1902	Mobile, Ala.

FORMER STUDENTS

Katie Bowen also teaches	Waugh, Ala.
Benjamin Jones	Waugh, Ala.
Nelson Judkins	Cecil, Ala.
Gomine Judkins	Cecil, Ala.
Wm. Plato, also black smith	Waugh, Ala.
James Pinckett, carpenter	Waugh, Ala.
Ossie Williams	Waugh, Ala.
James Garrison	Waugh, Ala.

Nelson Garrison	Waugh, Ala.
John Mitchell also painter	Waugh, Ala.
*Wallace Campbell blacksmith	Fitzpatrick, Ala.
*R. T. Phillips blacksmith	

This is a letter from a Negro farmer in the south:

ISAAC P. MARTIN—

Merryweather Co—near Stenson

Father belonged to Peter Martin near about 3 miles from where he was born—never did own any land. Went to work planting at 9—Worked 9 to 25—Had six or eight months schooling—Went one month in a year. School lasted about three months. Used Blue Back Speller got as high as Baker; Got as far as subtraction—Did not know anything outside of reading—Did not know what a newspaper was.

Father taught us to work corn, cotton sweet potatoes—He was a—farmer—Had eleven children all worked—about 1880 they began to grow up and leave the farm—go on some other plantation—all married.

My older brother and all the younger children got more schooling Brother next younger—Payne's Institute Ga.—finished preaching in Americus Georgia. I had a cousin to come here—He wanted to buy—here—He was interested in machine shop—He was down in Opelika. He met more boys on their way here, inquiring around to get down this far and get in.

I had saved up $200 in the bank. I was going to buy land. Went into day school a Preparatory about 800 or 900 students. The first work was in harness & shoe shop—Lewis Adams was in charge—I came there walking. I wanted to get away from the farm. Going around town I saw that everyone looked better than on the farm—I wanted to be something. Went in twice a year. We had plenty country churches. Rabbits, squirrels, ducks, possums—Geography, reading, Wentworth's Arithmetic. Miss Hunt and Miss Logan were one of my teachers. I read lots about Hiawatha. There was a number of little boys in the shop—they used to call me "Pop." They were ahead of me. Went to Blacksmith Shop. Worked about four months. Then went to work in Wheelwright. I learn a good deal about blacksmith and wood work. I find both these trade very handy.

I was here three weeks before I could eat in the dining room—had to go to restaurant—I was ashamed.

I was here only one term. Came in 1895—left in 96—Never came back until tonight. My mother sent for me—My mother was awful sick. My class was so low that I was ashamed to come back. I weighed 240 pounds. I went back home until 1898—on farm. I got to read my newspapers. I subscribed for the semi-monthly Atlanta Journal—I could read that.

I saw advertised and so much money paid out for wages—I thought I would go into business. I started grocery store and meat market—I had $2,500 made on farm. Father used to run us off the farm at 20 so I rented some land.

I was born 1870. I had been working for myself for years. 1898 I came to Birmingham. I failed in grocery business. "Credit." I made a lot of friends all over town. . . . .
. . . .
They had lots of money but they owed a lot. It take lot to feed them. Took three years and little over to get all of money.

Worked for Tenn. Coal and Iron Co. I leased some land from the Republic Iron and Steel Co. Leased 64 acres outside of Pratt City and went to trucking. I bought two mules for $40. It was a sale. They were old run down mules. They were blind—I worked there until I grew something. Farm about a mile from Pretts. Paid $1.50 per acre—now I pay $7. The company would not sell. I peddle vegetables to people here—ran two wagons—now I run three. Got new feed for horses. By fall had lots of stuff. Married in 1900—year after went to Birmingham. Second year I was able to buy two good mules—Had two good wagons made. Fall of second year had another which made three. Running three now. I employ six people— 3 men and 3 women all the time. I drive the wholesale wagon.

I raise between $3,500 and $4,000 worth of stuff each year. Have since the second year. I sell about $2,000 a year above expenses. Production increases every year. I learned all I know about trucking since then. I have fifteen head of cattle. Eight milking cows. I raise three crops. That is the highest. Third crop is not worth so much. 90,000 cabbages this year. Got the plants from South Carolina. I bought a piece of land in Oklahoma for $3,000 outside of 22 miles from Muskogee. Land rents now for $300. I own a lot in Red Bird. Have 2 children. 14 & and 17. They go to school.

Won county prize year before last—196 bushels—this year received State prize 200 bushels. Plant eight and ten acres of cotton, 14 acres corn. Raise all my fodder. Three-fourths acres of new sugar cane, 150 gals. of syrup. I make butter $30 per hundred. $40 retail. I take two or three little farm journals and take the bulletin.

These letters addressed to R. E. Park and to Booker T. Washington give information about the estate of John McKee:

Estate of
JOHN MCKEE,   }
    Deceased. }

HON. BOOKER T. WASHINGTON,
Tuskegee Institute,
Alabama,

Dear sir:

Your favor has been received and in reply thereto I would state that the State Appraiser fixed the valuation in Estate of the late Colonel John McKee as follows:

Gross valuation of Personal estate,	$ 71,644.29
Gross valuation of real estate in Pennsylvania,	$ 271,188.33
Making together,	$ 342,832.62
Net valuation of the above,	$ 212,831.86

Of this $46,500. is in unimproved real estate from which, at this time, no income is derived.

In addition to the above the Estate owns the following from which no income (or but a nominal income) is derived:—a lot in Gloucester County, New Jersey, valued at One hundred Dollars ($100),—a large area of land in Atlantic County, New Jersey, known as McKee City, assessed for taxation at twenty-thousand six hundred and fifty Dollars ($20,650) and a tract of coal and mineral lands in Kentucky, which Colonel McKee always considered would turn out to be valuable and would eventually realize a considerable sum. It is assessed for taxation for 1909 at Seventy thousand Dollars ($70,000)—

In brief the testamentary directions of Colonel McKee are to accumulate the rents and income of his estate until the decrease of all his children and grand-children, meanwhile improving (under certain conditions) his unimproved real estate. Upon the death of all his children and grand-children, the estate is to be made use of in the establishment and maintenance of a college for the education of colored and white fatherless boys.

Very truly yours,
JOSEPH P. McCULLEN

February 23, 1909.

MR. ROBERT E. PARK,
Tuskegee Institute, Ala.

Dear Sir:

Yours of the 13th inst., post marked the 16th inst., has been received. You state you would be glad to have any information I can give you about Mr. McKee, particularly in regard to the amount of the estate he left at the time of his death.

The value of Mr. McKee's estate has been variously estimated from $1,000,000 to $4,000,000. I am not able to give a more exact estimate, as I have not seen any inventory made by his executors. He owned more than 300 houses in this city, all unencumbered. He also owned oil and coal lands in Kentucky and West Virginia, and lands in Bath and Steuben Counties, N.Y. As to his personal characteristics, I would suggest that you see the Philadelphia Press of April 20, 1902. If you desire a more exact estimate of the value of his estate, I would suggest that you write Joseph P. McCullen, Jr., No. 1008 Land Title Building, this city.

Yours truly,
T. J. MINTON.

The following letter from Colonel James Lewis to Booker T. Washington gives valuable information about Thomy Lafon and incidentally about other persons in New Orleans:

New Orleans, La., Jany. 25/09.

COLONEL JAMES LEWIS,

Dear Sir:

In answer to your letter of 14th instant, will say that the delay in my answer was caused by my desire to obtain and furnish to you all informations regarding the late Mr. Thomy Lafon.

The baptismal records in the archive of the Cathedral at that time written in Spanish attest that the late Mr. Thomy Lafon was born in this city on December 28th, 1810. He died at his home, corner Ursulines & Robertson Streets, on December 23rd, 1893, at the ripe age of 83 years. His body rests in the St. Louis cemetery on Esplanade Avenue. He was a man of dignified appearance and affable manners. In early life he taught school; later he operated a small dry goods store in Orleans Street until near into 1850. He was never married. Sometime before the war of Secession he had started his vast fortune by loaning money at advantageous rates of interest and by the accumulation of his savings. Toward the close of his career he became attached to the lamented Archbishop Janssens and began his philanthropies. By the terms of his will, dated April 3rd, 1890, he provided amply for his aged sister and some friends, and wisely distributed the bulk of his estate among public charitable institutions of New Orleans. His legacy was appraised at $413,000.00 divided in securities and realty.

In recognition of his charity, the City of New Orleans named after him one of its public schools.

Before his death he had established an asylum for orphan boys called the Lafon Asylum, situated in St. Peter Street between Claiborne Avenue & N. Derbigny Street. To this Asylum he bequeathed a sum of $2000, and the revenues, amounting to $275 per month of a large property situated corner Royal & Iberville Streets.

Other legacies were to the

Charity Hospital of New Orleans	$10,000
" " Ambulance Dept	3,000
Lafon Old Folk's Home	5,000
Little Sisters of the Poor	5,000
Shakespeare Almshouse	
Catholic Institution for indigent orphans	2,000

and the following property:

1st.	St. Claude St. bet. St. Philip & Ursulines Sts., valued at	$1500
2nd.	Robertson St. bet. St. Philip & Ursulines Sts., valued at	2000

3rd.	Burgundy St. bet. Hospital & Barracks Sts., valued at	2000	
4th.	Union St. between Royal & Dauphine Sts., valued at	2000	
	St. John Berchman Asylum for girls, under the care of Holy family		2000

and the following property:

1st.	Burgundy St., No. 528, worth about	$1500	
2nd.	Dumaine St., Nos. 2129/31, worth about	2500	
3rd.	Galvez St., No. 828, worth about	1800	
4th.	Toulouse St., Nos. 726/28, worth about	2500	
5th.	Tulane Ave., No. 1402, worth about	4000	
	Asylum for old indigents, corner Tonti & Hospital Streets		15000

and the following property:

1st.	St. Andrew St., 1536/38 valued at	6000	
2nd.	Baronne St., No. 722 valued at	4000	
3rd.	Baronne St. Nos. 732/36 valued at	8000	
4th.	Canal & Villere Sts. valued at	6000	
5th.	Canal St., old No. 176 valued at	30000	
	An another cash		$ 2000
	Society of the Holy Family, Orleans St		10000
	Straight University of New Orleans		3000
	Southern University of New Orleans		3000
	New Orleans University of New Orleans		3000
	Society of Jeunes Amis, New Orleans		3000
	Eye, Ear Nose & Throat Hospital		3000
	Mother St. Clair of the Convent of the Good Shepherd		20000

All of which cash legacies were doubled.

Yours respectfully,
(Signed) P. A. BACAS

The Conflict and Fusion of Cultures with Special Reference to the Negro[1]

Under ordinary circumstances the transmission of the social tradition is from the parents to the children. Children are born into society and take over its customs, habits, and standards of life simply, naturally, and without conflict. But it will at once occur to any one that the life of society is not always continued and maintained in this natural way, by the succession of parents and children. New societies are formed by conquest and by the imposition of one people upon another. In such cases there arises a conflict of cultures and as a result the process of fusion takes place slowly and is frequently not complete. New societies are frequently formed by colonization, in which case new cultures are grafted on to older ones. The work of missionary societies is essentially one of colonization in this sense.

Finally we have societies growing up, as in the United States, by immigration. These immigrants, coming as they do from all parts of the world, bring with them fragments of divergent cultures. Here again the process of assimilation is slow, often painful, not always complete. In the case where societies are formed and maintained by adoption, that is by immigration, the question arises: How far is it possible for a people of a different race and a different culture to take over the traditions and social inheritance of another and an alien people? What are the conditions which facilitate this transmission and, in general, what happens when people of different races and cultures are brought together in the intimate relations of community life?

Robert E. Park, "The Conflict and Fusion of Cultures With Special Reference to the Negro," *The Journal of Negro History* IV:2 (April 1919), pp. 111–33.

[1] This address was delivered before the American Sociological Society convened in annual session at Richmond in 1918.

These questions have already arisen in connection with the education of the Negro in America and with the work of foreign missions. If the schools are to extend and rationalize the work they are already doing in the Americanization of the immigrant peoples, questions of this sort may become actual in the field of pedagogy. This paper is mainly concerned with the Negro, not because the case of the Negro is more urgent than or essentially different from that of the immigrant, but because the materials for investigation are more accessible.

Admitting, as the anthropologists now seem disposed to do, that the average native intelligence in the races is about the same, we may still expect to find in different races certain special traits and tendencies which rest on biological rather than cultural differences. For example, over and above all differences of language, custom or historic tradition, it is to be presumed that Teuton and Latin, the Negro and the Jew—to compare the most primitive with the most sophisticated of peoples—have certain racial aptitudes, certain innate and characteristic differences of temperament which manifest themselves especially in the objects of attention, in tastes and in talents. Is the Jewish intellectual, for example, a manifestation of an original and peculiar endowment of the Jewish race or is he rather a product of traditional interest and emphasis characteristic of Jewish people—a characteristic which may be explained as an accommodation to the long-continued urban environment of the race?[2] Is the Negro's undoubted interest in music and taste for bright colors, commonly attributed to the race, to be regarded as an inherent and racial trait or is it merely the characteristic of primitive people? Is Catholicism to be regarded as the natural manifestation of the Latin temperament as it has been said that Protestantism is of the Teutonic?

Here are differences in the character of the cultural life which can scarcely be measured quantitatively in terms of gross intellectual capacity. Historical causes do not, it seems, adequately account for them. So far as this is true we are perhaps warranted in regarding them as modifications of transmitted tradition due to innate traits of the people who have produced them. Granted that civilization, as we find it, is due to the development of communication and the possibility of mutual exchange of cultural materials, still every special culture is the result of a selection and every people borrows from the whole fund of cultural materials not merely that which it can use but which, because of certain organic characteristics, it finds stimulating and interesting.

The question then resolves itself into this: How far do racial characteristics and innate biological interests determine the extent to which one racial group can and will take over and assimilate the characteristic features of an alien civilization? How far will it merely take over the cultural forms, giving them a

[2] "The City: Suggestions for the Investigation of Human Behavior in the City Environment," *American Journal of Sociology*, V, 44, March, 1915, p. 589.

different content or a different inflection? This problem, so far as it is related to the lives of primitive peoples, has already been studied by the ethnologists. Rivers, in his analysis of the cultures of Australian people, has found that what we have hitherto regarded as primitive cultures are really fusions of other and earlier forms of culture.[3] The evidence of this is the fact that the fusion has not been complete. In the process of interchange it frequently happens that what Rivers calls the "fundamental structure" of a primitive society has remained unchanged while the relatively formal and external elements of alien culture only have been taken over and incorporated with it.

There are indications also that, where cultural borrowings have taken place, the borrowed elements have for the people who have taken them over a meaning different from what they had for the people from whom they were borrowed. W. J. McGee, in an article entitled "Piratical Acculturation," has given an interesting illustration of this fact.[4] McGee's observations of the Beri Indians go to show that they imitated the weapons of their enemies, but that they regarded them as magical instruments and the common people did not even know their names. There are numerous other illustrations of this so-called "piratical acculturation" among the observations of ethnologists. It is said that the Negroes in Africa, when they first came into possession of the white man's guns, regarded them as magical instruments for making a noise and used them, as the Germans used the Zeppelins and the newspapers, merely to destroy the enemy's morale.

No doubt the disposition of primitive peoples is to conceive everything mystically, or animistically, to use the language of ethnology, particularly where it concerns something strange. On the other hand, when the primitive man has encountered among the cultural objects to which civilization has introduced him, something which he has been able to make immediately intelligible to himself, he has at once formed a perfectly rational conception of it. Some years ago at Lovedale, South Africa, the seat of one of the first successful industrial mission schools, there was an important ceremony to which all the native African chiefs in the vicinity were formally invited. It was the introduction and demonstration of the use of the plow, the first one that had ever been seen in those parts. The proceedings were followed with great interest by a large gathering of natives. When the demonstration was finished one old chief turned to his followers and said with great conviction : "This is a great thing which the white man has brought us. One hoe like that is worth as much as ten wives." An African chief could hardly have expressed appreciation of this one fundamental device of our civilization in more pragmatic or less mystical terms. The wise old chief grasped the meaning of the plow at once, but this was because he had been pre-adapted by earlier experience to do so.

[3] Rivers, "Ethnological Analysis of Cultures," *Nature*, Vol. I, 87, 1911.]

[4] W. J. McGee, *Piratical Acculturation*.

It is the subjective, historic and ultimately, perhaps, racial and temperamental factor in the lives of peoples which makes it difficult, though not impossible, perhaps, to transmit political and religious institutions to people of a different racial type and a different social tradition. William James' essay, "On a Certain Blindness in Human Beings," in which he points out how completely we are likely to miss the point and mistake the inner significance of the lives of those about us, unless we share their experience, emphasizes this fact. If then the transmission and fusion of cultures is slow, incomplete and sometimes impossible, it is because the external forms, the formulas, technical devices of every social tradition can be more easily transmitted than the aims, the attitudes, sentiments and ideals which attach to them [and] are embodied in them. The former can be copied and used; the latter must be appreciated and understood.

For a study of the acculturation process, there are probably no materials more complete and accessible than those offered by the history of the American Negro. No other representatives of a primitive race have had so prolonged and so intimate an association with European civilization, and still preserved their racial identity. Among no other people is it possible to find so many stages of culture existing contemporaneously. It has been generally taken for granted that the Negro brought a considerable fund of African tradition and African superstition from Africa to America. One not infrequently finds in the current literature and even in standard books upon the Negro, references to voodoo practices among the Negroes in the Southern States. As a matter-of-fact the last authentic account which we have of anything approaching a Negro nature worship in the United States took place in Louisiana in 1884. It is described by George W. Cable in an article on "Creole Slave Songs" which appeared in the *Century Magazine* in 1886. In this case it seems to have been an importation from the West Indies. I have never found an account of a genuine instance of voodoo worship elsewhere in the United States, although it seems to have been common enough in the West Indies at one time.

My own impression is that the amount of African tradition which the Negro brought to the United States was very small. In fact, there is every reason to believe, it seems to me, that the Negro, when he landed in the United States, left behind him almost everything but his dark complexion and his tropical temperament. It is very difficult to find in the South today anything that can be traced directly back to Africa. This does not mean that there is not a great deal of superstition, conjuring, "root doctoring" and magic generally among the Negroes of the United States. What it does mean is that the superstitions we do find are those which we might expect to grow up anywhere among an imaginative people, living in an intellectual twilight such as exists on the isolated plantations of the Southern States. Furthermore, this superstition is in no way associated, as it is in some of the countries of Europe, southern Italy for example, with religious beliefs and practices. It is not part of

Negro Christianity. It is with him, as it is with us, folklore pure and simple. It is said that there are but two African words that have been retained in the English language. One of these is the word Buckra, from which comes Buckra Beach in Virginia. This seems remarkable when we consider that slaves were still brought into the United States clandestinely up to 1862.[5]

The explanation is to be found in the manner in which the Negro slaves were collected in Africa and the manner in which they were disposed of after they arrived in this country. The great markets for slaves in Africa were on the West Coast, but the old slave trails ran back from the coast far into the interior of the continent, and all the peoples of Central Africa contributed to the stream of enforced emigration to the New World. In the West Indies a good deal was known among slave-traders and plantation owners about the character and relative value of slaves from different parts of Africa, but in the United States there was less knowledge and less discrimination. Coming from all parts of Africa and having no common language and common tradition, the memories of Africa which they brought with them were soon lost.

There was less opportunity in the United States also than in the West Indies for a slave to meet one of his own people, because the plantations were considerably smaller, more widely scattered and, especially, because as soon as they were landed in this country, slaves were immediately divided and shipped in small numbers, frequently no more than one or two at a time, to different plantations. This was the procedure with the very first Negroes brought to this country. It was found easier to deal with the slaves, if they were separated from their kinsmen.

On the plantation they were thrown together with slaves who had already forgotten or only dimly remembered their life in Africa. English was the only language of the plantation. The attitude of the slave plantation to each fresh arrival seems to have been much like that of the older immigrant towards the greenhorn. Everything that marked him as an alien was regarded as ridiculous and barbaric.[6] Furthermore, the slave had in fact very little desire to return to his native land. I once had an opportunity to talk with an old man living just outside of Mobile, who was a member of what was known as the African colony. This African colony represented the cargo of one of the last slave

[5] There is or was a few years ago near Mobile a colony of Africans who were brought to the United States as late as 1860. It is true, also, that Major R. R. Moton, who has succeeded Booker T. Washington as head of Tuskegee Institute, still preserves the story that was told him by his grandmother of the way in which his great-grandfather was brought from Africa in a slave ship.

[6] *Domestic Manners and Social Condition of the White, Coloured and Negro Population of the West Indies,* by Mrs. Carmichael, Vol. I. (London, Wittaker, Treacher and Co.), p. 251. "Native Africans do not at all like it to be supposed that they retain the customs of their country and consider themselves wonderfully civilized by being transplanted from Africa to the West Indies. Creole Negroes invariably consider themselves superior people, and lord it over the native Africans."

ships successful in landing in this country just at the opening of the war. The old man remembered Africa and gave me a very interesting account of the way in which he was captured and brought to America. I asked him if he had ever wished to return. He said that a missionary who had been in their country and spoke their language had visited them at one time. This missionary offered to send them back to Africa and even urged them to go. "I told him," said the old man, "I crossed the ocean once, but I made up my mind then never to trust myself in a boat with a white man again."

The fact that the Negro brought with him from Africa so little tradition which he was able to transmit and perpetuate on American soil, makes that race unique among all peoples of our cosmopolitan population. Other peoples have lost, under the disintegrating influence of the American environment, much of their cultural heritage. None have [sic] been so utterly cut off and estranged from their ancestral land, traditions and people. It is just because of this that the history of the Negro offers exceptional materials for determining the relative influence of temperamental and historical conditions upon the process by which cultural materials from one racial group are transmitted to another; for, in spite of the fact that the Negro brought so little intellectual baggage with him, he has exhibited a rather marked ethnical individuality in the use and interpretation of the cultural materials to which he has had access.

The first, and perhaps the only distinctive institution which the Negro has developed in this country is the Negro church, and it is in connection with his religion that we may expect to find, if anywhere, the indications of a distinctive Afro-American culture. The actual conditions under which the African slaves were converted to Christianity have never been adequately investigated. We know, in a general way, that there was at first considerable opposition to admitting the Negro into the church because it was feared that it would impair the master's title to his slaves. History records too that the house servants were very early admitted to churches and that in many cases masters went to considerable pains to instruct those servants who shared with them the intimacy of the household.[7] It was not, however, until the coming of the new, free and evangelistic types of Christianity, the Baptists and the Methodists, that the masses of the black people, that is, the plantation Negroes, found a form of Christianity that they could make their own.

How eagerly and completely the Negro did take over the religion of these liberal denominations may be gathered from some of the contemporary writings, which record the founding of the first Negro churches in America. The first Negro church in Jamaica was founded by George Liele, shortly after the close of the Revolutionary War. George Liele had been a slave in Savannah,

---

[7] The Society for the Propagation of the Gospel in Foreign Parts was founded in 1701 and the efforts to Christianize the Negro were carried on with a great deal of zeal and with some success.

but his master, who was a Tory, emigrated to Jamaica upon the evacuation of that city. Andrew Bryan in Savannah was one of Liele's congregation. He was converted, according to the contemporary record, by Liele's exposition of the text "You must be born again!" About eight months after Liele's departure, Andrew began to preach to a Negro congregation, "with a few white." The colored people had been permitted to erect a building at Yamacraw, but white people in the vicinity objected to the meetings and Bryan and some of his associates were arrested and whipped. But he "rejoiced in his whippings" and holding up his hand declared "he would freely suffer death for the cause of Jesus Christ." Bryan's master interceded for him and "was most affected and grieved" at his punishment. He gave Bryan and his followers a barn to worship in, after Chief Justice Osbourne had given them their liberty. This was the origin of what was probably the first Negro church in America.

George Liele and Andrew Bryan were probably not exceptional men even for their day. The Rev. James Cook wrote of Bryan: "His gifts are small but he is clear in the grand doctrines of the Gospel. I believe him truly pious and he has been the instrument of doing more good among the poor slaves than all the learned doctors in America."[8] The significant thing is that, with the appearance of these men, the Negroes in America ceased to be a mission people. At least, from this time on, the movement went on of its own momentum, more and more largely under the direction of Negro leaders. Little Negro congregations, under the leadership of Negro preachers, sprang up wherever they were tolerated. Often they were suppressed, more often they were privately encouraged. Not infrequently they met in secret.

In 1787 Richard Allen and Absolom [sic] Jones had formed in Philadelphia the Free African Society, out of which four year later, in 1790, arose the first separate denominational organization of Negroes, the African Methodist-Episcopal Church. George Liele, Andrew Bryan, Richard Allen, and the other founders of the Negro church were men of some education, as their letters and other writings show. They had had the advantage of life in a city environment and the churches which they founded were in all essentials faithful copies of the denominational forms as they found them in the churches of that period.

The religion of the Negroes on the plantation was then, as it is today, of a much more primitive sort. Furthermore, there were considerable differences in the cultural status of different regions of the South and these differences were reflected in the Negro churches. There was at that time, as there is today, a marked contrast between the Upland and the Sea Island Negroes. Back from the coast the plantations were smaller, the contact of the master and slave were more intimate. On the Sea Islands, however, where the slaves were and still are more completely isolated than elsewhere in the South, the

---

[8] JOURNAL OF NEGRO HISTORY, Vol I, 1916, p. 70.

Negro population approached more closely to the cultural status of the native African. The Sea Islands were taken possession of in the first years of the war by the Federal forces and it was here that people from the North first came in contact with the plantation Negro of the lower South. They immediately became interested in the manners and customs of the Island Negroes, and from them we have the first accurate accounts of their folk-lore and sayings.

The Sea Island Negroes speak a distinct dialect and retain certain customs which are supposed to be of African origin. It is, however, in their religious practices that we have the nearest approach to anything positively African. This has undoubtedly the characteristics of primitive ritual. But this does not mean that it is African in origin. It seems to me more likely that it is to be interpreted as a very simple and natural expression of group emotion, which is just beginning to crystallize and assume a formal character. The general tone of these meetings is that of a religious revival in which we expect a free and uncontrolled expression of religious emotion, the difference being that in this case the expression of the excitement is beginning to assume a formal and ritualistic character.

In the voodoo practices, of which we have not any accurate records, the incantations that were pronounced by the priests, contain strange, magic words, scraps of ancient ritual, the meanings of which are forgotten. Lafcadio Hearne [sic. Hearn], who knew the Negro life of Louisiana and Martinique intimately and was keen on the subject of Negro folk-lore, has preserved for us this scrap from an old Negro folk song in which some of these magic words have been preserved. Writing to his friend Edward Krehbiel he says:

"Your friend is right, no doubt about the
'Tig, tig, malaborn
La Chelerna che tango
Redjoum!'

"I asked my black nurse what it meant. She only laughed and shook her head. 'Mais c'est voodoo, ca; je n'en sais rien!' 'Well,' said I, 'don't you know anything about Voodoo songs?' 'Yes,' she answered, 'I know Voodoo songs; but I can't tell you what they mean.' And she broke out into the wildest, weirdest ditty I ever heard. I tried to write down the words; but as I did not know what they meant I had to write by sound alone, spelling the words according to the French pronunciation."[9]

So far as I know there are, among the plantation hymns, no such remains of ancient ritual, mystical words whose meanings are unknown, no traces whatever of African tradition. If there is anything that is African about the

[9] *Afro-American Folksongs A Study in Racial and National Music,* by Henry Edward Krehbiel. (New York and London, G. Schirmer), p. 37. From a letter of Lafcadio Hearne [sic].

Negroes' Christianity, it is not African tradition but the African temperament which has contributed it. I assume, therefore, that what we find in the most primitive form of Negro Christianity is not the revival of an older and more barbaric religion but the inception of a new and original form of Christianity.

An interesting fact in regard to the religious practices of the Negroes of the Sea Islands, which has not, so far as I know, been recorded in any of the descriptions of that people, is the existence among them of two distinct religious institutions; namely, the church and the "praise house." The praise house is the earlier institution and represents apparently a more primitive and more characteristically Negro or African type. In slavery days, the church was the white man's place of worship. Negroes were permitted to attend the services and there was usually a gallery reserved for their use. Churches, however, were relatively few and not all the slaves on the plantation could attend at any one time. Those who did attend were usually the house servants. On every large plantation, however, there was likely to be, and this was characteristic of the Sea Island plantations, a "praise house" where the slaves were permitted to worship in their own peculiar way. It was here that the "shout" took place. After the Civil War, churches were erected and regular congregations of the Negro denominations were formed. The Negro churches, however, never wholly displaced the praise houses on Port Royal and some of the other islands. It is a singular fact that today, among the Negroes of Port Royal, at any rate, no one is converted in church. It is only in the praise houses that Negroes get religion. It is only through the praise house that one enters the church. The whole process involves, as I have been informed, not merely an "experience," the precise nature of which is not clear, but also an examination by the elders to determine whether the experience is genuine, before candidates are admitted in good standing as members of the congregation.

On the whole the plantation Negro's religion was a faithful copy of the white man's. It was content rather than the form which suffered sea change in the process of transmission from the white man to the black. What this content was, what new inflection and color the Negro slave imparted to the religious forms which he borrowed from his master we may, perhaps, gather from a study of the plantation hymns. These folksongs represent, at any rate, the naïve and spontaneous utterance of hopes and aspirations for which the Negro slave had no other adequate means of expression. The first and most interesting account we have of these Negro spirituals is that of Col. Thomas Wentworth Higginson, in his *Army Life in a Black Regiment.*[10] He collected them from the lips of his own black soldiers as they sang them about the campfire at night. He was almost the first to recognize that these rude plantation hymns

[10] *Army Life in a Black Regiment,* by Thomas Wentworth Higginson. Boston, Fields, Osgood and Co., 1870.

represented a real literature, the only literature the American Negro has produced, until very recent times.

Col. Higginson has compared the Negro spirituals to the Scotch ballads
and to the folk songs of other races. It is, however, not so much their similar-
ities as their differences which are interesting and significant. Negro folk
songs are ruder and more primitive. The verses, often but not always rhymed
are, as in the case of the example given below, composed almost entirely of
single phrases, followed by a refrain, which is repeated again with slight
modifications, ending, not infrequently, in an exclamation.

> An' I couldn't hear nobody pray,
>   O Lord!
> Couldn't hear nobody pray.
>   O—way down yonder
>   By myself,
> I couldn't hear nobody pray.
>
> In the valley,
>   Couldn't hear nobody pray,
> On my knees,
>   Couldn't hear nobody pray,
> With my burden,
>   Couldn't hear nobody pray,
> An' my Saviour,
>   Couldn't hear nobody pray.
>
> O Lord!
> I couldn't hear nobody pray,
>   O Lord!
> Couldn't hear nobody pray.
>   O—way down yonder
>   By myself,
> I couldn't hear nobody pray.
>
> Chilly waters,
>   Couldn't hear nobody pray,
> In the Jordan,
>   Couldn't hear nobody pray,
> Crossing over,
>   Couldn't hear nobody pray,
> Into Canaan,
>   Couldn't hear nobody pray.

In Negro folk songs the music and expression are everything. The words, often striking and suggestive, to be sure, represent broken fragments of ideas, thrown up from the depths of the Negroes' consciousness and swept along upon a torrent of wild, weird and often beautiful melody. One reason the verses of the Negro folk songs are so broken and fragmentary is that the Negroes were not yet in secure possession of the English language. Another explanation is the conditions under which they were produced. The very structure of these verses indicate [sic] their origin in the communal excitement of a religious assembly. A happy phrase, a striking bit of imagery, flung out by some individual was taken up and repeated by the whole congregation. Naturally the most expressive phrases, the lines that most adequately voiced the deep unconscious desires of the whole people, were remembered longest and repeated most frequently. New lines and variations were introduced from time to time. There was, therefore, a process of natural selection by which the best, the most representative verses, those which most adequately expressed the profounder and more permanent moods and sentiments of the Negro were preserved and became part of the permanent tradition of the race.

Negro melodies still spring up on the plantations of the South as they did in the days of slavery. The Negro is, like the Italian, an improviser, but the songs he produces today have not, so far as my knowledge goes, the quality of those he sang in slavery. The schools have introduced reading, and this, with the reflection which writing enforces, is destroying the folk songs of the Negro, as it has those of other races.

Not only are the Negro folk songs more primitive—in the sense I have indicated—than the folk songs of other peoples with which we are familiar but the themes are different. The themes of the Scotch ballads are love and battles, the adventures and tragedies of a wild, free life. The Negro songs, those that he has remembered best, are religious and other worldly. "It is a singular fact," says Krehbiel, "that very few secular songs—those which are referred to as 'reel tunes,' 'fiddle songs,' 'corn songs' and 'devil songs,' for which slaves generally expressed a deep abhorrence, though many of them no doubt were used to stimulate them while in the field—have been preserved while 'shout songs' and other 'speritchils' have been kept alive by the hundred."[11]

If it is the plantation melodies that, by a process of natural selection, have been preserved in the traditions of the Negro people, it is probably because in these songs they found a free and natural expression of their unfulfilled desires. In the imagery of these songs, in the visions which they conjure up, in the themes which they again and again renew, we may discern the reflection of dawning racial consciousness, a common racial ideal.

The content of the Negro folk songs has been made the subject of a careful investigation by Howard Odum in his *Study of the Social and Mental Traits*

[11] Krehbiel, *Afro-American Folksongs,* p. 16.

of the Negro. He says: "The Negro's fancies of 'Heaven's bright home' are scarcely exceeded by our fairy tales. There are silver and golden slippers, crowns of stars, jewels and belts of gold. There are robes of spotless white and wings all bejeweled with heavenly gems. Beyond the Jordan the Negro will outshine the sun, moon and stars. He will slip and slide the golden street and eat the fruit of the trees of paradise. . . . With rest and ease, with a golden band about him and with palms of victory in his hands and beautiful robes, the Negro will indeed be a happy being. . . . To find a happy home, to see all the loved ones and especially the Biblical characters, to see Jesus and the angels, to walk and talk with them, to wear robes and slippers as they do, and to *rest forever,* constitute the chief images of the Negro's heaven. He is tired of the world which has been a hell to him. Now on his knees, now shouting, now sorrowful and glad, the Negro comes from 'hanging over hell' to die and sit by the Father's side."[12]

In the imagery which the Negro chooses to clothe his hopes and dreams, we have, as in the musical idiom in which he expresses them, reflections of the imagination and the temperament of Africa and the African. On the other hand, in the themes of this rude rhapsodical poetry—the House of Bondage, Moses, the Promised Land, Heaven, the apocalyptic visions of Freedom—but Freedom confined miraculously and to another world—these are the reflections of the Negro's experience in slavery.

The Negro's songs of slavery have been referred to by Du Bois in his *Soul [sic] of Black-Folk* as sorrow songs, and other writers have made the assertion that all the songs of the slaves were in a plaintive minor key. As a matter of fact, investigation has shown that actually less than twelve per cent of Negro songs are in a minor.[13] There are no other folk songs, with the exception of those of Finland, of which so large a percentage are in the major mood. And this is interesting as indicating the racial temperament of the Negro. It tends to justify the general impression that the Negro is temperamentally sunny, cheerful, optimistic. It is true that the slave songs express longing, that they refer to "hard trials and great tribulations," but the dominant mood is one of jubilation, "Going to sing, going to shout, going to play all over God's heaven."

Other worldliness is not peculiar to the religion of the slave. It is a trait which the slave encountered in the religion of his master. But in the Negro's conception of religion it received a peculiar emphasis. In fact, these ecstatic visions of the next world, which the Negro slave songs portrayed with a directness and simplicity that is at once quaint and pathetic, are the most significant features of the Negro's songs of slavery.

---

[12] Studies in History, Economics, and Public Law, edited by The Faculty of Political Science of Columbia University, Vol. 37, New York, 1910, No. 3—*Social and Mental Traits of the Negro,* by Howard W. Odum, Ph.D., p. 91.

[13] Krehbiel, *Afro-American Folksongs.*

It is interesting to note in this connection that nowhere in these songs do we discover the slightest references to Africa. They reflect no memories of a far off happier land. Before the Negro gained his emancipation Africa had, so far as he was concerned, almost ceased to exist. Furthermore, the whole tone and emphasis of these songs and of all other religious expressions of the American Negro are in marked contrast with the tone and emphasis of African religious ideas. The African knew of the existence of another world, but he was not interested in it. The world, as the African understood it, was full of malignant spirits, diseases and forces with which he was in constant mortal struggle. His religious practices were intended to gain for him immunity in this world, rather than assurance of the next. But the Negro in America was in a different situation. He was not living in his own world. He was a slave and that, aside from the physical inconvenience, implied a vast deal of *inhibition*. He was, moreover, a constant spectator of life in which he could not participate; excited to actions and enterprises that were forbidden to him because he was a slave. The restlessness which his situation provoked found expression, not in insurrection and rebellion—although, of course, there were Negro insurrections—but in his religion and in his dreams of another freer world. I assume, therefore, that the reason the Negro so readily and eagerly took over from the white man his heaven and apocalyptic visions was because these materials met the demands of his peculiar racial temperament and furnished relief to the emotional strains that were provoked in him by the conditions of slavery.

So far as slavery was responsible for the peculiar individuality of the Negro's religion we should expect that the racial ideals and racial religion would take on another and a different character under the influence of freedom. This, indeed, is what seems to me is taking place. New ideals of life are expressed in recent Negro literature and slowly and imperceptibly those ideas are becoming institutionalized in the Negro church and more particularly in the cultural ideals of the Negro school. But this makes another chapter in the history of Negro culture in America.

I have sought in this brief sketch to indicate the modifications, changes and fortune which a distinctive racial temperament has undergone as a result of encounters with an alien life and culture. This temperament, as I conceive it, consists in a few elementary but distinctive characterstics, determined by physical organization and transmitted biologically. These characteristics manifest themselves in a genial, sunny and social disposition, in an interest and attachment to external, physical things rather than to subjective states and objects of introspection; in a disposition for expression rather than enterprise and action. The changes which have taken place in the manifestations of this temperament have been actuated by an inherent and natural impulse, characteristic of all living things, to persist and maintain themselves in a changed environment. Such changes have occurred as are likely to take place in any organism in its struggle to live and to use its environment to further and complete its own existence.

The general principle which the Negro material illustrates is that the racial temperament selects out of the masses of cultural materials, to which it had access, such technical, mechanical and intellectual devices as meet its needs at a particular period of its existence. It clothes and enriches itself with such new customs, habits, and cultural forms as it is able, or permitted to use. It puts into these relatively external things, moreover, such concrete meanings as its changing experience and its unchanging racial individuality demand.

Everywhere and always the Negro has been interested rather in expression than in action; interested in life itself rather than its reconstruction or reformation. The Negro is, by natural disposition, neither an intellectual nor an idealist like the Jew, nor a brooding introspective like the East Indian, nor a pioneer and frontiersman like the Anglo-Saxon. He is primarily an artist, loving life for its own sake. His metier is expression rather than action. The Negro is, so to speak, the lady among the races.

In reviewing the fortunes of the Negro's temperament as it is manifested in the external events of the Negro's life in America, our analysis suggests that this racial character of the Negro has exhibited itself everywhere in something like the rôle of the *wish* in the Freudian analysis of dream life. The external cultural forms which he found here, like the memories of the individual, have furnished the materials in which the racial wish, that is, the Negro temperament, has clothed itself. The inner meaning, the sentiment, the emphasis, the emotional color which these forms assumed as the result of their transference from the white man to the Negro, these have been the Negro's own. They have represented his temperament—his temperament modified, however, by his experience and the tradition which he has accumulated in this country. The temperament is African, but the tradition is American.

I present this thesis merely as a hypothesis. As such its value consists in its suggestion of a point of view and program for investigation. I may, however, suggest some of the obvious practical consequences. If racial temperament—particularly when it gets itself embodied in institutions and in *nationalities,* that is, social groups based upon race—is so real and obdurate a thing that education can only enrich and develop it but not dispose of it, then we must be concerned to take acount of it in all our schemes for promoting naturalization, assimilation, Americanization, Christianization, and acculturation generally.

If it is true that the Jew, as has been suggested, just because of his intellectuality is a natural born idealist, internationalist, doctrinaire, and revolutionist, while the Negro, because of his natural attachment to known, familiar objects, places and persons, is preadapted to conservatism and to local and personal loyalties; if these things are true, we shall eventually have to take account of them practically. It is certain that the Negro has uniformly shown a disposition to loyalty, during slavery to his master, and during freedom to the South and the country as a whole. He has maintained this attitude of loyalty, too, under very discouraging circumstances. I once heard Kelly Miller, the most philosophical of the leaders of his race, say in a public speech that one of the greatest hardships the Negro suffered in this country was due to the fact that he was not permitted to be patriotic.

Of course, all these alleged racial characteristics have a positive as well as a negative significance. Every race, like every individual, has the vices of its virtues. The question remains still to what extent so-called racial characteristics are actually racial, that is, biological, and to what extent they are the effect of environmental conditions. The thesis of this paper, to state it again, is: (1) That fundamental temperamental qualities, which are the basis of interest and attention, act as selective agencies and as such determine what elements in the cultural environment each race will select, in what region it will seek and find its vocation, in the larger social organization; (2) that, on the other hand, technique, science, machinery, tools, habits, discipline and all the intellectual and mechanical devices with which the civilized man lives and works, remain relatively external to the inner core of significant attitudes and values which constitute what many call the will of the group. This racial will is, to be sure, largely social, that is modified by social experience, but it rests ultimately upon a complex of inherited characteristics, which are racial.

It follows from what has been said that the individual man is the bearer of a double inheritance. As a member of a race, he transmits by interbreeding a biological inheritance. As a member of society or a social group, on the other hand, he transmits by communication a social inheritance. The particular complex of inheritable characters, which characterizes the individuals of a racial group constitutes the racial temperament. The particular group of habits, accommodations, sentiments, attitudes and ideals transmitted by communication and education constitute a social tradition. Between this temperament and this tradition there is, as has been generally recognized, a very intimate relationship. My assumption is that temperament is the basis of the *interests;* that as such it determines in the long run the general run of attention, and this, eventually, determines the selection in the case of an individual of his vocation, in the case of the racial group its culture. That is to say, temperament determines what things the individual and the groups will be interested in; what elements of the general culture, to which they have access, they will assimilate; what, to state it in pedagogical terms, they will learn.

It will be evident at once that where individuals of the same race and hence the same temperament are associated, the temperamental interests will tend to reinforce one another, and the attention of members of the group will be more completely focused upon the specific objects and values that correspond to the racial temperament. In this way racial qualities become the basis for nationalities, a nationalistic group being merely a cultural and eventually political society founded on the basis of racial inheritances. On the other hand, when racial segregation is broken up and members of a racial group are dispersed and isolated, the opposite effect will take its place. This explains the phenomena which have frequently been the subject of comment and observation, that the racial characteristics manifest themselves in an extraordinary way in large homogeneous gatherings. The contrast between a mass meeting of one race and a similar meeting of another is particularly striking. Under such circumstances characteristic racial and temperamental differences appear that would otherwise pass entirely unnoticed.

When the physical unity of a group is perpetuated by the succession of parents and children, the racial temperament, including fundamental attitudes and values which rest on it, are preserved intact. When however, society grows and is perpetuated by immigration and adaptation, there ensues, as a result of miscegenation, a breaking up of the complex of the biologically inherited qualities which constitute the temperament of the race. This again initiates changes in the mores, traditions and eventually in the institutions of the community. The changes which proceed from modification in the racial temperament will, however, modify but slightly the external forms of the social traditions but they will be likely to change profoundly their content and meaning. Of course, other factors, individual competition, the formation of classes, and especially the increase of communication, all coöperate to complicate the whole situation and to modify the effects which would be produced by racial factors working in isolation. All these factors must be eventually taken account of, however, in any satisfactory scheme of dealing with the problem of Americanization by education. This is, however, a matter for more complete analysis and further investigation.

Life Experience:
Its Relation to Sociology

Methods of Teaching

*Impressions and a Verdict**

One of the best things that has been said about method is Cooley's remark about methods of research. "A working methodology" he said, "is a residue from actual research, a tradition of laboratories and work in the field: the men who contributed to it did so unconsciously, by trying to find out something that they ardently wanted to know."

I think one may fairly apply Cooley's dictum to methods of teaching. The best methods are likely to be those that the teacher has worked out for himself in the effort to teach; that is, to transmit to his pupils, under the conditions which the classroom imposes, some body of information, of ideas or of practices which represent, presumably, the accepted tradition in his particular field of study.

There is always likely to be too much routine and too little imagination, too much discipline and too little self-expression in our educational procedures. I say this with a certain degree of reservation because I know that in certain instances methods designed to encourage self-expression, on the part of pupils have resulted in something like nervous prostration in teachers—not to mention the incidental destruction of the school room furniture.

I am, of course, all for such self-expression as the so-called progressive education encourages but not on the part of the students merely. Teachers, like students, are inclined to regard their textbooks as sacred literature,—the last word on a subject rather than the first.

Reprinted from *Social Forces* XX:1 (October 1941). "Methods of Teaching: Impressions and a Verdict" by Robert E. Park. Copyright © The University of North Carolina Press.

*Read before the Sixth Annual Meeting of the Southern Sociological Society in Atlanta, Georgia, April 4, 1941.

In my own experience the most effective and the most inspiring teachers have employed the most unconventional and the least formal methods. If I am less disposed than I might otherwise have been to accept orthodox methods of teaching it is because I am convinced that the influence which an uninhibited teacher, with insight and understanding, can exercise upon a pupil, though often emphasized has rarely been overestimated. My own case as [sic] an illustration.

When I entered the University of Michigan in 1883 I was 19 years old. I had learned in school, during the fourteen years, off and on, in which I have [sic] been a pupil, little or nothing. This I discovered shortly after my arrival. It was true I had read much, but not by any means the best, even of what was accessible to me. Probably the most stimulating stuff I had encountered up to that time was Bob Ingersoll's lectures, "The Ten Mistakes of Moses," and a protracted series of rather ribald debates on the subject of evolution, carried on by a society of young radicals in our town. That debating society seems to have played about the same role in my intellectual life that the debates of the Hell Fire club did in that of Benjamin Franklin, when he was a boy in New England. Our town was in Minnesota, but was settled by New Englanders.

However, I did discover geometry while I was in high school and found it exciting. I made a sort of game of it, trying to work out the problems, as far as possible, without referring to the demonstrations in the text. Otherwise I was not interested in school, the result being that when I entered the University I was, for all practical purposes, an ignoramus.

The teacher who "pulled the kivers off and woke me up," as an old colored man once put it, was Calvin Thomas, who was just then making his reputation as a German scholar and teacher. He was the first real scholar, as I realized later, I had ever met. The others were just teachers. German was his subject but I learned much more than German from him. After the first ten days in freshman German we had a written quiz. On that quiz he gave me a score of ten on a scale of 100. Incidentally he informed me, in a note at the bottom of my paper, that if I was six times as good a student at the end of the semester as I was then he could not possibly pass me. That note changed my career. I had been a football player, and an outdoors boy. I became a student and a consistent burner of the midnight oil. I found, almost for the first time, that I I [sic] could be interested in what was going on in school. My interest in going to college had not been, originally, intellectual but practical. I intended to be an engineer. I became instead a student of philosophy, and was presently possessed with a devouring curiosity to know about the world, and all that man had thought and done.

I think the very best teacher—at least the very best lecturer—I ever studied under was Georg Friedrich Knapp, at the University of Strassburg. He was,—believe it or not,—at once a statistician and a historian, and his most popular course was a history of European, and particularly German, agriculture. Among other things I got to know and to understand from him the

German peasant. In fact I gained from his lectures a knowledge of peasant life so complete and intimate as I would never have believed possible to have of any people with whom one had not lived. These lectures were delightfully anecdotal, and at the same time amazingly informing, the product of an acute mind and an extraordinary amount of patient, scholarly investigation. It was, however, the art with which they were presented that impressed me most.

Knapp used to put a complete analysis of his lectures on the board. This analysis itself was a work of art. With this outline and his exposition of the subject, including the anecdotes with which he illustrated it, one felt that one never need look at a book on the subject again. One did, however, want to go and see and learn from first hand observation more about the people of which he had spoken. That course, aside from what it taught me about teaching, was an immensely stimulating introduction to, and orientation in, a field of study in which I have been interested ever since, namely, peasant economy and peasant life.

When I came South a year or two later to make the acquaintance of the Negro peasant, I found, to put Mr. Kipling's phrase in reverse, that the things you learn from the whites will help you a lot with the brown and the black. Finally, and this is a mere detail, I recall that in concluding his course of lectures he referred us, as further introduction to a more detailed study of the subject, not to a scientific treatise but to a novel, *Der Bitner Bauer,* which I purchased and read with interest. It suggested an idea by which I have ever since greatly profited, namely the value of realistic fiction and of literary description in bringing into view the more intimate and human aspects of life, giving the student in this way, not the authentic knowledge he is seeking, but at any rate that "acquaintance with" the situation and the subject that is as indispensable to the sociologist as it is to the historian.

Another of my teachers was William James and I learned about methods of teaching from him, mainly, I think, because he had no methods,—at least no formal methods,—at all. James did not lecture, he merely discoursed, and though he did, in one of the courses, use a textbook, it was a textbook on theology and he used it, as it seemed to me, somewhat like a red flag to a bull, to excite the class and start discussion. Once started discussion went on in a very effective but irregular way, not wholly unlike one of the so-called "bull sessions" with which students are familiar. At any rate what one learned was not what one got out of the textbook, but what one got out of the discussion. And what did one get out of these discussions? Certainly nothing that could by any extension of that term be described as erudition. Our discussions were neither historical nor doctrinal. They were, perhaps metaphysical. At any rate they remained entirely in what Santayana would call "the realm of the spirit." What one got from them was not knowledge, certainly not knowledge in the ordinary sense of that word, but insight and enlightenment.

What made them memorable were the occasional and seemingly casual remarks with which James would from time to time illuminate the subject of discussion. I remember an occasion when, after listening patiently to a prolonged debate about evolution and progress, he remarked, wearily in a kind of aside: "Progress! Progress is a terrible thing. How much effort, how much suffering, how much disillusionment it has cost us first and last." As he went on to elaborate this theme we found ourselves looking down in retrospect the long vista of evolutionary history in the course of which man had arisen to his rather precarious preeminence on our little planet, with something less, at least, than the enthusiasm with which we had previously looked forward to its continuation in the future. After that, somehow, we lost interest in the debate and, as for me, I have never had the same interest in progress since. Is this an instance of James' method or is it just his temperament? I am sure I do not know.

I recall another apparently casual remark of James that cleared up a rather extensive area of confusion in my mind. One of the things we discussed in this course was the proof for the existence of God. It seems a little quaint to me now that anyone should want a proof of the existence of God or find any comfort in it after he got it. But Professor Royce, who was James' colleague and neighbor in Cambridge, formulated and published such a proof while I was at Harvard. To me it all seemed a little mystifying, like taking a rabbit out of a hat, and I was neither impressed nor convinced by the argument. At any rate the proofs for the existence of God was [sic] a live topic in the department of philosophy at Harvard at that time. So it was that we found ourselves one day discussing the attributes of God. What were they? Someone suggested that one of God's attributes was infinity. Infinite in what? Infinite in space? Infinite in time? And what would that mean anyway? "Infinitely old," said James, and that remark banished once and for all, so far as I was concerned, any further interest in the attributes of God. It did more than that. It banished scholasticism. From that time on logic, and formal knowledge of every sort, ceased to have for me that interest or the authority they once had. Ideas were no longer to be anywhere or in any sense a substitute or a surrogate for reality and the world of things. Thenceforth my interest was in science rather than philosophy.

A great many things seemed to happen in James' classes. I recall that one day a grandson of Brigham Young who was a student at Harvard reported in the seminar on abnormal psychology on Mormonism. This was at a time when James was writing his lectures on "Varieties of Religious Experience." Another time this seminar went in a body to visit an insane hospital at Providence, Rhode Island. James discovered among the patients an old friend. This friend was walking about in the hospital garden, on the arm of an attendant, in a great state of exaltation, telling how he was now directing the stars in their movements and, in general, managing the affairs of the universe. James immediately took his arm and walking along in a most natural way, listened sympathetically and with real interest, as if he expected, as I believe he did, some new light from this insane man on this wild and irrational universe of ours, in which, in spite of all the order man had so far discovered in it, anything, it seems, may happen. This was characteristic of James' interest in everything human and of his radically empirical view of things in general.

The most memorable event in any of James' courses, as I now recall, was his reading in one of his classes, I do not now remember which, a paper he had just finished writing entitled "A Certain Blindness in Human Beings," published later, and very properly it seems to me, as an addendum to his "Talks to Teachers." I mention it here because I am convinced that this address, in preference to anything else that James or anyone else has written, should be required reading for sociologists and for teachers. James' purpose in writing the paper was theoretic rather than practical or pedagogical. It was for him, the expression of an article of faith.[1] To me, however, it is the most radical statement of the difficulty and the necessity,—considering that the very existence of society, as we know it, depends upon our ability to achieve understanding and consensus,—of communication in a society composed of individuals as egocentric as most of us naturally are. When I speak of the necessity of understanding in society I mean such an understanding as is embodied in tradition and is necessary to the transmission of a culture from each successive generation to the next, this being, according to Dewey, the essence of the educational process.

I did not realize when I sat down to write this paper that before I got through, it would turn out to be a chapter in an autobiography. However, I am not now writing my memoirs. I am mentioning here merely those from whom I learned somethings about methods. John Dewey was another of these.

One thing I now recall as characteristic of Dewey's method of teaching is that his students always seemed to have had the notion that he and they were somehow engaged in a common enterprise. With him learning was always, so it seemed, an adventure; an adventure which was taking us beyond the limits of safe and certified knowledge into the realm of the problematic and unknown. We always had a conviction, at the very least, that something was doing and that we were going somewhere, although we did not always know just where.

Dewey was not a particularly thrilling lecturer but he was an inspiring leader, and under his leadership we moved forward with a confidence, even though we were not sure of our destination.

I referred earlier to the fact that the educational process, as we know it, goes on under conditions that are imposed by the classroom. What are those conditions? I will mention merely one.

A class is, ordinarily, a mere aggregation of individuals engaged in a more or less enthusiastic contest for the approval of the teacher, and ultimately, for

[1] James believed, as I once heard him say, that the most real thing is a thing that is most keenly felt rather than the thing that is most clearly conceived. This was where he differed with his colleague Royce.

grades. Such an aggregation is not,—as under certain conditions it might be,—an organized or collective unit, engaged in an organized and planned pursuit of knowledge.

Under these circumstances the easiest, and perhaps the only thing to do, is to intensify the competition for place and rank, making the work of the class a kind of game, trusting that now and then, here and there, some individual will be lit up by an idea and begin the pursuit of knowledge on his own account. If no one is lit up; if there is no pursuit, no adventure, no thrills, nothing that impels the student to venture off the beaten track; if every one in the class moves along with the herd, progress will be slow; and interest,—the interest which participation in a common enterprise usually inspires,—will flag, eventually evaporate. Worst of all the knowledge so acquired is likely to be purely formal and verbal.

Under these conditions what the student gets in school is information rather than insight; definitions rather than ideas; conclusions and convictions that close minds rather than facts that reorient them. Under the insidious influences of the classroom hypotheses, which are intended to raise questions and theories, which are designed to guide research, frequently take the form of doctrines,—doctrines which, since they give us, or seek to, a final and authoritative statement of truth,—tend invariably to terminate investigation and discourage that disinterested curiosity which is characteristic of children and of science, particularly pure science, if science is ever pure. Doctrines have their function, but they are practical rather than theoretical.

Dewey and James were pragmatists. What I learned from them was the value of experiment and experience as distinguished from exposition and of research as opposed to scholasticism, as a method of education in the social as well as the physical sciences.[2]

It was from Dewey that I got, to use a newspaper phrase, my first great "assignment," the assignment to investigate the nature and social function of the newspaper. I have been working on that assignment ever since.

Another man, whom I knew longer and from whom I learned more than from any of my other teachers, was Booker Washington. After two years at Harvard and four years abroad where I had gone to study the newspaper, I finally finished my education, as I told the students of that institution a few weeks ago, at Tuskegee. I may as well tell how that happened. After six years of philosophy I was a little weary of the academic atmosphere. I wanted to renew my connection with the world of men and things. It happened that the foreign secretary of the Baptist Missionary Association, Dr. Barbour, had just returned from abroad with some very gruesome evidences of the atrocities of

---

[2] The Method of scholasticism is dialectic, i.e., discussion. Its function is to make ideas with which we operate clear and consistent. But thinking is more fruitful when it is in touch, at least, with an empirical world, that is a world of chance and change.

King Leopold's rule in the Belgian Congo. He wanted some one to help him advertise conditions in that part of the world. As a result I became the first secretary of the Congo Reform Association. I was at that time very little of a missionary, and my experience as a newspaper man had convinced me that reform was not enough. But the Congo looked to me like a "good story."

In the course of the campaign to arouse public opinion on the subject of the Congo natives, I sought out everyone in the United States who knew anything about the so-called Congo Free State and anyone else who could be interested in the fate of the natives there. It was in this way that I met Booker Washington. By the time I met him, however, I had become convinced that conditions in the Congo were not the result of mere administrative abuses. Rather they were the conditions which one was likely to meet wherever a European people had invaded the territory of a more primitive folk in order to uplift, civilize, and incidentally, exploit them. I said something about my theory to Washington. I told him I believed the evils of Leopold's regime in the Congo, were endemic, i.e., one of the more or less inevitable incidents of the civilizing process. He did not seem interested. His mind was essentially pragmatic and he was rather allergic to theories of any sort. When, however, I told him that I was thinking of going to Africa; that there was, I had heard, at Lovedale, South Africa an industrial school for natives, and that, if there was any solution of the Congo problem it would probably be some form of education, he invited me to come to Tuskegee. I went to Tuskegee to stay a few weeks, but I remained for seven years.

One reason I stayed as long as I did was because I had been convinced shortly after my arrival that the problem of the American Negro was merely an aspect or a phase of the native problem in Africa; it was, in short, a problem which, like slavery, had arisen as an incident in an historical process and as a phase of the natural history of civilization. This was, also—although he would not have stated it in such formidable terms,—Booker Washington's conception of the matter. It was, in fact, from him that I first gained some adequate notion of how deep-rooted in human history and human nature social institutions were, and how difficult, if not impossible it was, to make fundamental changes in them by mere legislation or by legal artifice of any sort. It was the first time I realized that social problems, in so far as they are not problems of administration or of policy, are problems of fundamental human nature and culture.

During those seven winters I was at Tuskegee I went all over the South. I did not associate to any extent with white folks but I did get pretty thoroughly acquainted with the upper levels of the Negro world, about which southern white people at that time knew very little. On the other hand I gained very little knowledge, except indirectly, about that nether world of Negro life with which white men, particularly if they grew up on a southern plantation, knew a great deal. These seven years were for me a sort of prolonged internship during which I gained a clinical and first hand knowledge of a first class social problem.

My apprenticeship was too long, no doubt. If learning is to be adventure it cannot be at the same time a vocation. If we are to make of education a voyage of exploration we must eventually return to base, in order to give an accounting of our discoveries. However, the time I spent at Tuskegee was never dull. In fact it was crowded with events and I have never regretted the experience.

For one thing I was increasingly impressed, while I was there, that I was in the unique position of seeing, as it were from the inside, the intricate workings of an important and significant historical process,—a process by which, within the wider cultural framework of American national life, a new racial and cultural minority, or as Washington once put it, "a nation within a nation," was visibly emerging, that is taking new form and substance, as the result of a struggle to raise its status.

At Tuskegee I was, it seemed, at the very center of the Negro world. I had the access to most everything that was likely to throw light on the processes that were slowly but inevitably changing Negro life and the South. I even used to have some of the letters referred to me that were hard to answer, because they were based on some of the numerous and typical misunderstandings of the racial situation. I learned much about the race problem in my effort to analyze the ideological misinterpretations upon which these letters were based.

If I got more than I otherwise would out of my experience it was not merely that I had the opportunity, but because I had the preparation that enabled me to learn from what I saw and heard. Returning from Europe I was no longer a newspaper man but a student. It was as a student, participating in a great enterprise, but sufficiently detached to see it in its more general social and sociological significance, that I looked at the Negro and the South.

During all this time I was exploring and discovering what was for me an entirely new world, a world which up to that time had remained veiled in misapprehension and misunderstanding, and there was, it seemed, no end to it. Every year, every month the situation seemed to change. Things were, to be sure, changing, but not as rapidly as they seemed. It was I who changed.

What was the source of this transfiguration of attitude and sentiment? It was not merely that I had gathered new impressions and more facts. It was that, from my wider experience I had gained new points of view and new insights. It is strange and a little disconcerting to observe what different aspects familiar and obvious objects may assume, if we see them from different points of view, or look at them out of different eyes. And this is particularly the case when the objects we are looking at are human beings whom we see and know, if at all, only through their faces, their customs, and their cultures. That this is so is due in part, no doubt, to that "certain blindness in human beings" of which James speaks, and to those distances—social distances, as we call them,—which separate individuals, living in one world from all those living in some other.

It seems to me now as I look back upon it that the methods of teaching I found in operation at Tuskegee were not only the most original but the most elemental and fundamental I have anywhere encountered. They were elemental because education, as Booker Washington conceived it, was not limited to students in school but included the great public of thoughtful men of both races, North and South. It was education designed to complete the work of emancipation and change the character of an institution that had grown up and become fixed in the habits, the customs, and ideology of a whole people.

I cannot go into any great detail, as I wish I might, in regard to the methods which Booker Washington devised to carry out his epic task. They included, among other things, the publication of a rural newspaper, a Negro Year Book, and an annual report on the statistics of lynching.

Most original of these educational devices, it seemed to me, was the Negro Farmers Conference. This conference which brought together annually the Negro farmers in Macon and the neighboring counties to discuss local affairs, gained in a short time such a reputation that it brought people together from all over the South.

Instead of attempting to instruct this gathering, or exhort it, Washington's method was to get from its members some sort of report, based on their own observation and experiences of the actual conditions of rural life, as they knew them in their own communities. In attempting thus to reverse the ordinary educational procedure it was necessary to inhibit some of the natural eloquence of those who wanted to make speeches and to bring to the fore the less articulate individuals, particularly those individuals who, because they had achieved something,—even if it was no more than raising a pig, or purchasing a mule,—had something to tell. What Washington and the conference wanted to know was, mainly, how they did it.

The information which this procedure brought forth, couched in the quaint, homely but eloquent language of the people themselves,—enlivened by anecdotes and illuminated by quaint humor and touches of pathos,—was the most moving and informing, not to say inspiring report on the state of the country and the human aspects of Negro life in the rural South that one could well imagine.

It was vastly more intimate, more suggestive and, at the same time, more actual than any formal investigation or report could possibly have been. It was more actual because it brought the participants face to face not merely with the facts but with the facts as they were reflected in the minds, the aspirations and sentiments of the people for whom these formal and physical conditions constituted the externals of a world.

As a method of instruction, the procedure of this conference, which lasted all day and was opened with prayer and enlivened with the singing of hymns,—hymns the people themselves had created,—has not, so far as my experience goes, been anywhere equaled by any more formal type of instruction. Not only were the Negro farmers present instructed and inspired by what they heard of what other men, living under the same condition as themselves, were doing to improve their lot, but other farmers in other places throughout the South, to whom the accounts of what had taken place at these meetings eventually circulated, were awakened and made curious about the new gospel, and the new realism with which that gospel viewed the Negro farmer's problems. Thus the circle of participants continued to widen from year to year throughout the South. Eventually these conferences brought into existence a form of oral or folk news, which, like the traditional folk ballads, tended as it circulated to assume the form of a folk literature.

It was the element of news in these conferences as it was, for example, in the rhetoricals at Tuskegee which made them locally famous. At these exercises, to which the whole school turned out, groups of students employed in one or the other of the several industries carried on by the school reported on the nature of their work, its function and importance in the total economy of the school. The students in this case were actually trying to communicate rather than to recite. The accounts which they gave of the tasks in which they were employed, were, therefore, always interesting as well as informing.

And then they were encouraged to dramatize the accounts they gave of their tasks. If it was the work of the printing office or the dairy which they were demonstrating they would seek in some ingenious way to reproduce or suggest the whole setting, even to milking a cow on the stage, if this was part of the drama. One time I recall the students employed in the Institute post office brought over practically all the furniture of the post office including a set of government mail bags. While some of the students were demonstrating how the mail was distributed, some one else read a paper telling how much mail the office handled and all the different countries from which it came, etc.

I was probably the more impressed by this sort of rhetorical exercise because it was so entertaining and instructive as compared with the Friday afternoon rhetoricals with their frigid little essays that I remembered of my own school days. Besides they had, as I have said, the element of news in them. They told us what was going on in the community.

News, as a form of knowledge, is a report of an event that gives one a new slant on a familiar theme. It presupposes the existence of a common interest or a common enterprise in which the community and the public to which the news is addressed participates. News is therefore never altogether new, otherwise it would not be intelligible. If its implications were not fairly obvious, news would not make people talk, and would not, therefore, get that wide and rapid circulation which news invariably achieves. It is when something that occurs in the class—something concerned with the lesson of course,—that makes students talk, that one knows that students have got something from the classroom.

Booker Washington was, I might add, an inveterate reader of the newspapers and invariably kept abreast of events inside or outside his world. It was,—more than anything else, I suspect,—the fact that he knew so well the world in which he lived that Washington was able to inspire so many people in America, besides his own students, with the conviction that at Tuskegee students and teachers were not merely learning and teaching, but participating in a great and significant enterprise, namely the education and elevation of a race.

It was this broader conception of education which led Washington to found the Negro Business League, not so much to advance Negro business as to educate the Negro people. It was also the reason for all his books, his magazine articles and his speeches—speeches which, though he repeated them over and over again from one end of the country to the other, were always new, because they were always the old themes interpreted in terms of the new events. This was at a time when the influence and prestige of Tuskegee was so great that outsiders, sometimes waggishly and sometimes scornfully, referred to the school as "the capitol of the Negro race."

I have gone into some detail in describing the Farmers Conference and some of the other educational devices which Booker Washington made use of at Tuskegee because they seemed to me to illustrate what every form of education might well strive to be, namely, at once a voyage of discovery, and a means and medium for an intelligent participation in the life of the community. That means one would not train students to be lawyers, doctors and teachers, merely, but rather encourage lawyers, doctors and teachers to be interested in medicine, law and education, considering each as an integral part of the cultural tradition in which all live and have their being. This would not relegate technical education to the status of a means or instrument of a successful career, but make it rather a method of participation in a way of life. And this is actually what Tuskegee, rather more than any school I ever knew, succeeded under Booker Washington, in doing.

It is a very curious fact, it seems to me, that a Negro who had been a slave, and was in any case a more or less self-educated man, should conceive and establish, not a school merely, but an industrial school, which put into operation methods of teaching, designed to educate men and women, less for any one specific occupation than for the actual business of life, that is to say, participation not merely in the economic life of the community but in all the varied interests that constitute the conscious life of a race or a people.

My conviction is that Washington was able to do this to the extent that he did because (1) he was identified with a people who had a problem; and because (2) he had a program which touched, directly, or indirectly, all the interests of the people for whom it was devised.

This suggestion that the school should be more intimately related to all the diverse interests of life of the student and the community, does not imply that schools, in order to give students more zest for the work in the classroom, must go into politics. God forbid. What it intends, at least, is that knowledge is and should be always finally and fundamentally practical. The fact is that science has invariably grown up about problems and that facts are, so to speak, only facts in a universe of discourse. A universe of discourse, I might add, is something which has come into existence to enable individuals associated in any one of the several sciences, or associated for any other common purpose, to think consistently and to act understandingly, and in some sort of concert.

But science is something more than a universe of discourse or a frame of reference; something more, in short, than an apparatus for systematic thought. Science is always concerned not merely with an ideal but a real world.

Sociology was bred in scholasticism. In so far as it retains that earlier orientation it seems concerned with ideas rather than things. Society, however, is not an idea, but a thing,—an organism, to be more specific. Societies grow, adapt themselves to conditions, compete among themselves, live like plants and animals. More than that they carry on wars and organized conflicts with one another, as animals do not.

Sociologists cannot solve their problems by dialectics merely, nor by making programs for other people to carry out. Sociology must be empirical and experimental. It must, to use Booker Washington's expression, "learn by doing"; it must explore, invent, discover, and try things out. So must students; so must education.

This paper started out to say something rather definite about methods of teaching. As I have had some experience as a student and a teacher, but very little acquaintance with current pedagogical doctrines, it seemed that it would be appropriate for me to review some of my experiences as a pupil before I attempted to discuss the methods I have myself found successful as a teacher. But I have, I find, drifted quite out of my course, as I originally charted it, and I have been more concerned with methods of learning than methods of teaching. The two things are, of course, related.

As I shall not have time to say anything about classroom methods based on my own experience as a teacher, it seems, I might, nevertheless, summarize in conclusion, my experience as a pupil. Of the teachers I have had from whom I learned most only one, Professor Friederich Knapp, it seems, had a method that could be described as systematic, such a method I mean as teachers are looking for when they talk professionally about teaching. The others all seemed, like a horse out in pasture, to be intent on cutting capers and escaping from the trammels which the classroom ordinarily imposes.

Education, however, must have methods, and knowledge must finally be presented in an orderly and systematic fashion. Otherwise knowledge becomes a mere personal possession which can be used but cannot be socialized, i.e., funded like science and transmitted from one generation to another in books.

The point which I am most interested in emphasizing is this: systematization of knowledge cannot be done successfully either by the teacher alone, even with the assistance of a textbook. The student must do some of the work of interpretation and formulation for himself. My experience is that he does not do this, and that he has never learned how.

INDEX

Palmer, A. Mitchell: censorship by, 20
Pan African Congress: DuBois speech before,
155–56n. 72
Pan-African Movement: and missionary work,
55
Pan-German League: colonialism in Africa,
156n. 78
Park, Robert E.: legacy, xv, 127–28, 135;
neglect of his pre-Chicago studies, xv,
xviii, 3, 141–42n. 38; biography, xv–xxi,
1, 61, 128, 173n. 37, 306–18; relationship
with other scholars, xvi, xix, 12, 20–23,
26, 37, 84, 131, 192, 202–03, 308–09; dissertation of, xvi, 28, 38; with Congo
Reform Association, xvi, 6, 57, 71,
311–12; and American Baptists, xvi, 63;
and Booker T. Washington, xvii, 57,
60–62, 82, 90, 117, 157n. 96, 162n. 45,
276–89, 312–16; Gothic perspective of,
xvi, xx, 11, 43, 57, 63–73, 73–76, 81–83;
viewed by other intellectuals, xviii, xx,
128, 132–33, 143n. 73; study of race relations, xvii–xx, 7–11, 26, 32–37, 95–104,
113–25, 133; and the civilizational process,
xviii–xix, 32, 95, 99, 107, 112, 116–17,
121–24; and concept of assimilation, xix,
33, 36, 95–102 105–08, 111–14, 119; and
the modern city, xx; on character of
Leopold II, xx, 7, 47, 51–52, 64–71, 82,
210–45; central themes in writings of, 1,
116; and sociology of religion, 1–2,
95–104, 110–12; on the problems of
democracy, 2–3; views on World Wars,
2–3, 16–17, 19–26, 27–29; pre-Chicago
studies of, 3–11; study of German militarism, 4–5, 13, 15–19, 30, 179–89; studies
of the Congo, 5–7, 41–80, 205–45;
ambivalence toward reformers, 9, 11, 90;
sociology of war, 13, 15–24, 27–31, 37–40;
on militarization, 12–13, 16–19, 21–23, 32,
36; and Bismarck's Kulturkampf, 13, 25, 36,
38, 130–31; on Moltke's military reorganization, 14–16, 37; on social conflict, 16,
95–104; on propaganda, 19–21, 115, 232,
234–35, 236–38; on censorship, 20; failure
to study American Indians, 24; on the state
and social evolution, 27–28; on Hitler's
control of the German state, 27–29; compared with Sumner, 28, 128; on the garrison state, 29–31, 33, 34–35; on the relation
between war and politics, 30–31; on the
status of Japanese in America, 32–33; contributions toward African liberation,
57–63; on progress as a terrible thing, 71;
unwitting compliance with Leopold's propaganda, 72; on capitalism, 74; on the
struggle with Communism, 74–75; analysis
of Sombart's work, 75, 190–95; and
humanistic sociology, 76; as stimulus for

study of African societies, 77; perspective
as romantic racialism, 77; contrasted with
Frazier, 78–79; studies of Winston-Salem,
83, 92–94, 97–100, 252–54, 262–75; study
of accommodation, 83–85, 92–94, 97–99,
102–03, 129, 200–01; on Protestantism,
83–85, 90, 130; on Atkins work in the
South, 88; and bi-racialism, 92, 98–100,
121, 124–25; on black social advancement,
94; on the new Occidental order, 95; on
the Tuskegee Institute, 101–02, 255–61;
conception of temperament, 106–12, 120,
132, 291–93, 302–05; on racial characteristics, 107–09; on black race consciousness,
114–20; missed Russian concern with
Africa, 117; on missions to Africa, 118–19;
on African customs in America, 119–20,
134; modernity as inevitable, 128; view of
the modern state, 131; challenges to his
assumptions, 132; concept of the marginal
man, 132; on society and social relationships, 201–04
Parsons, Talcott: concern about loyalties of
non-whites, 33; on Lutheranism, 89–90
Phillips, Ulrich Bonnell: historiography of,
132
Philosophy of rape: in Ward's justification of
racism, 7–8
Pickens, William: with the NAACP, 113
Pietism: inner-worldly ethic, 84; Weber's allu-
sions to, 84–85
Pilgrim's Progress: origins of muckraking, 63
Ploetz, Alfred: and scientific racism, 9
Polidori, John William: Gothic novelist, 46;
depiction of the vampire, 66–67
Political economy: Sombart's view, 190–92
Pois, Robert A.: on Meinecke's anti-semitism,
146n. 15
Polity: non-rational bases for, 2
Portugal: Congo slave trade, 222
Powdermaker, Hortense: on bi-racialism, 121
Pragmatism: of Dewey and James, 311
Prest, Thomas Pecket: fictionalized the vam-
pire, 153n. 22
Progress: idea of in Gothic sociology, 43; as a
terrible thing, 71, 309
Propaganda: German, during World War I,
19–22. See also Brussels Press Bureau
Protestantism: ethic, xvii; and the roots of capitalism, 45; role in Africa, 55–56, 119; as
two-faced, 82; in German social science,
83–84; contradictions and dilemmas in,
89–92; Park's ambivalence toward, 90;
modernizing effect on blacks, 94; and
Park's view of assimilation, 97; and race
temperament, 111, 291; and Congo atrocities, 130; universalizing principles, 130;
versus the state in the Congo, 205–06